NORTHERN THAILAND

CHIANG MAI AND BEYOND
A PHOTOGRAPHIC EXPLORATION

SCOTT SHAW

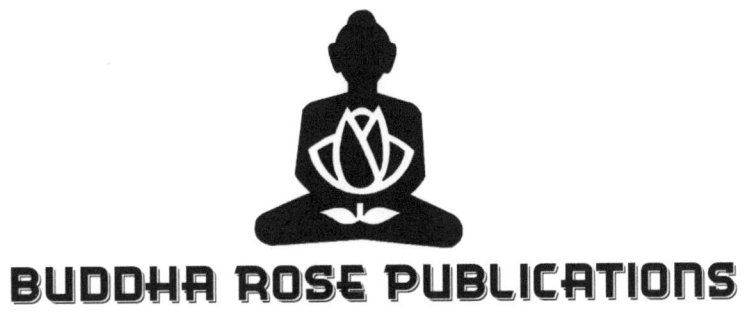

BUDDHA ROSE PUBLICATIONS

Northern Thailand: Chiang Mai and Beyond
A Photographic Exploration
Copyright © 2015 by Scott Shaw
www.scottshaw.com
ALL RIGHTS RESERVED
No part of this book can be reproduced in any
manner without the expressed written
permission of Scott Shaw or his representatives.

First Edition 2015

ISBN 10: 1-877792-83-7
ISBN 13: 978-1-877792-83-0

Printed in the United States of America

10 9 8 7 6 5 4 3 2 1

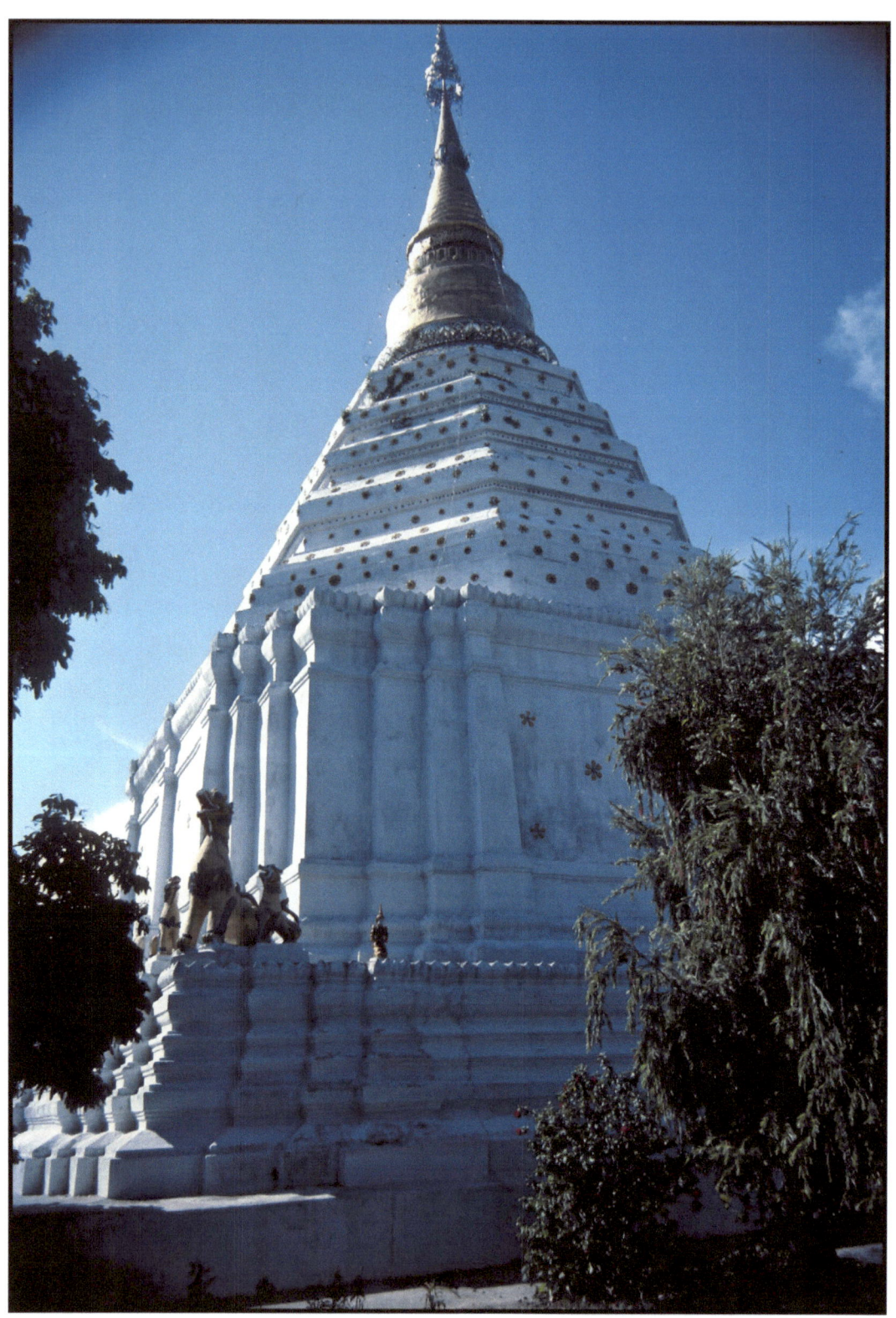

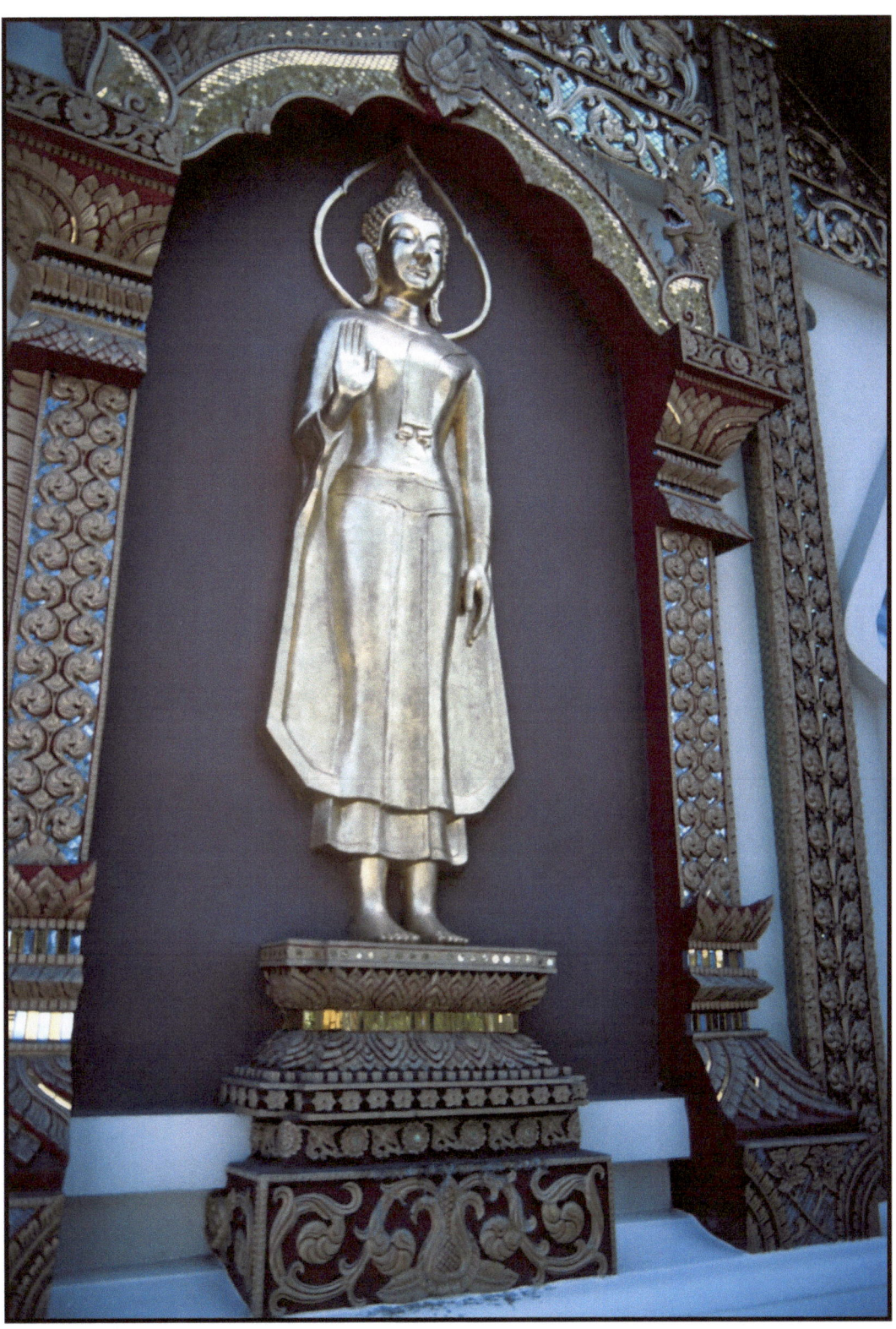

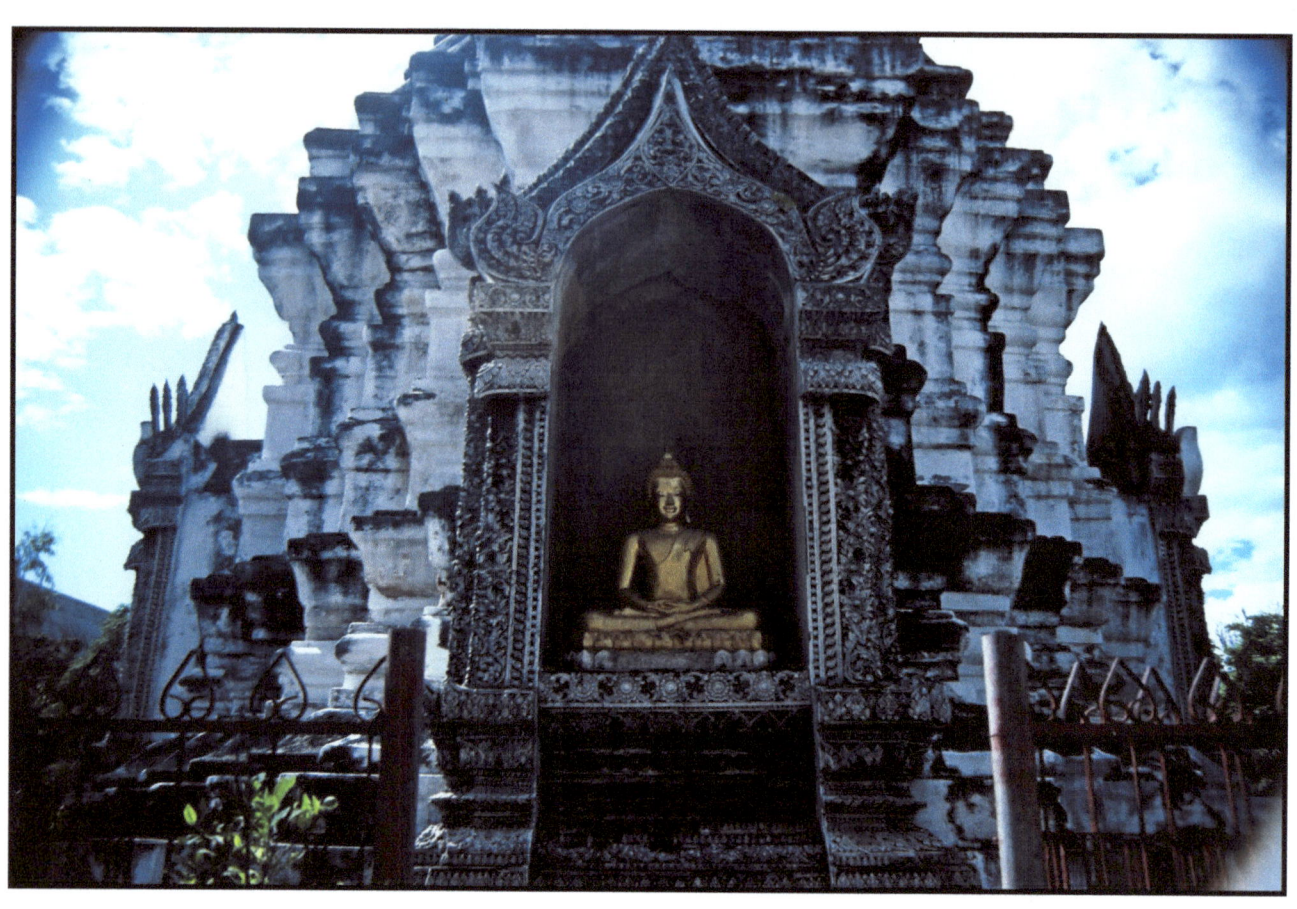

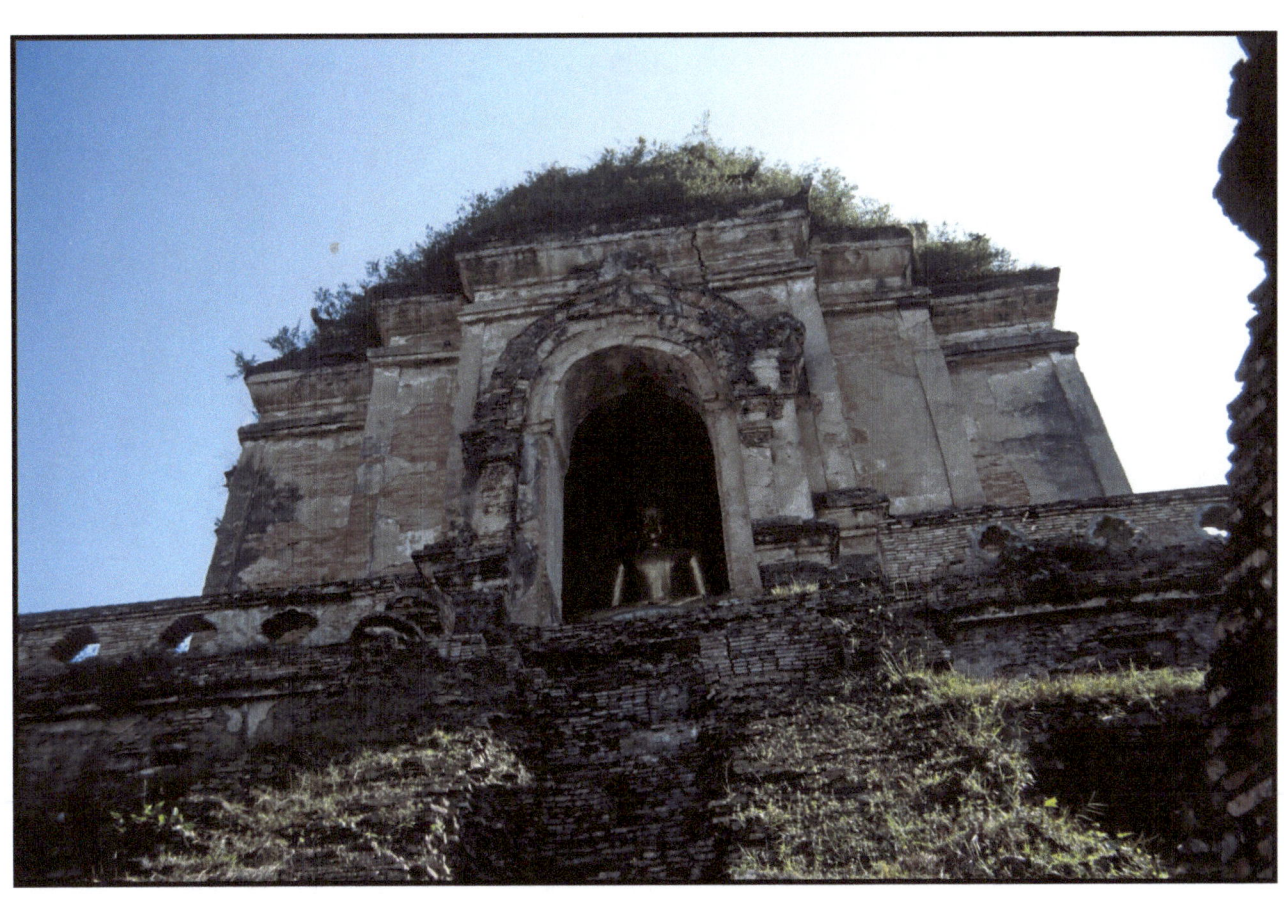

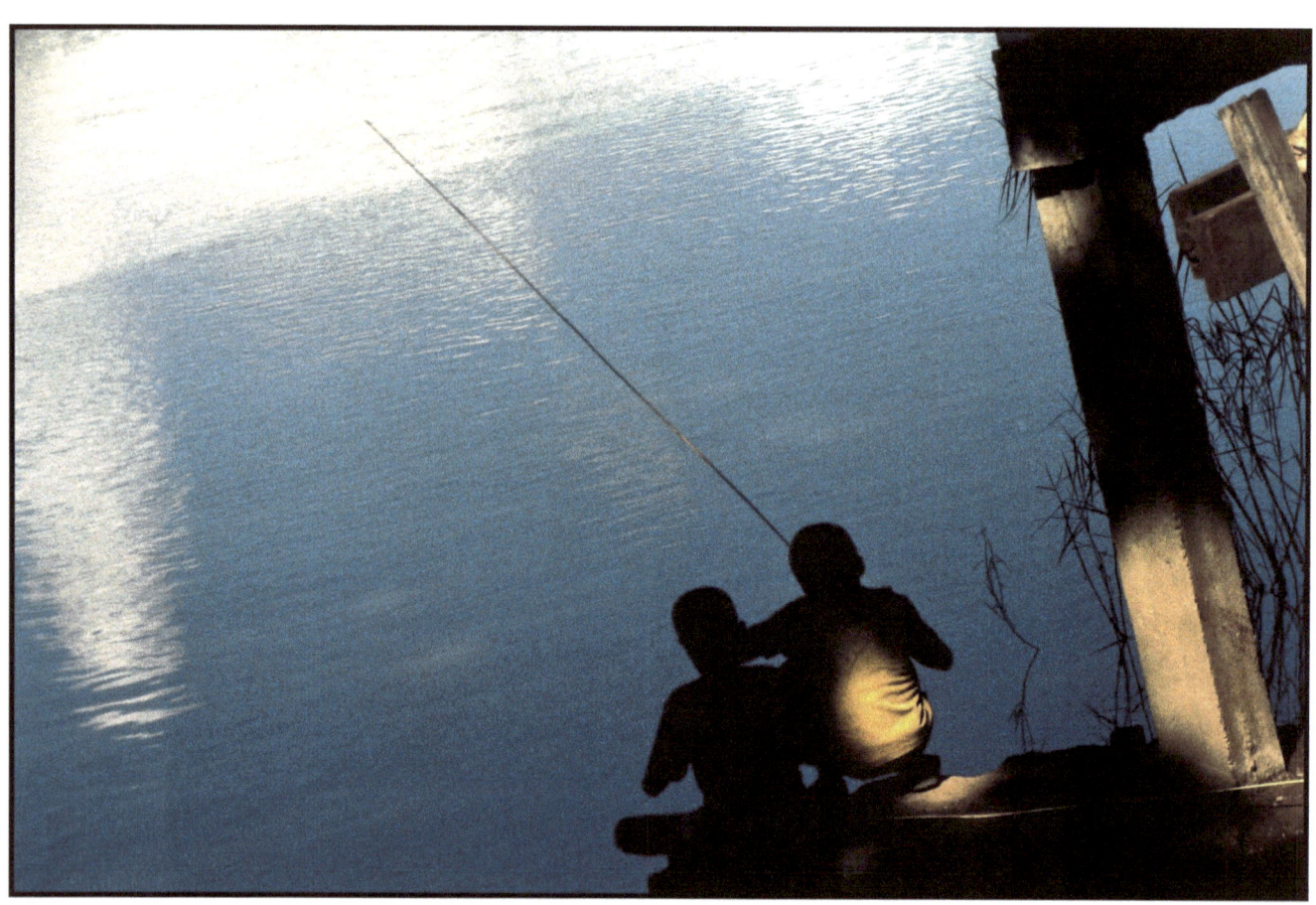

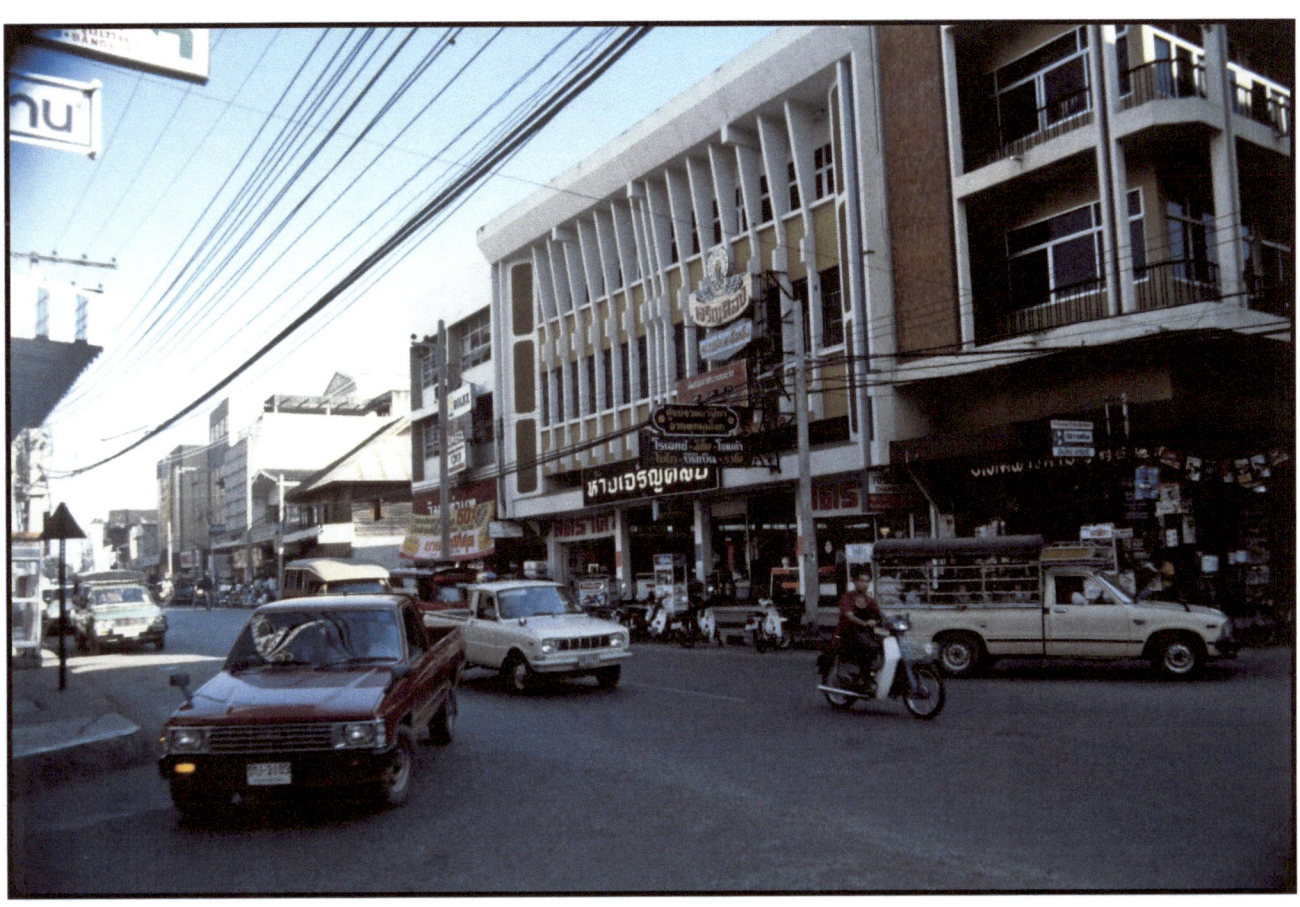

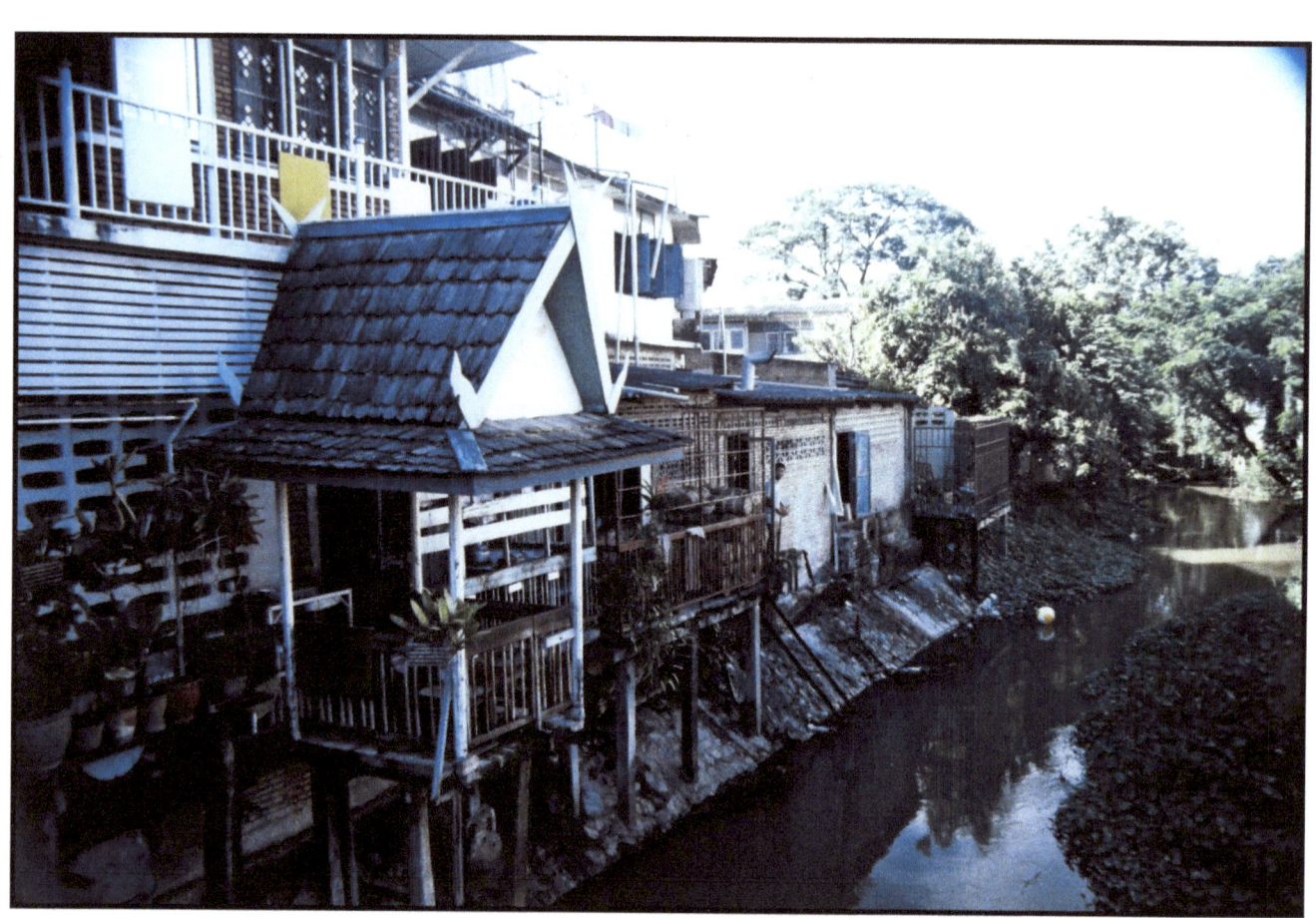

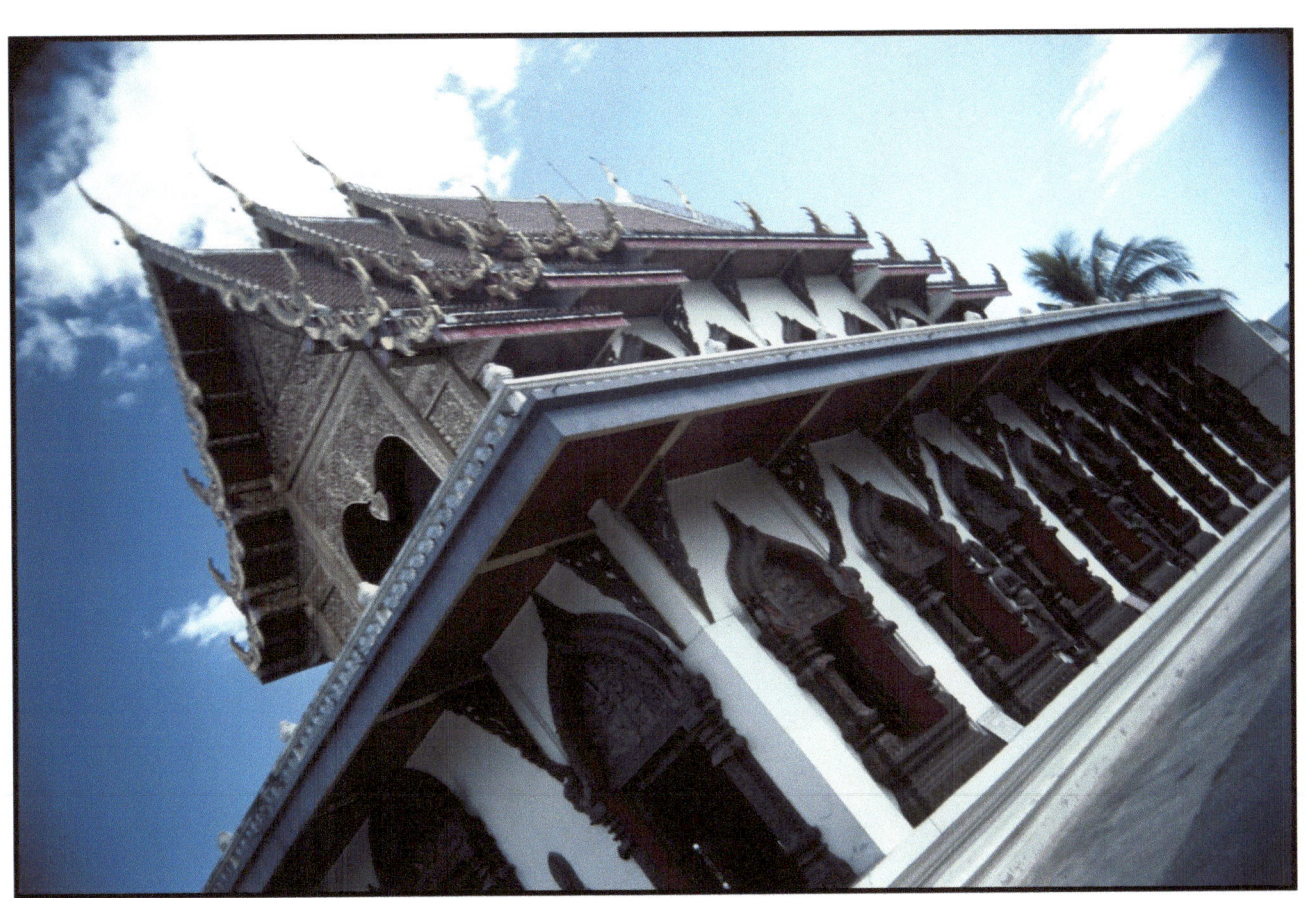

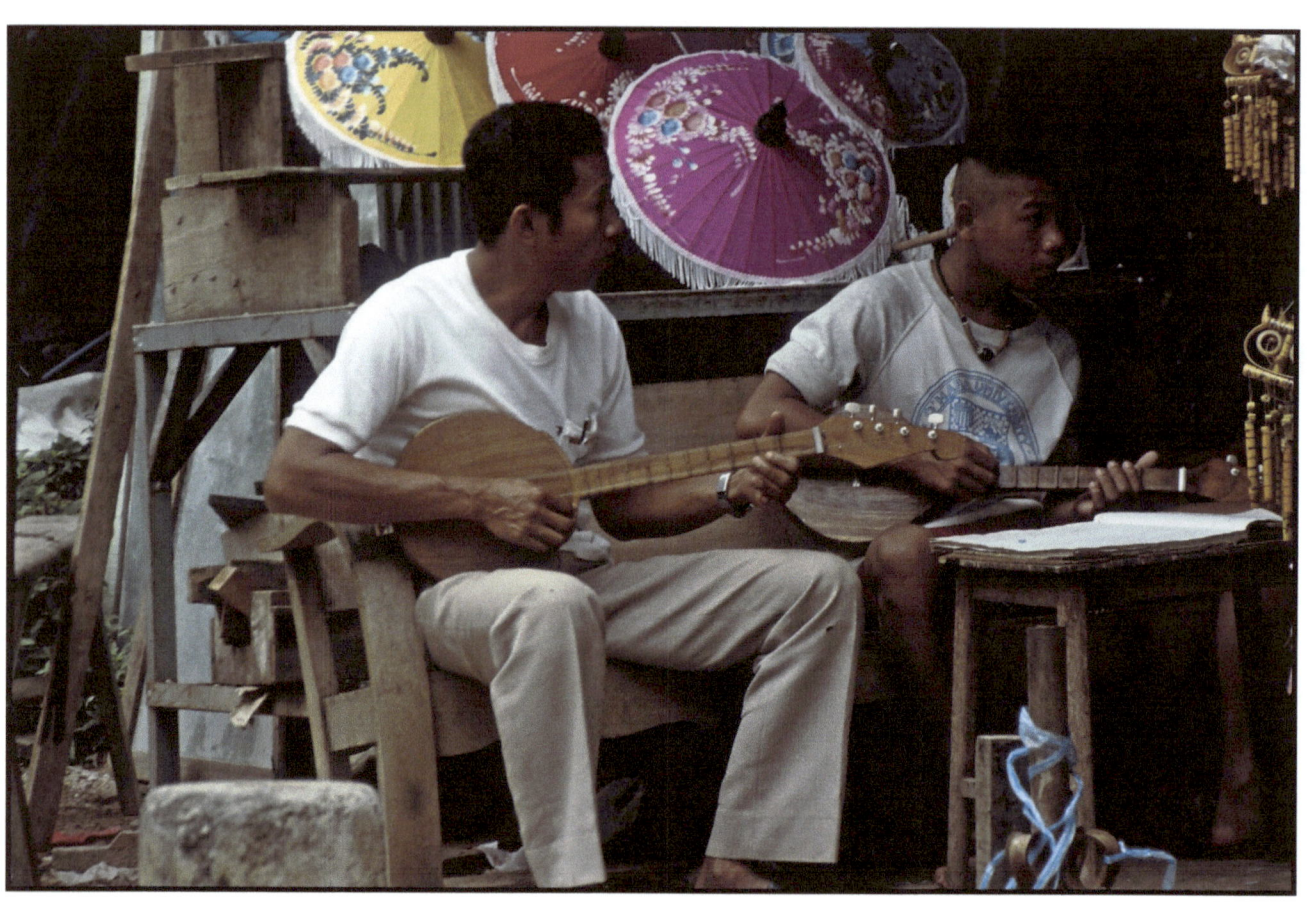

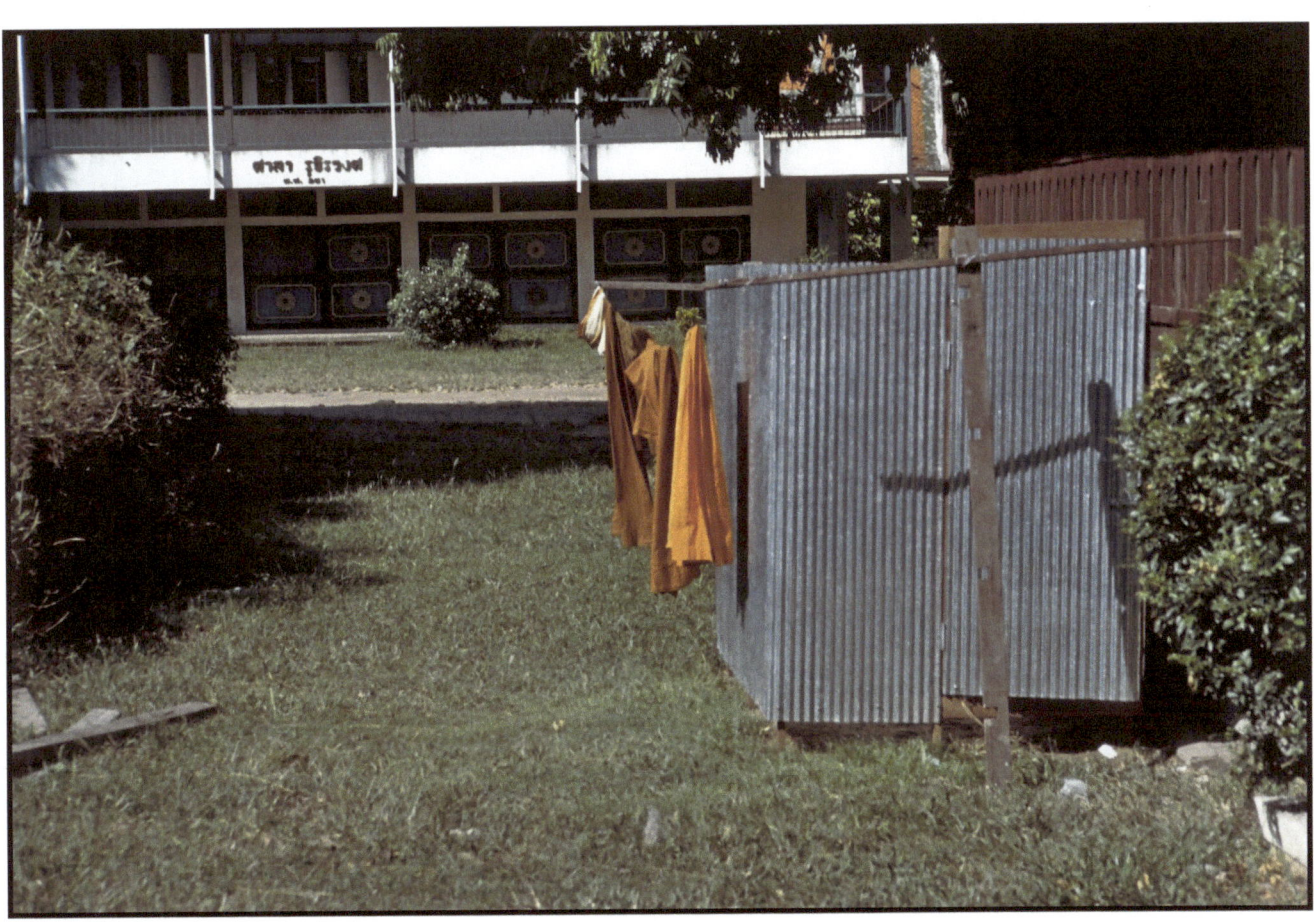

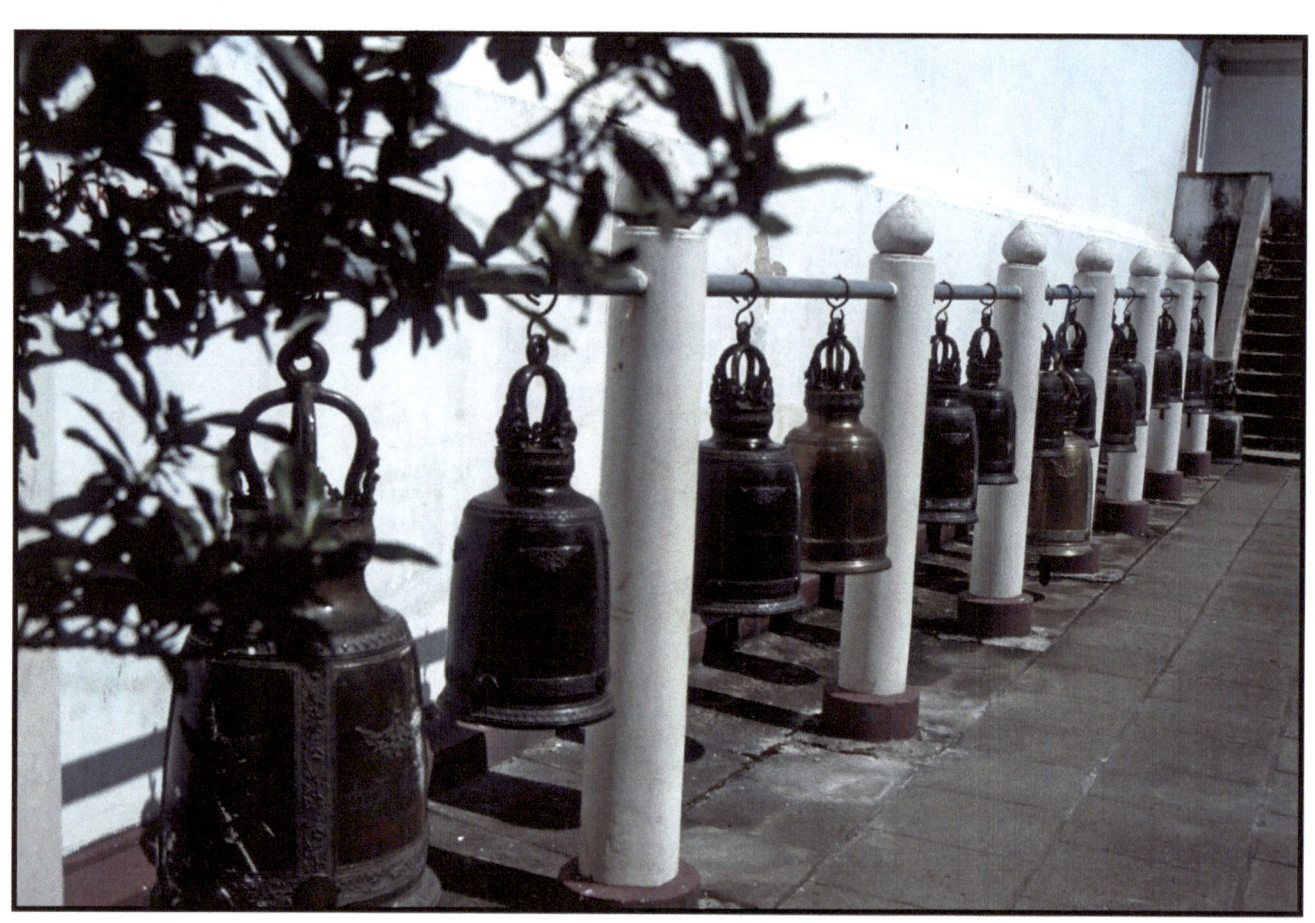

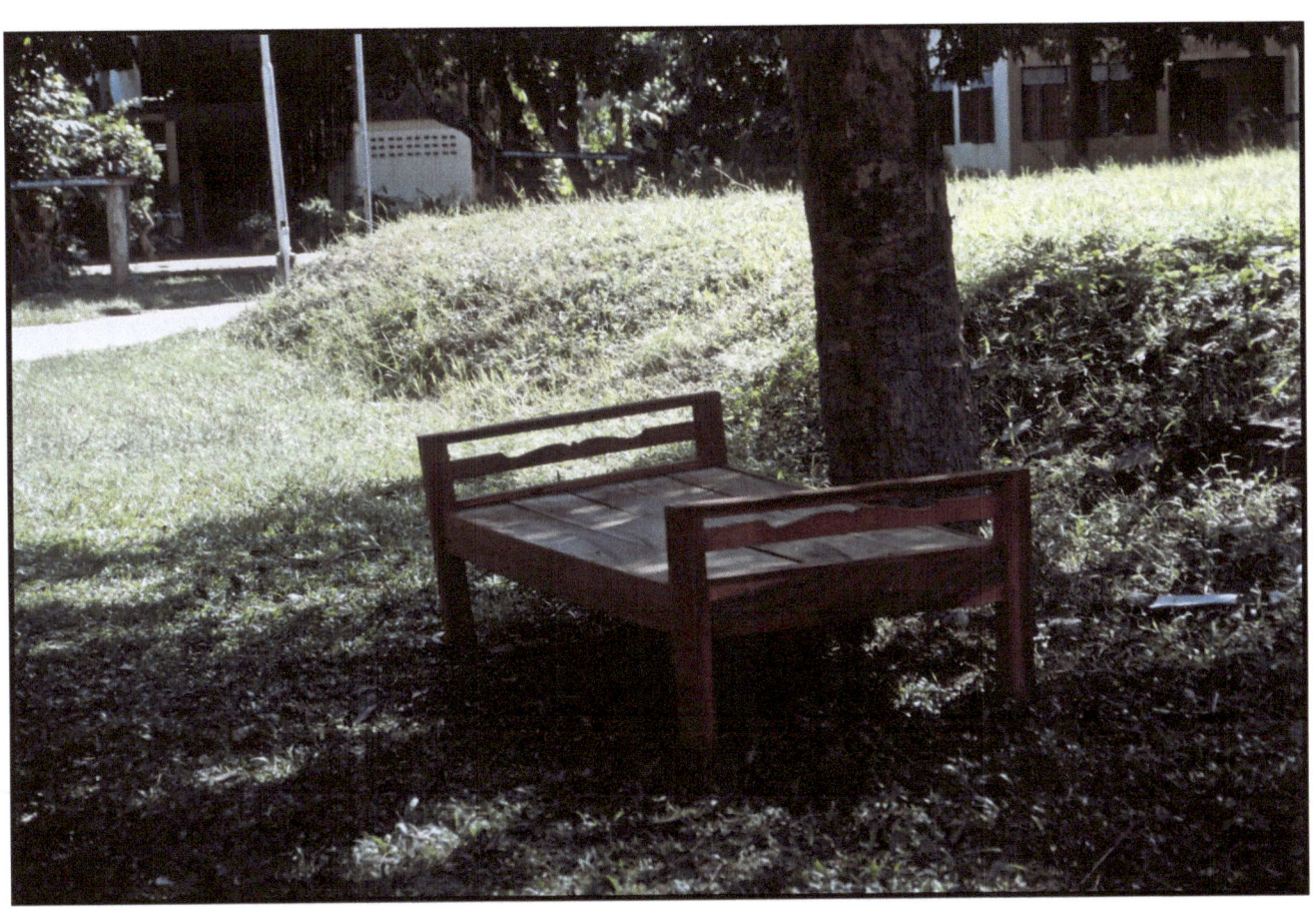

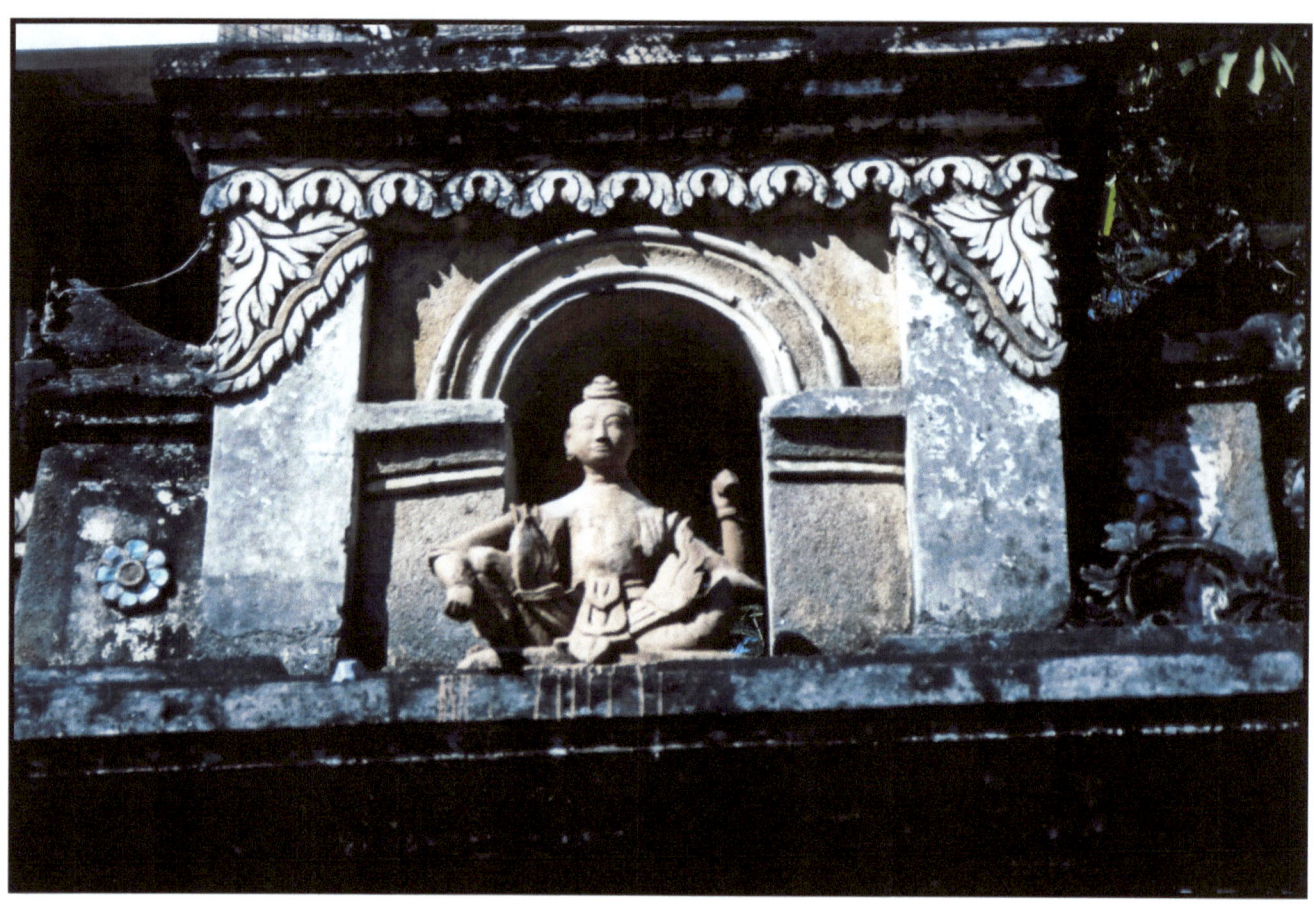

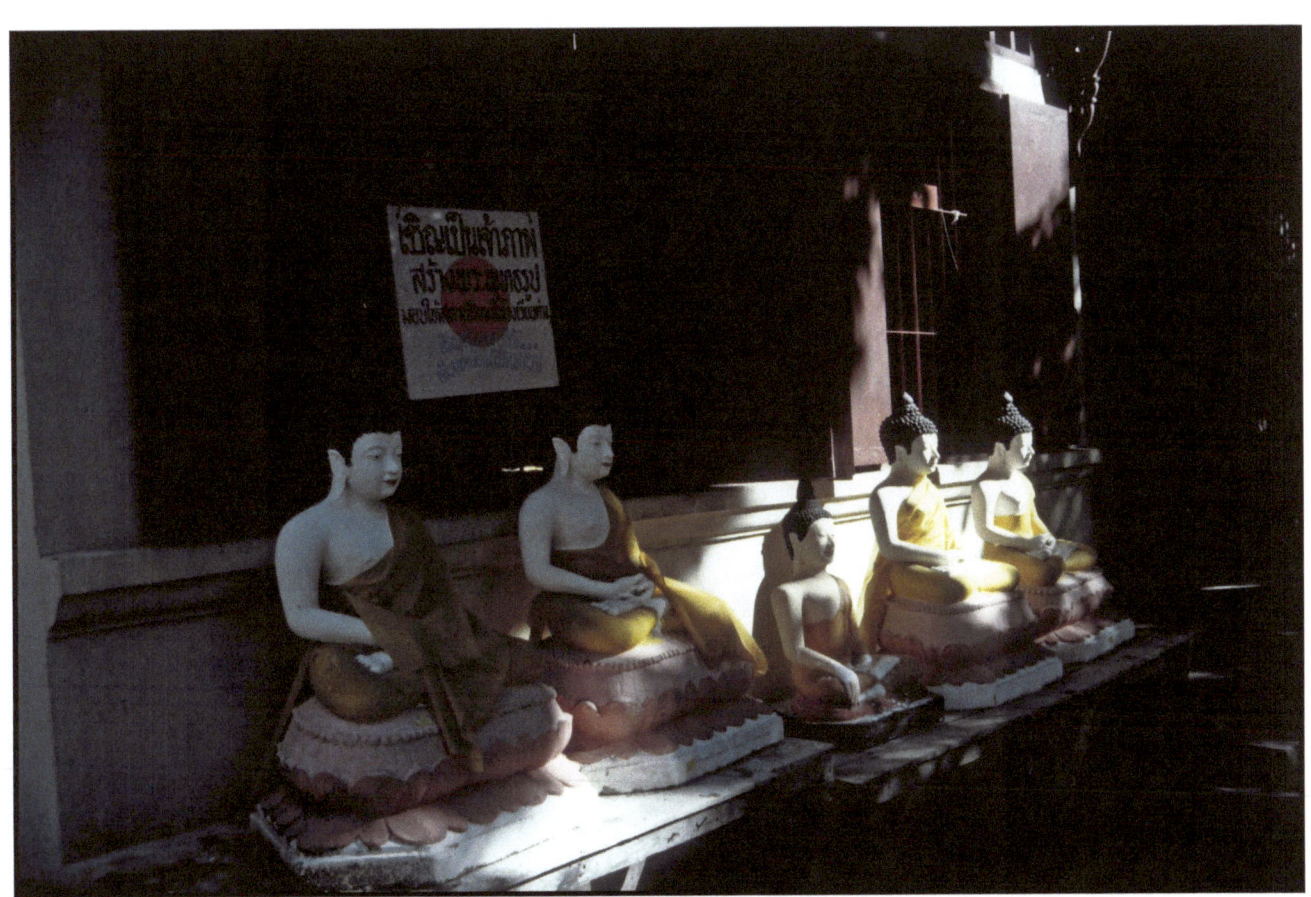

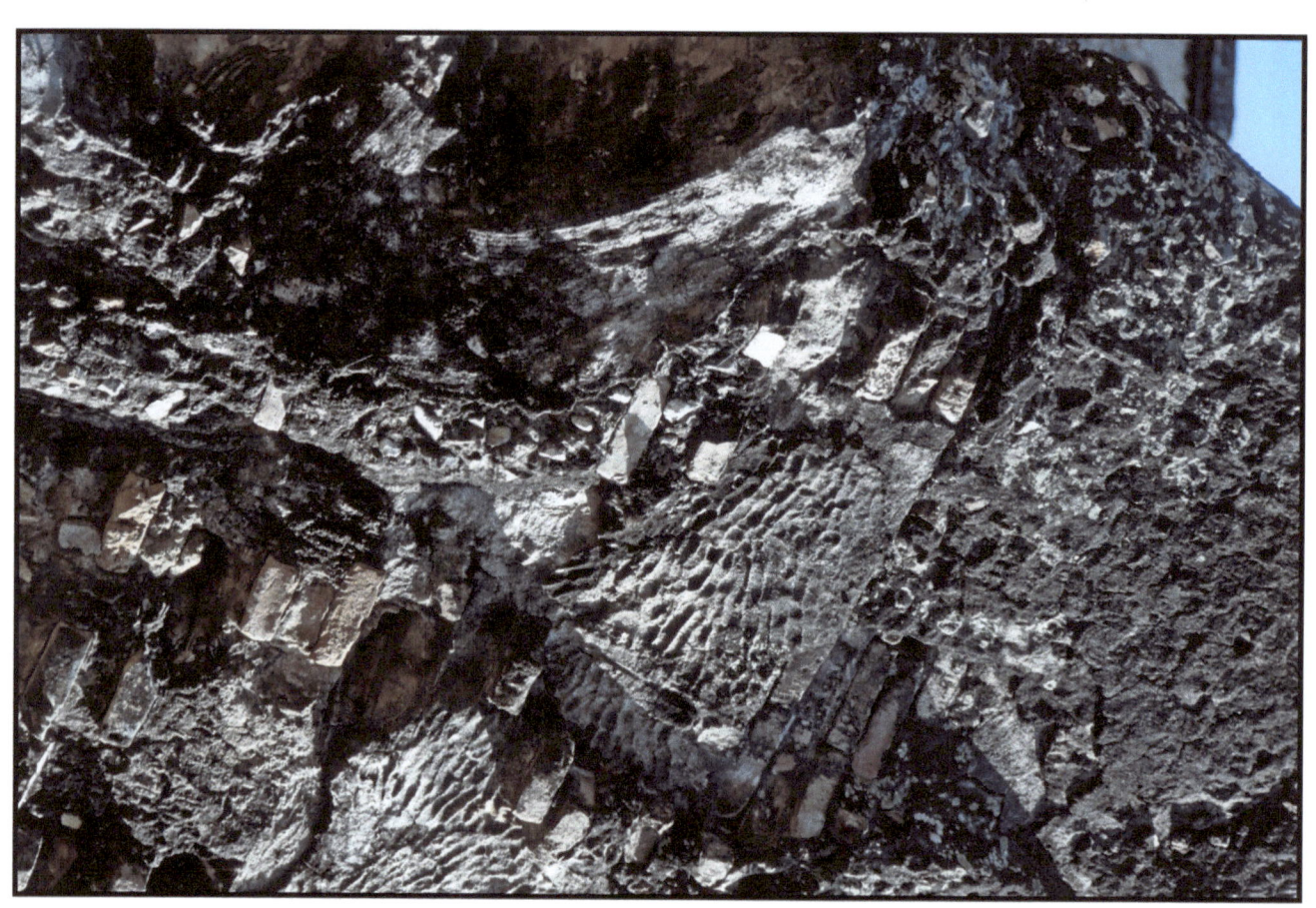

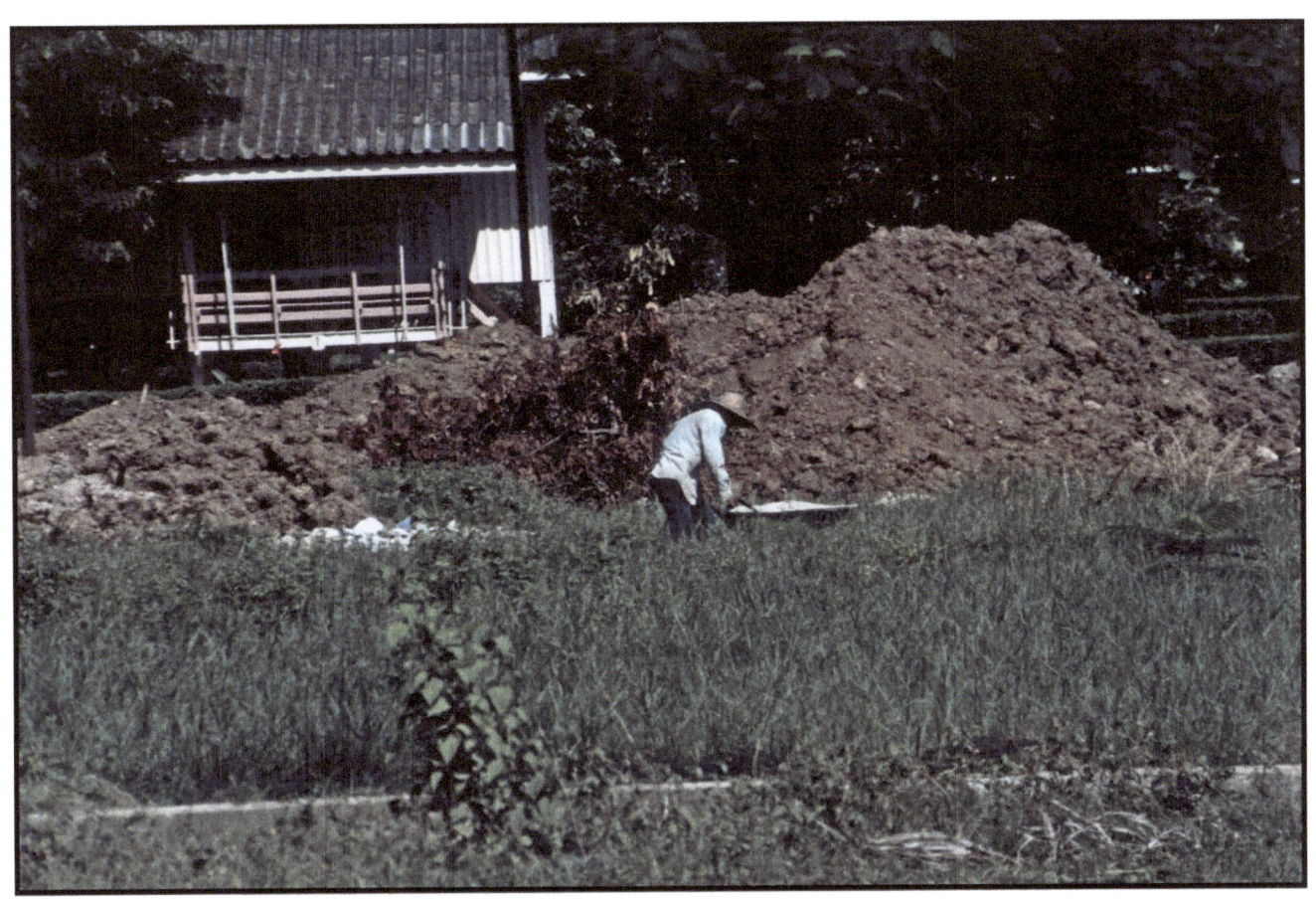

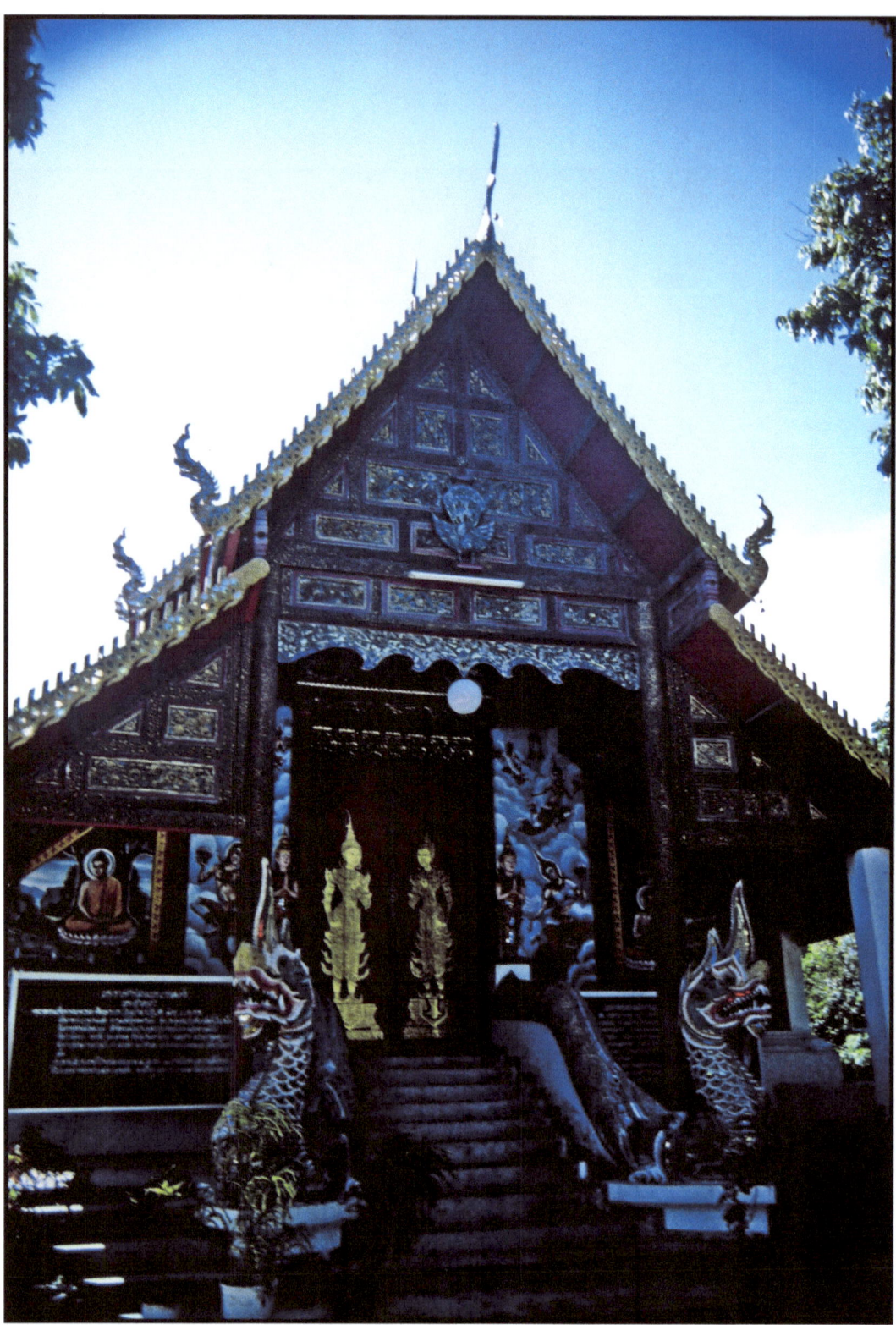

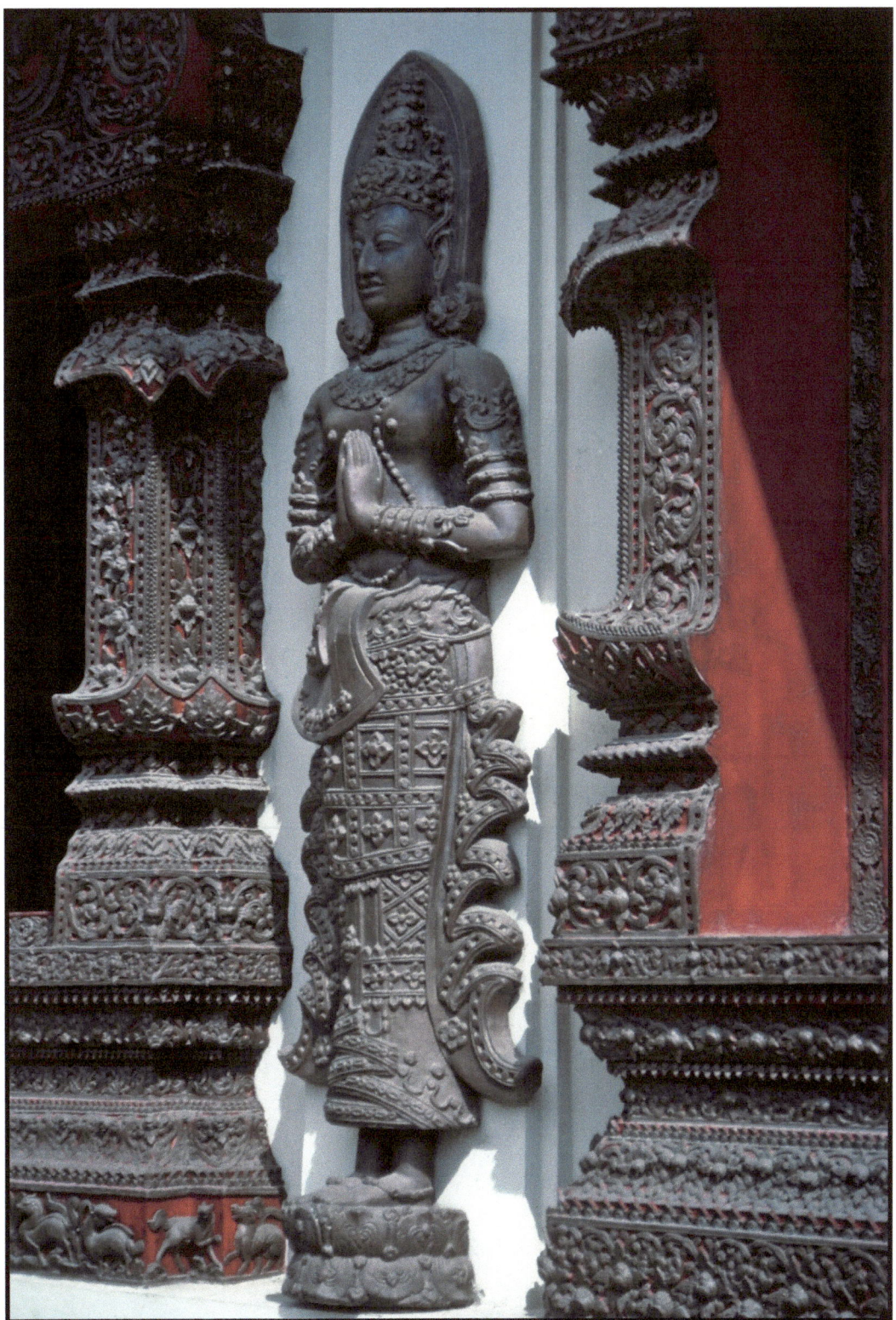

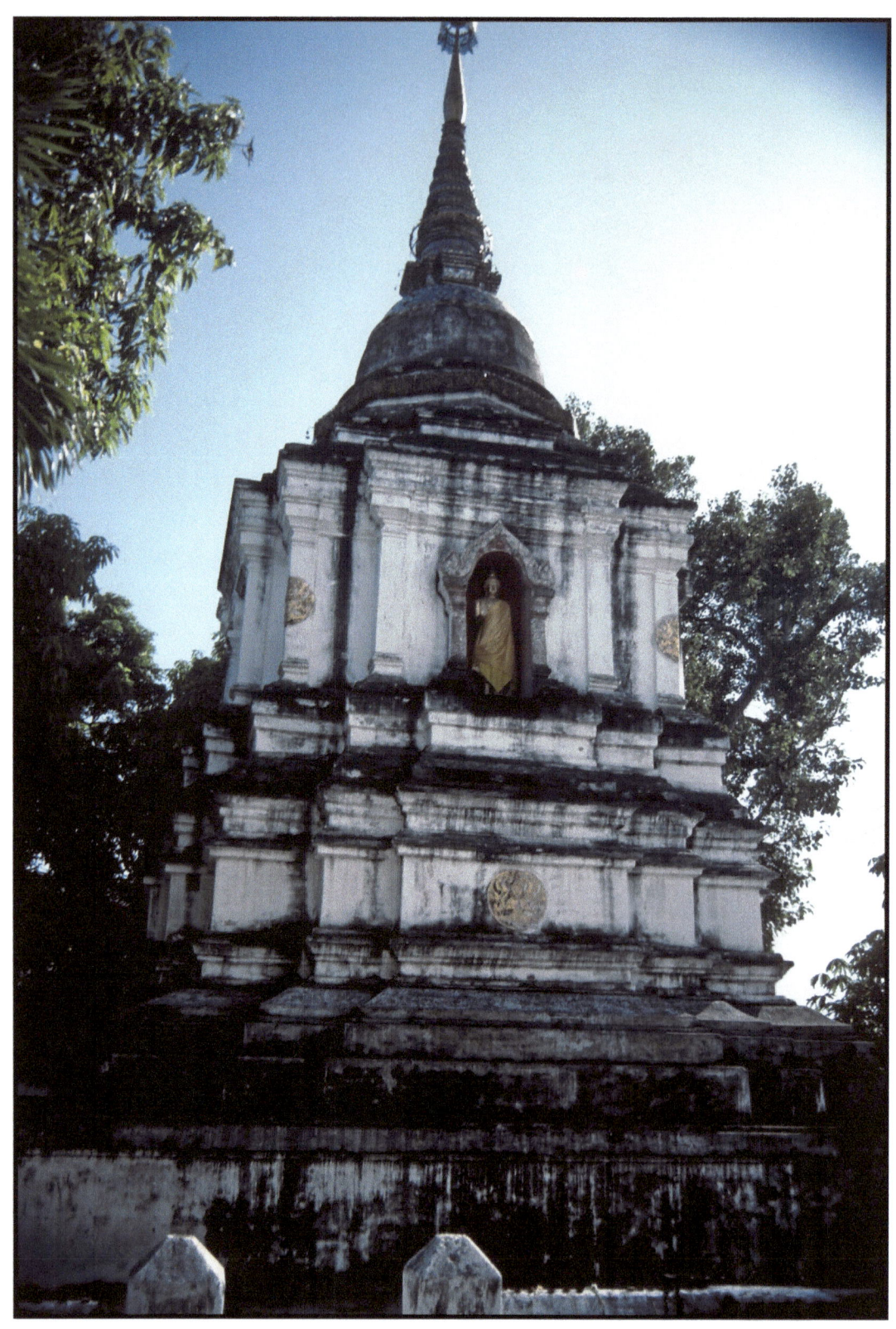

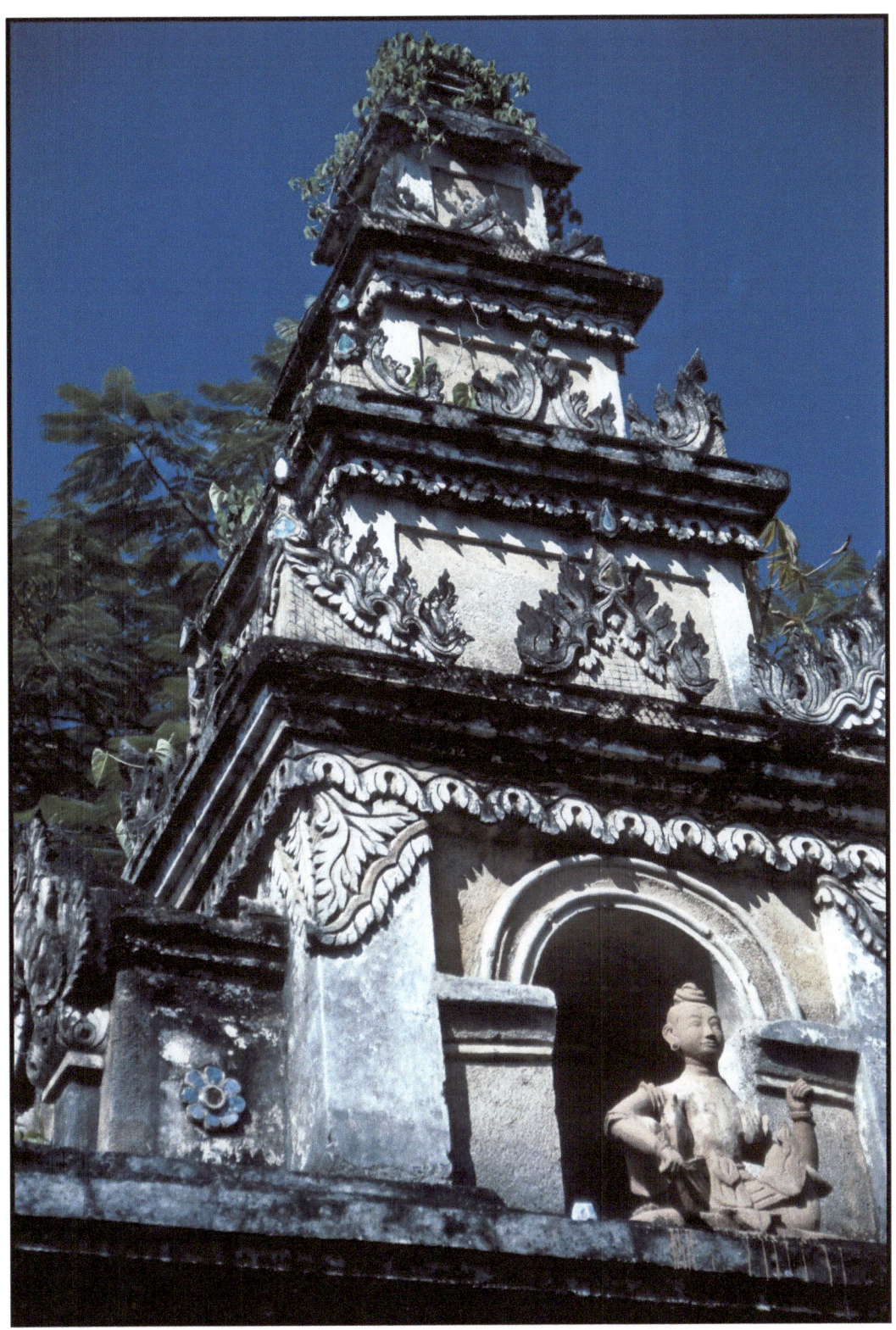

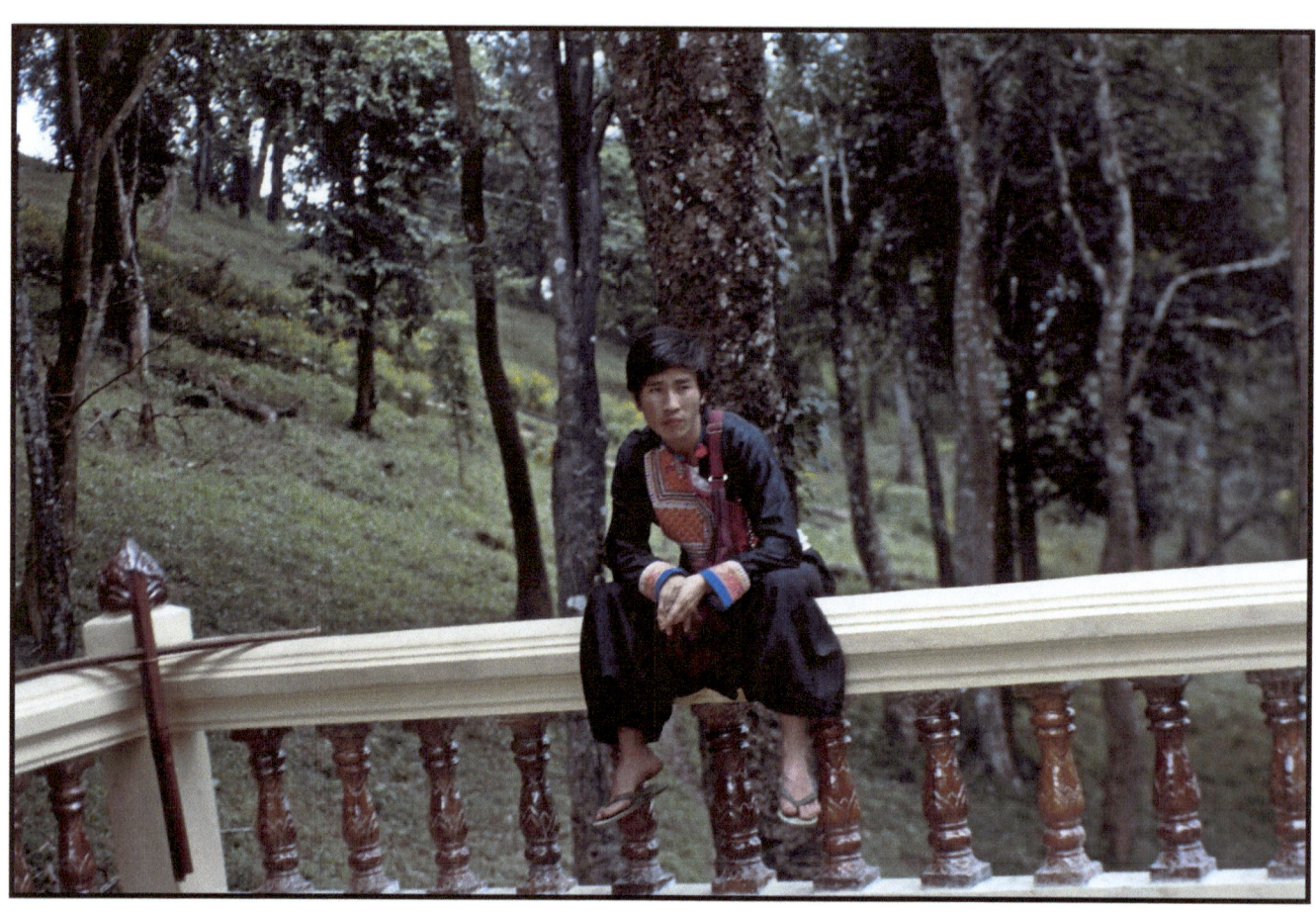

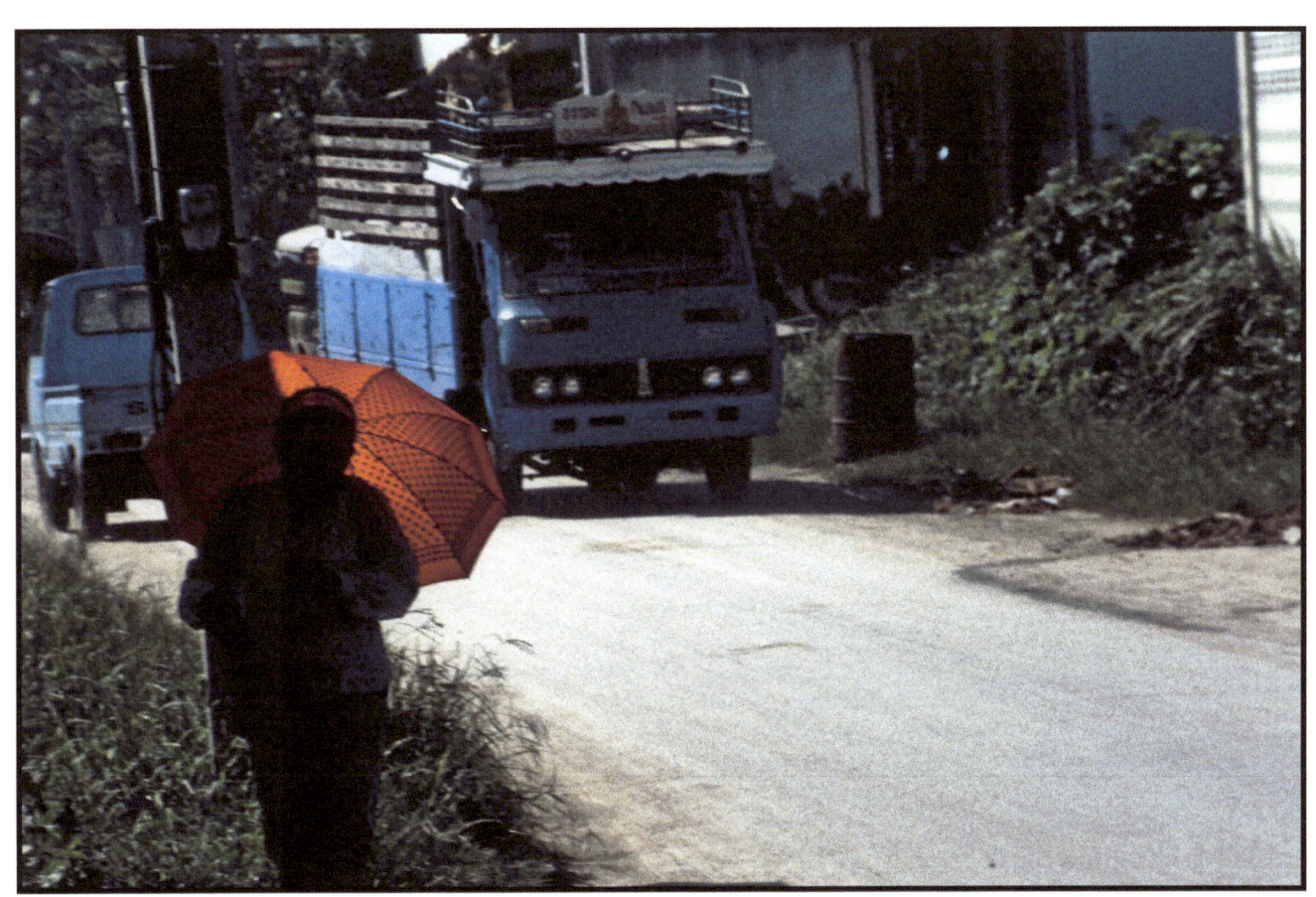

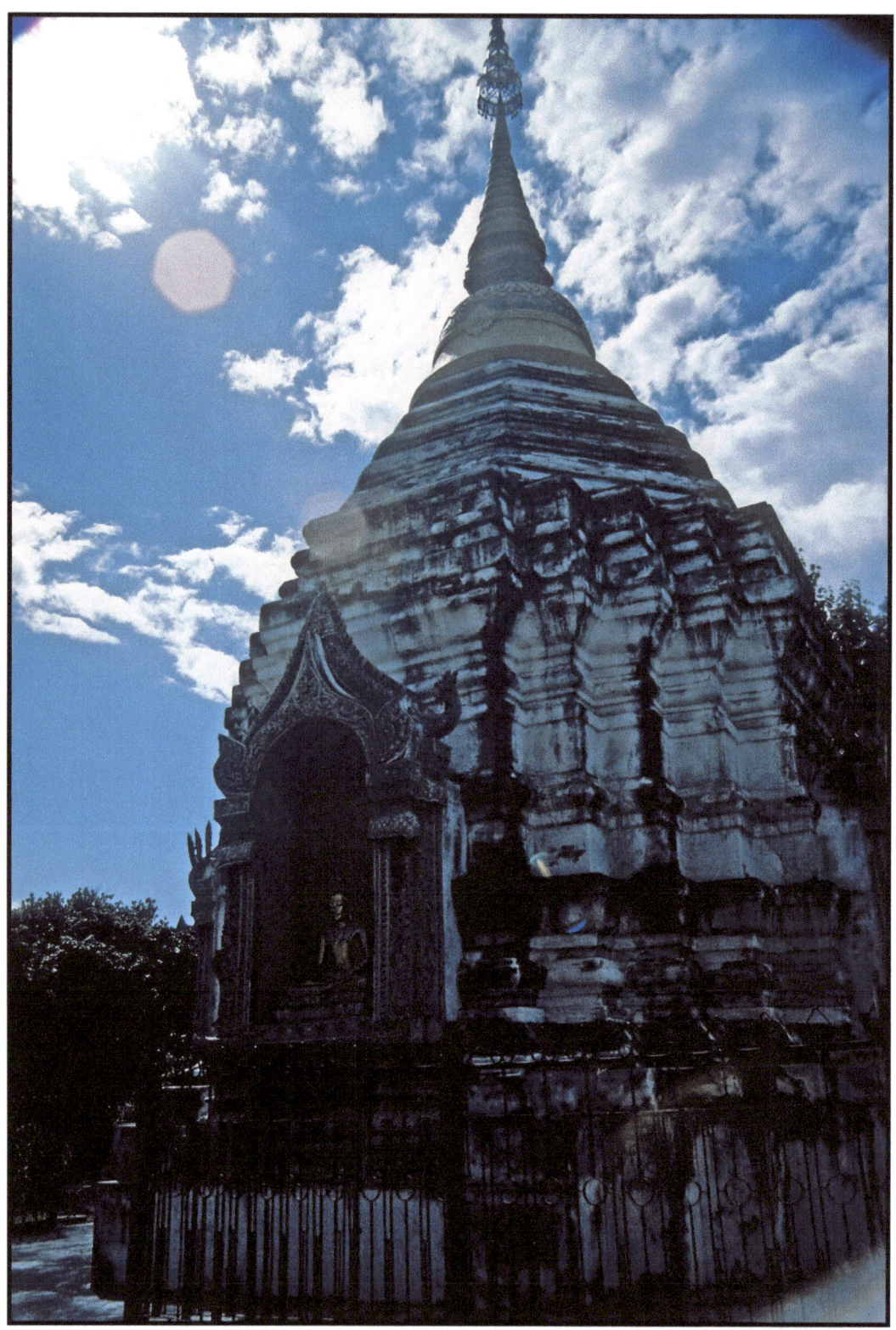

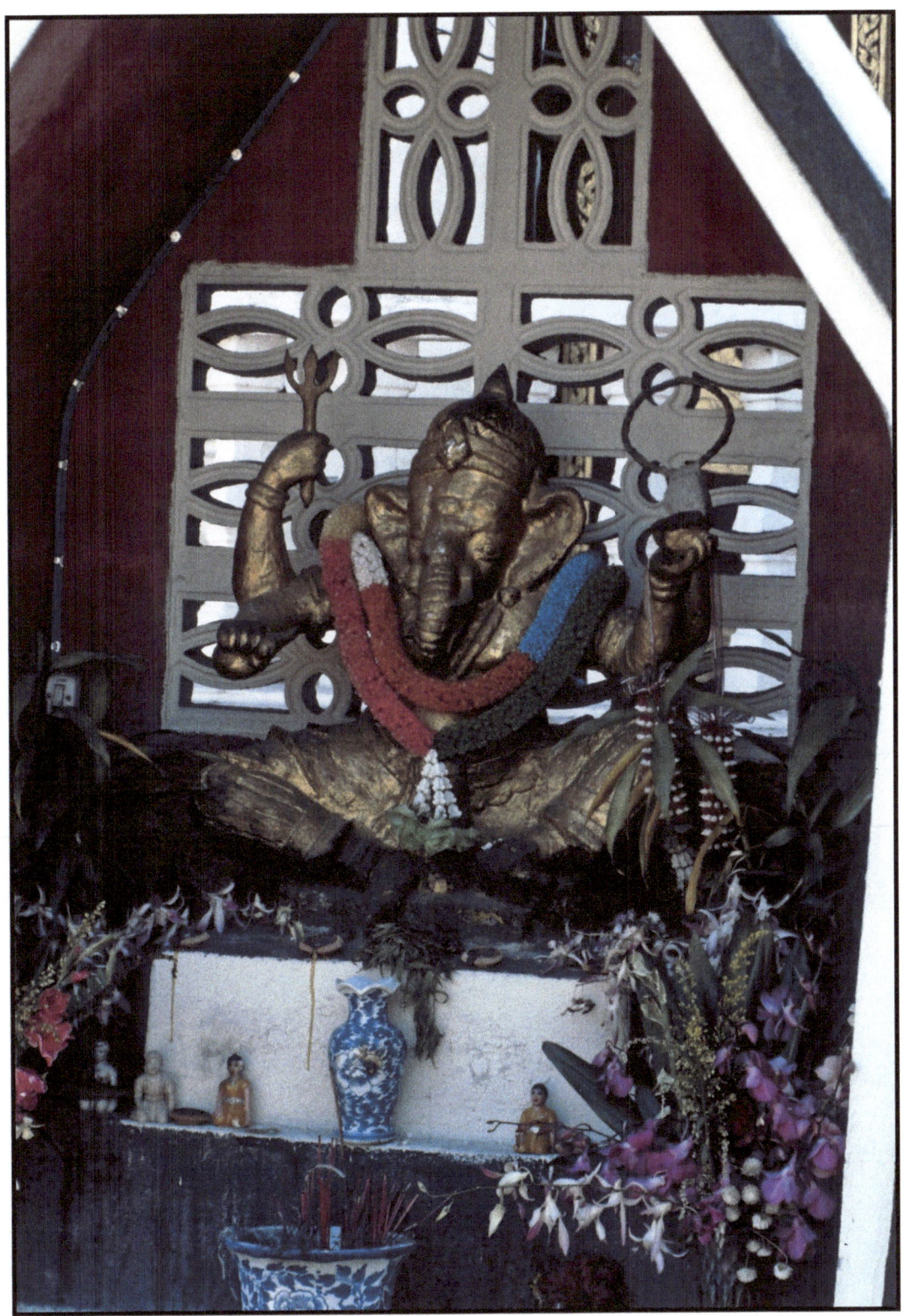

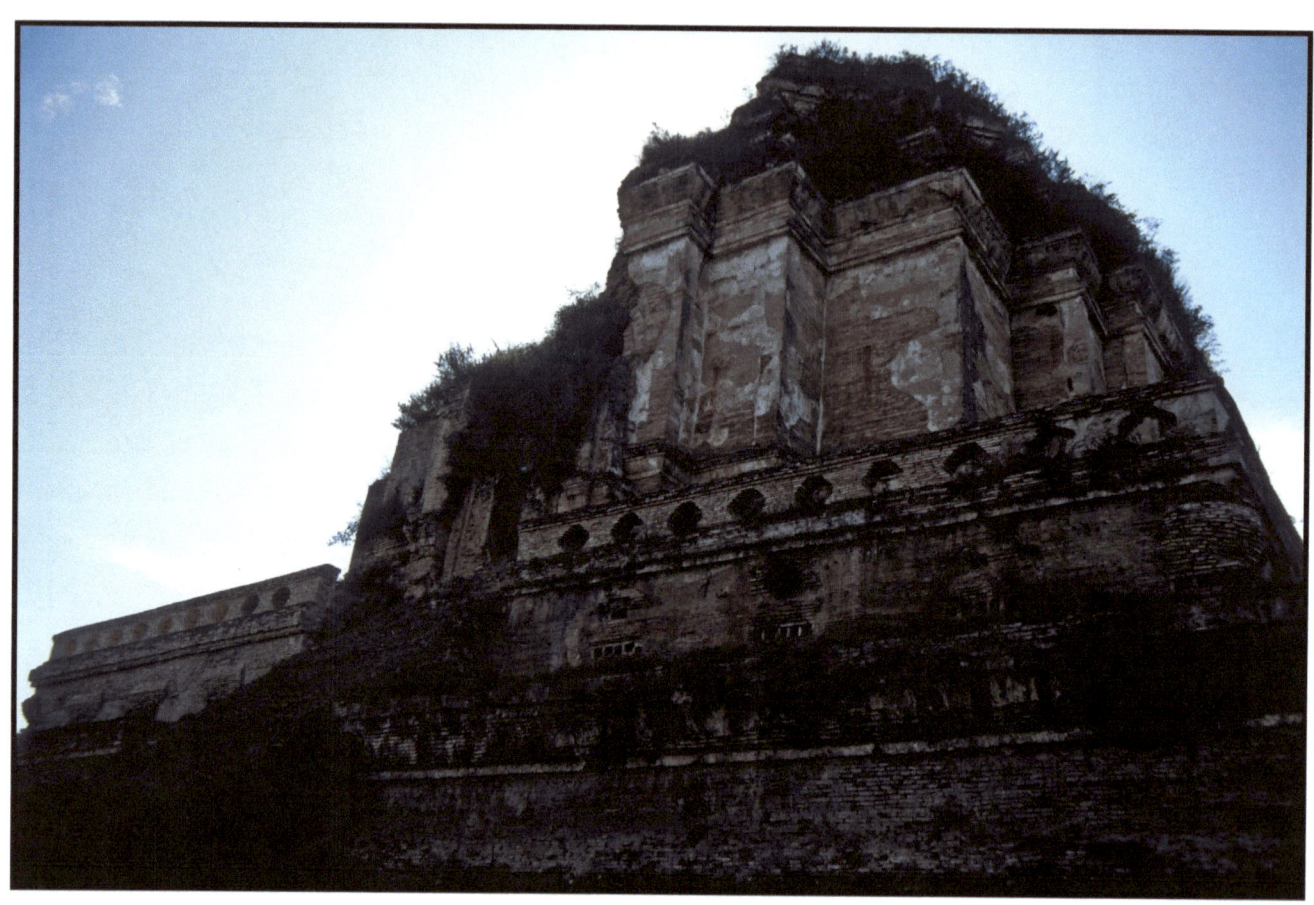

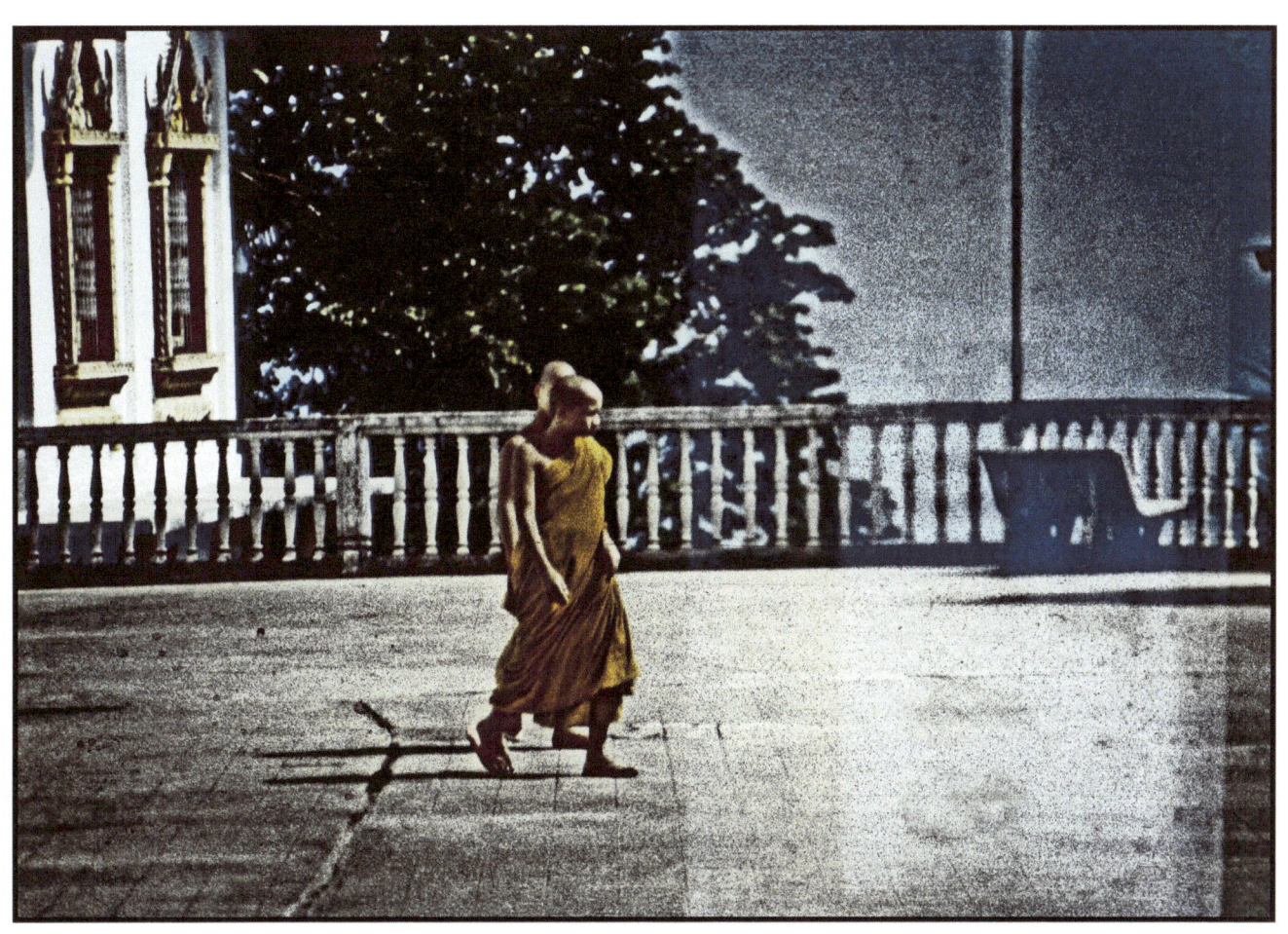

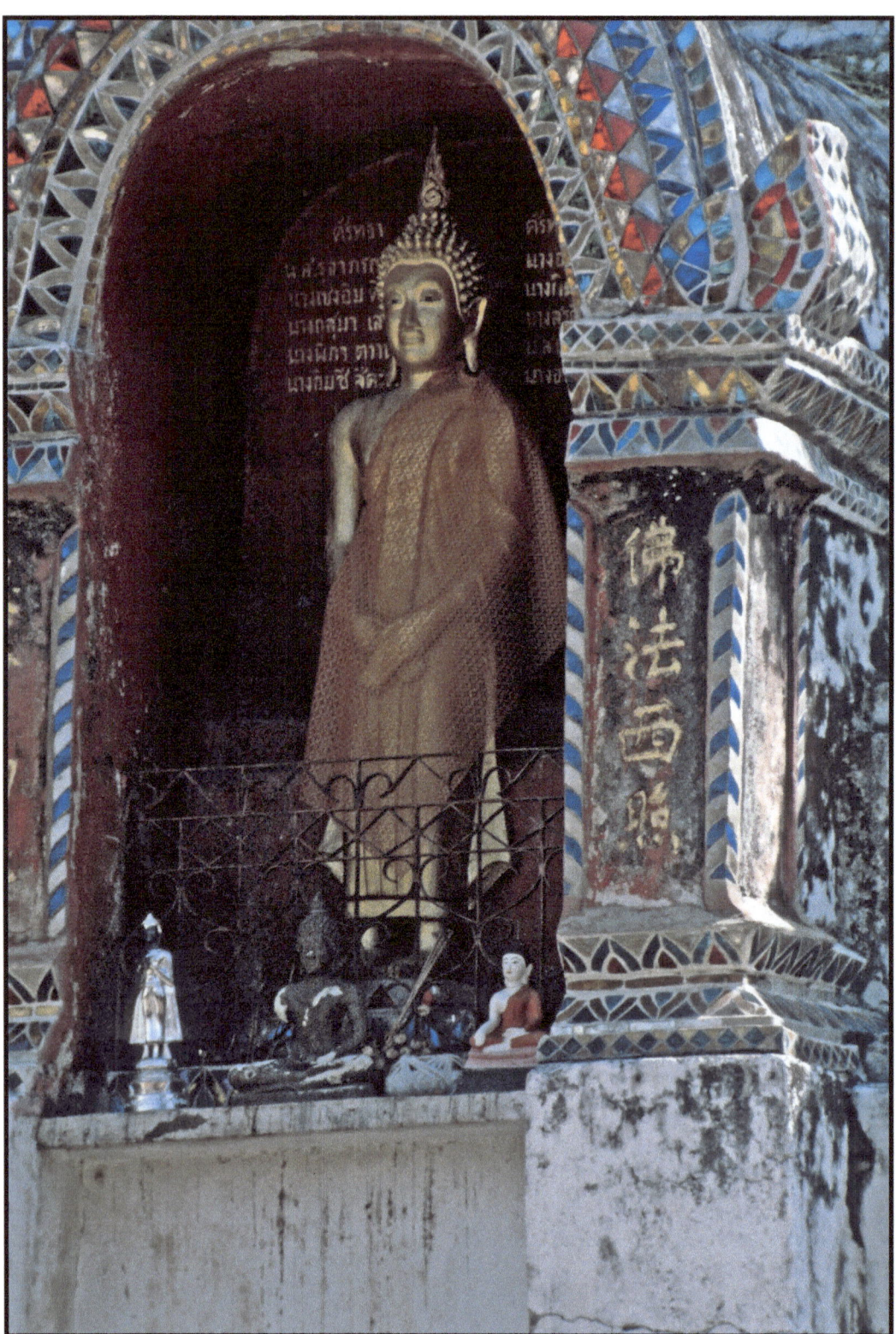

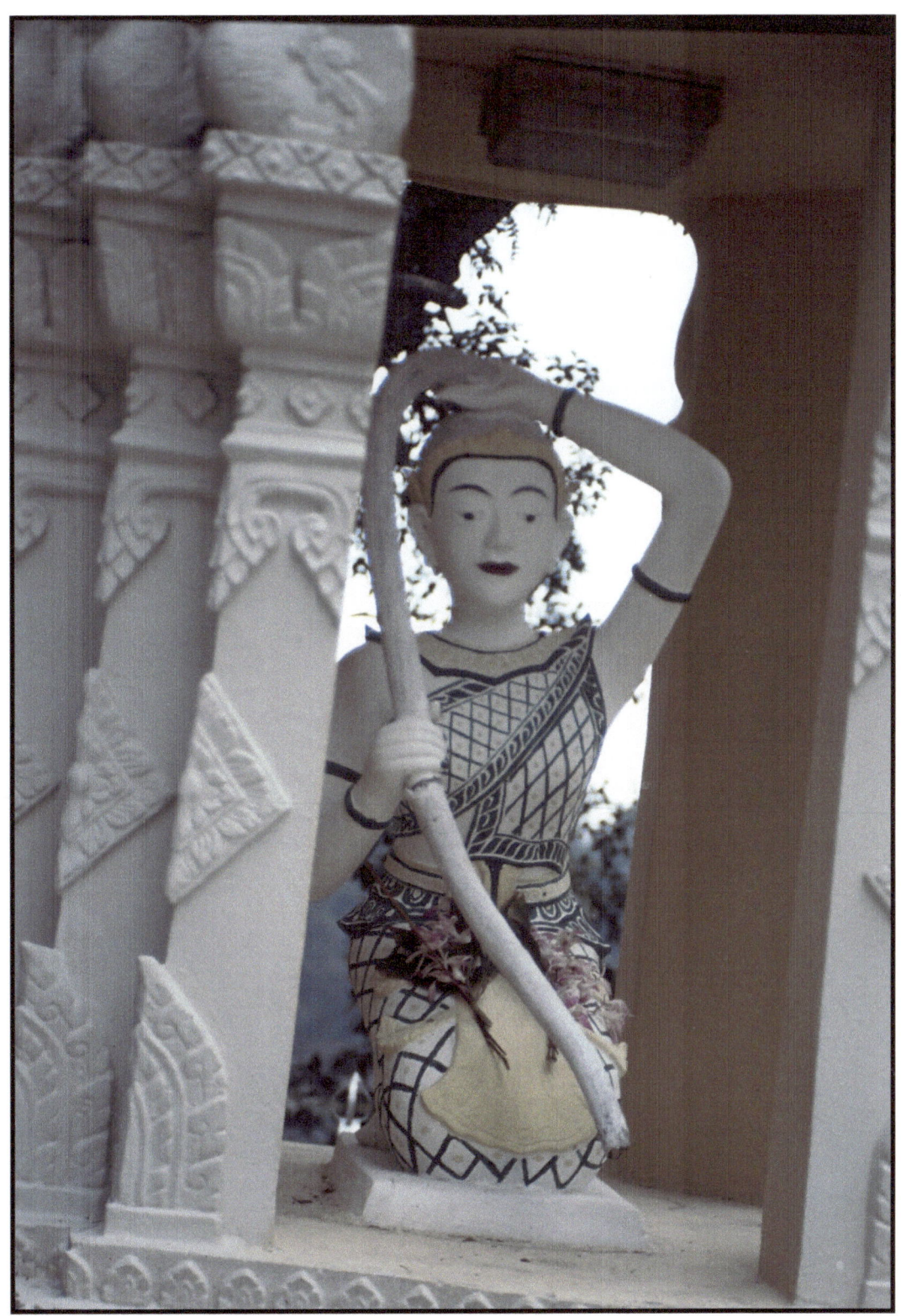

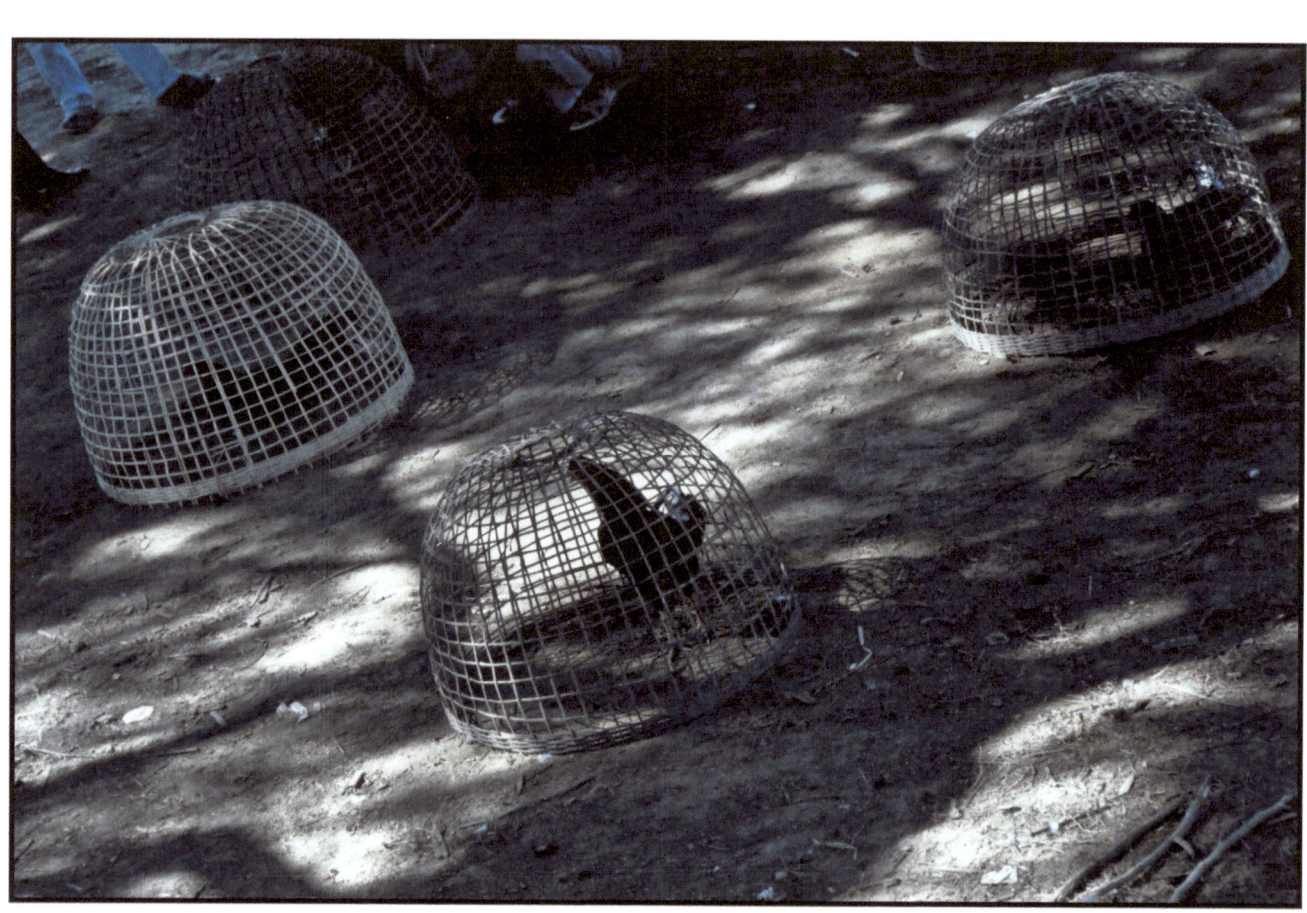

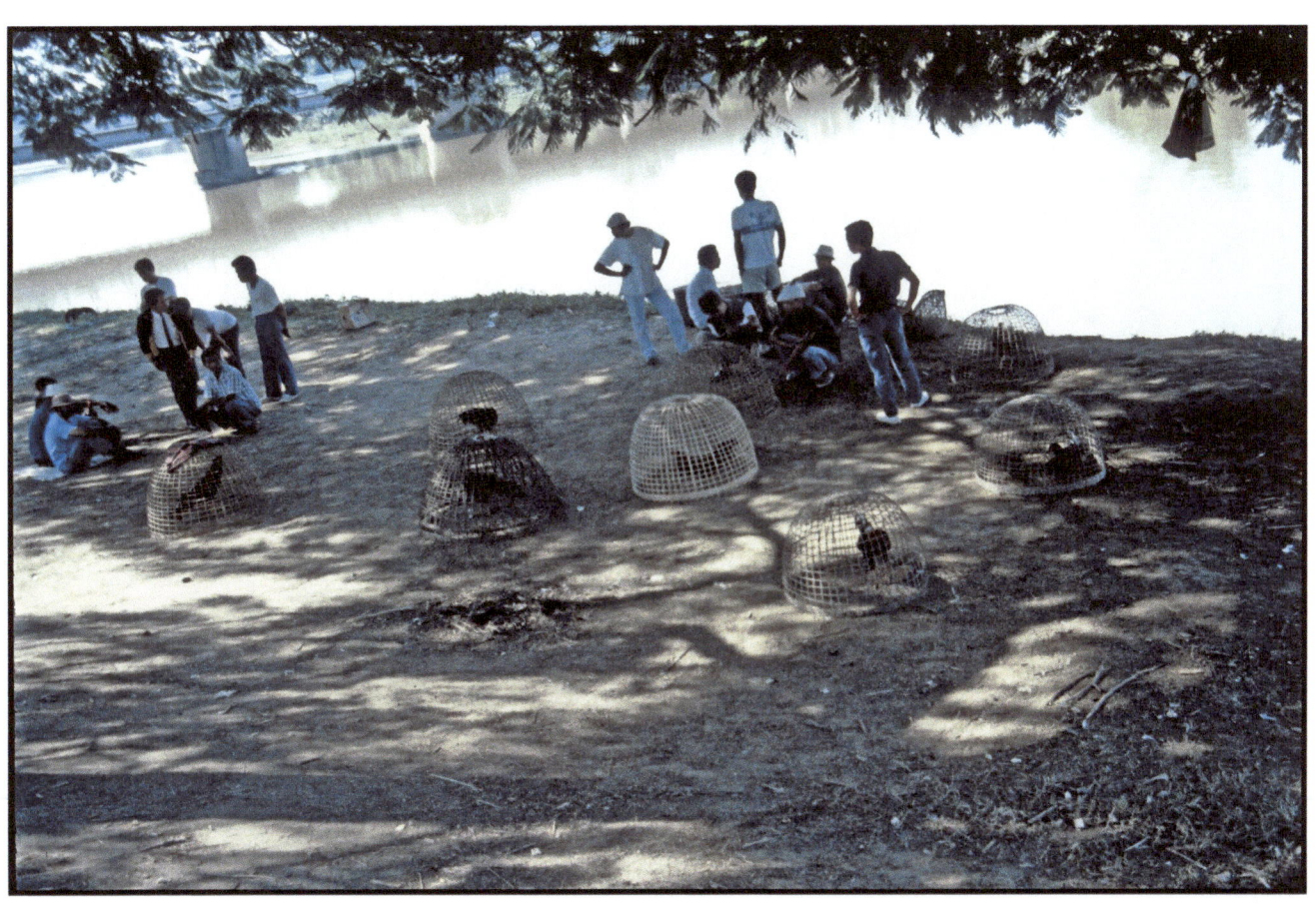

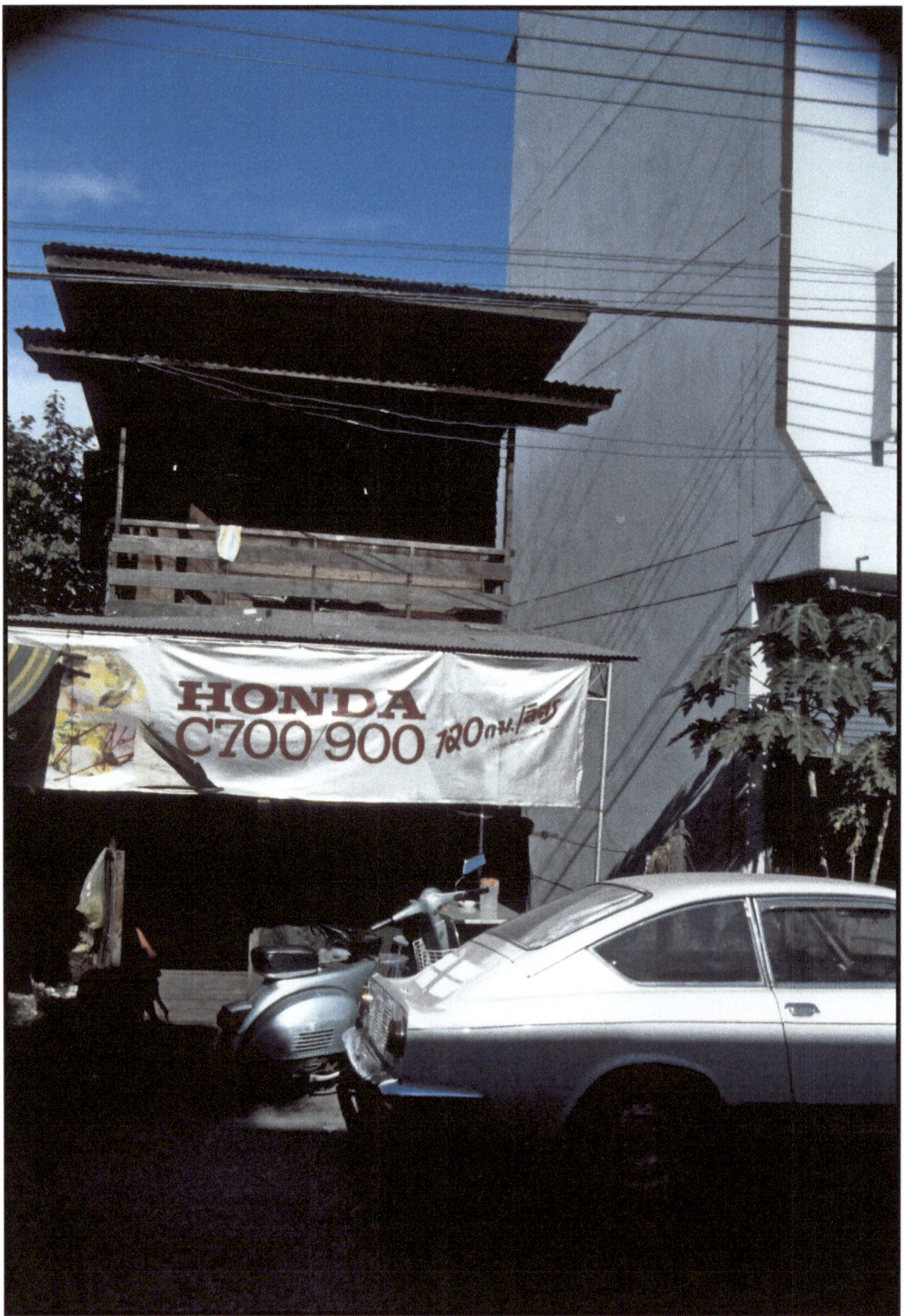

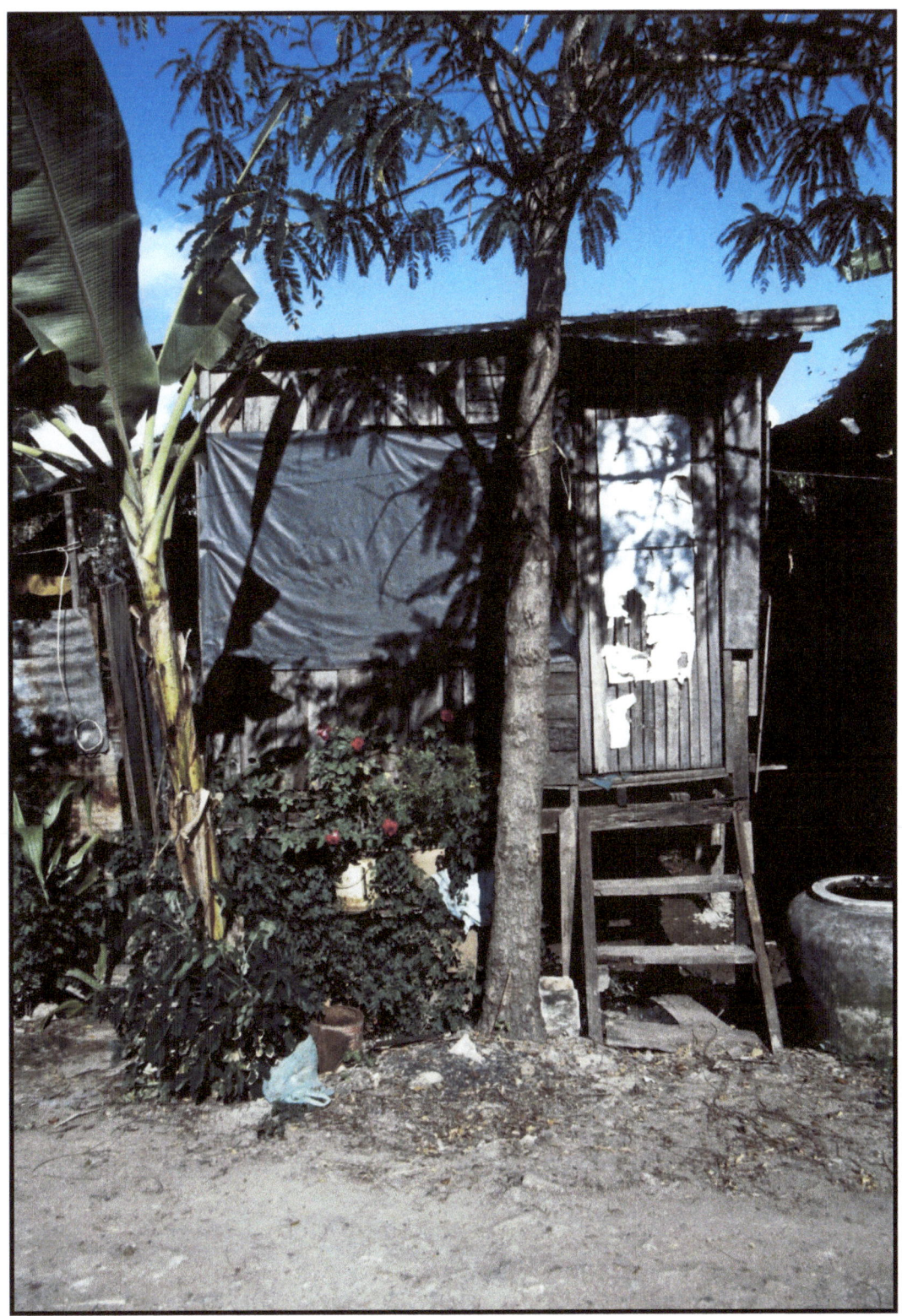

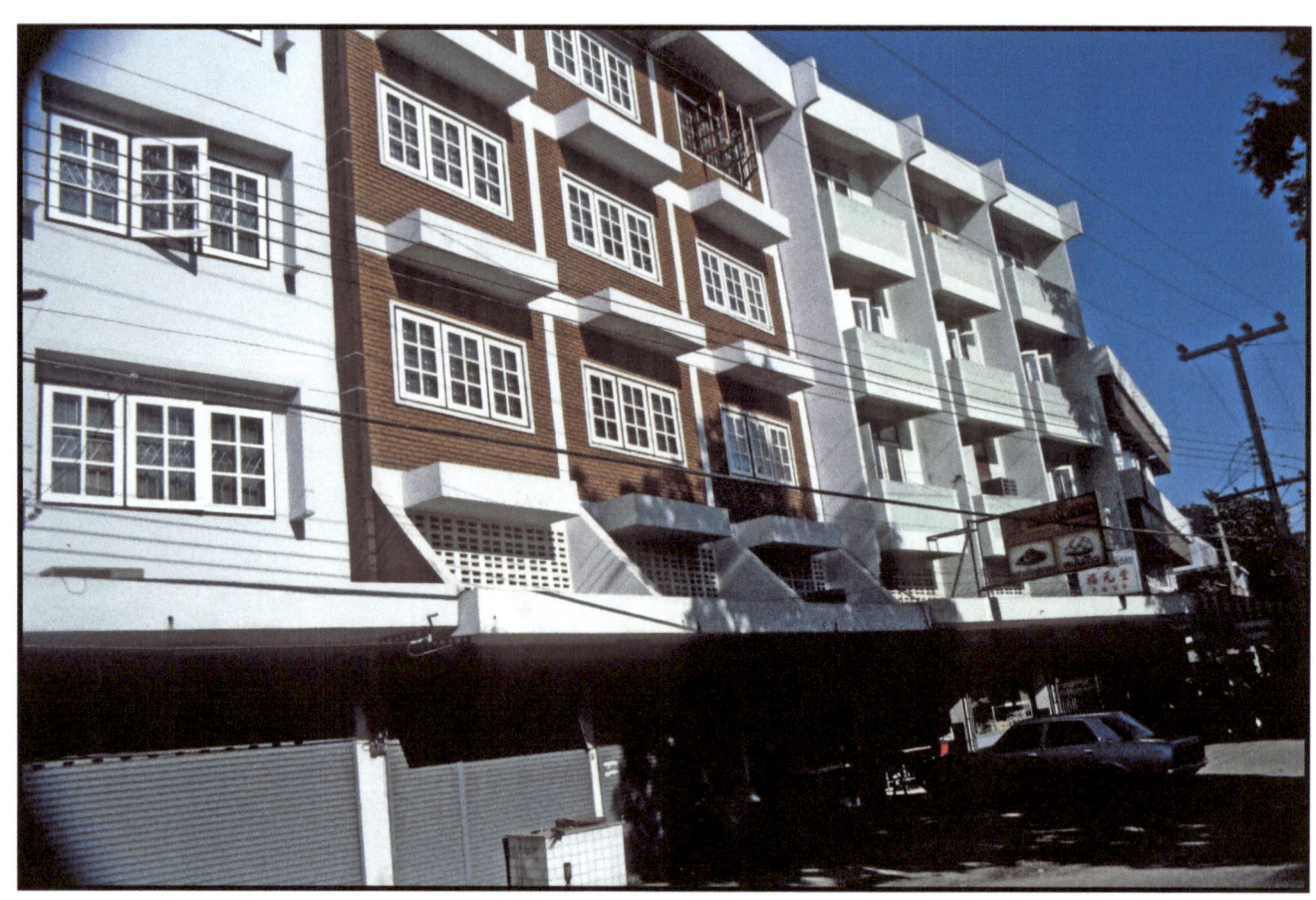

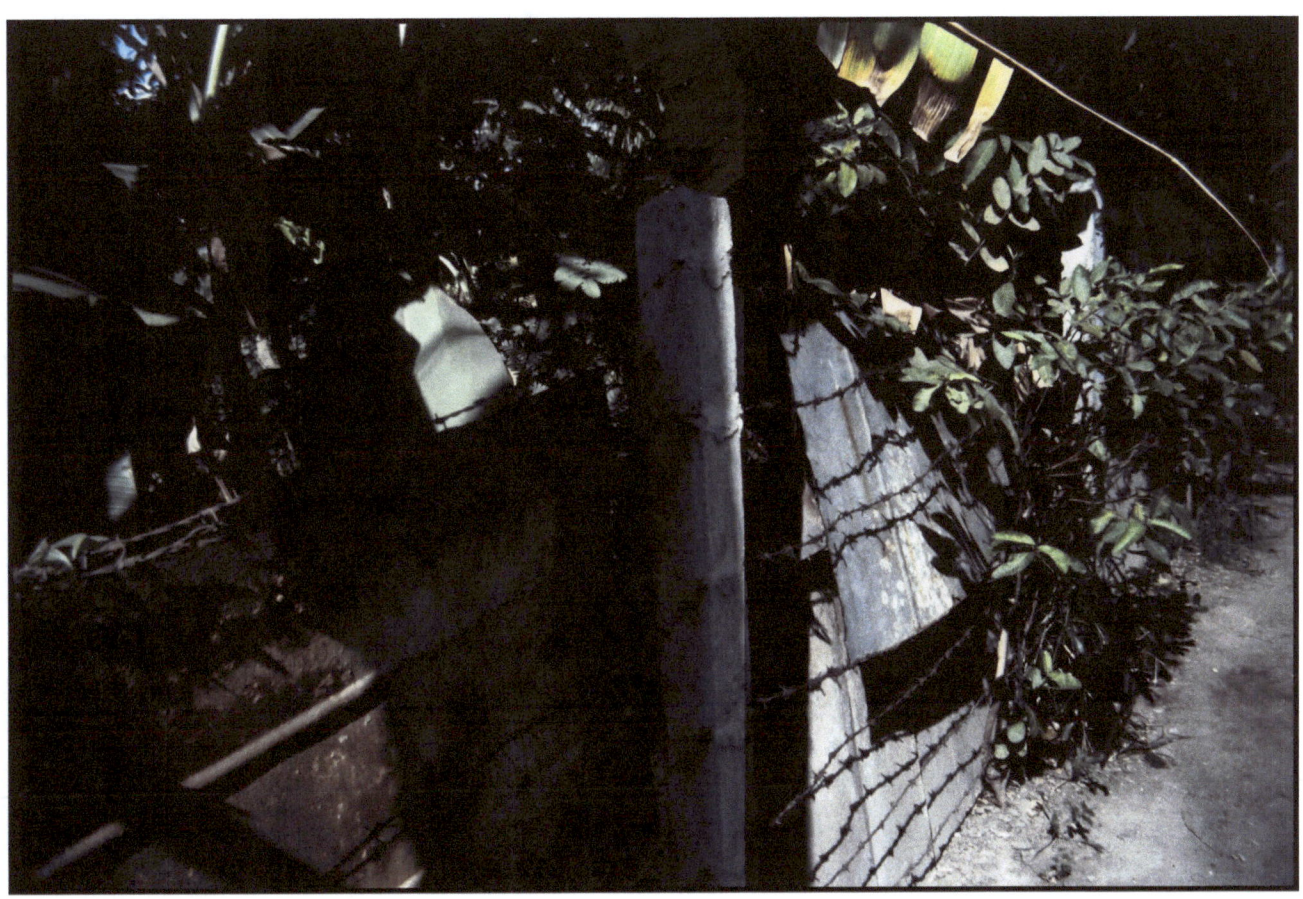

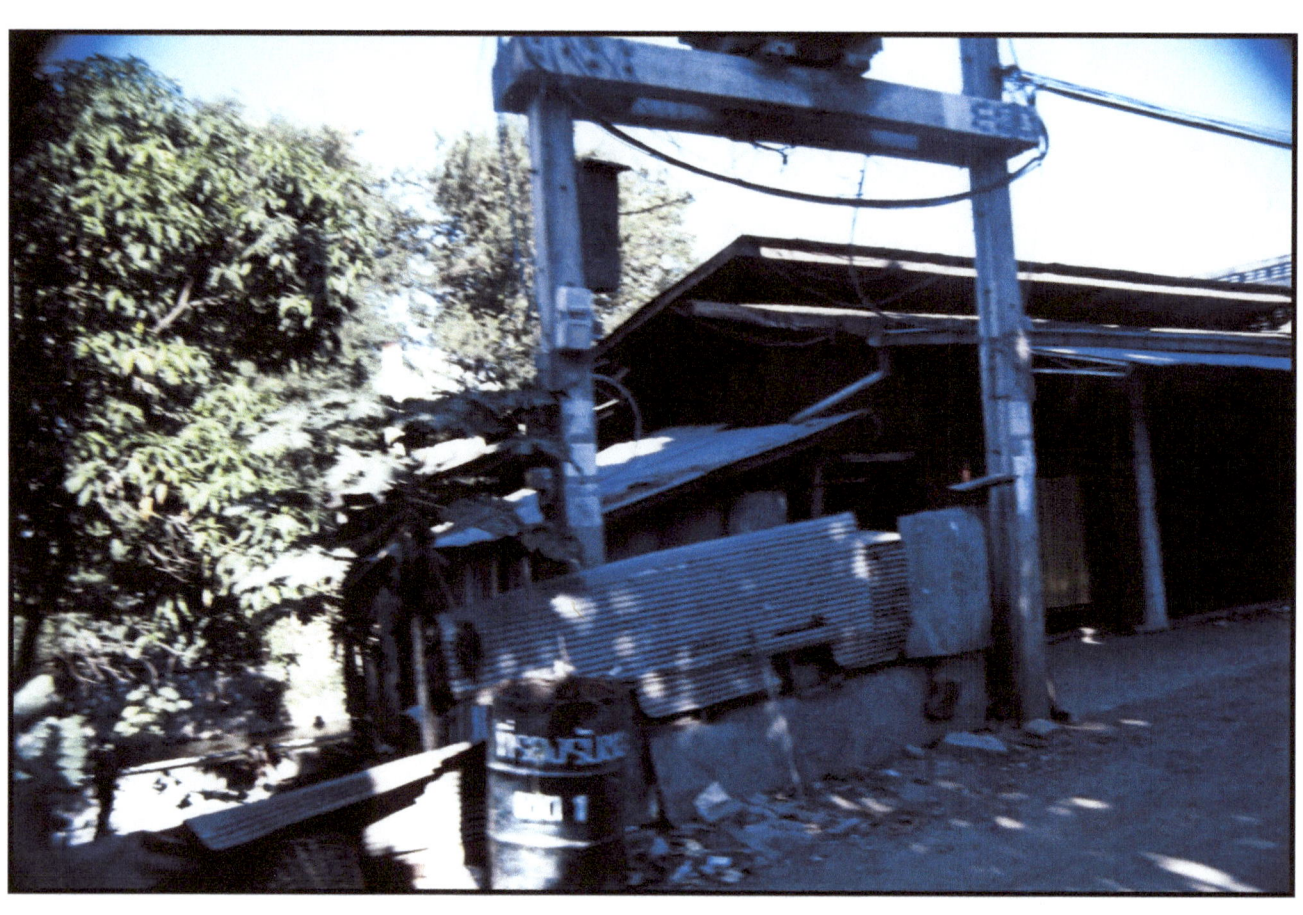

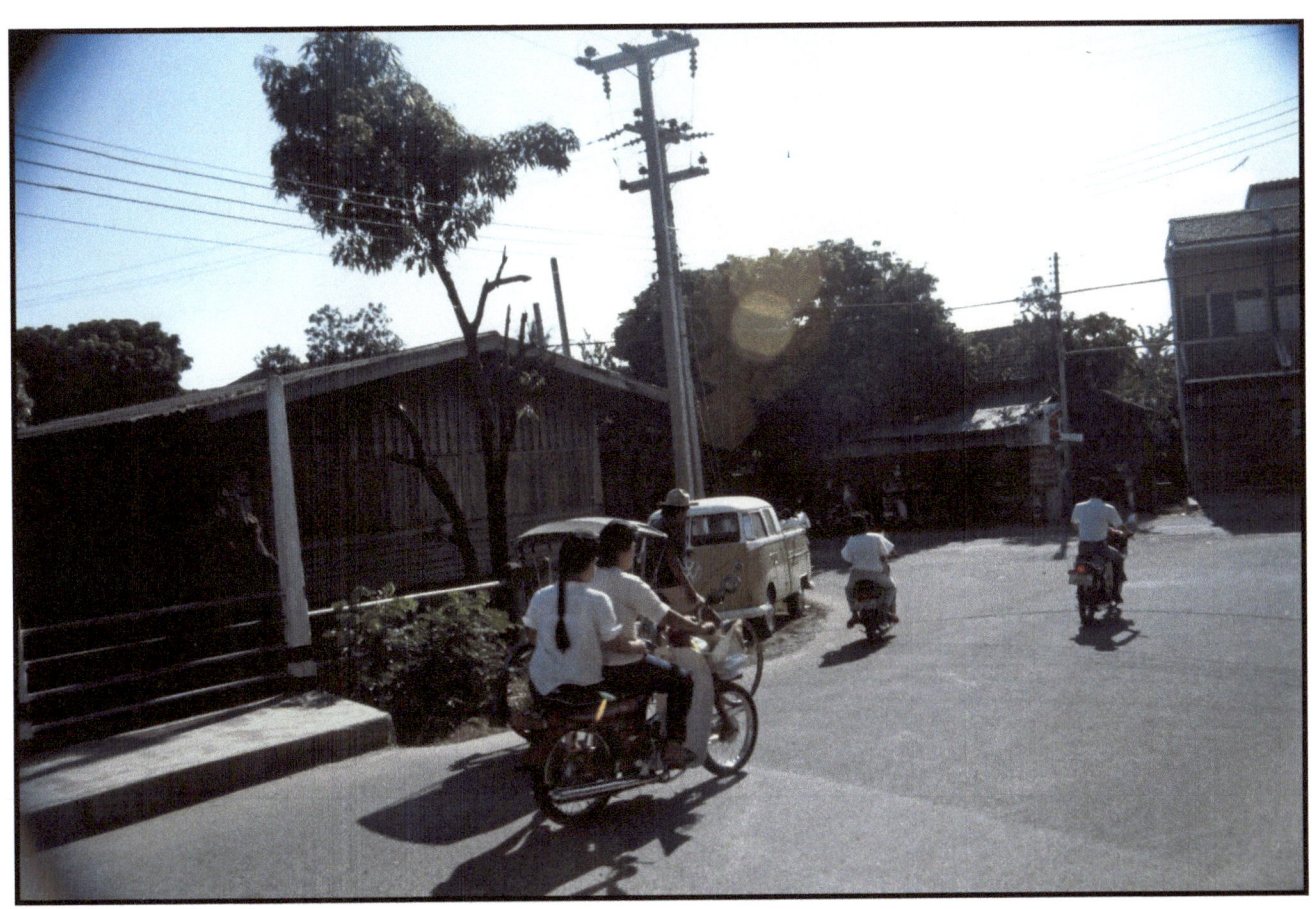

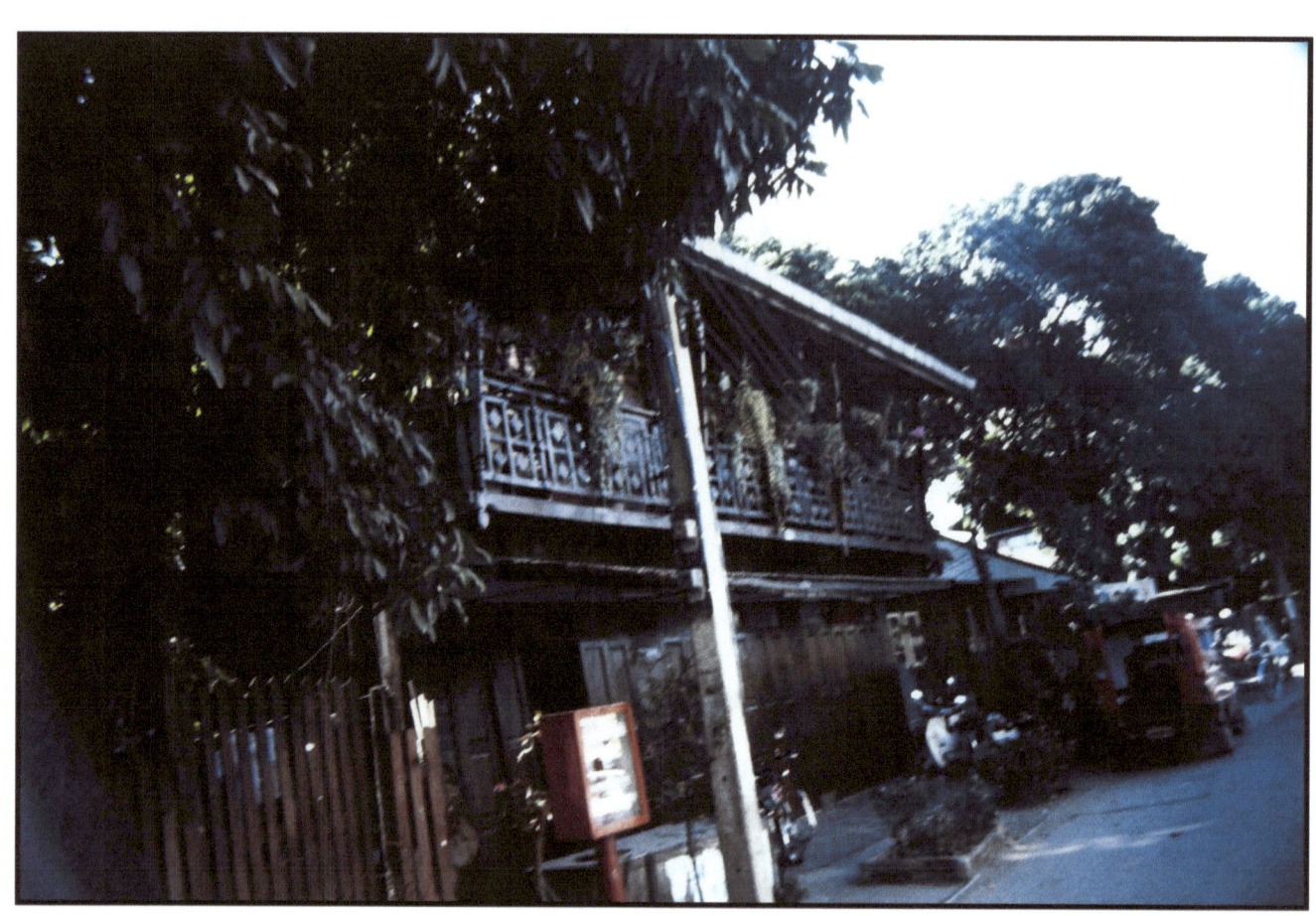

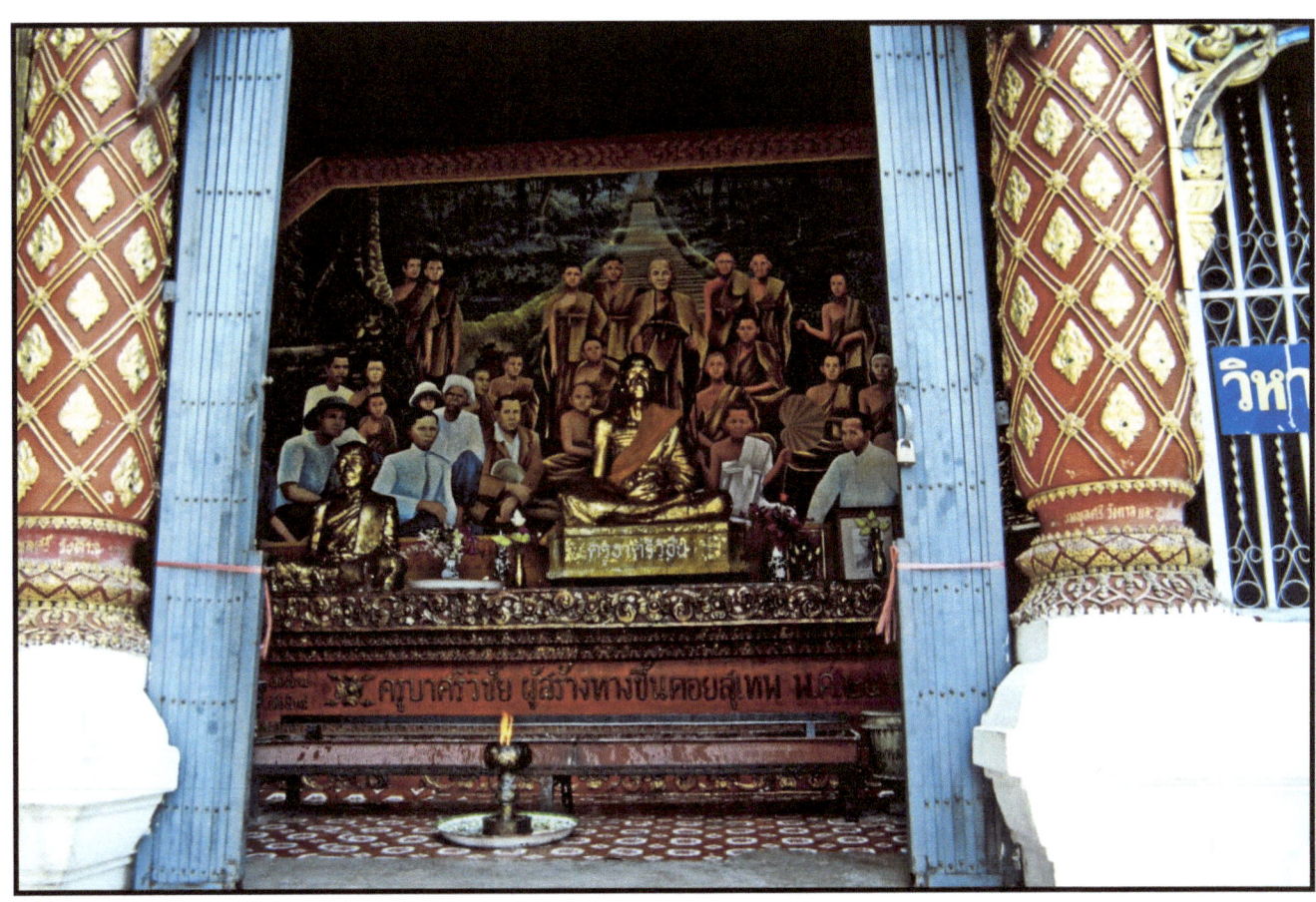

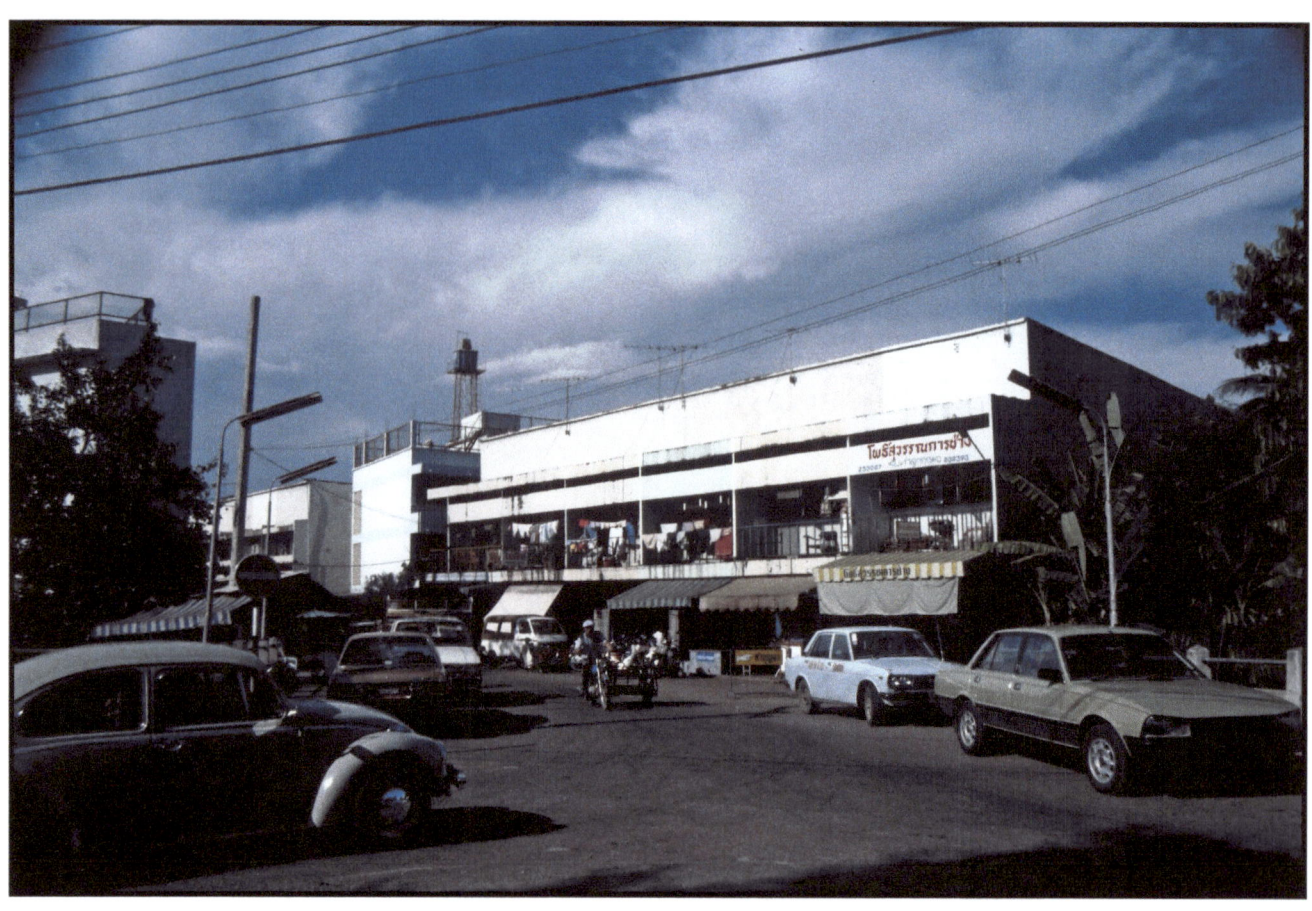

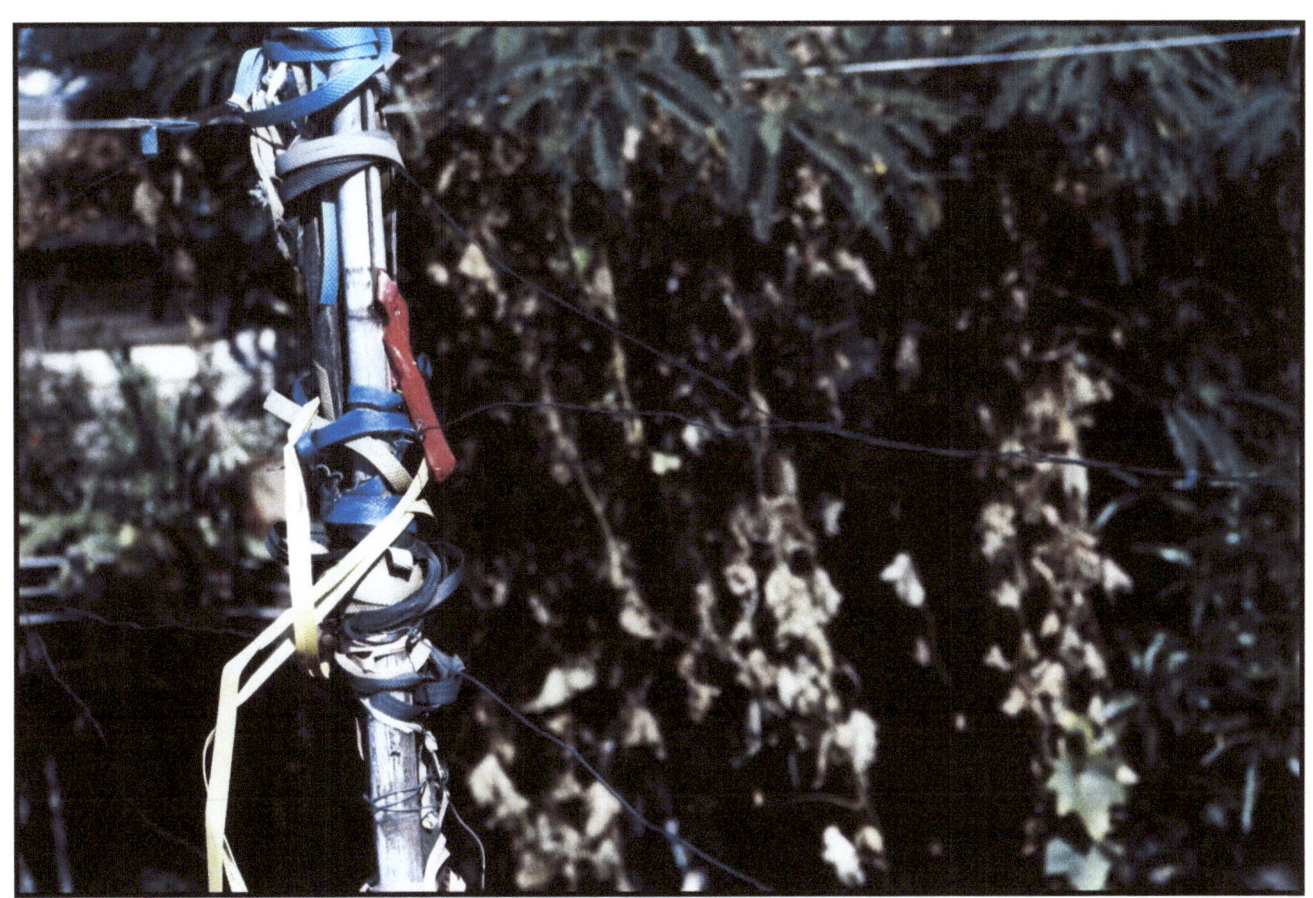

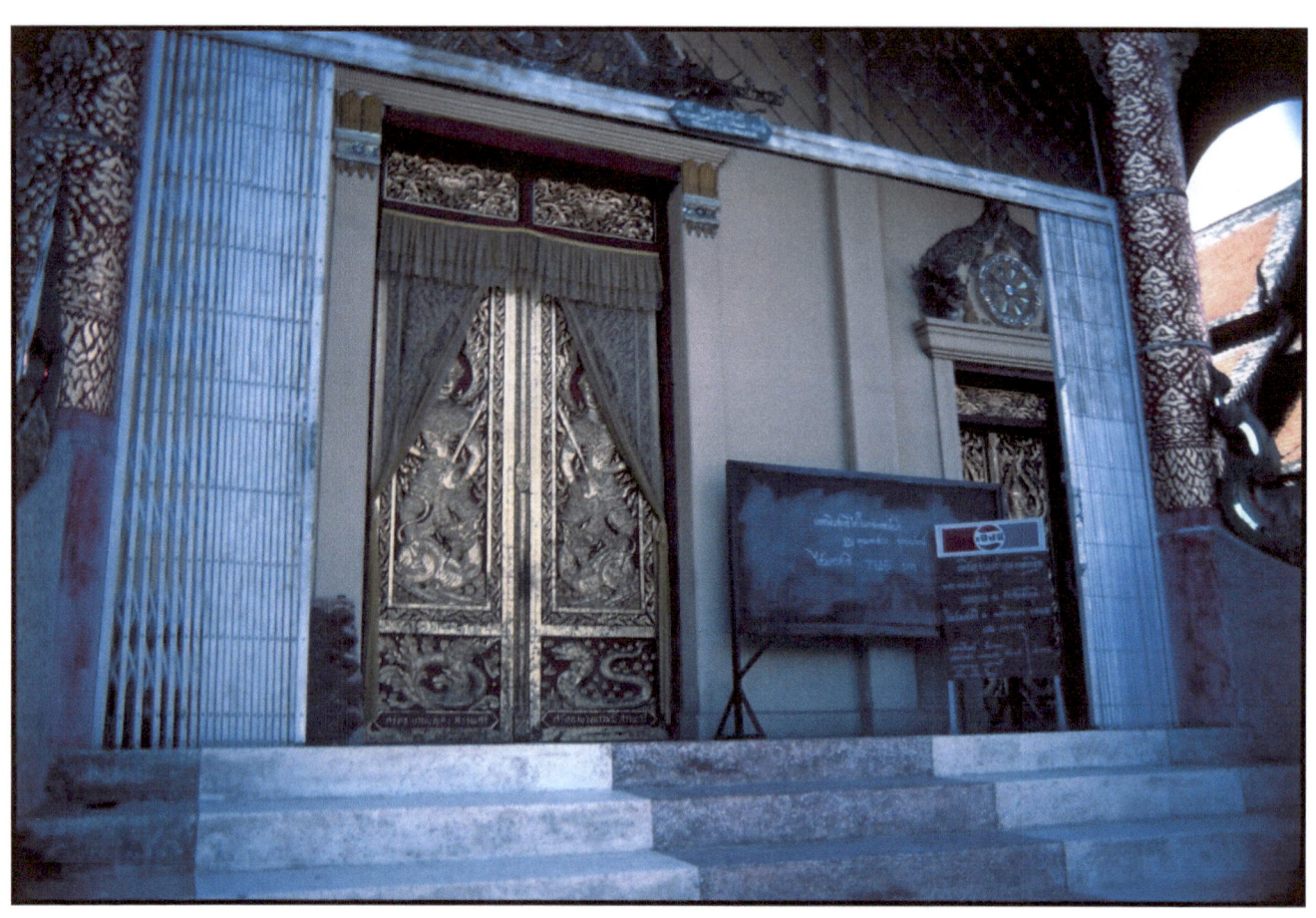

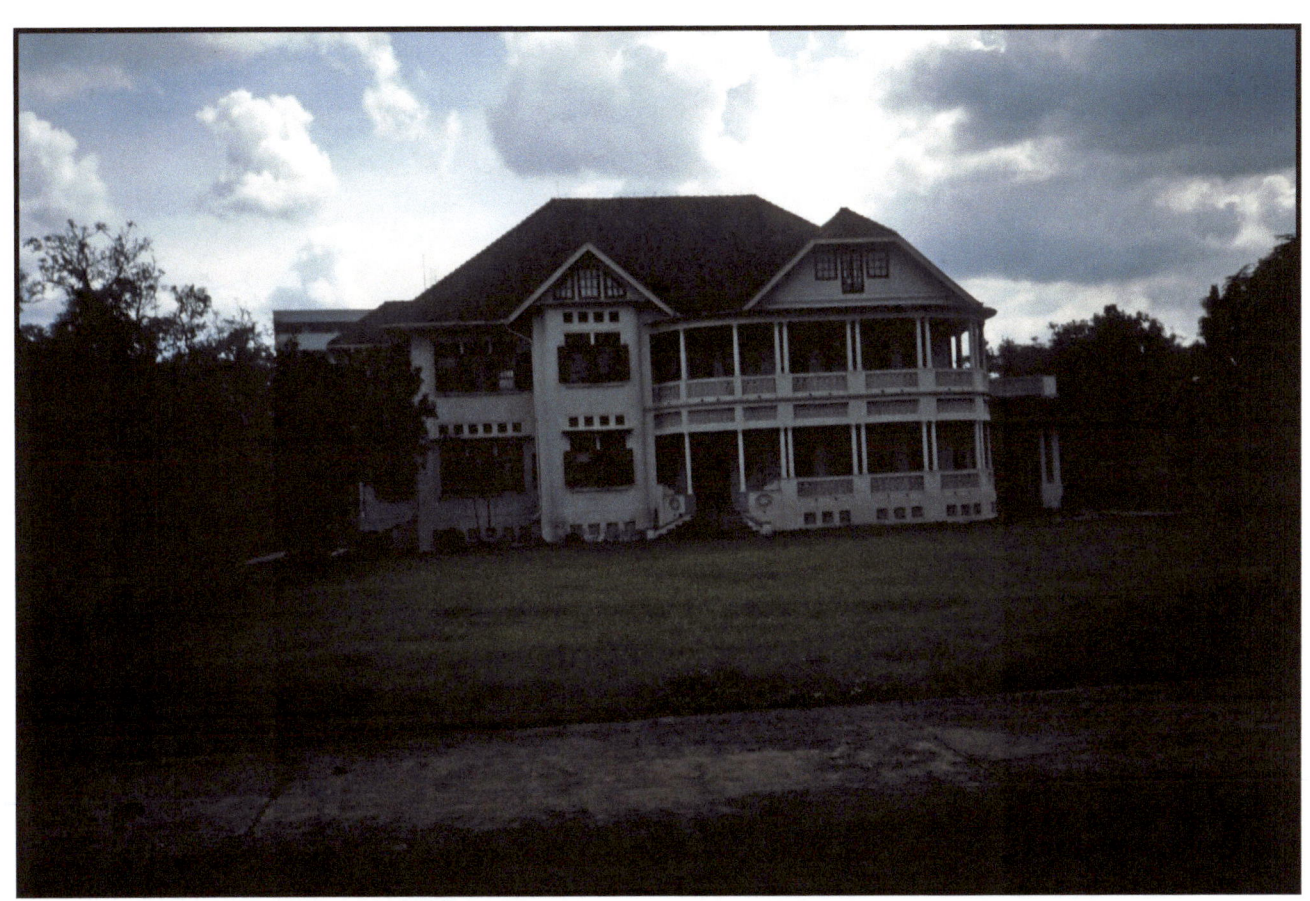

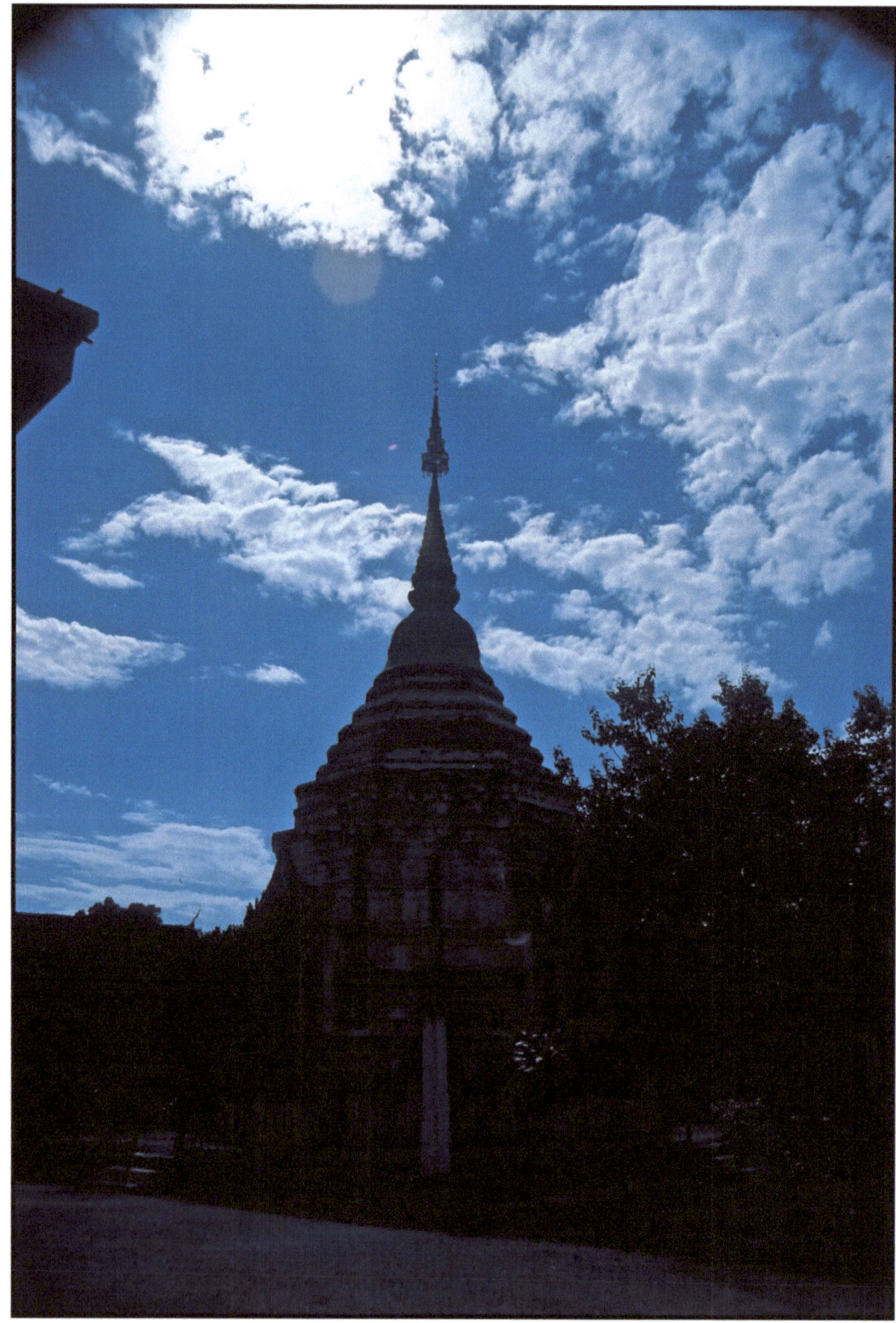

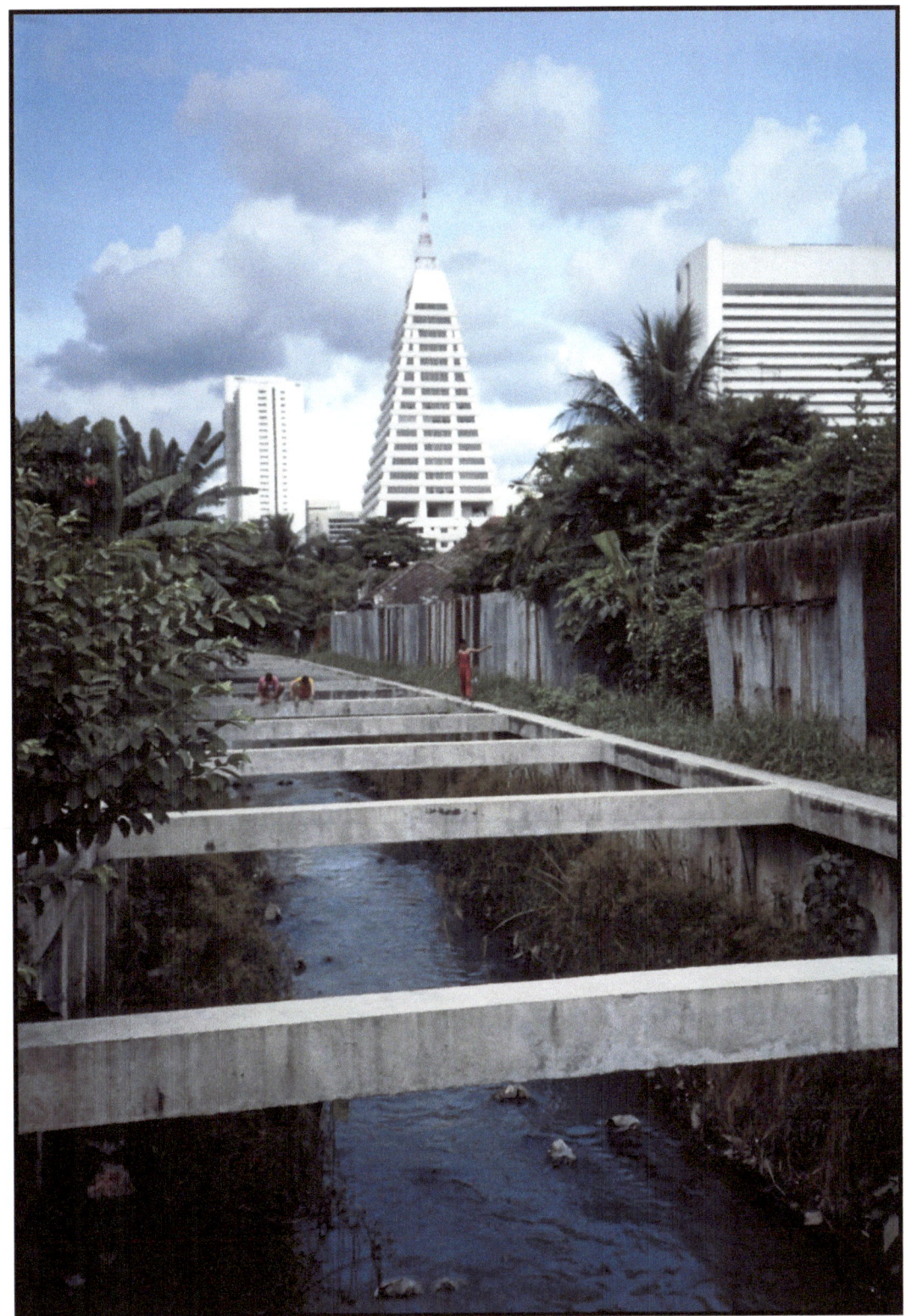

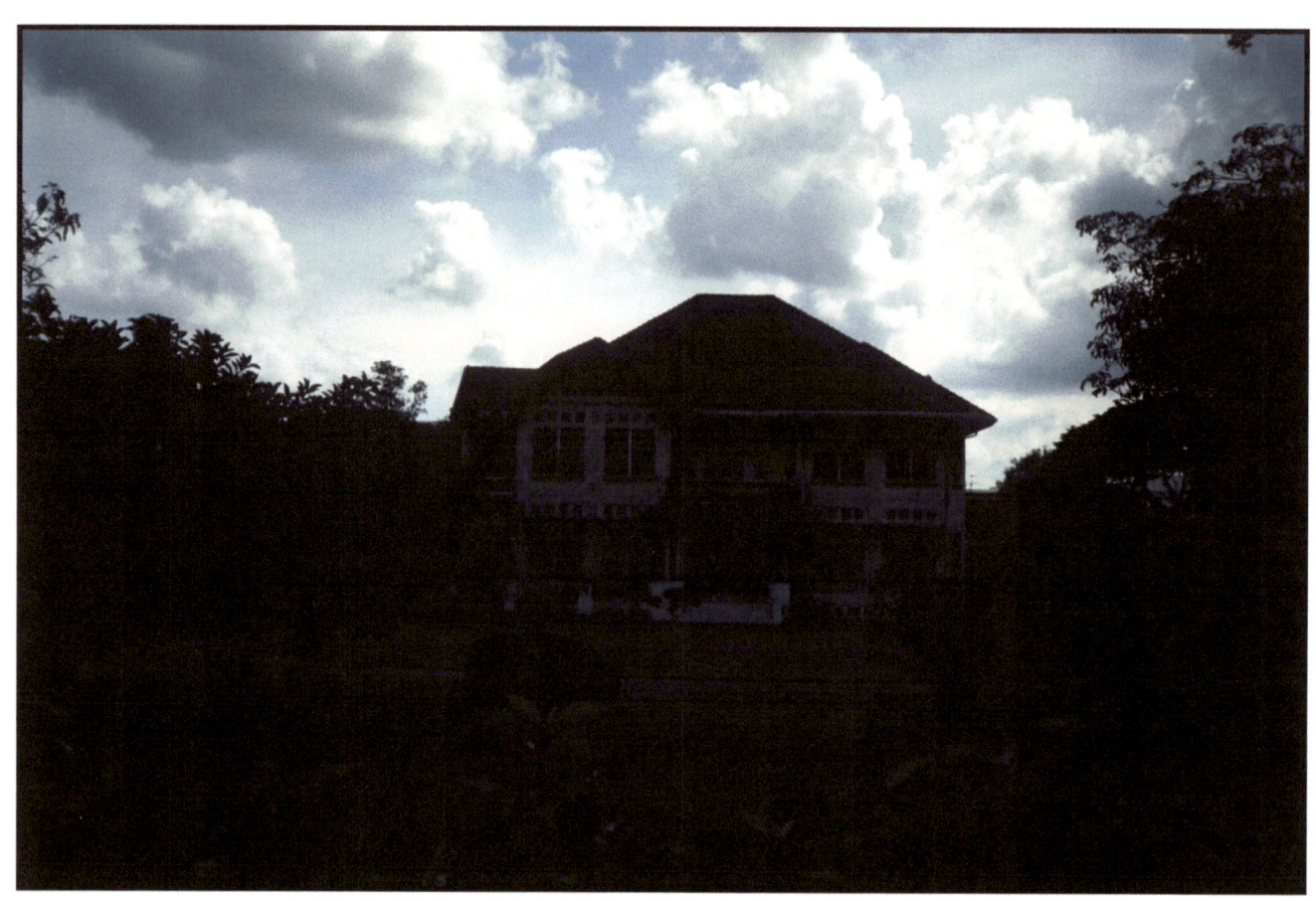

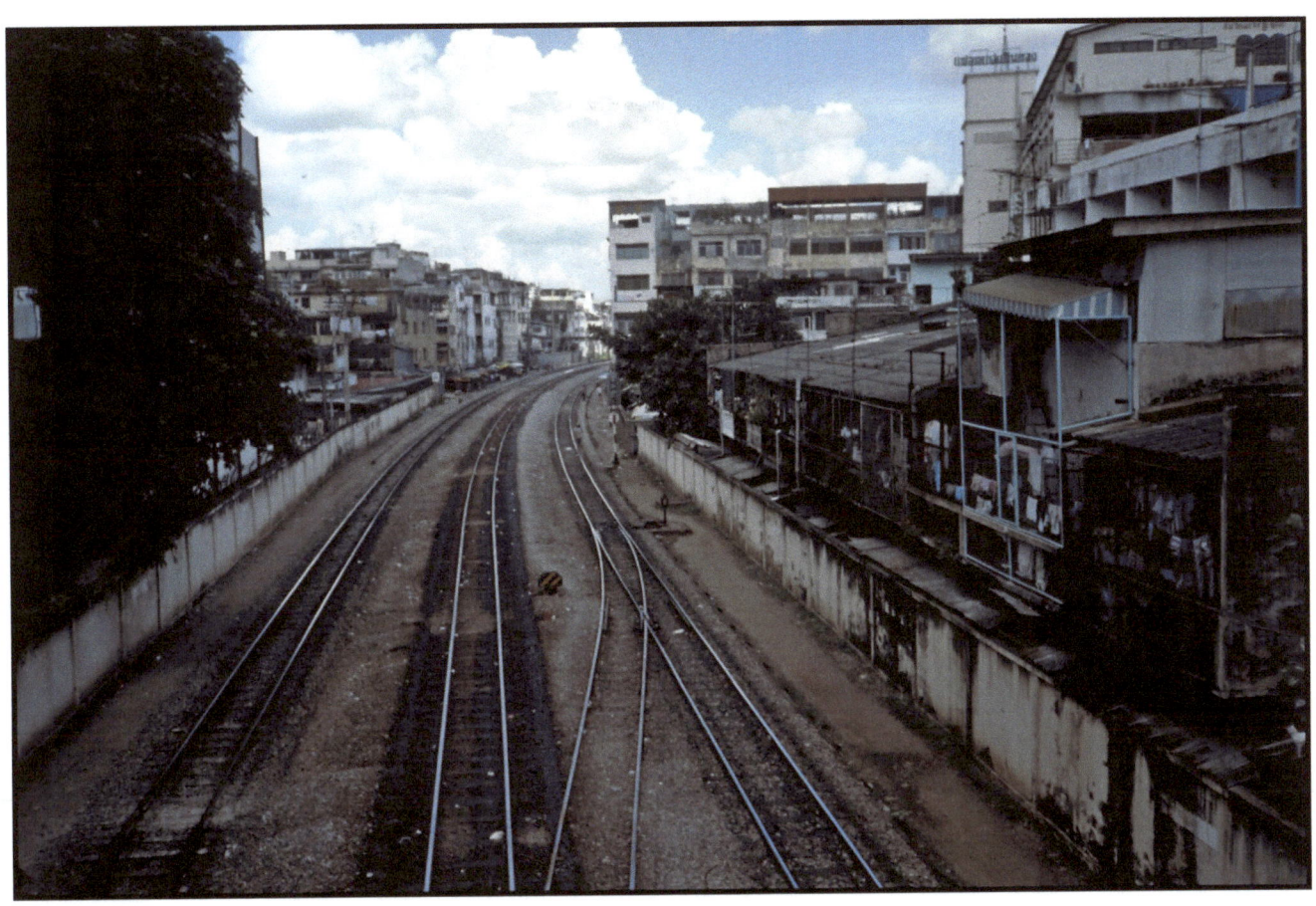

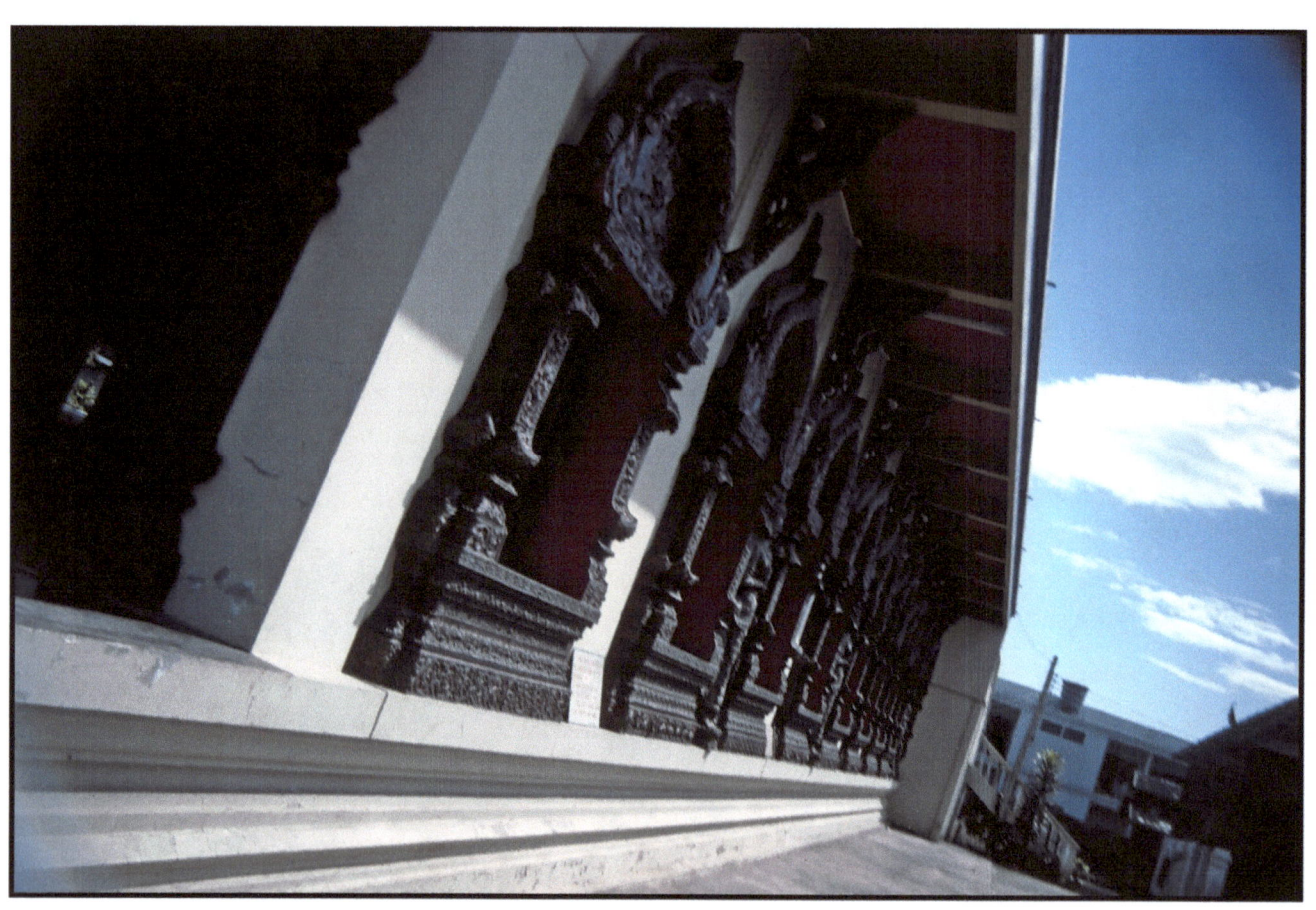

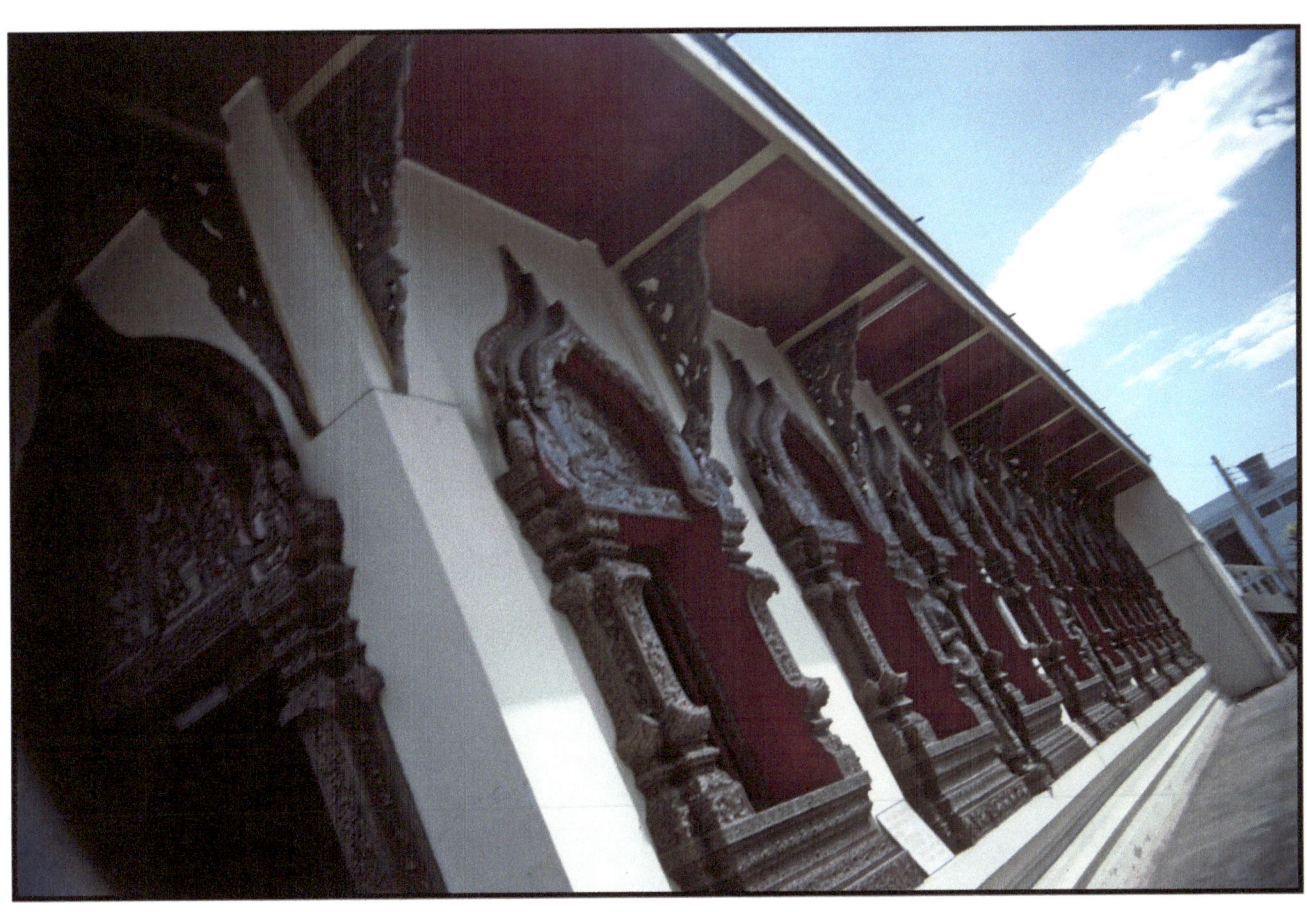

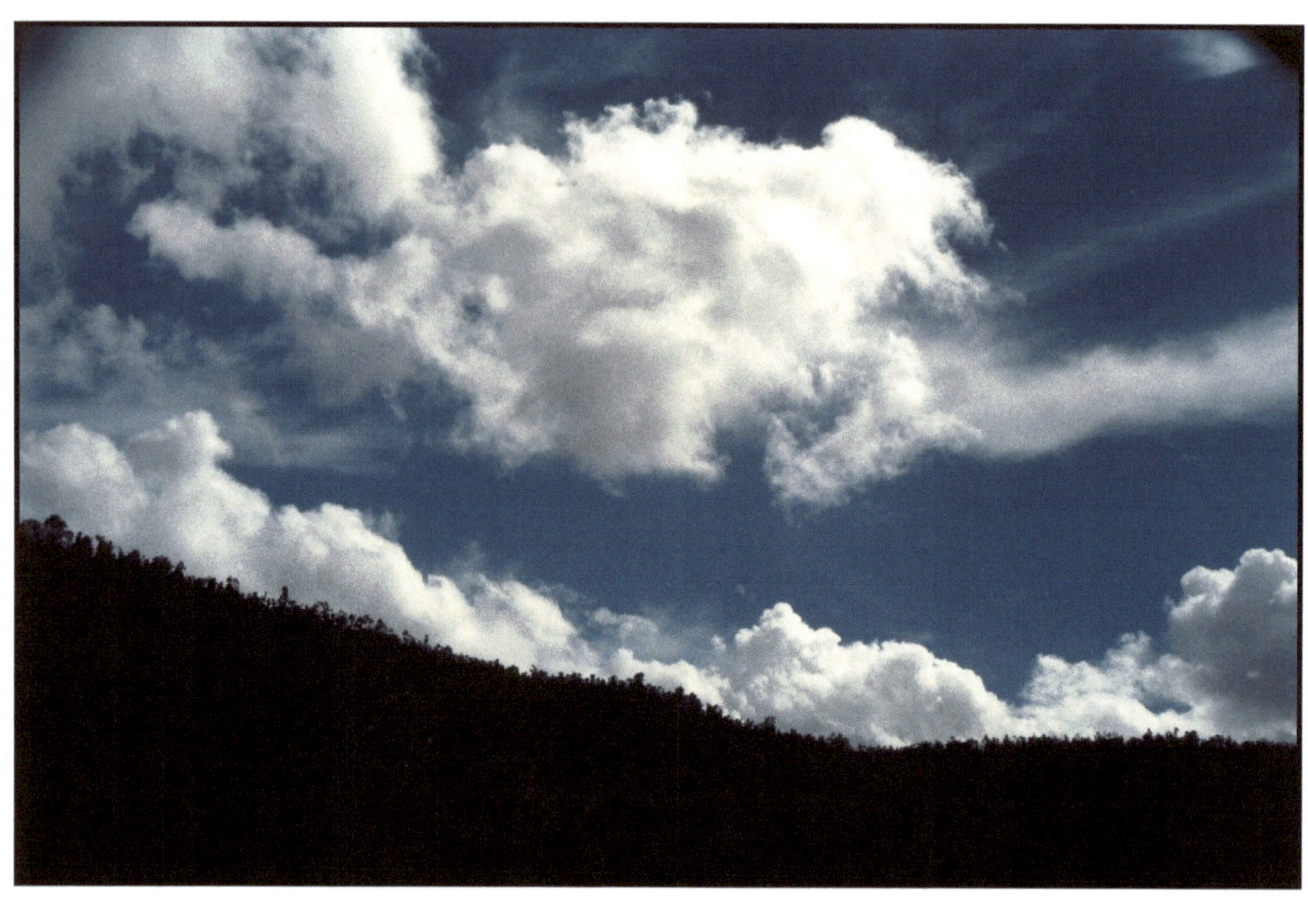

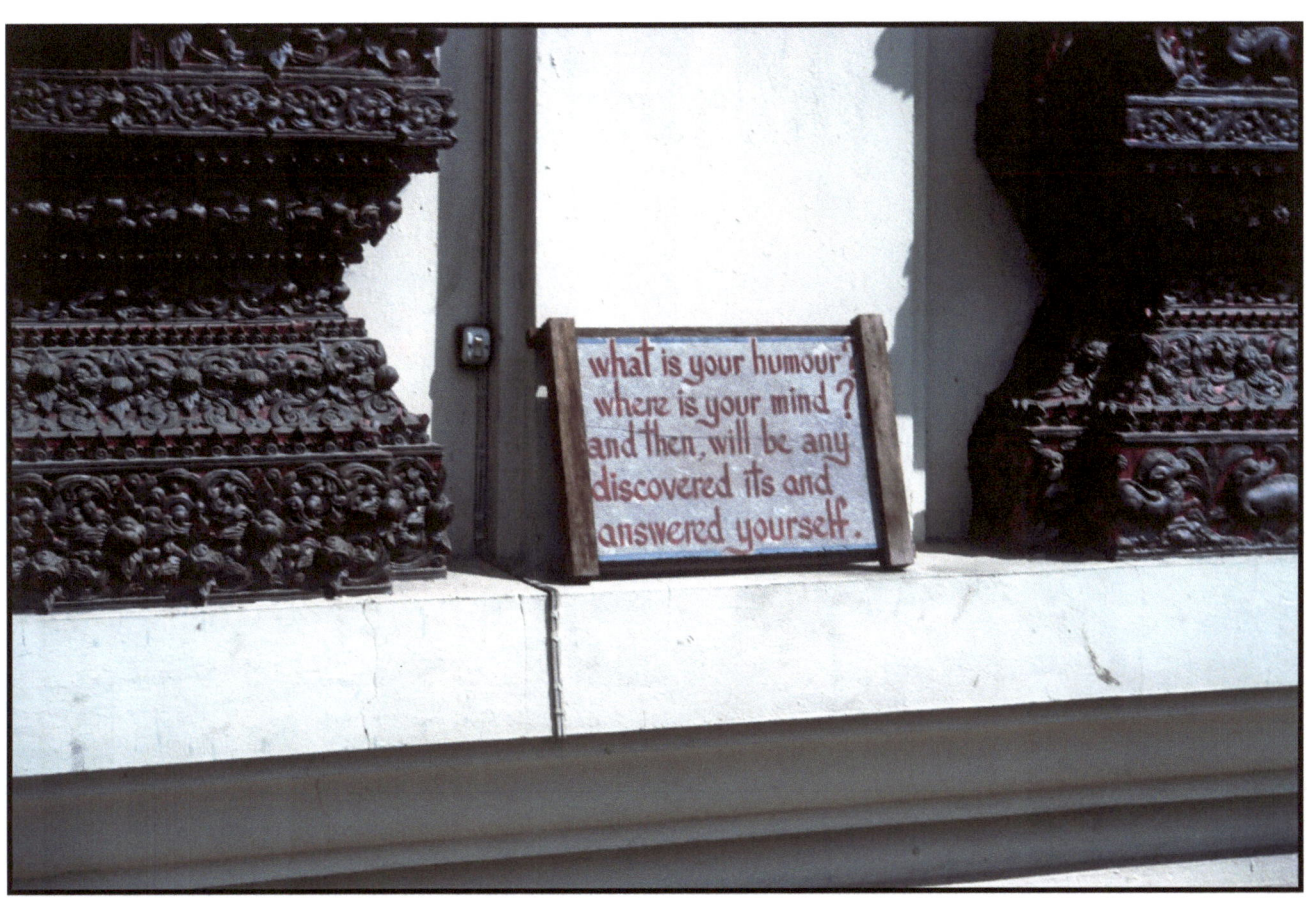

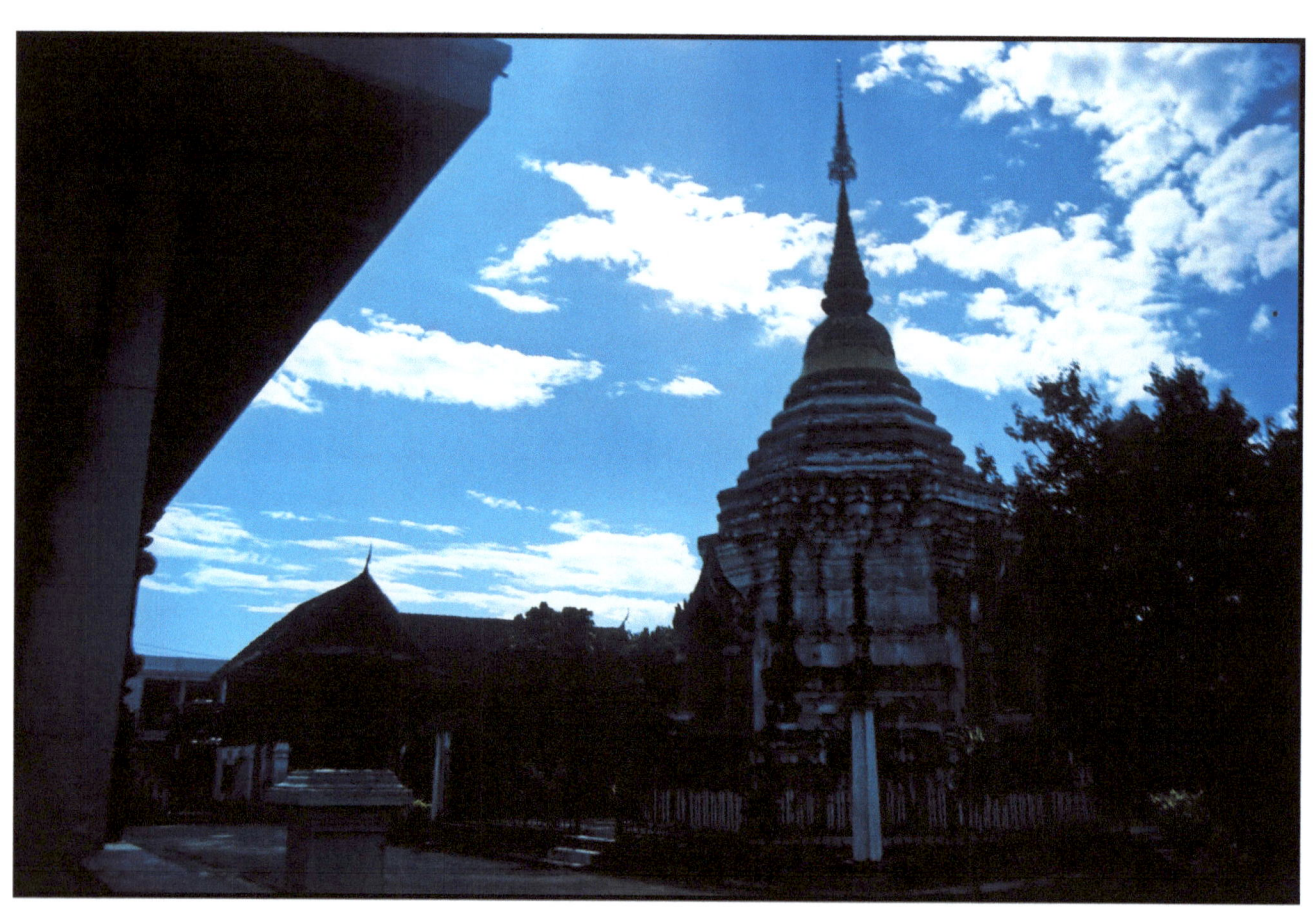

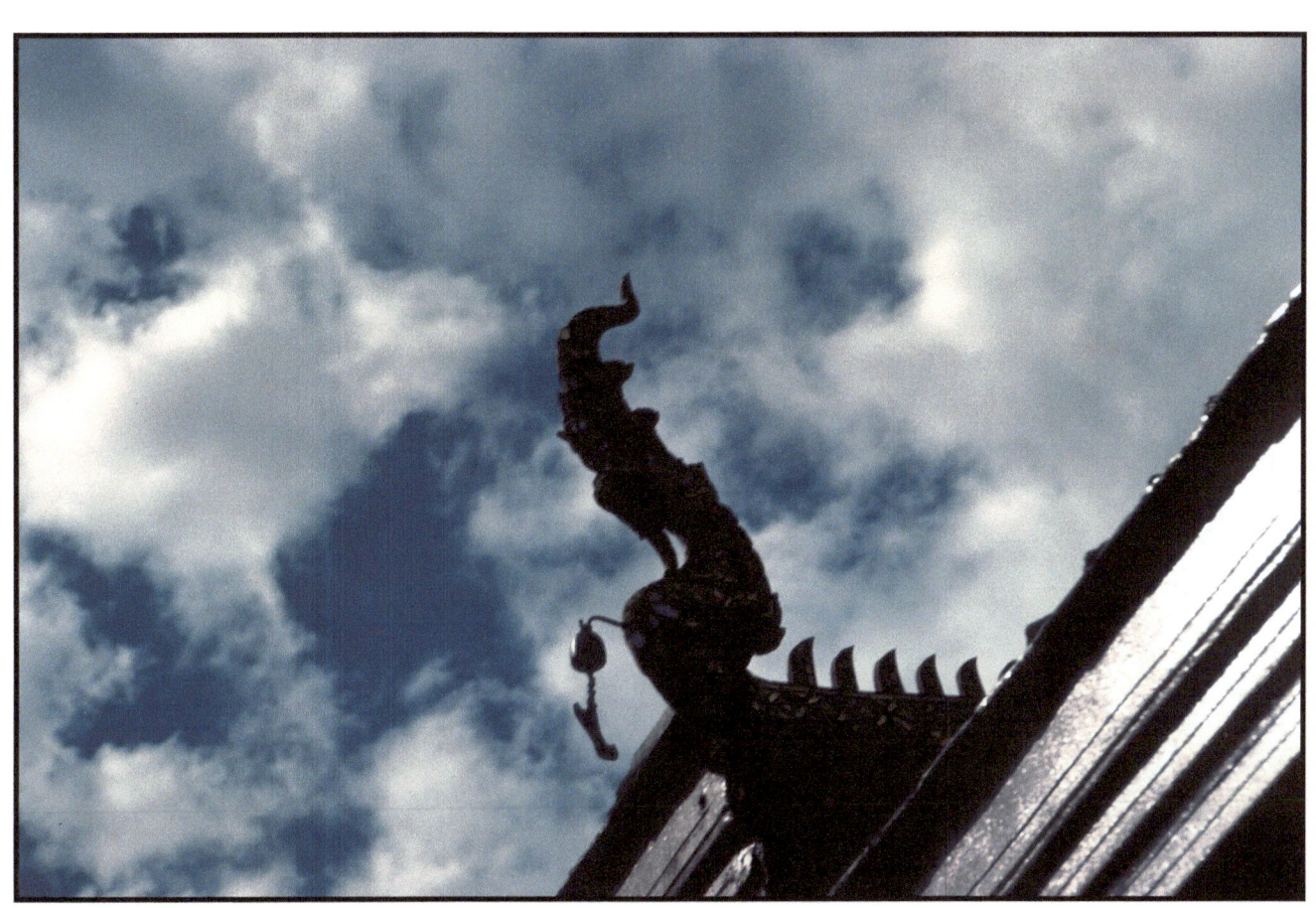

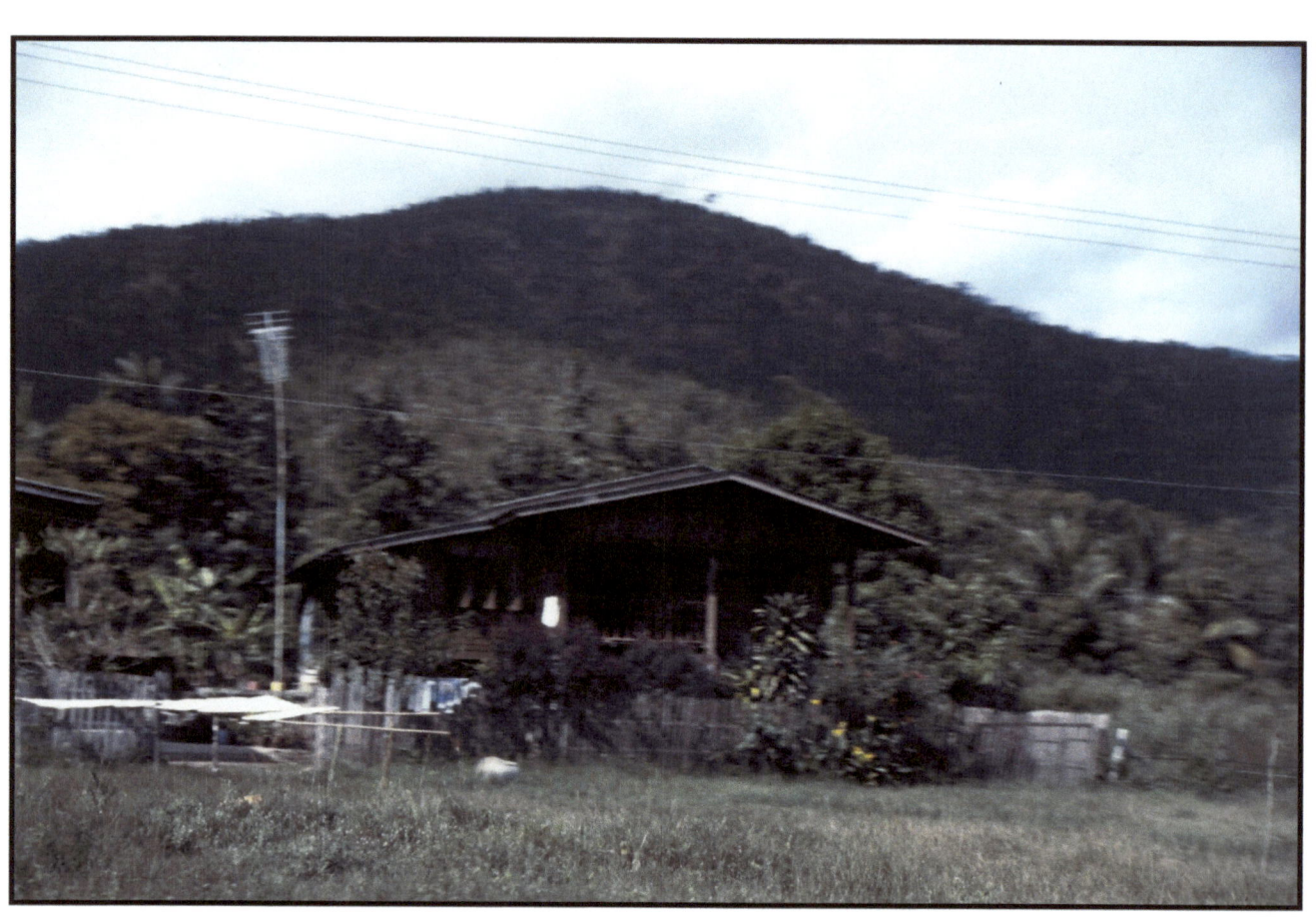

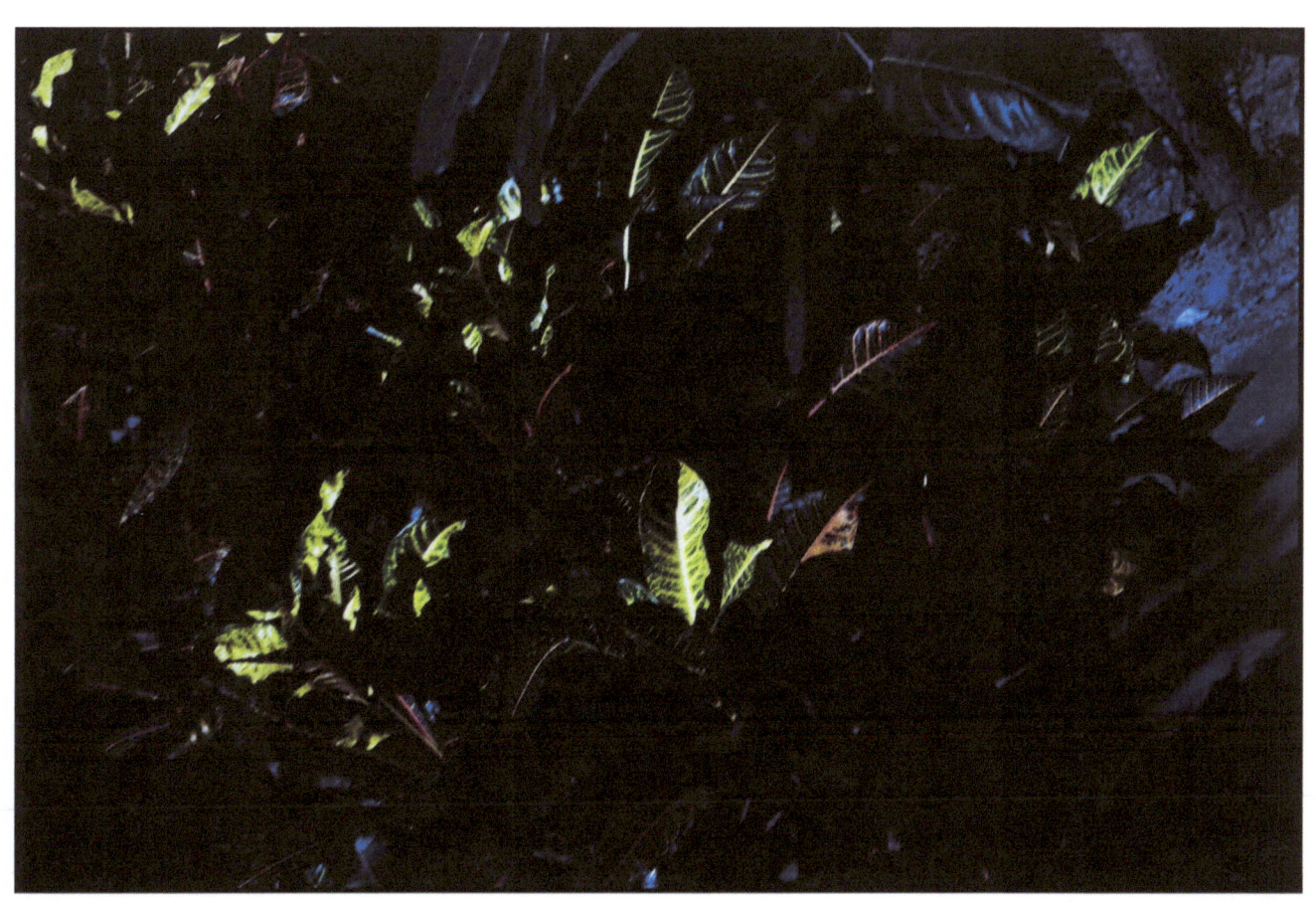

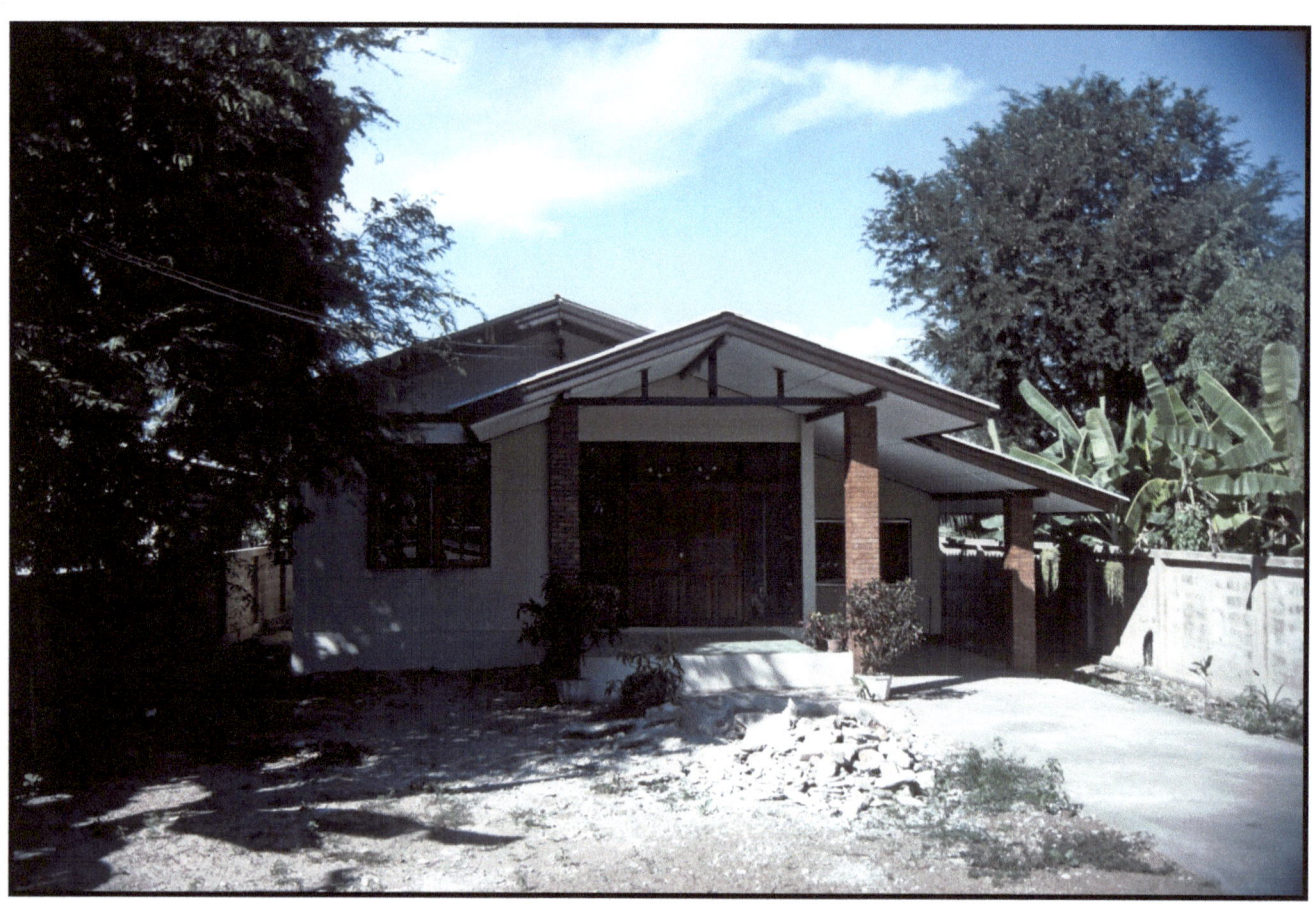

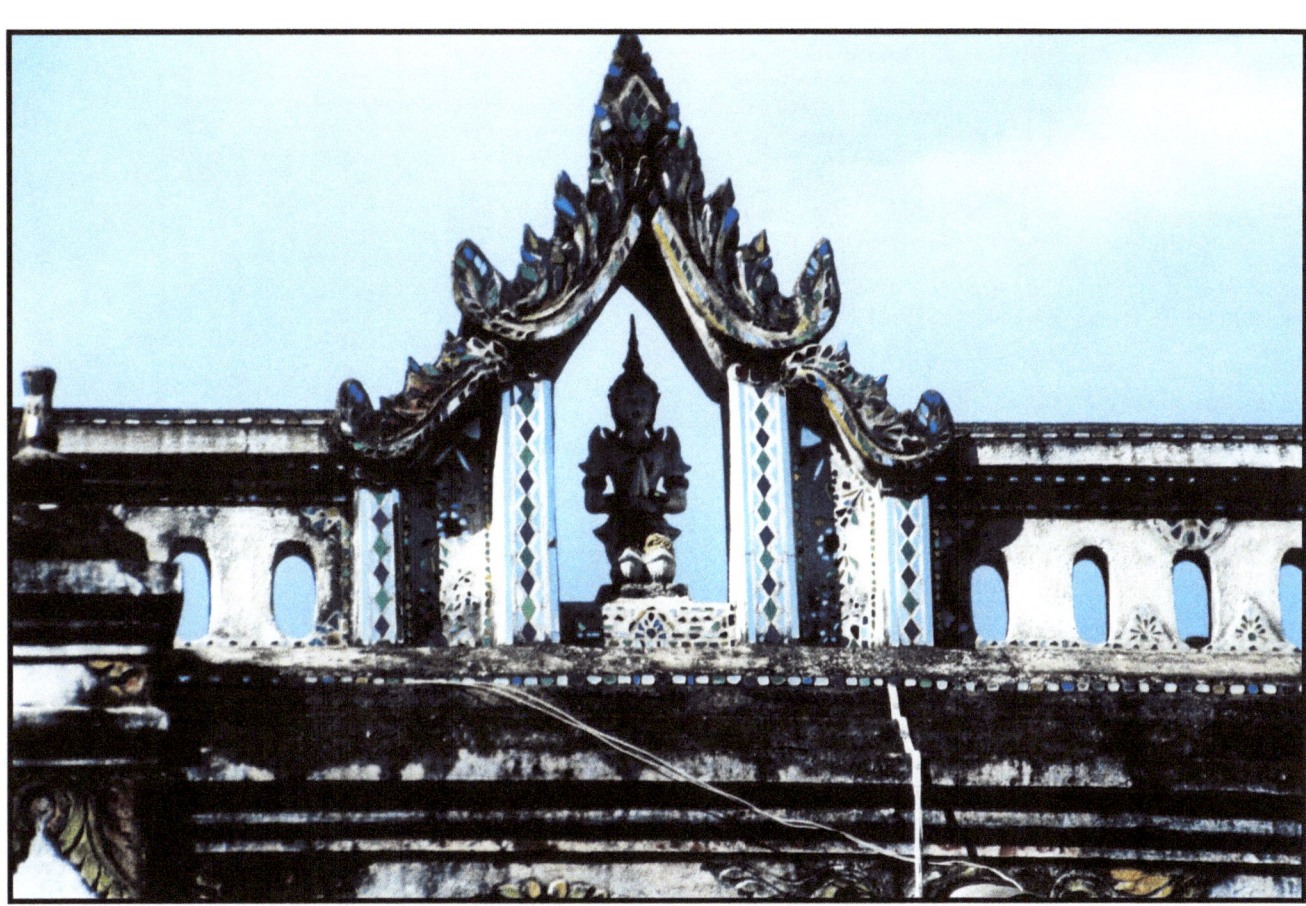

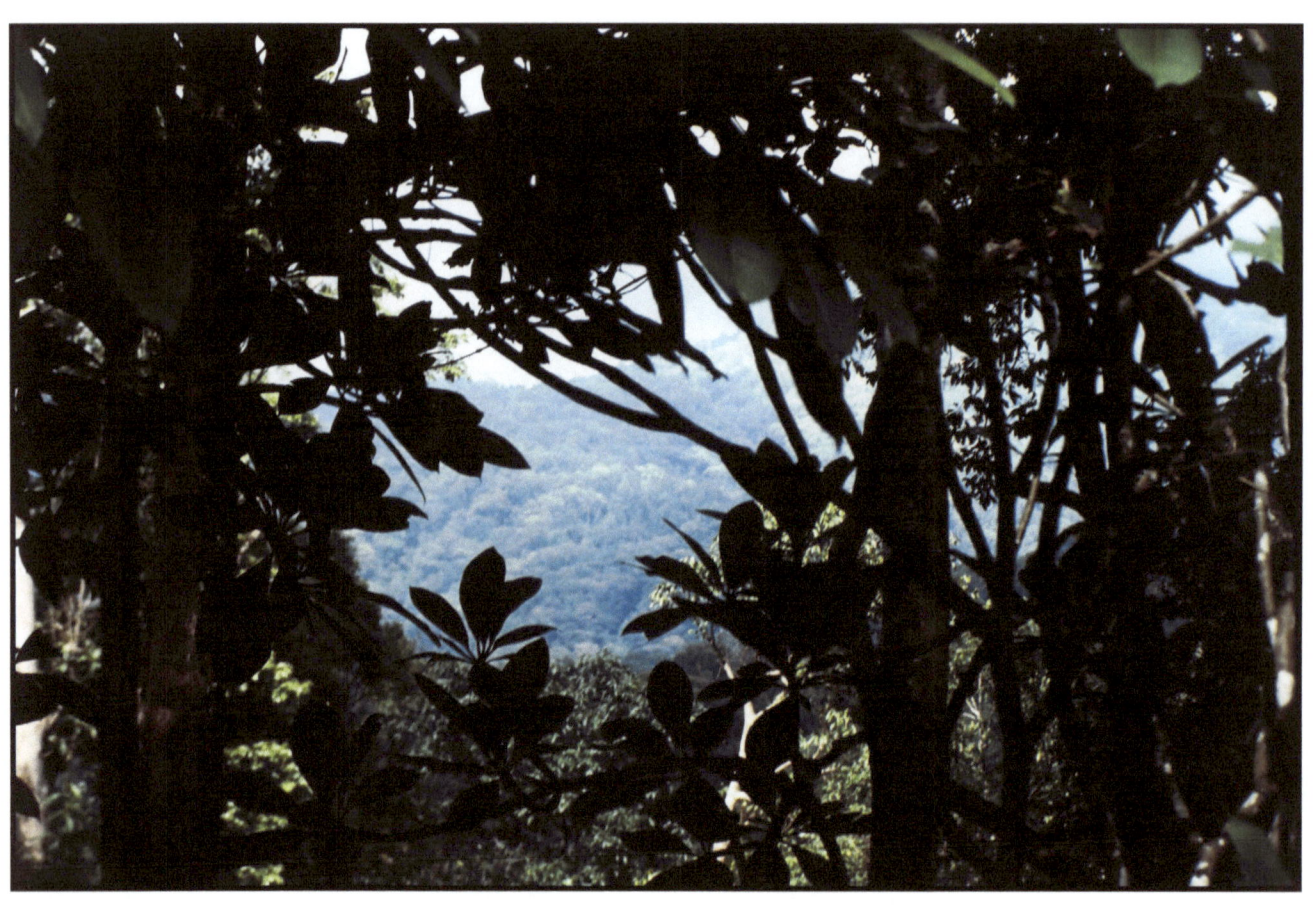

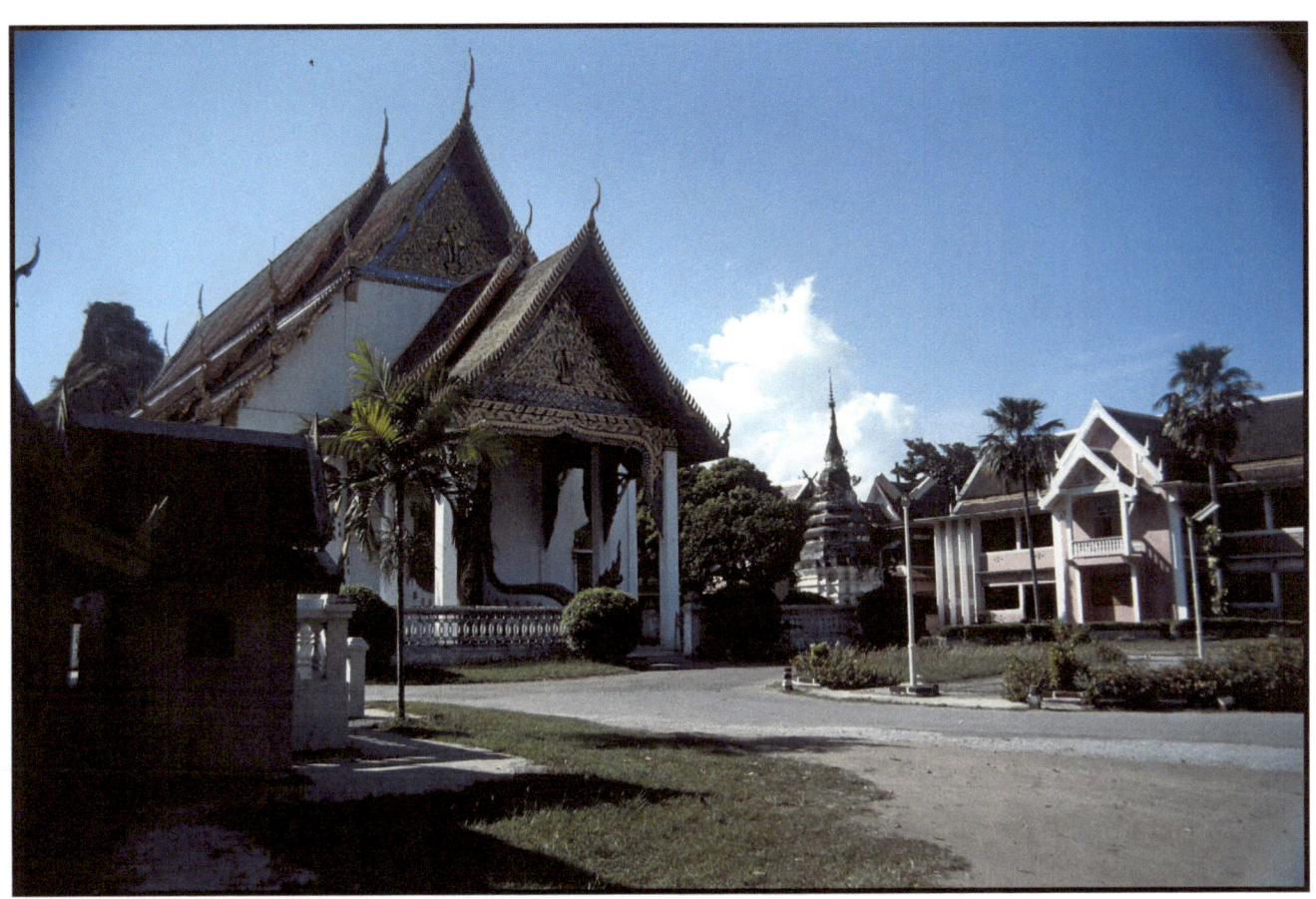

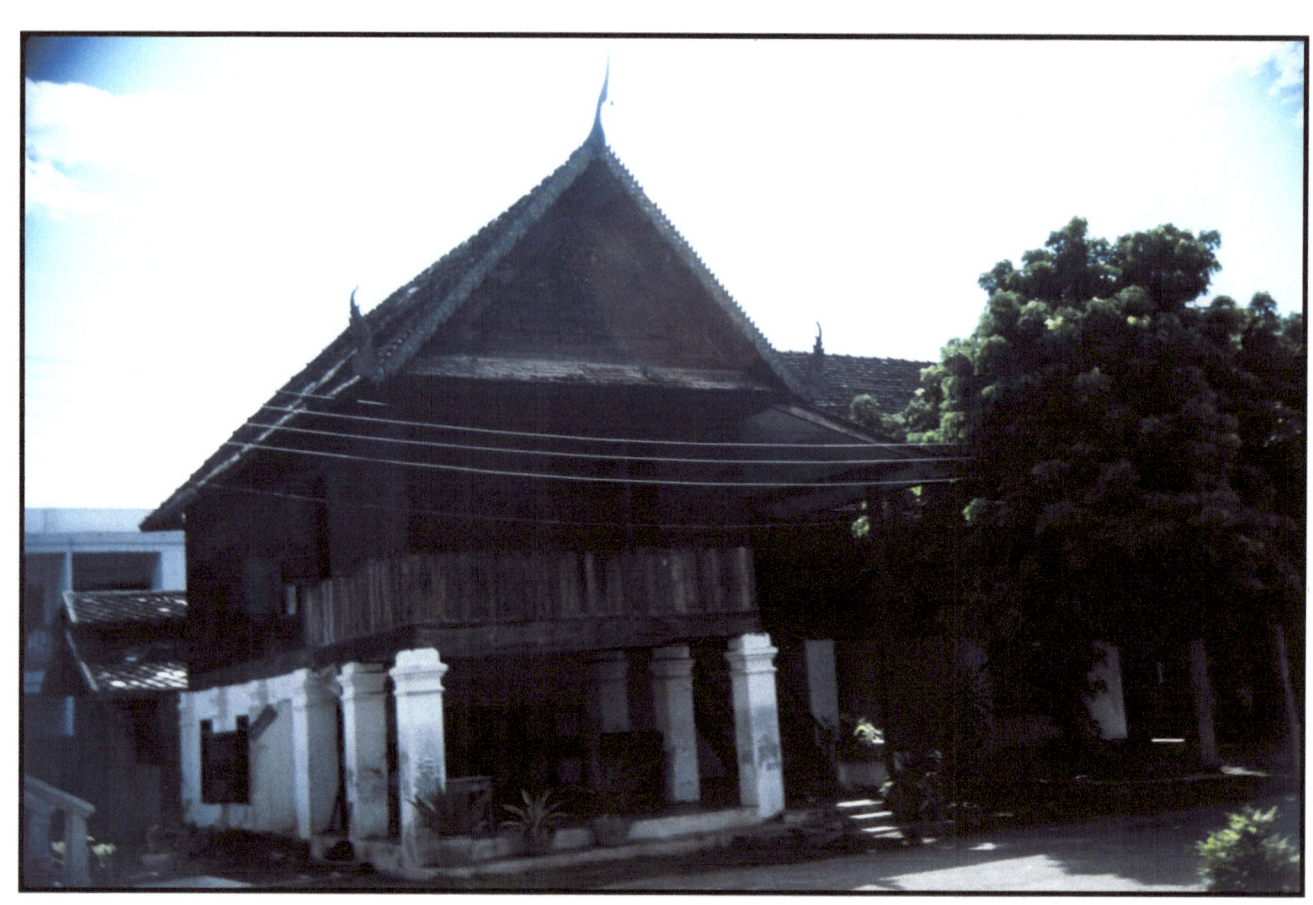

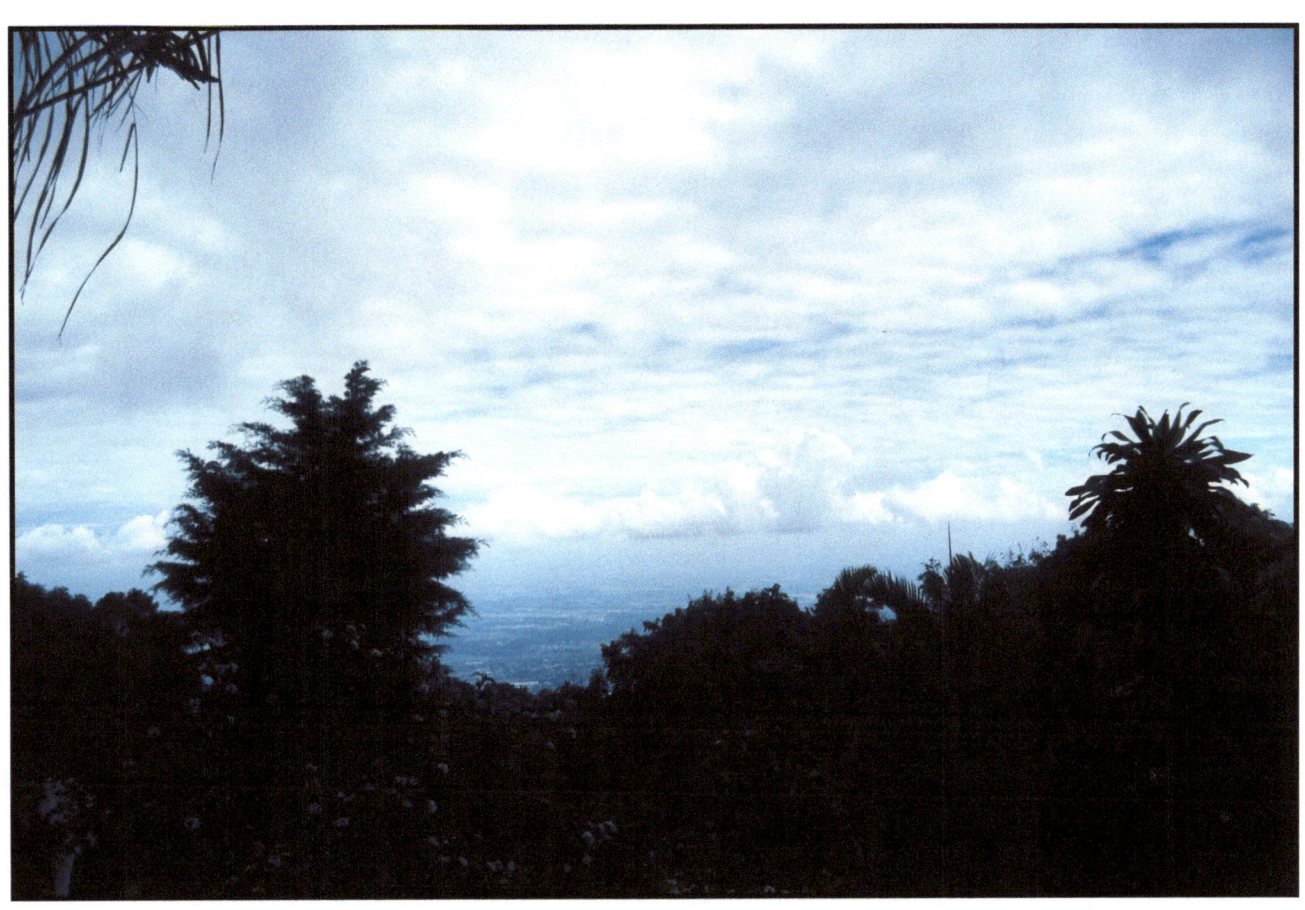

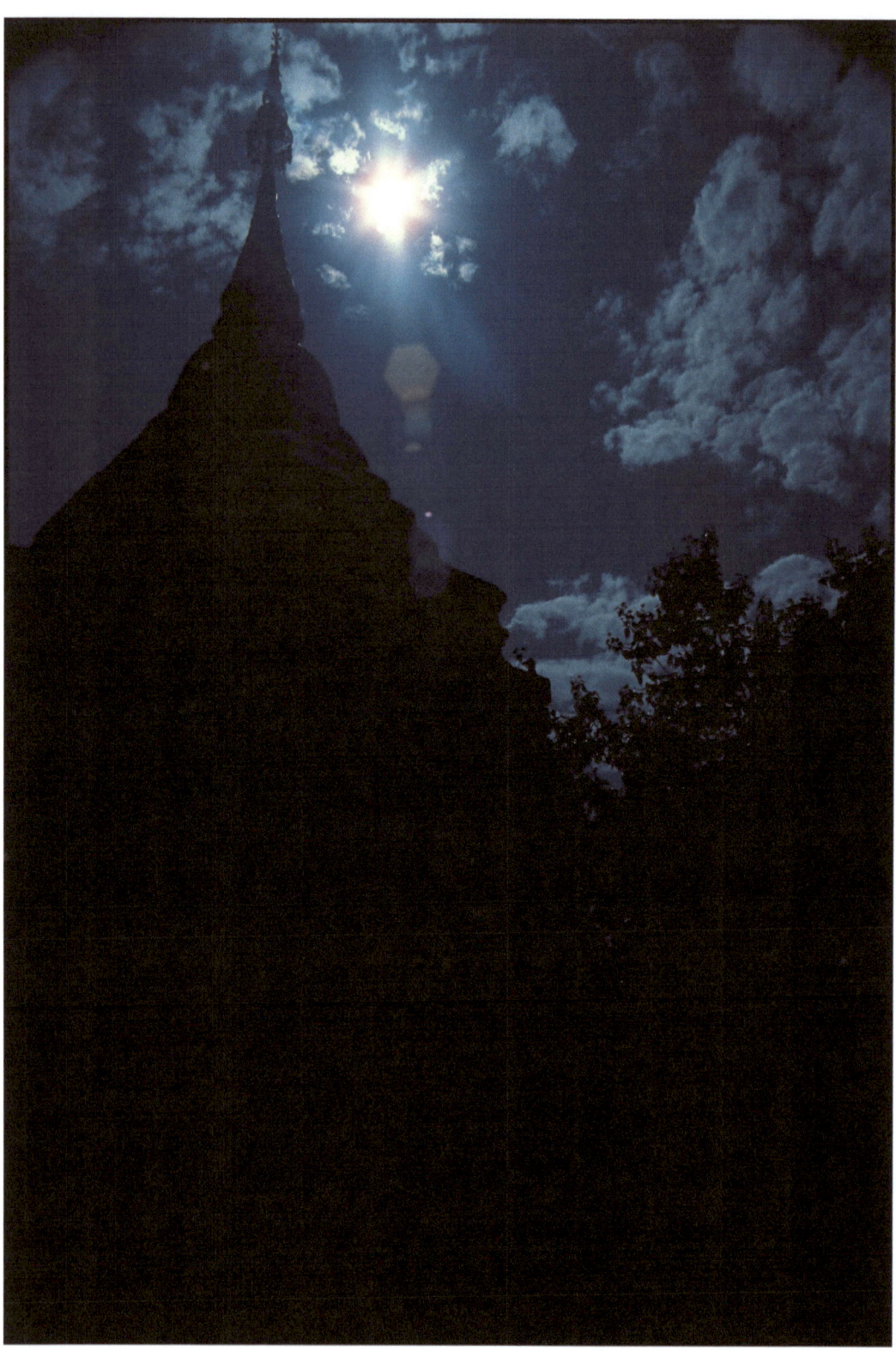

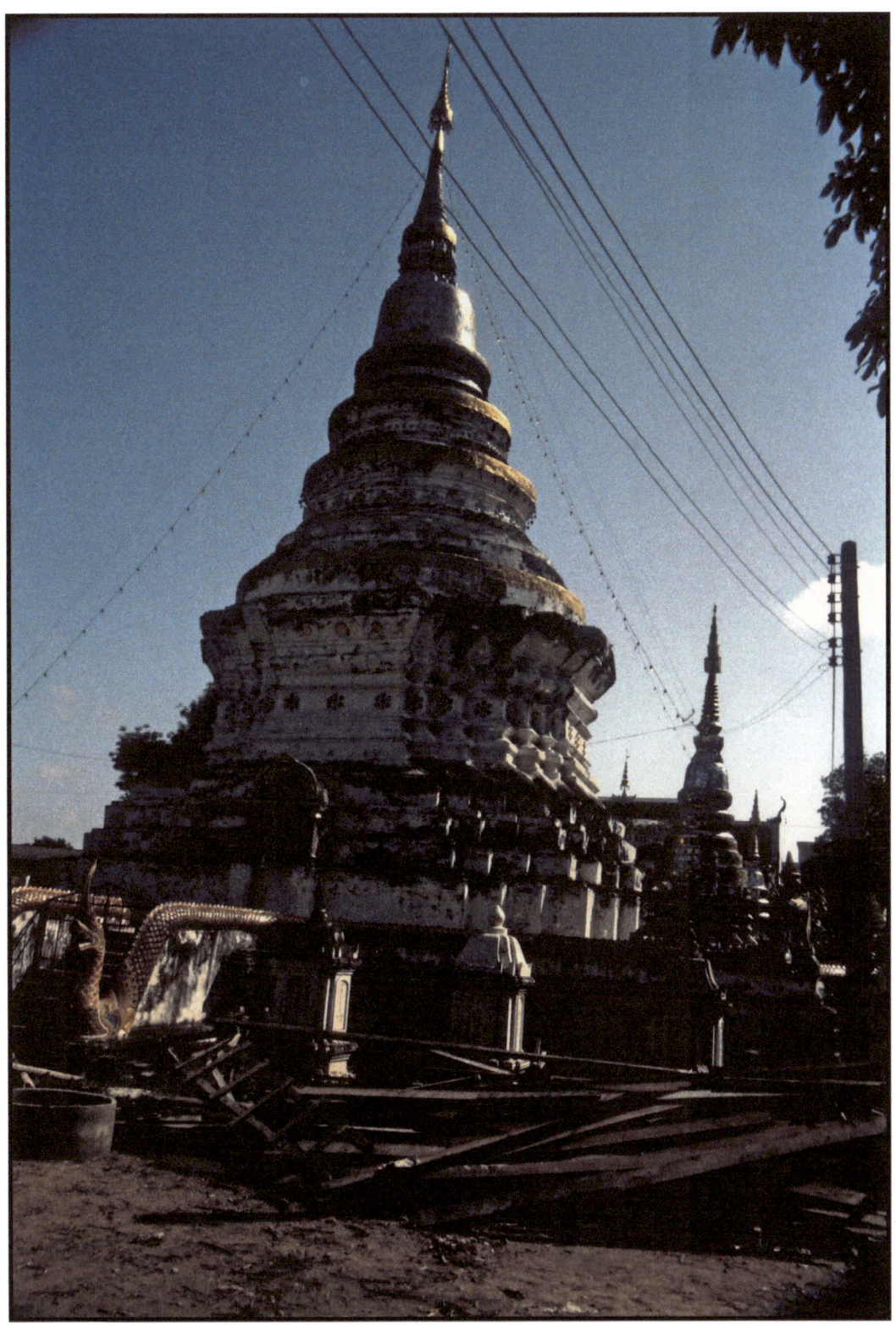

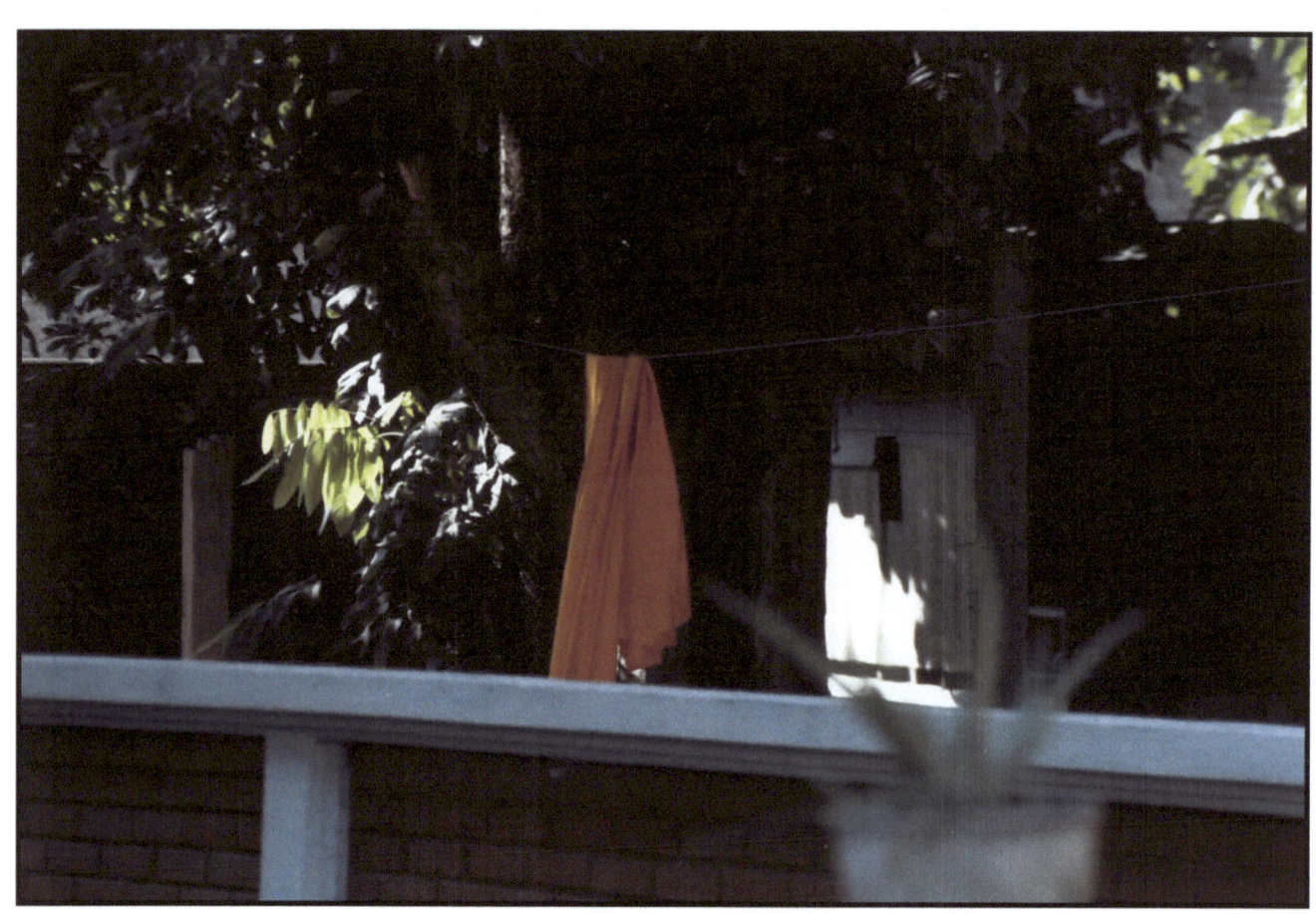

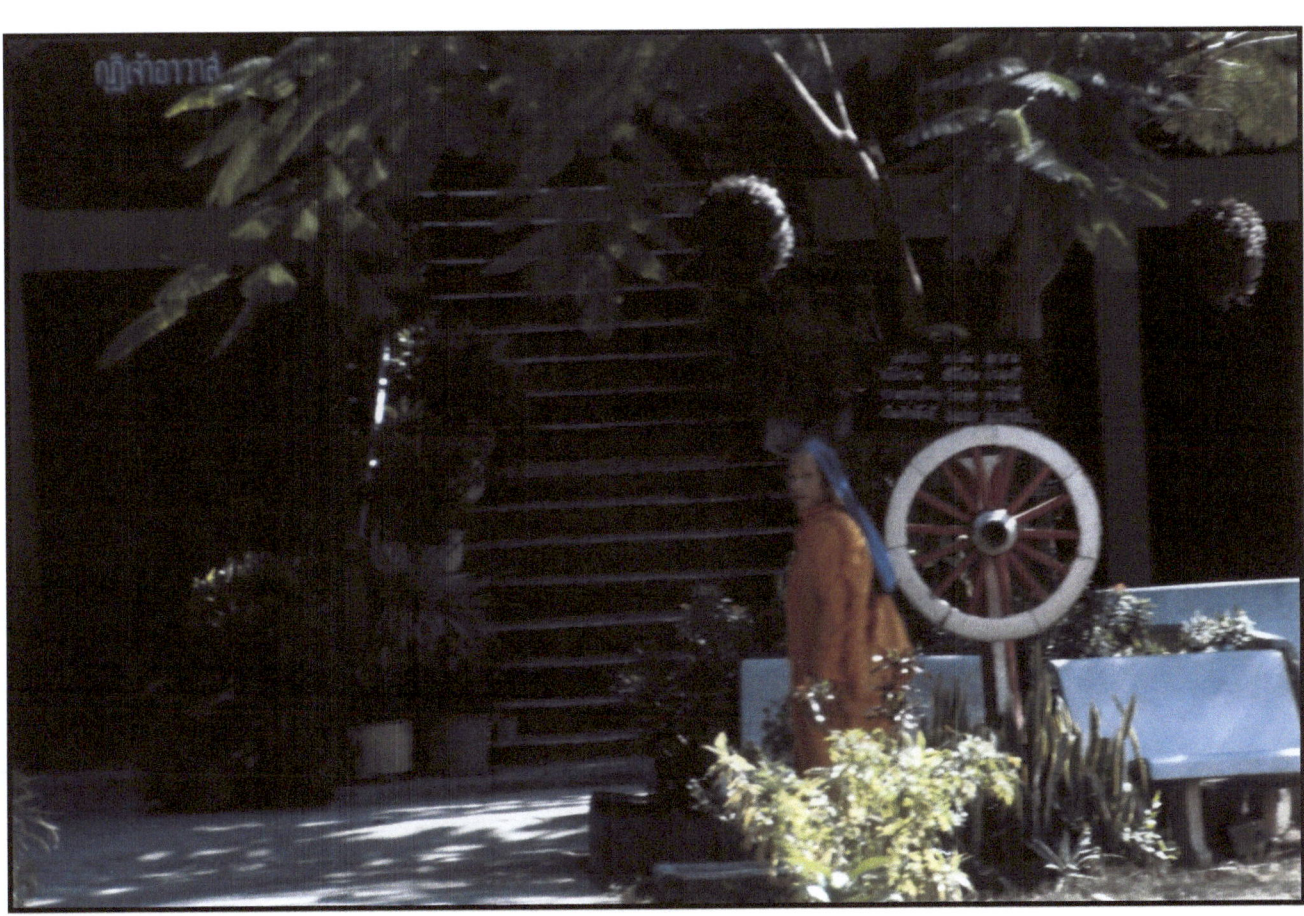

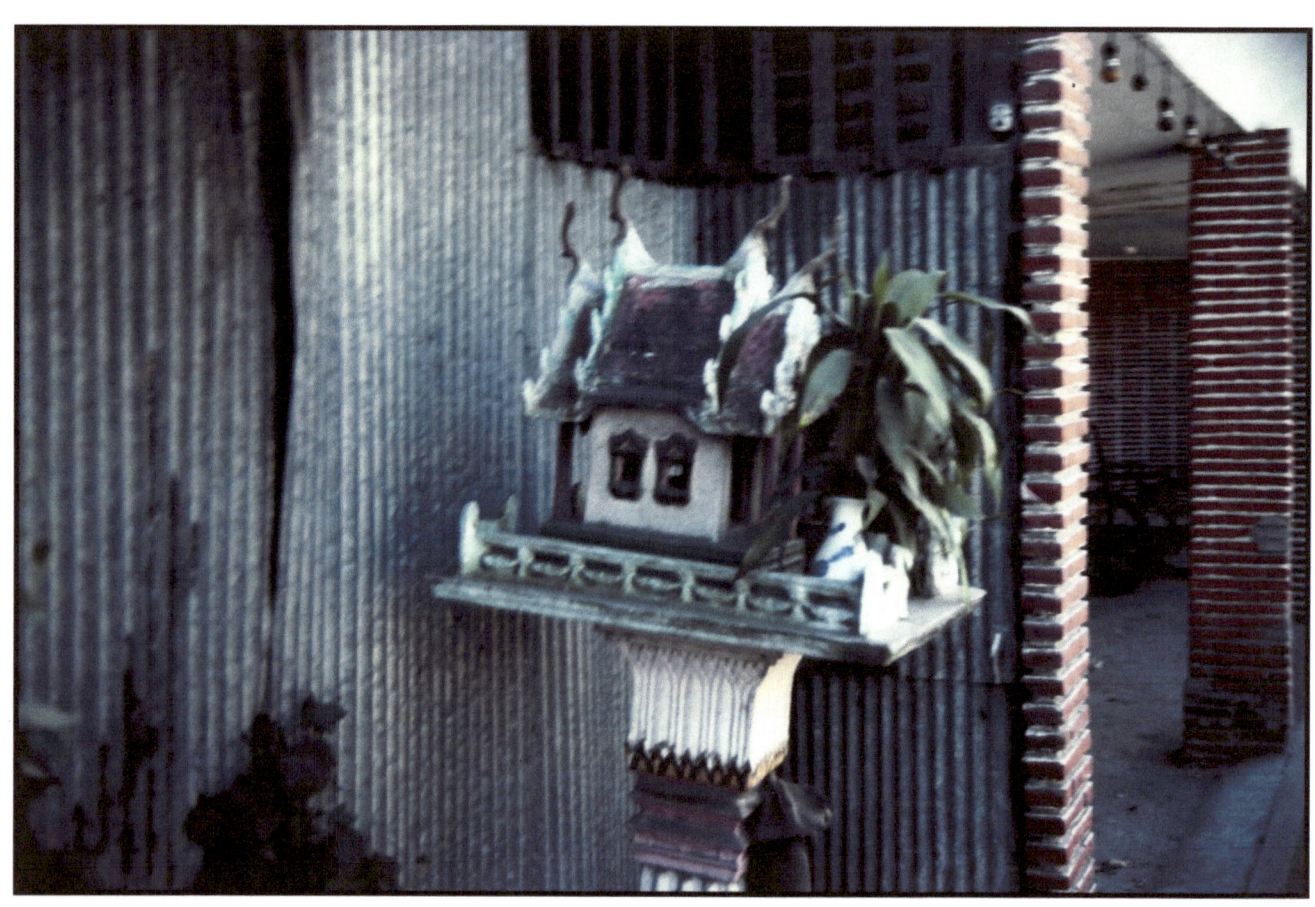

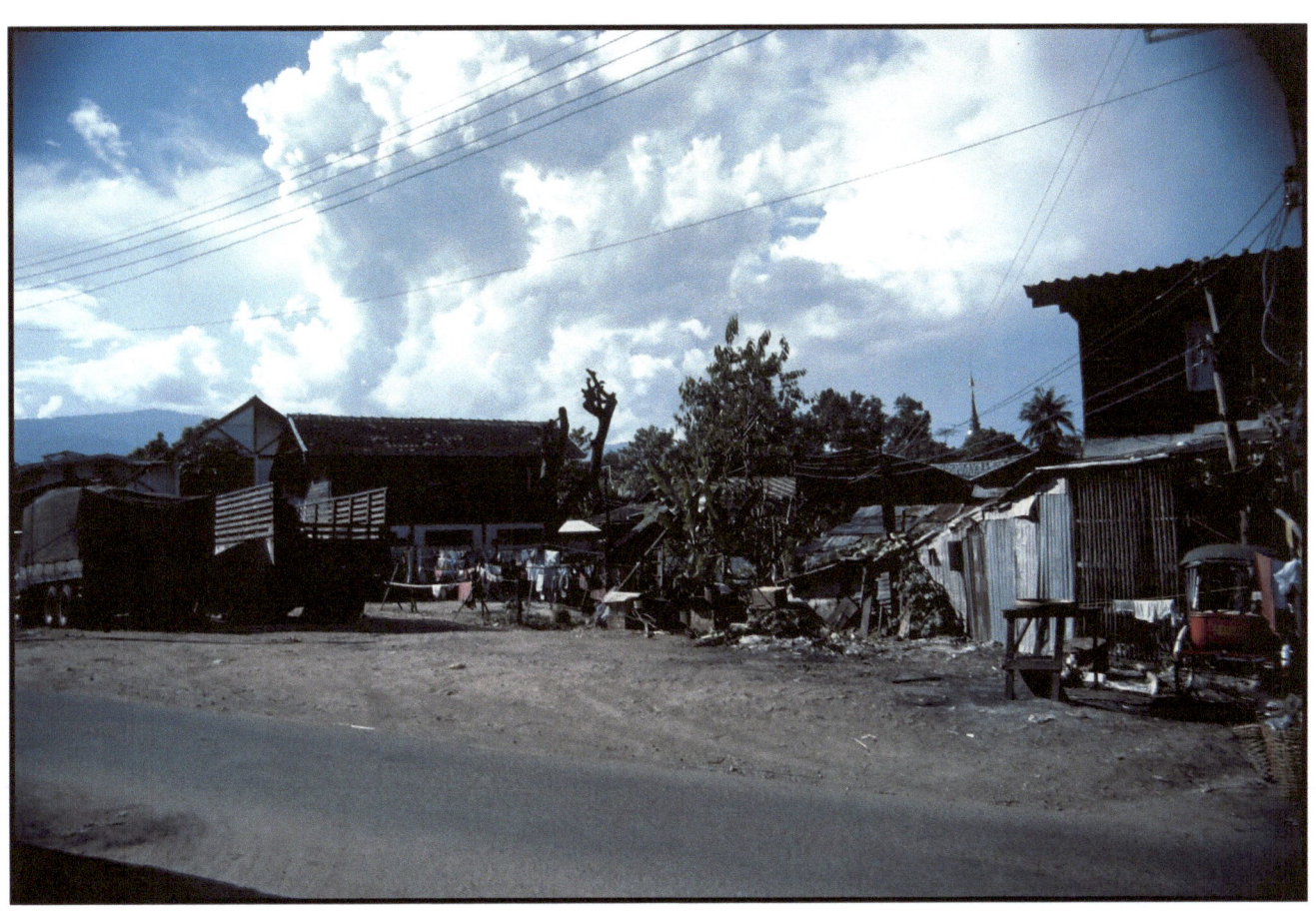

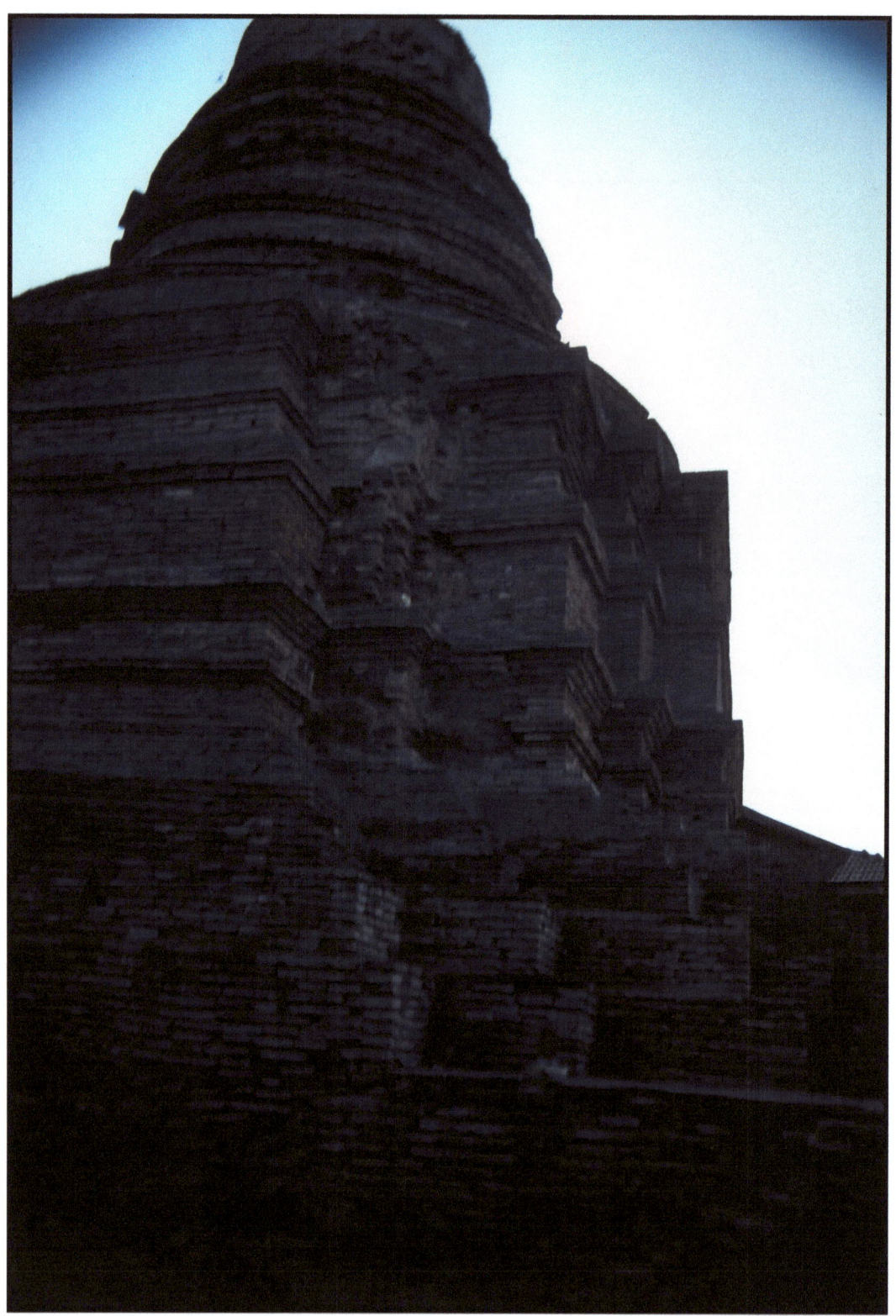

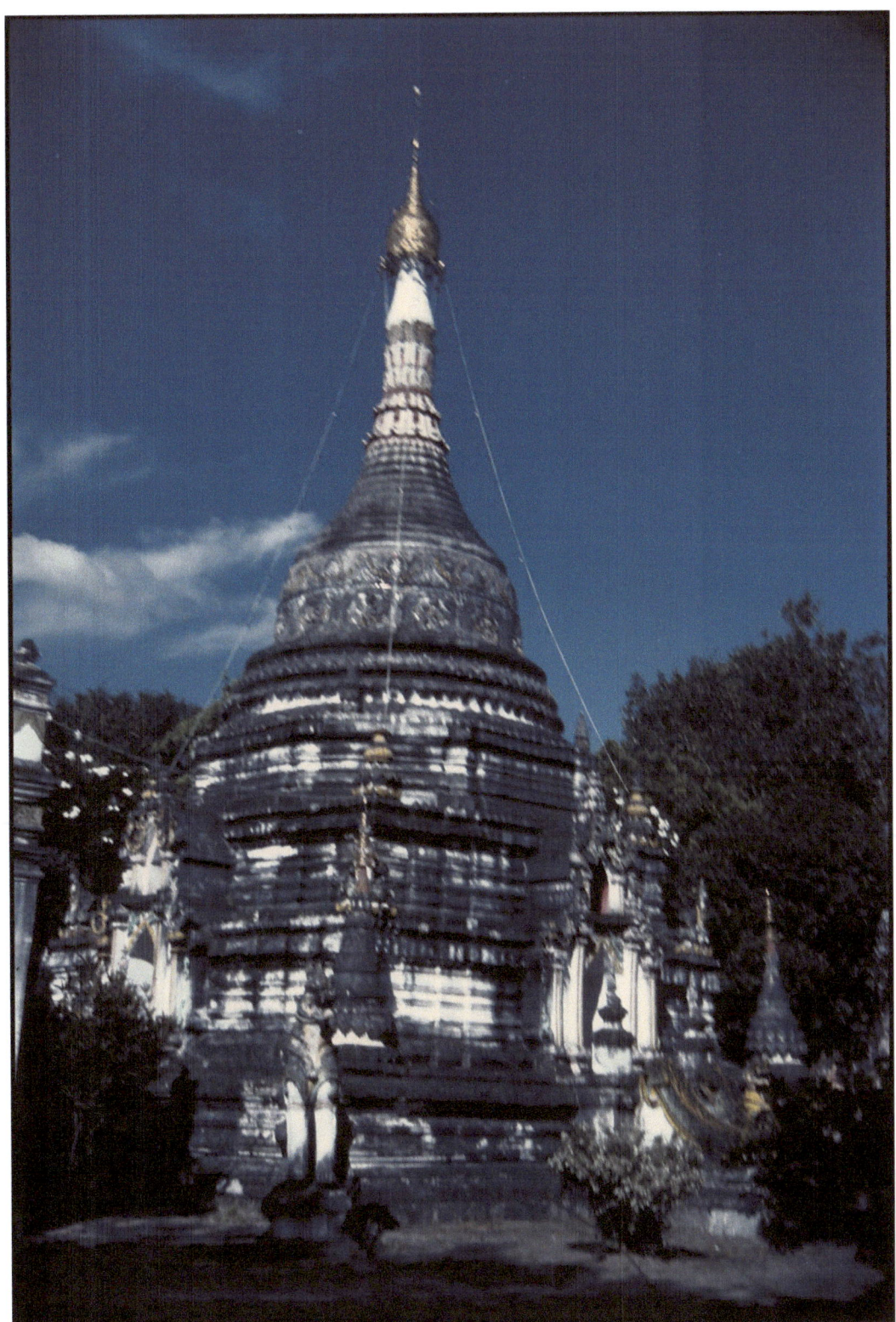

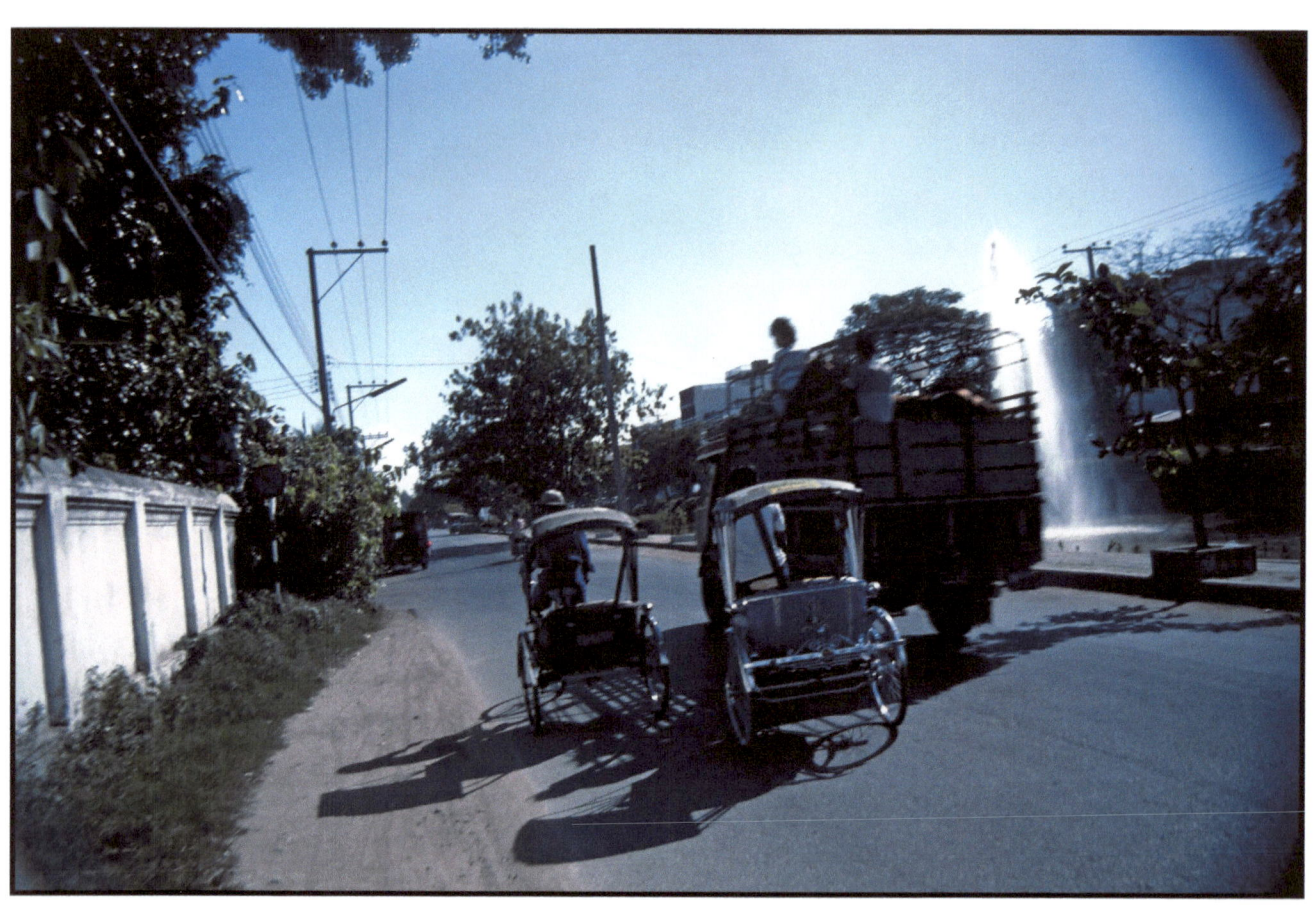

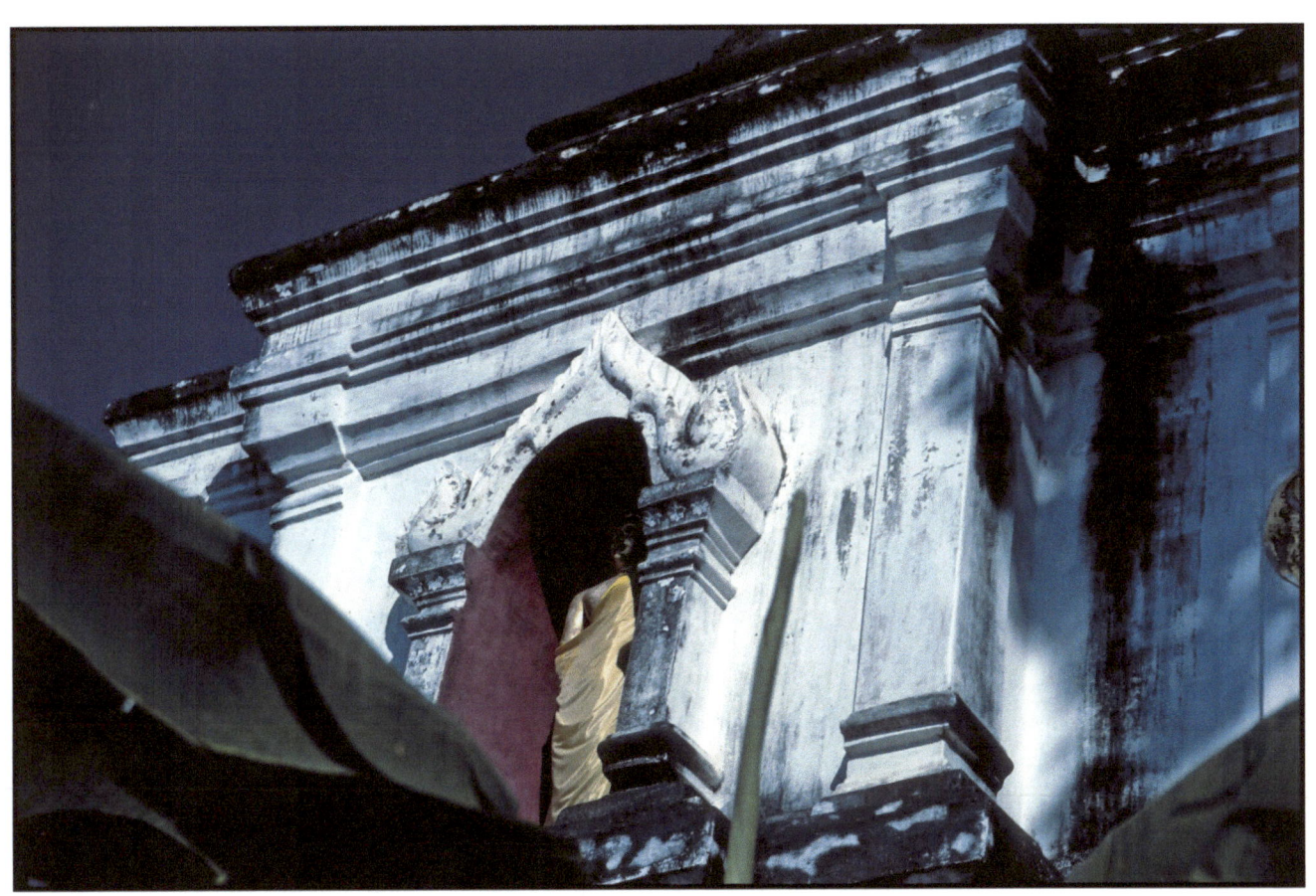

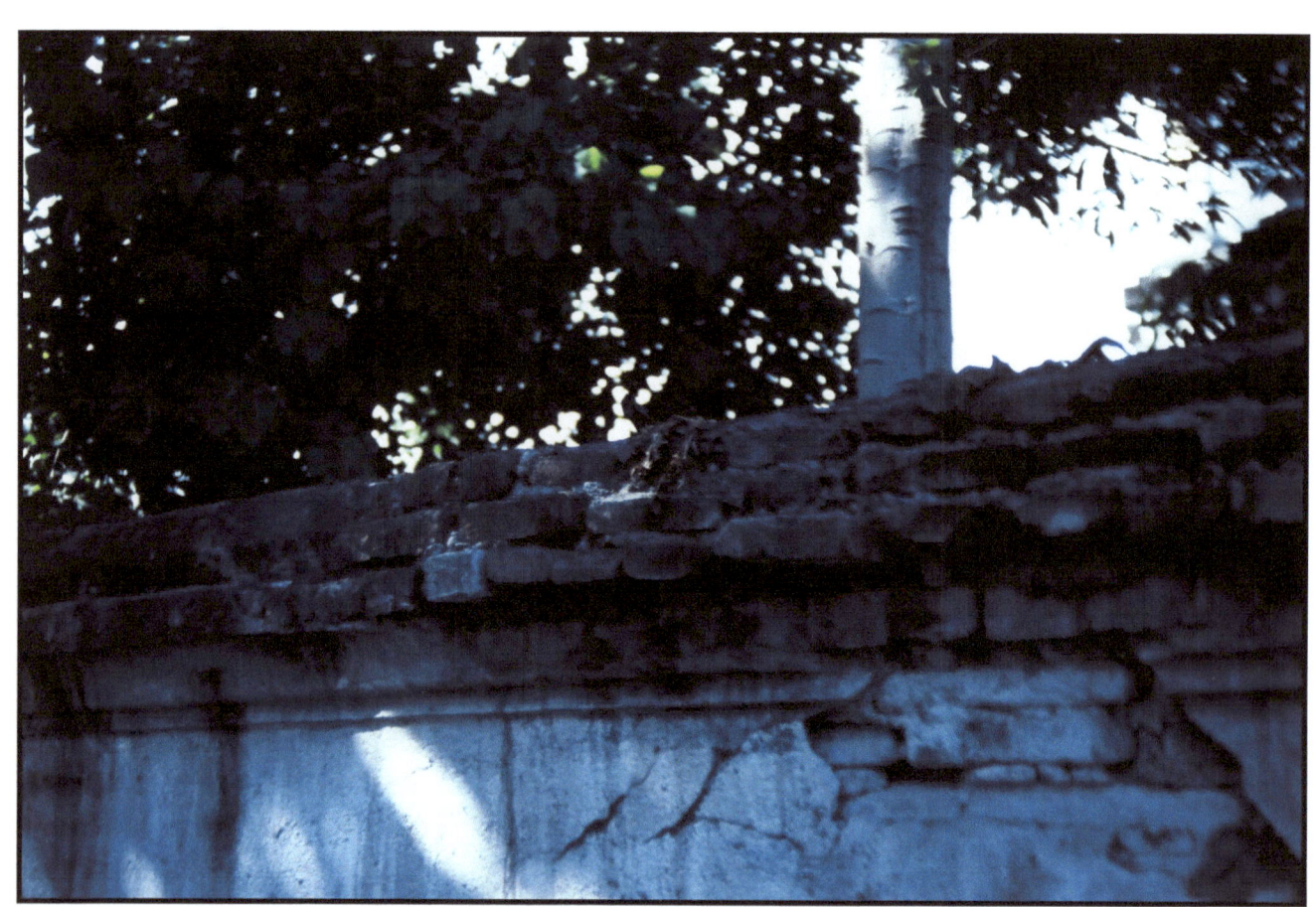

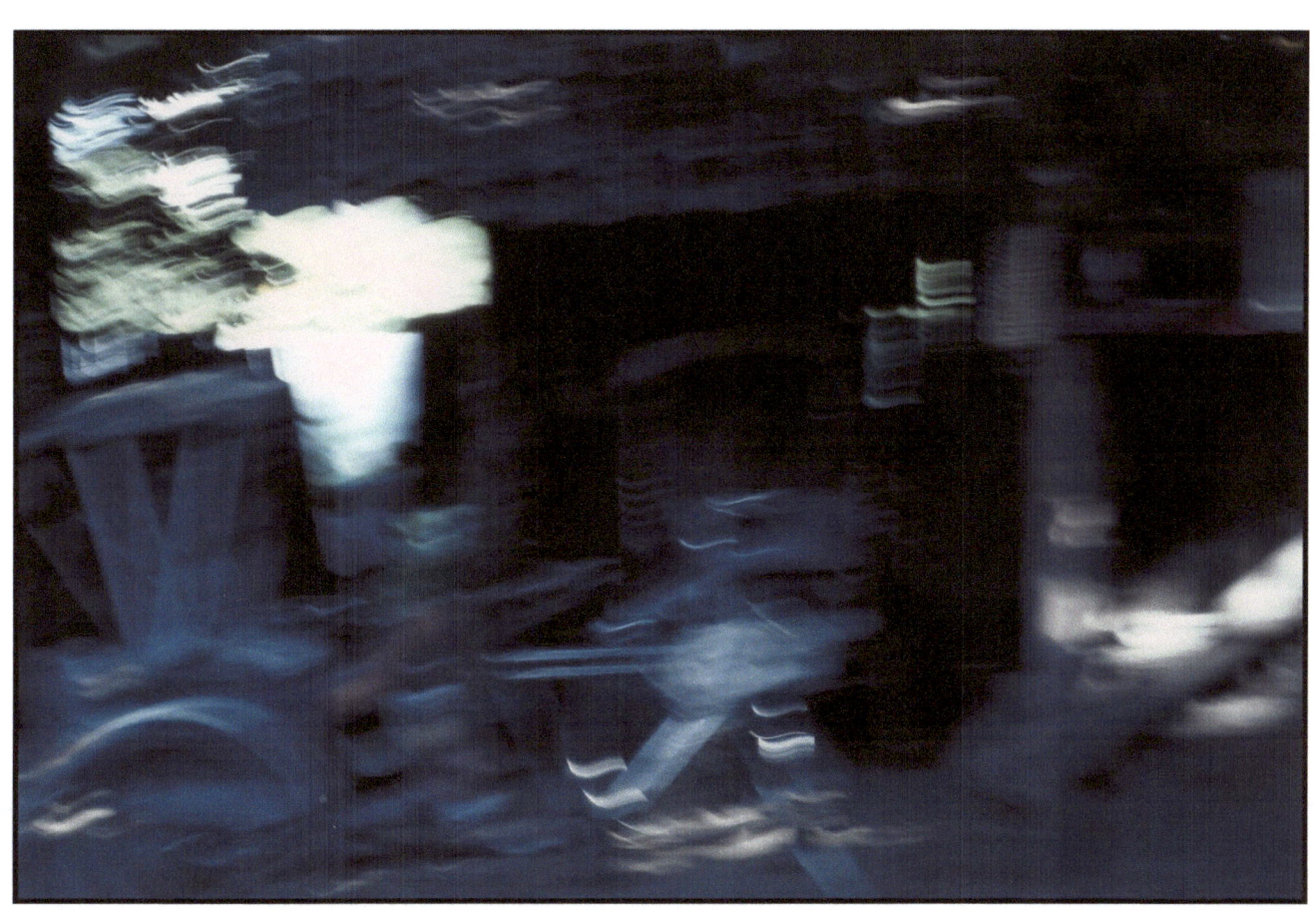

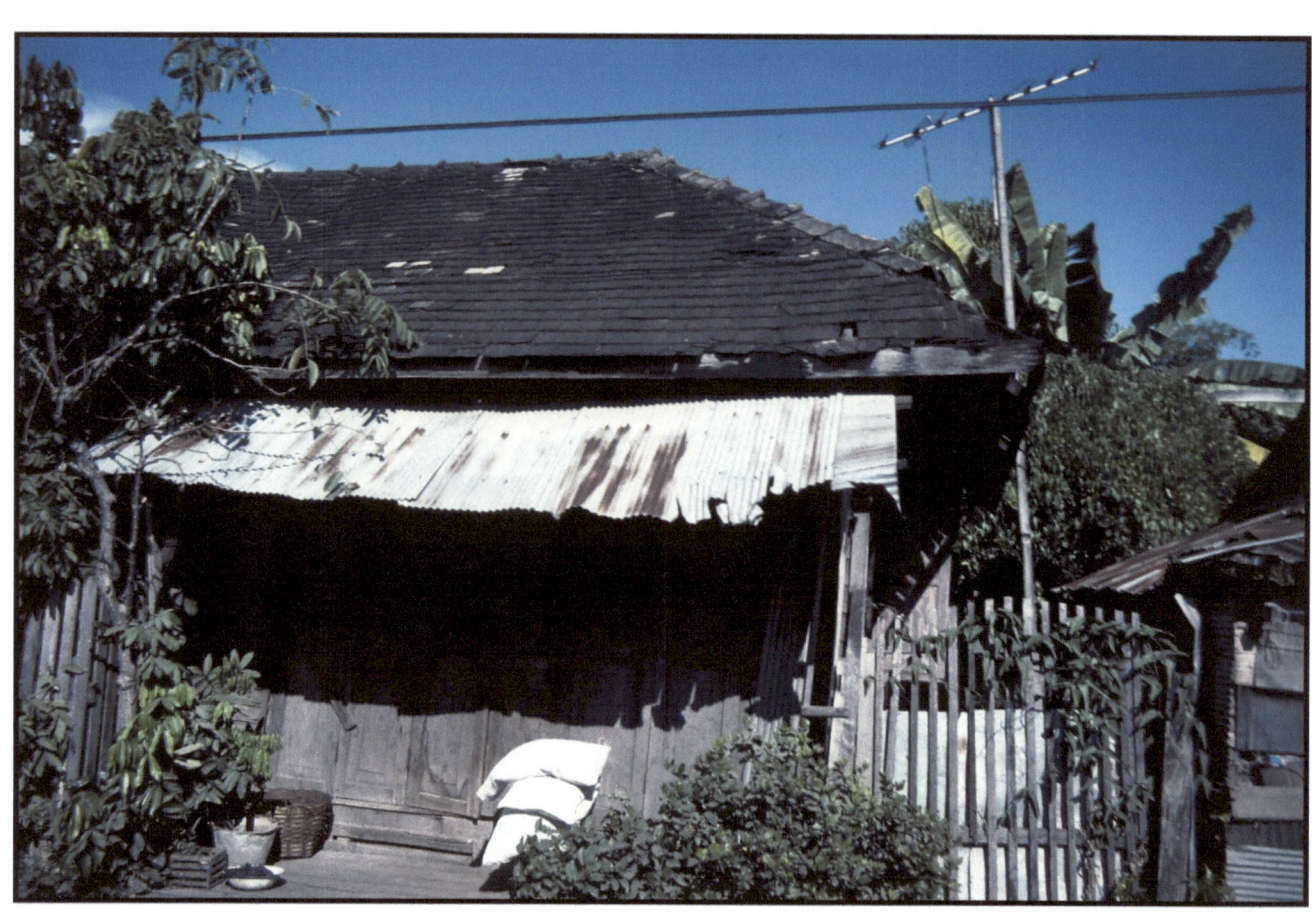

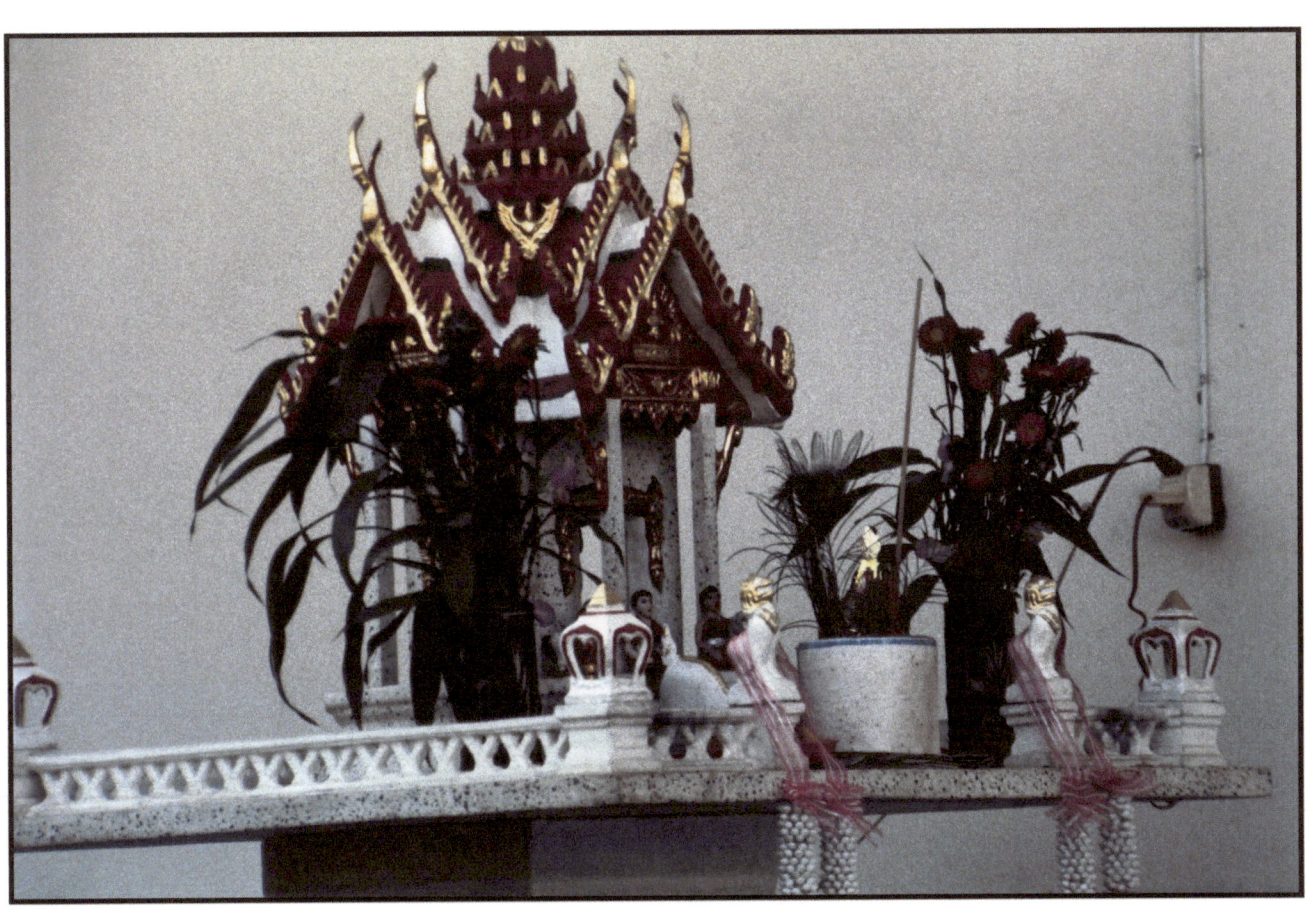

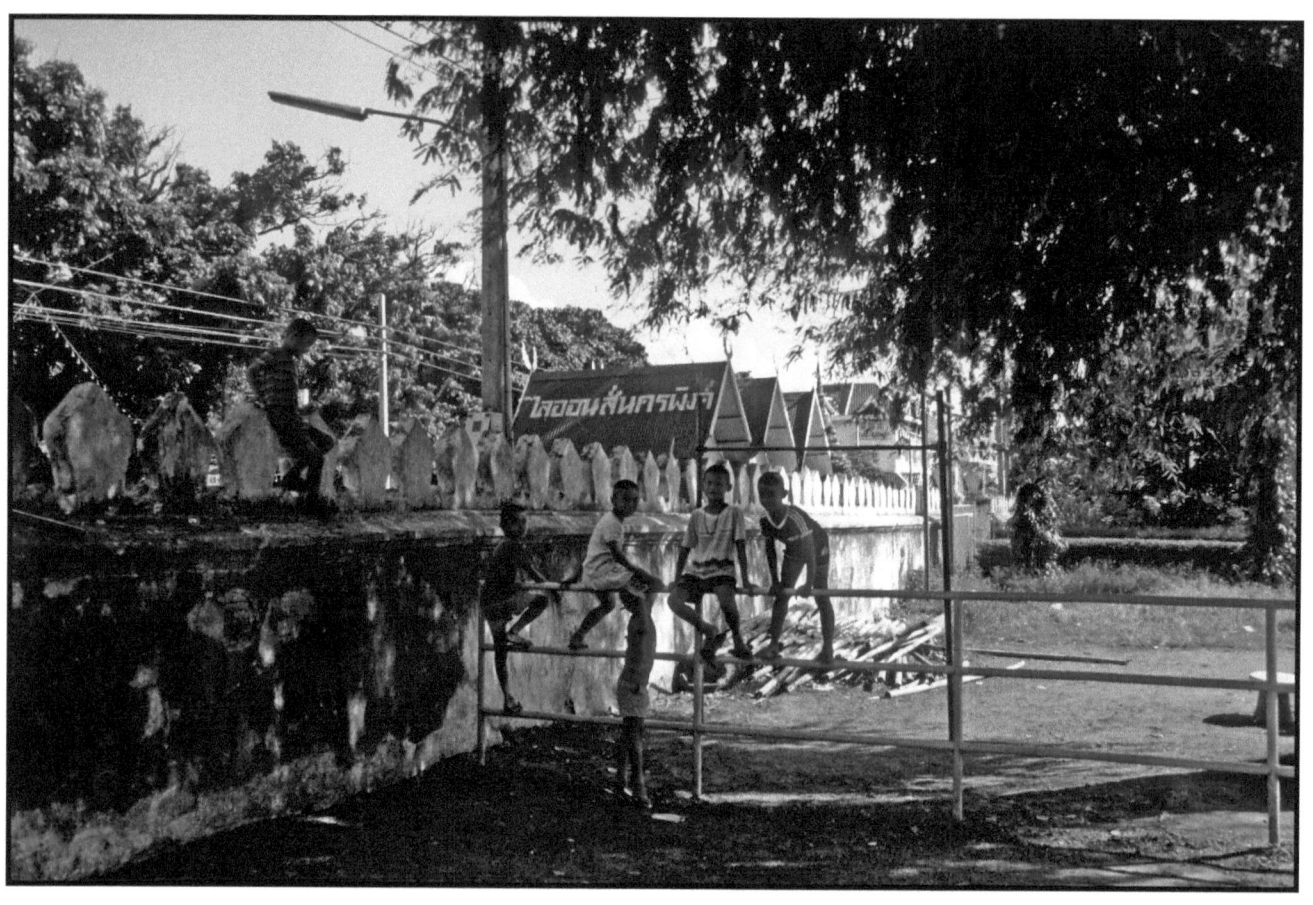

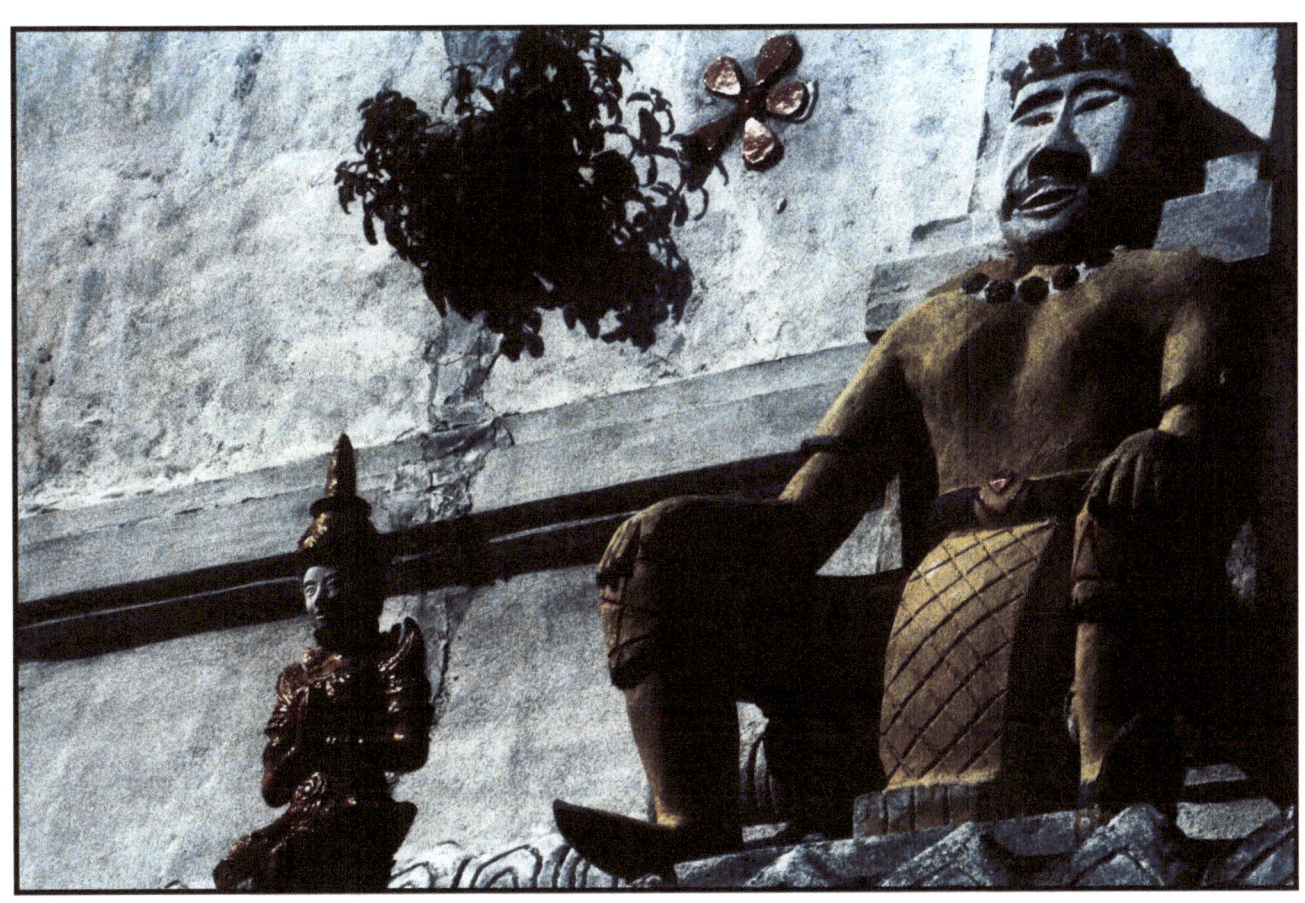

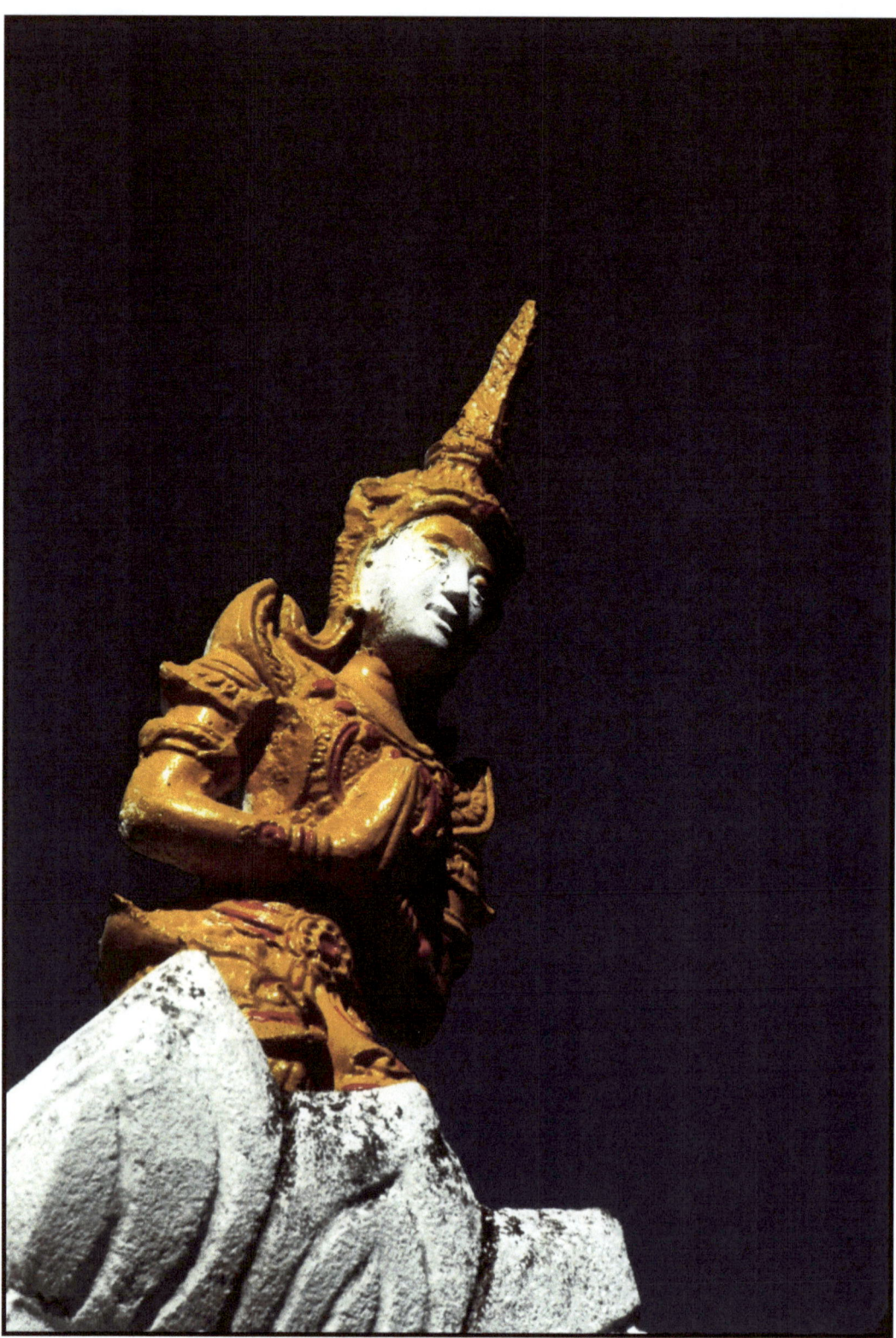

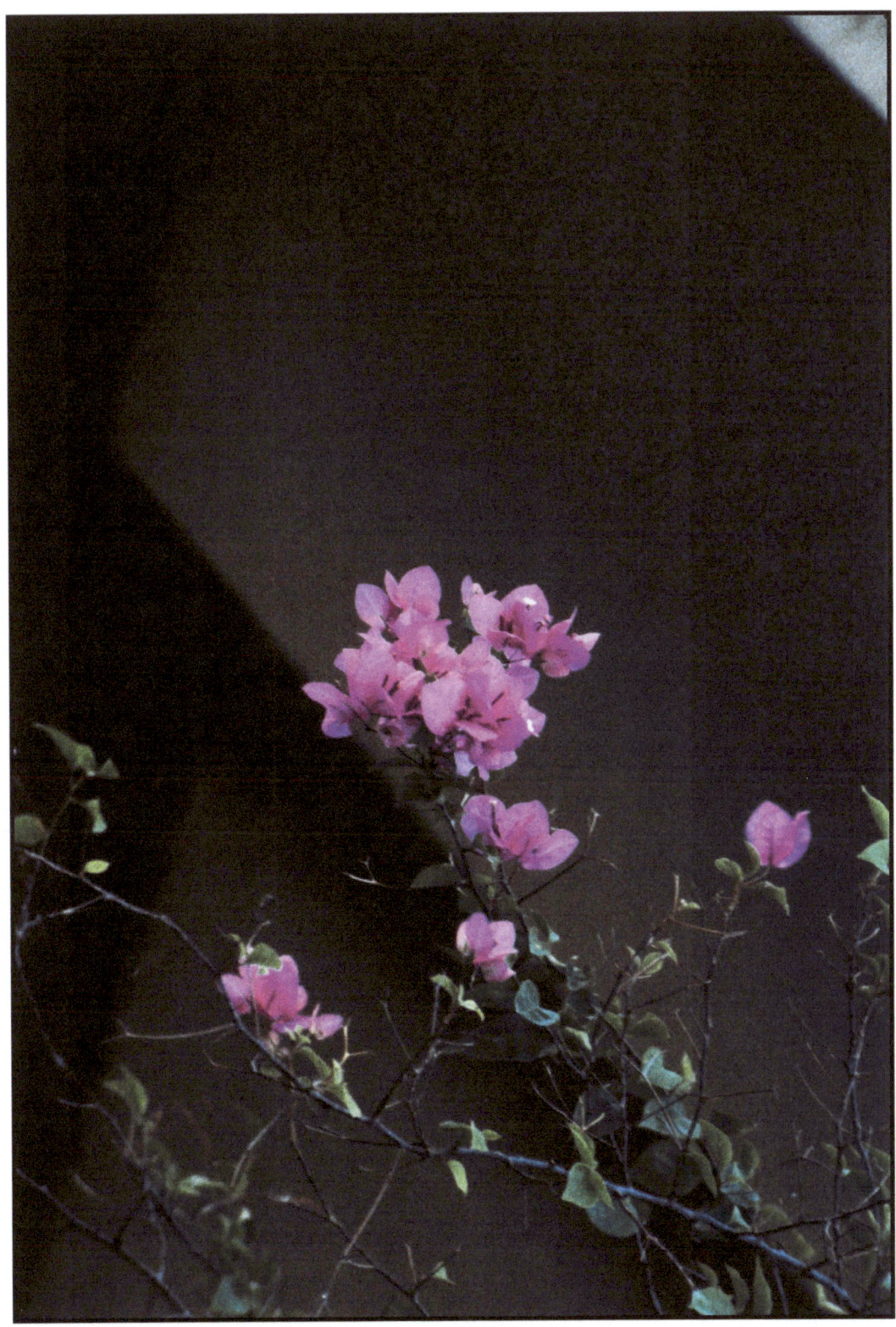

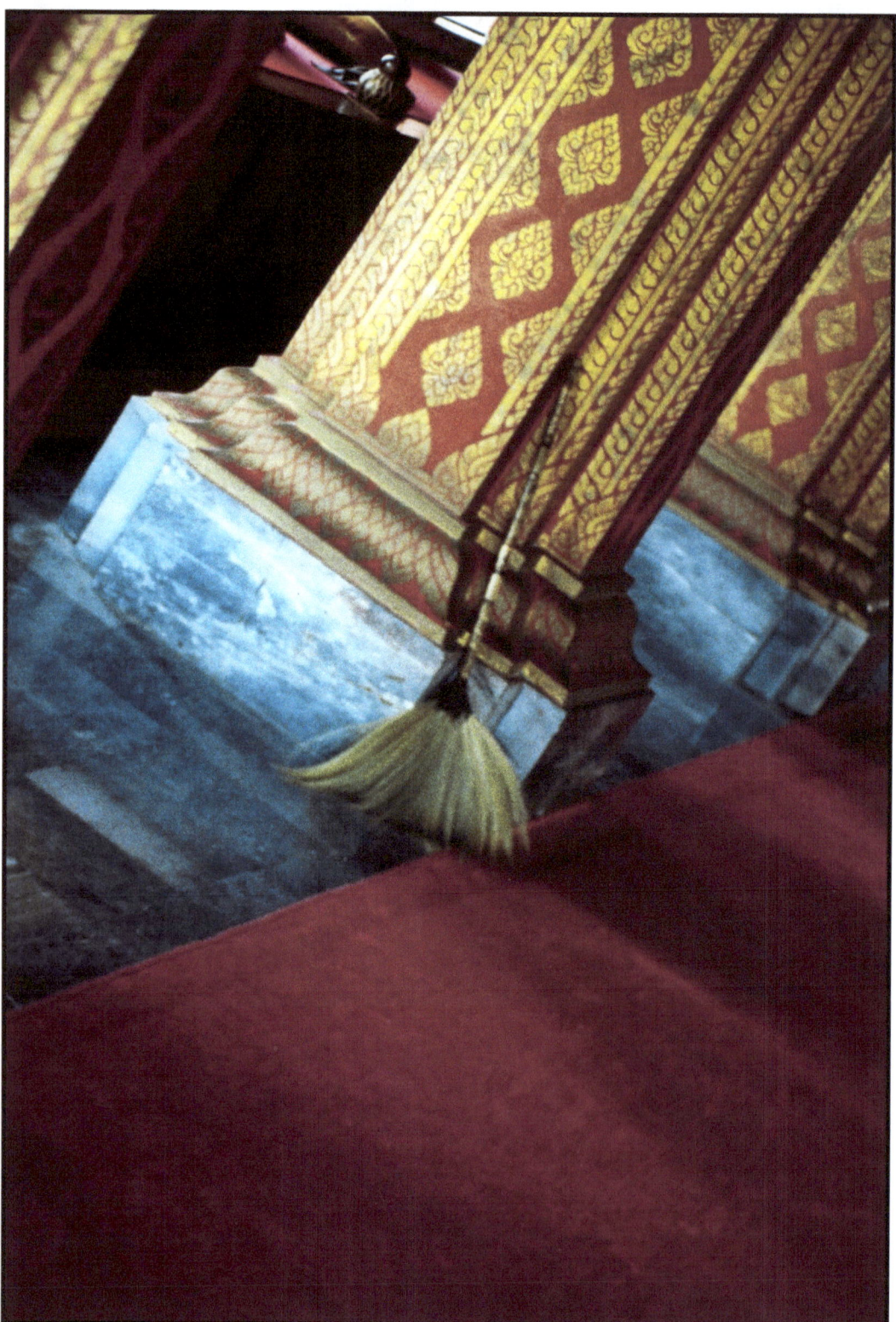

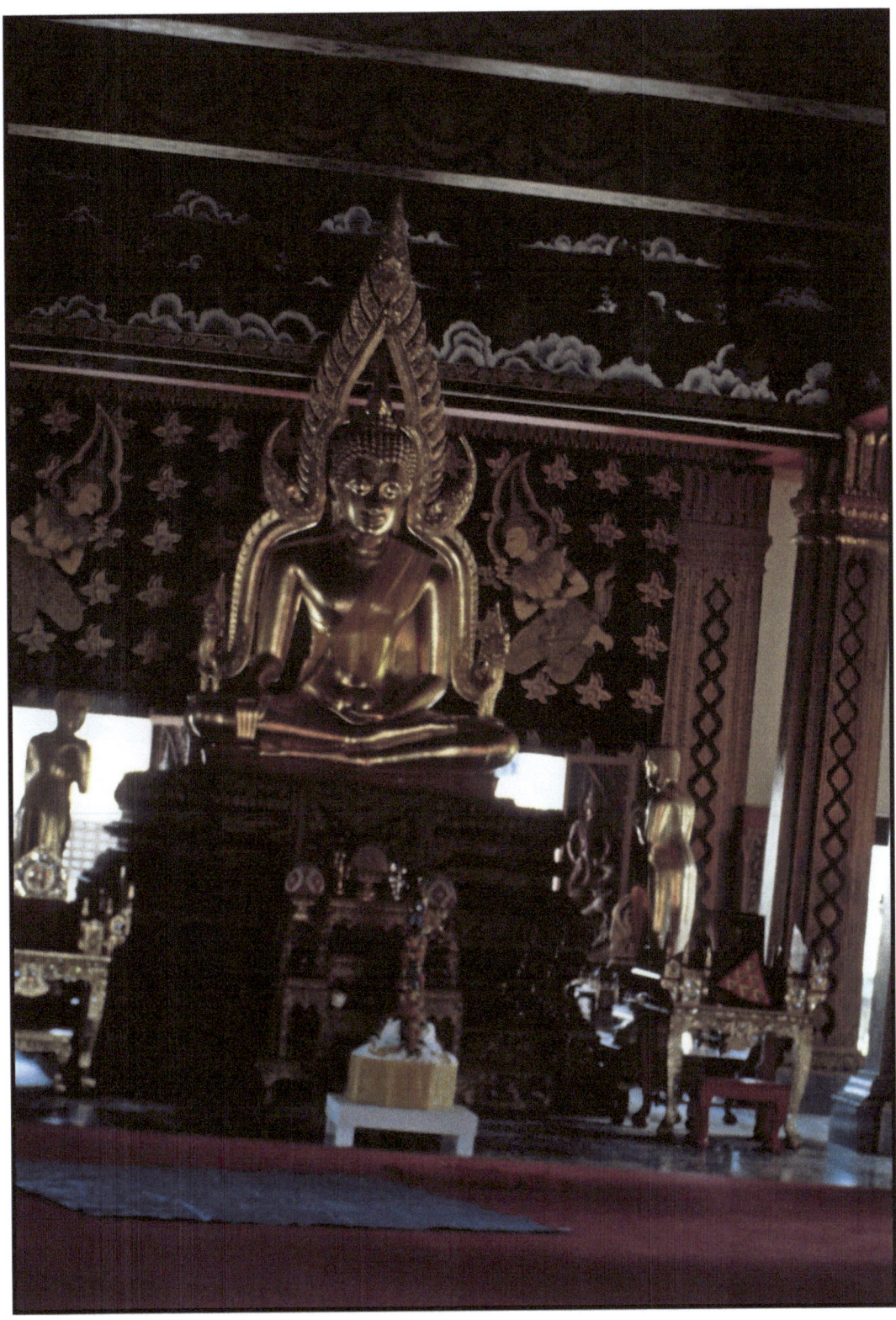

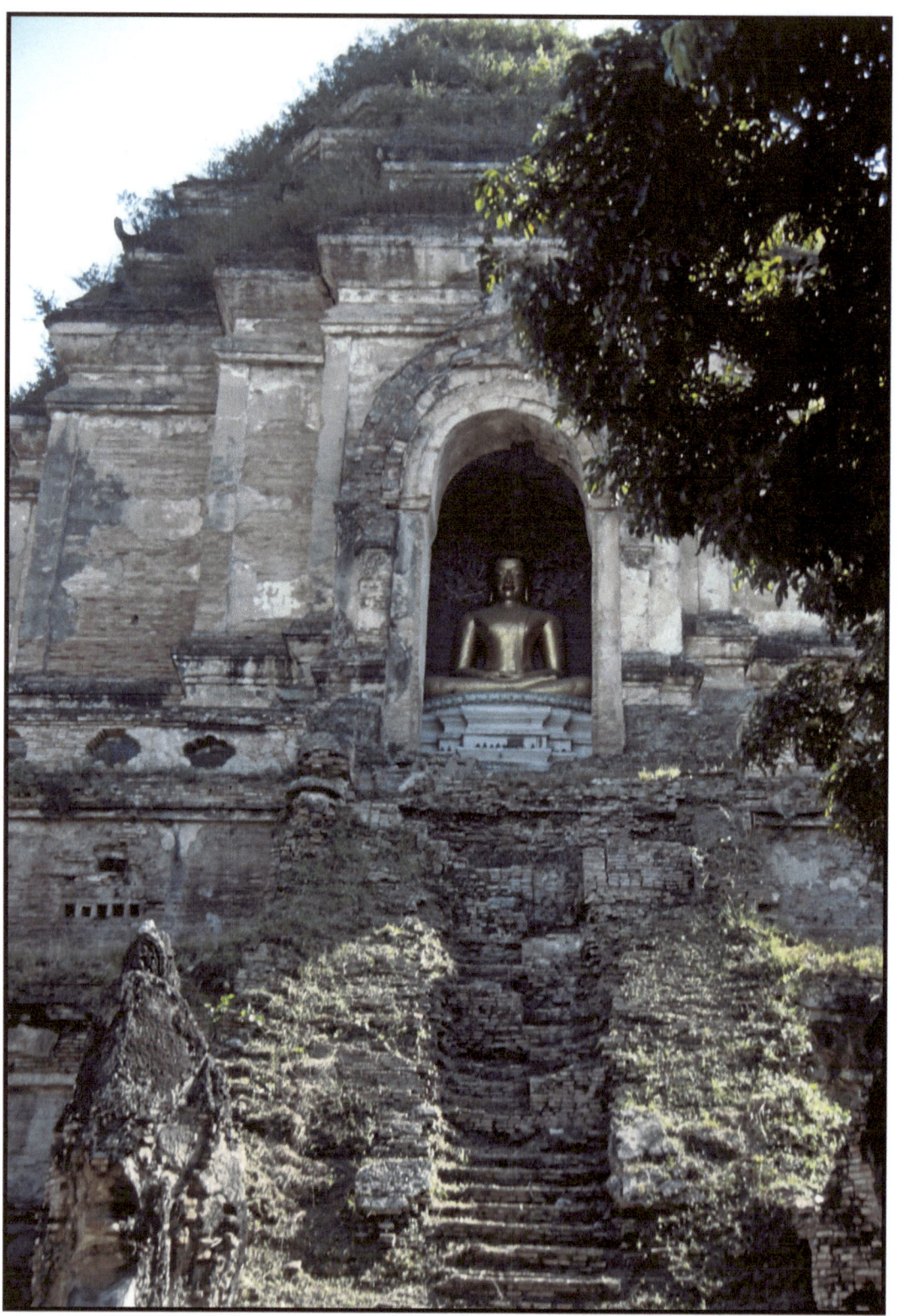

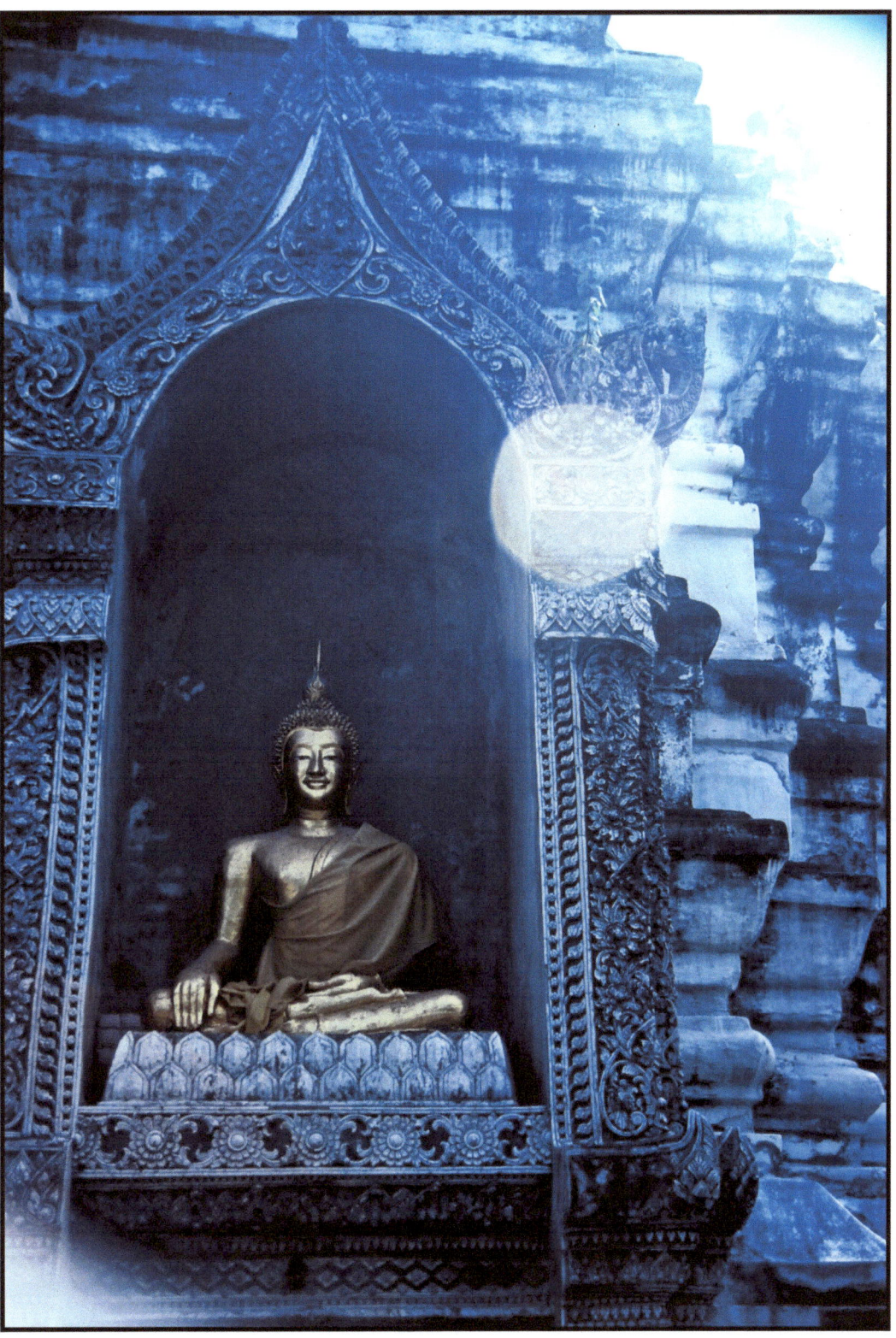

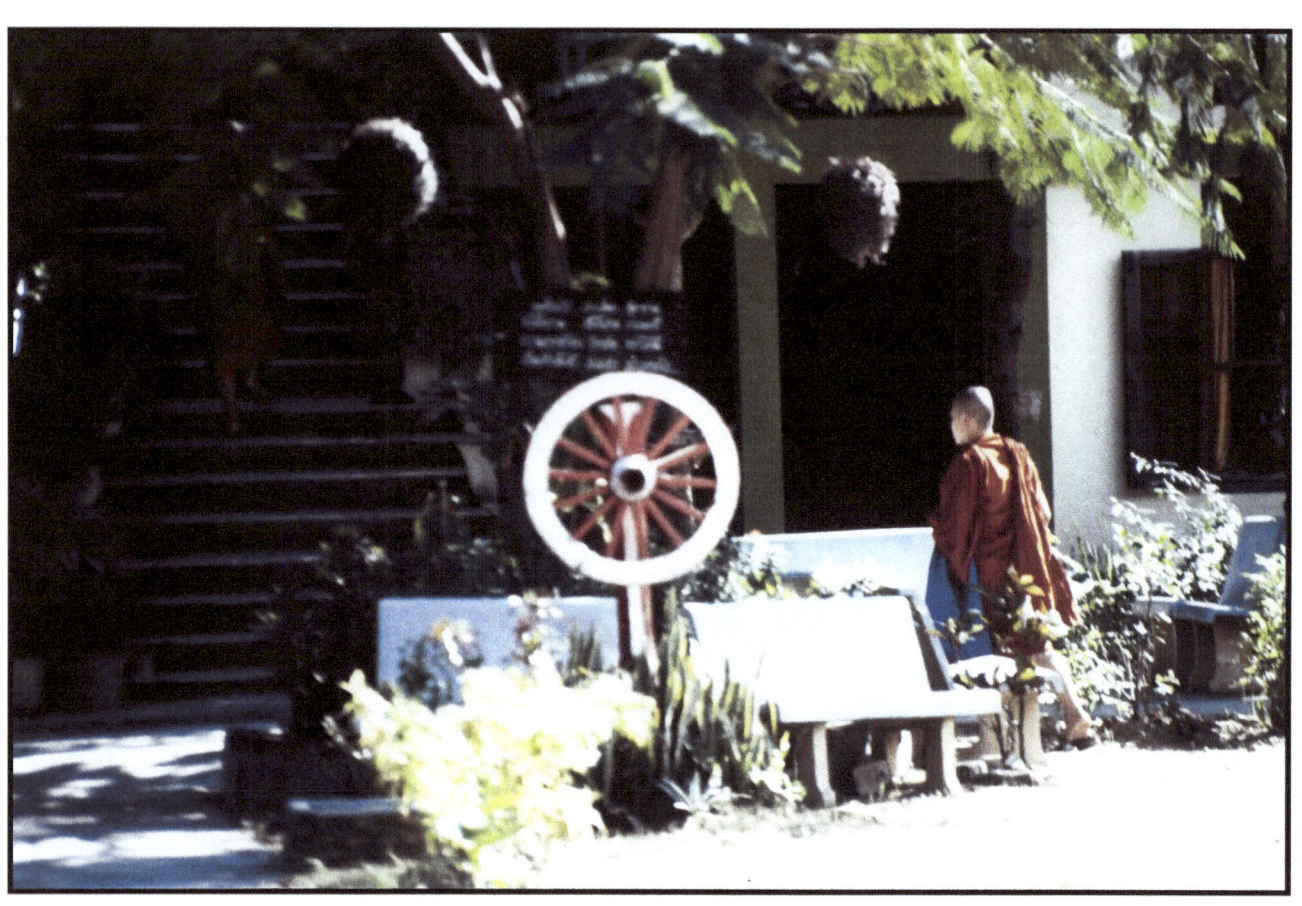

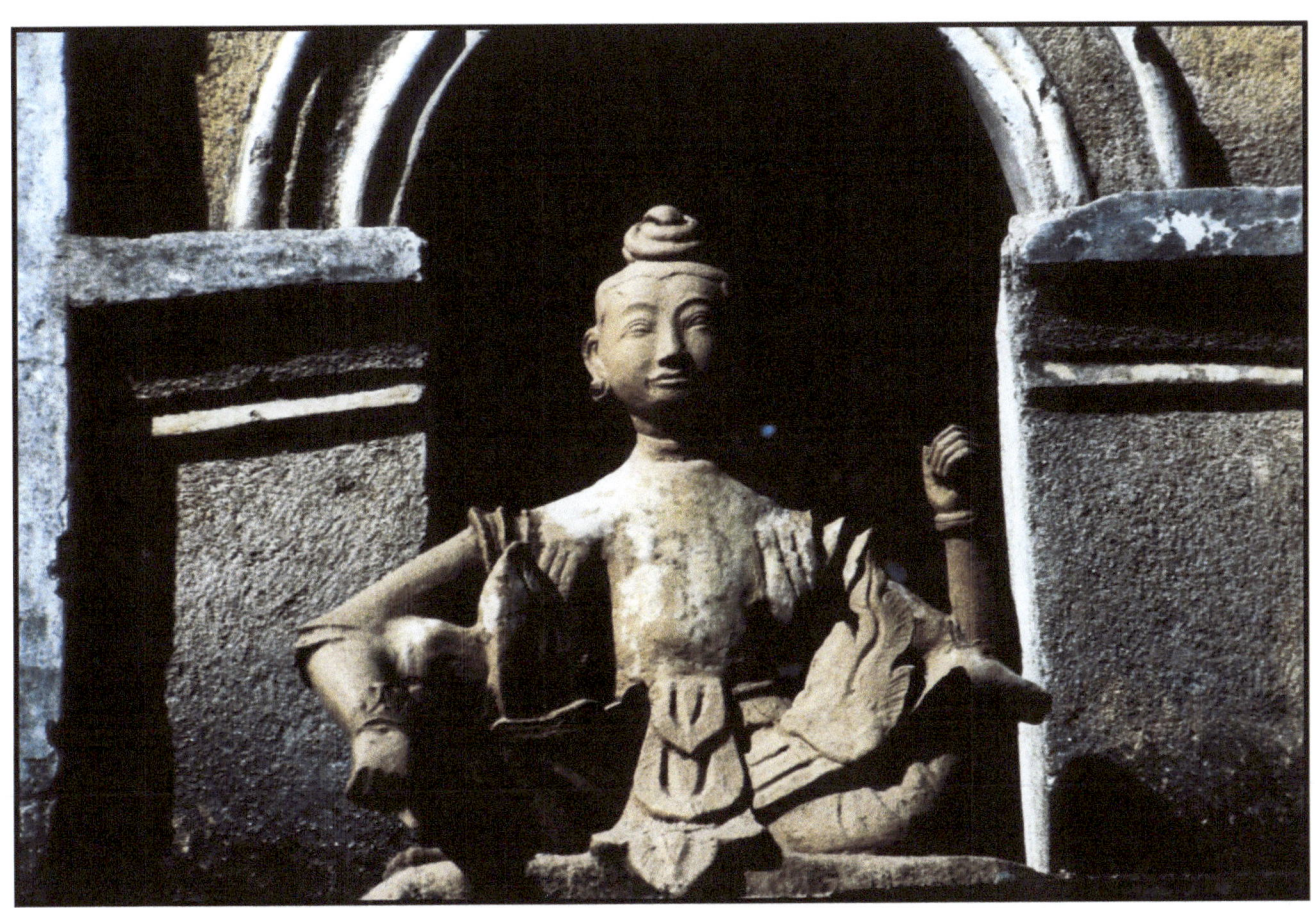

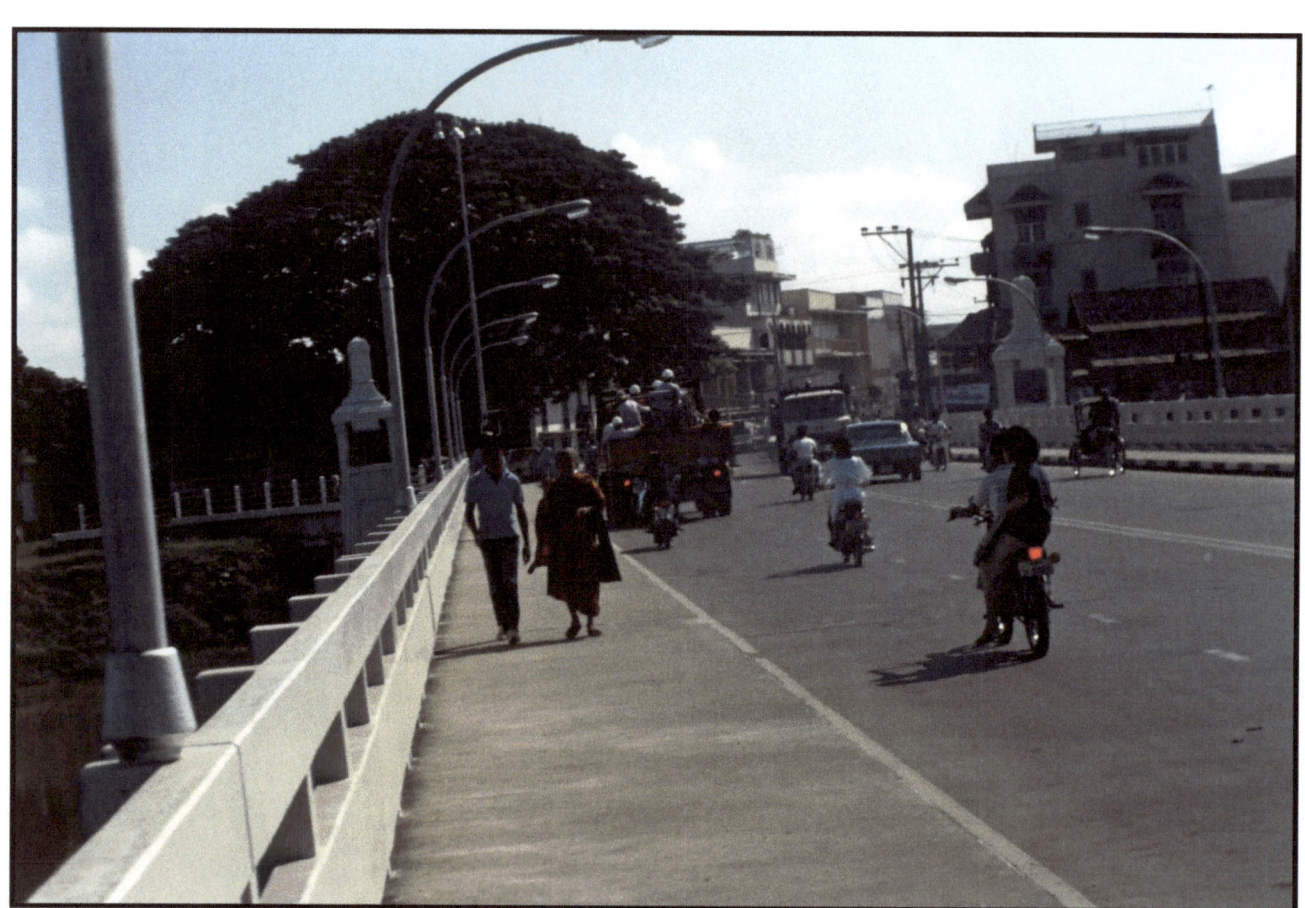

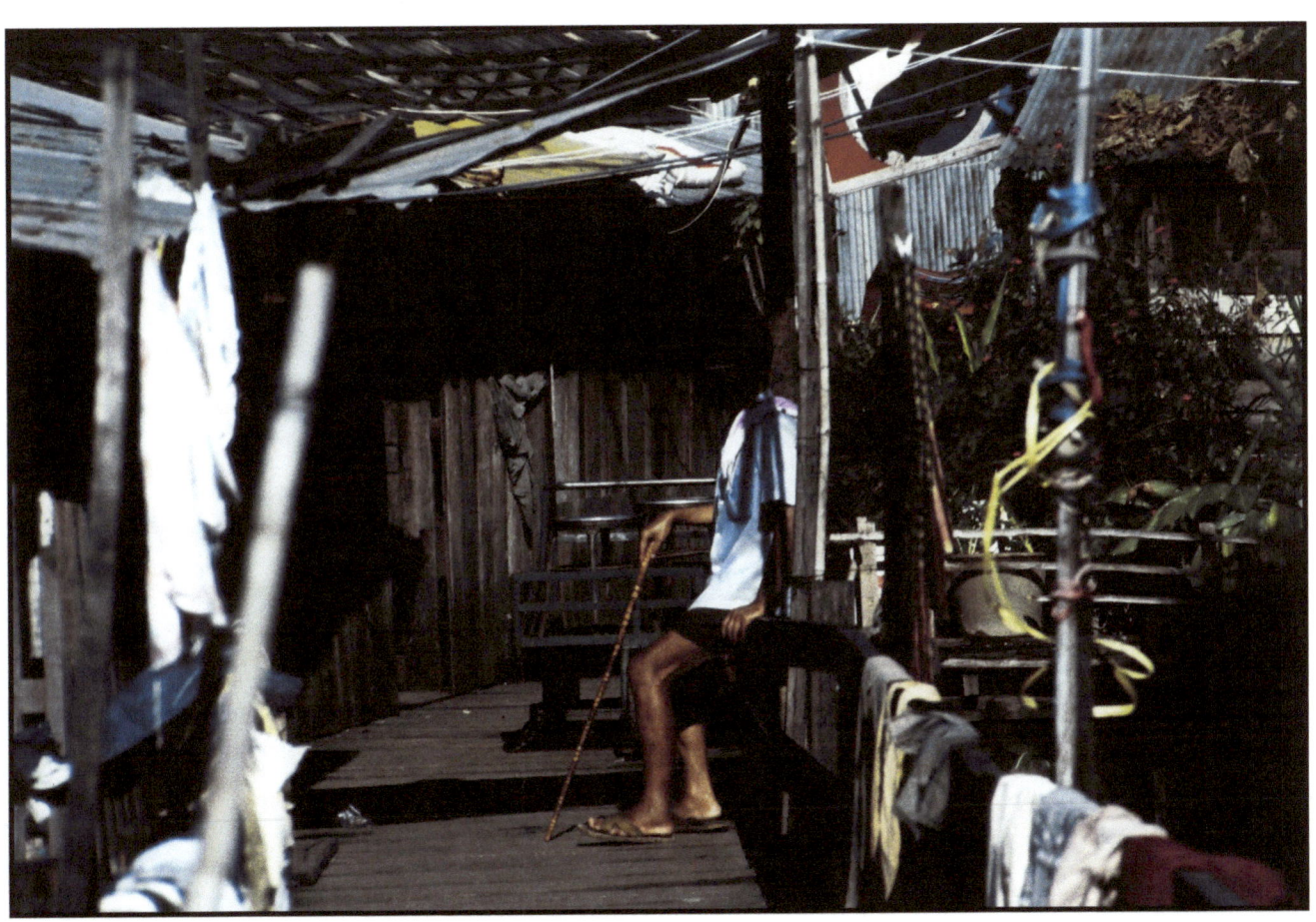

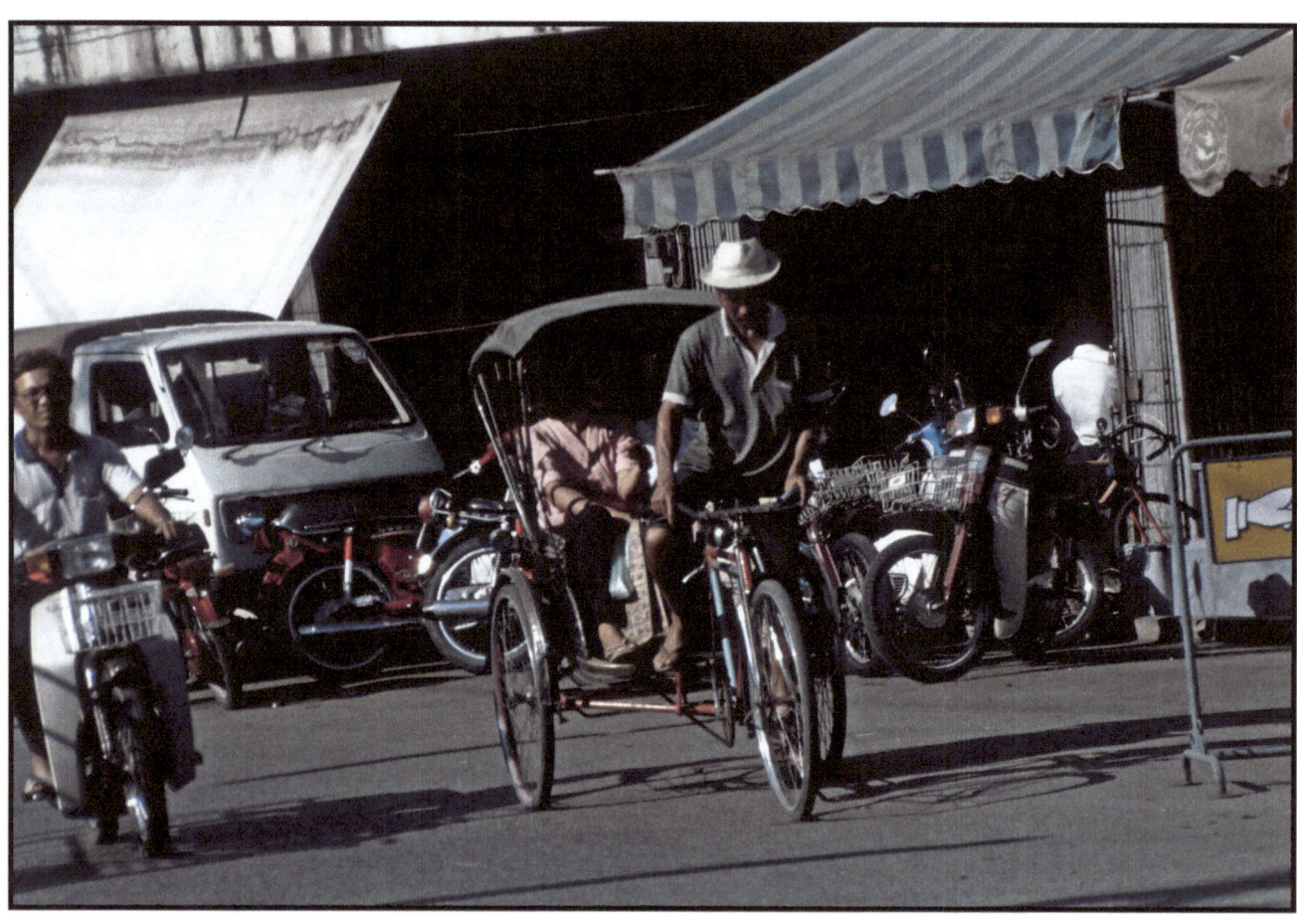

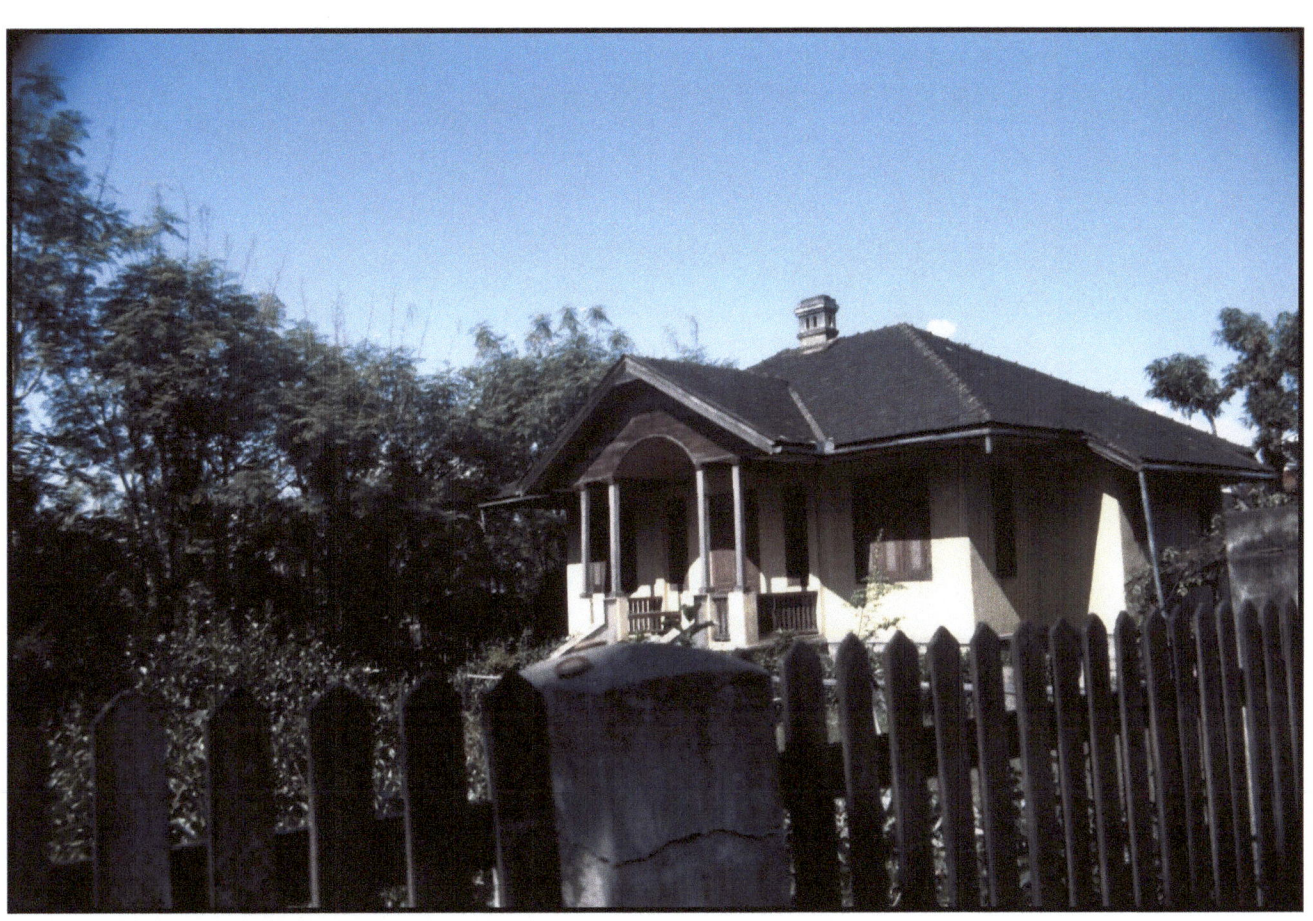

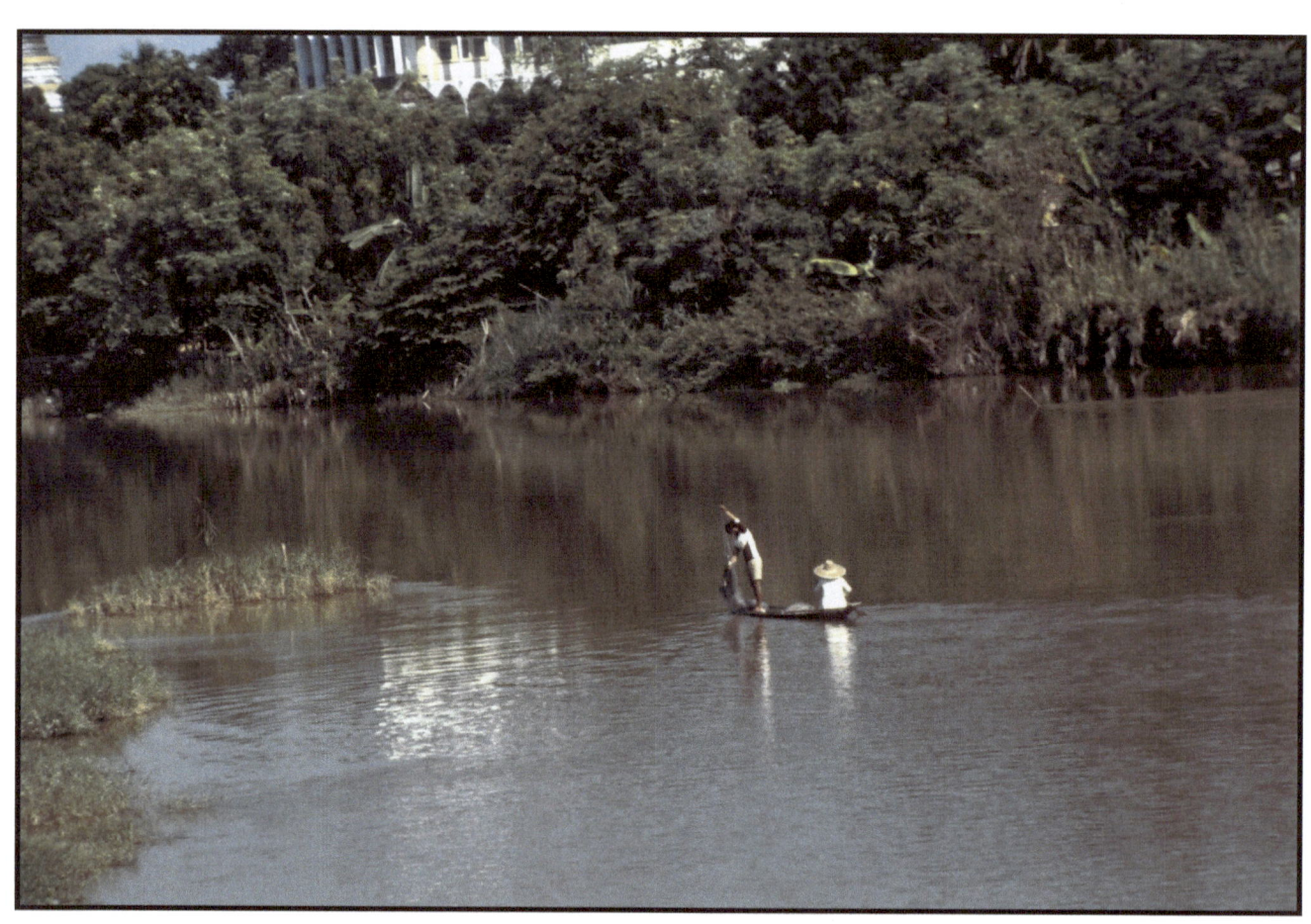

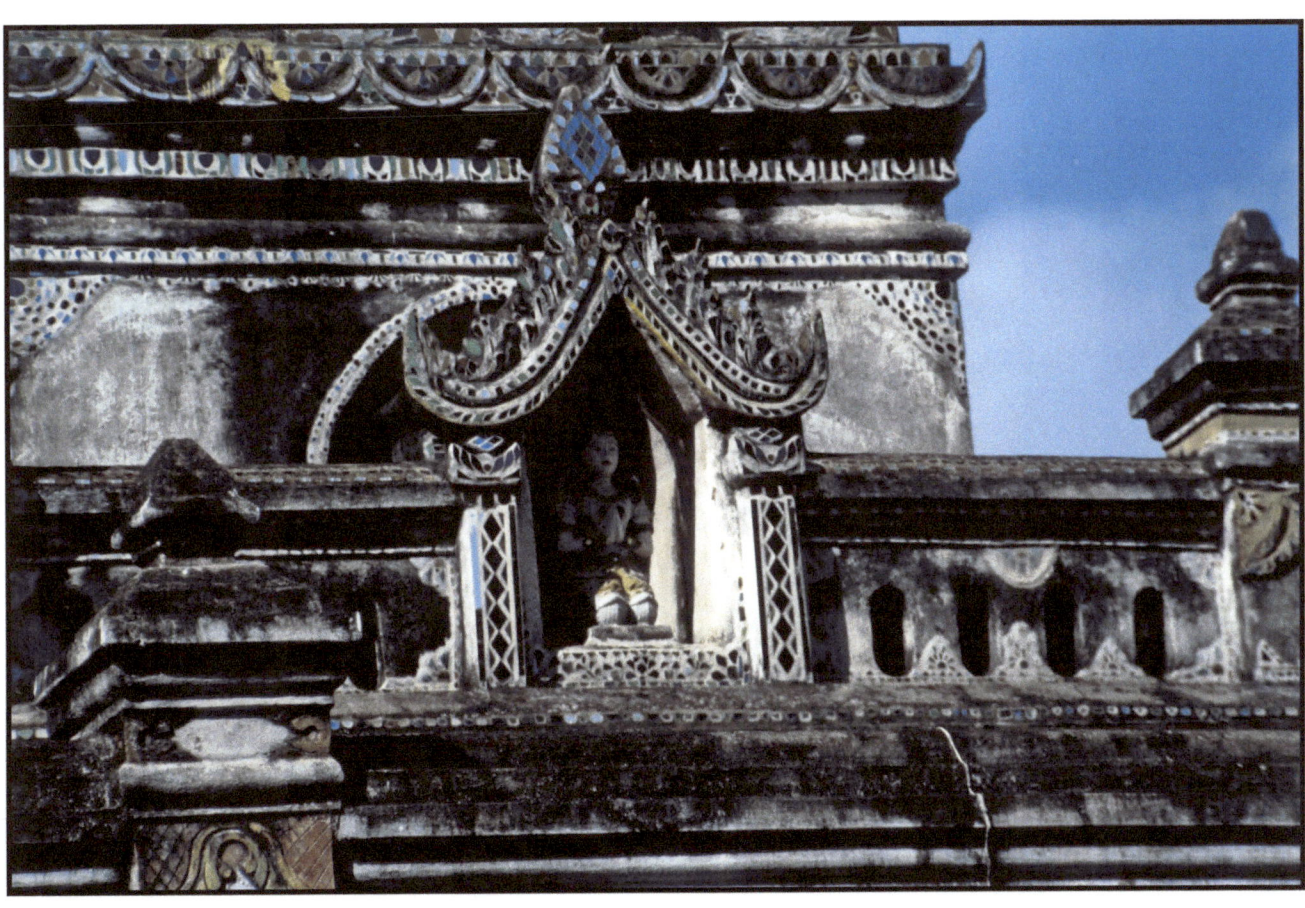

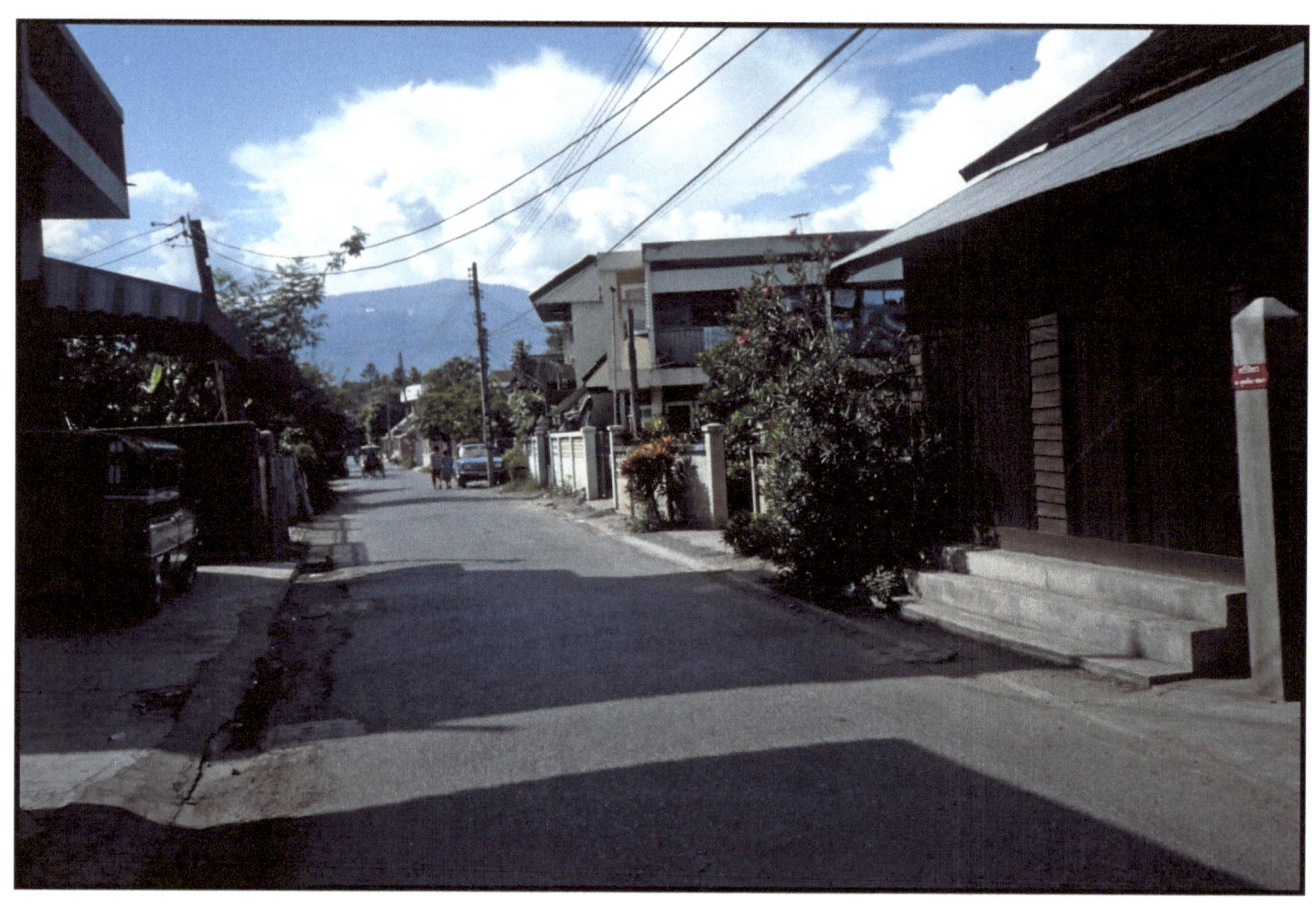

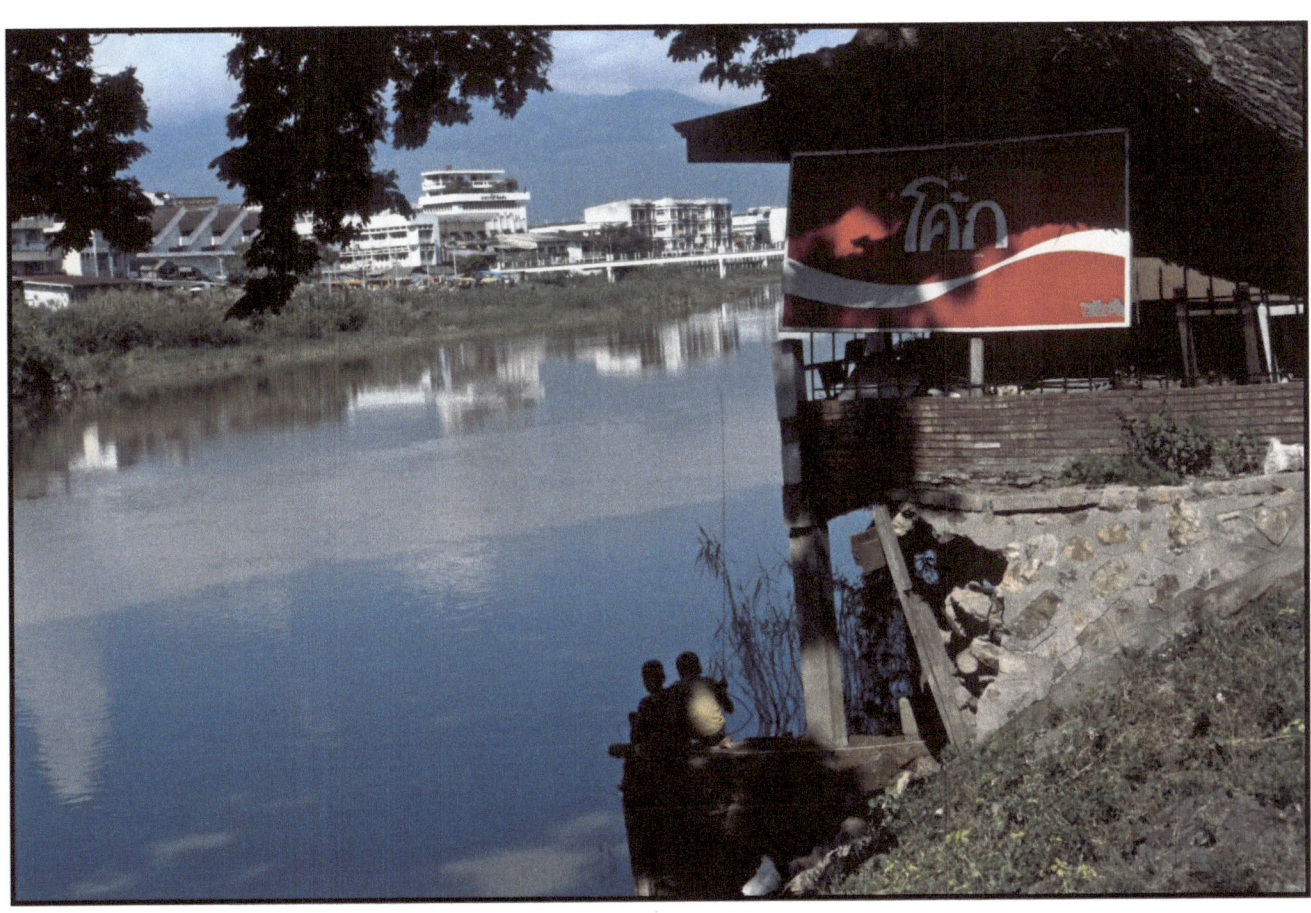

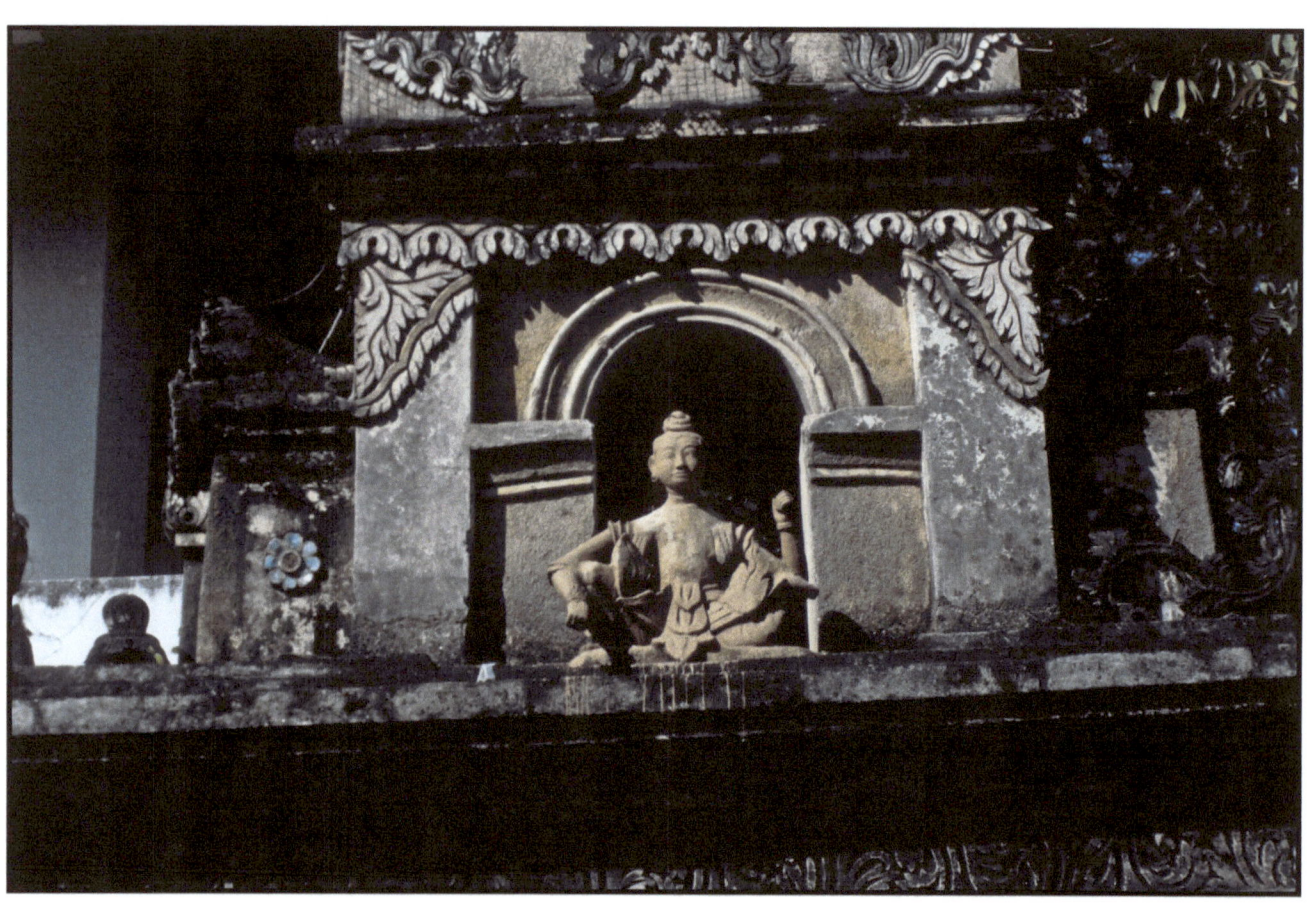

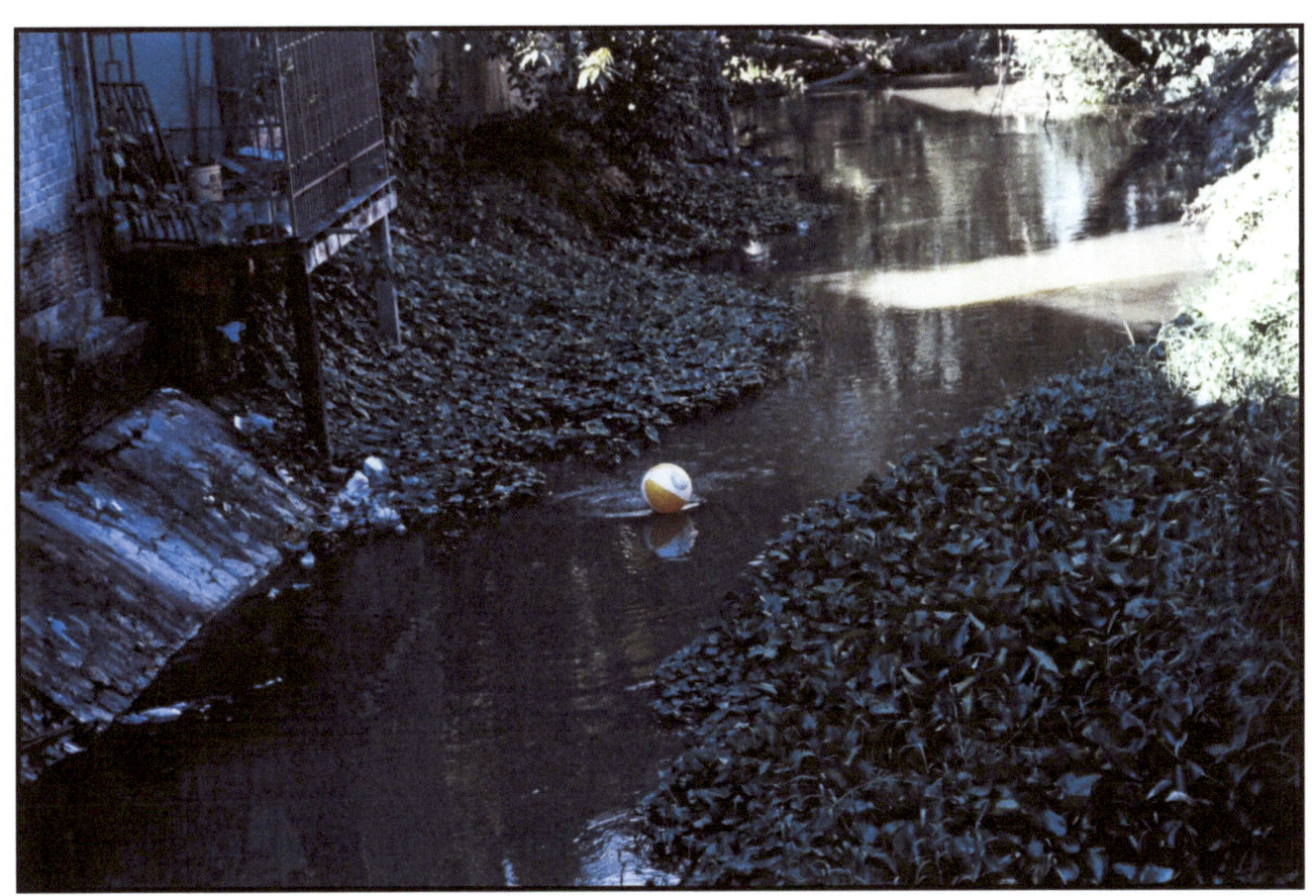

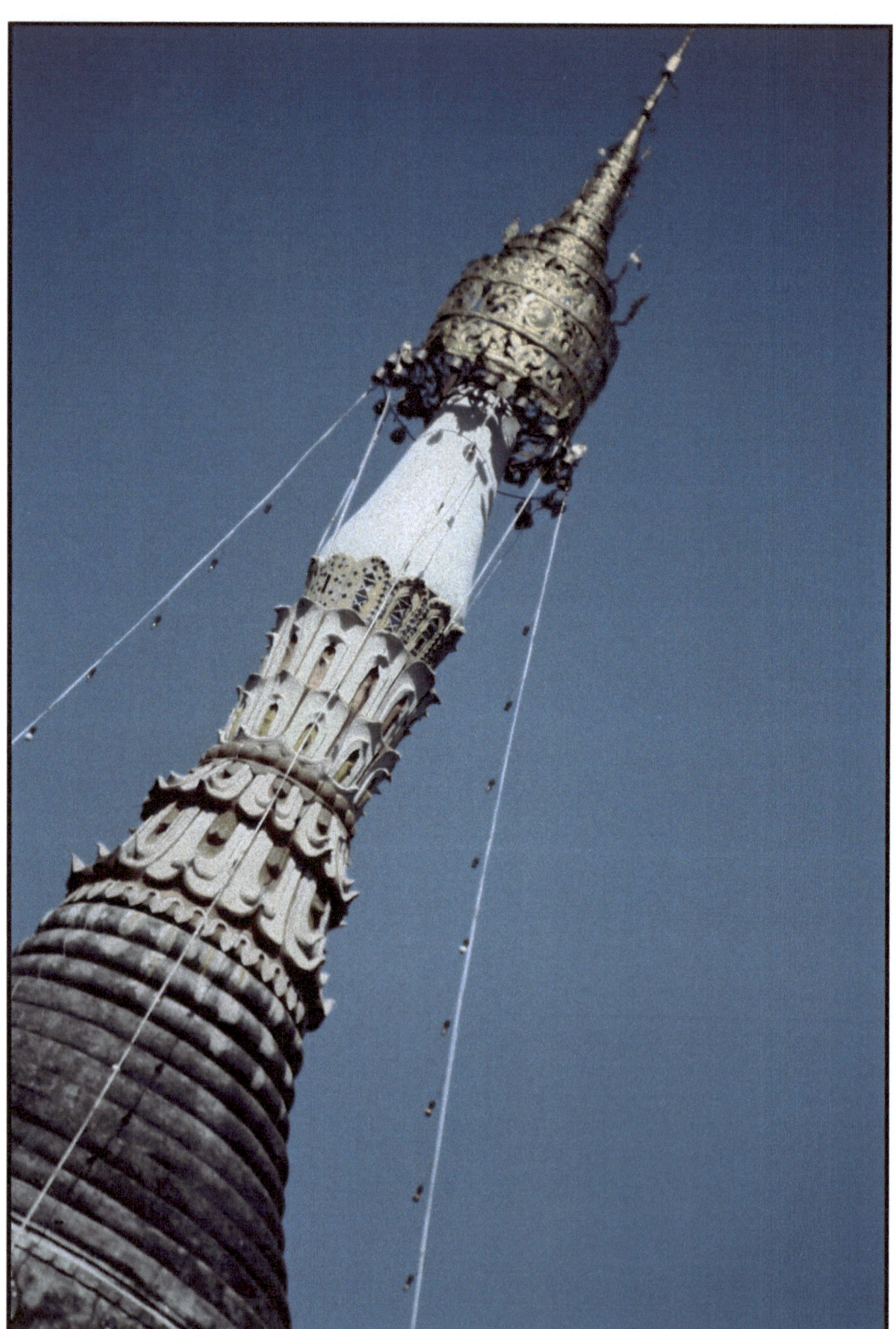

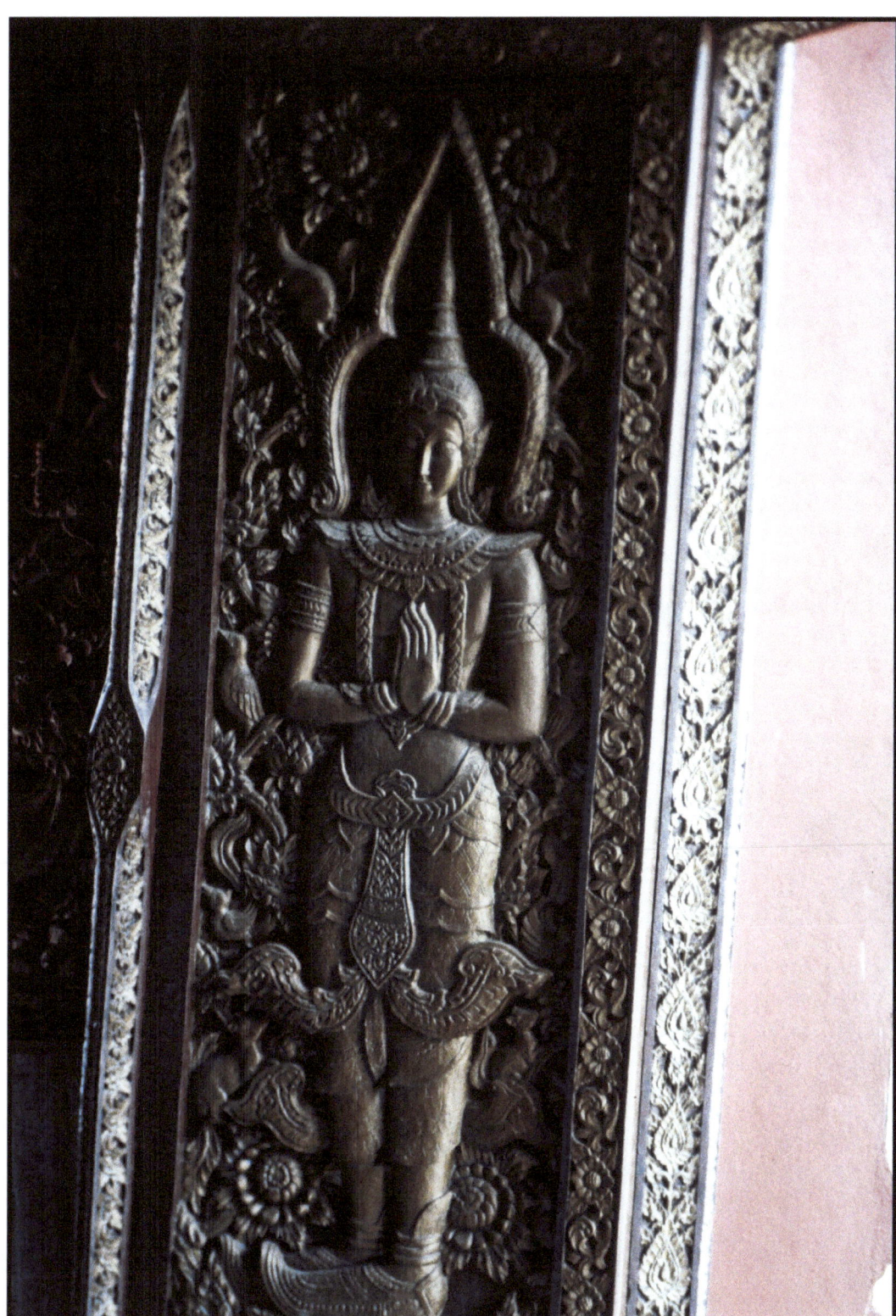

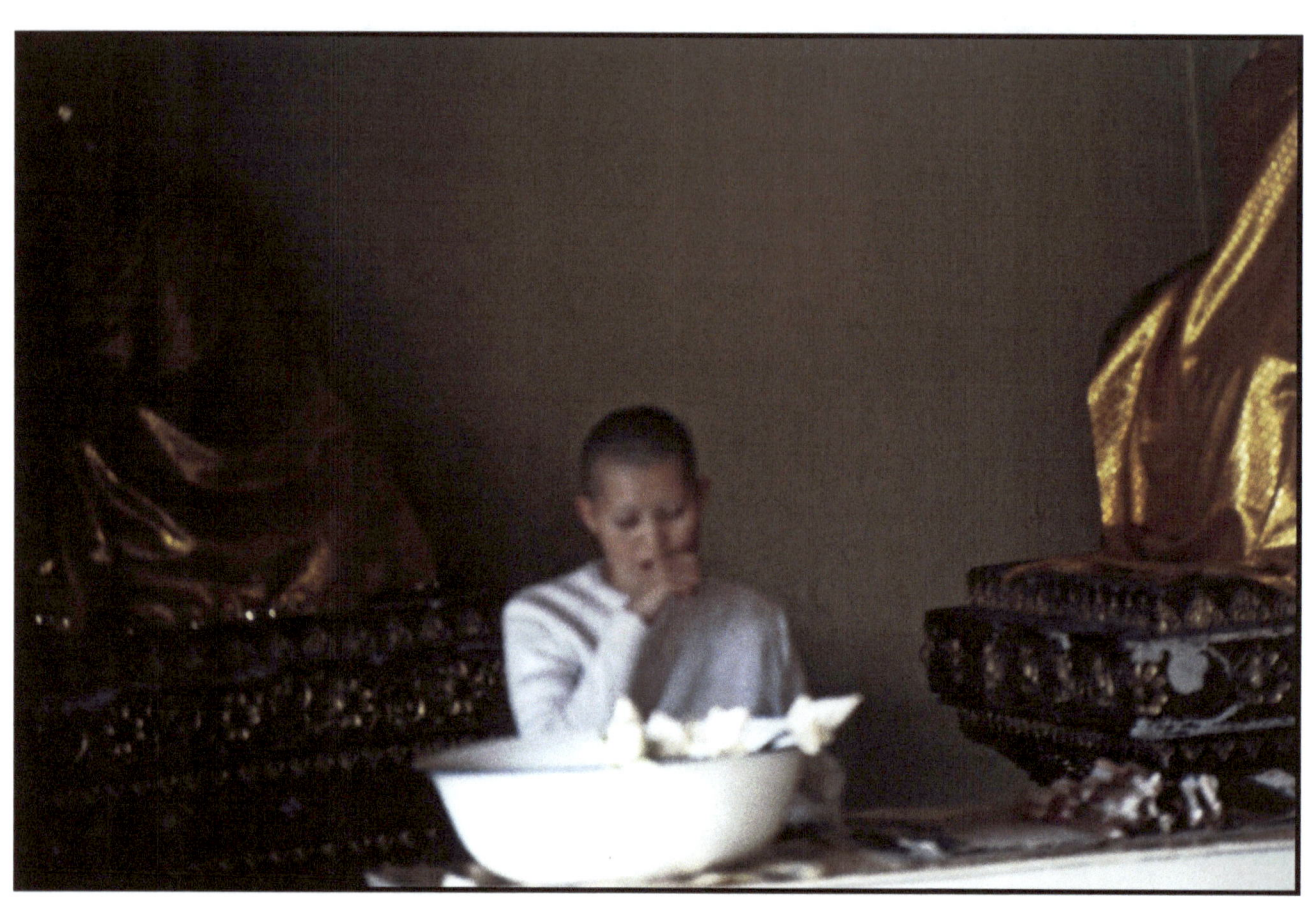

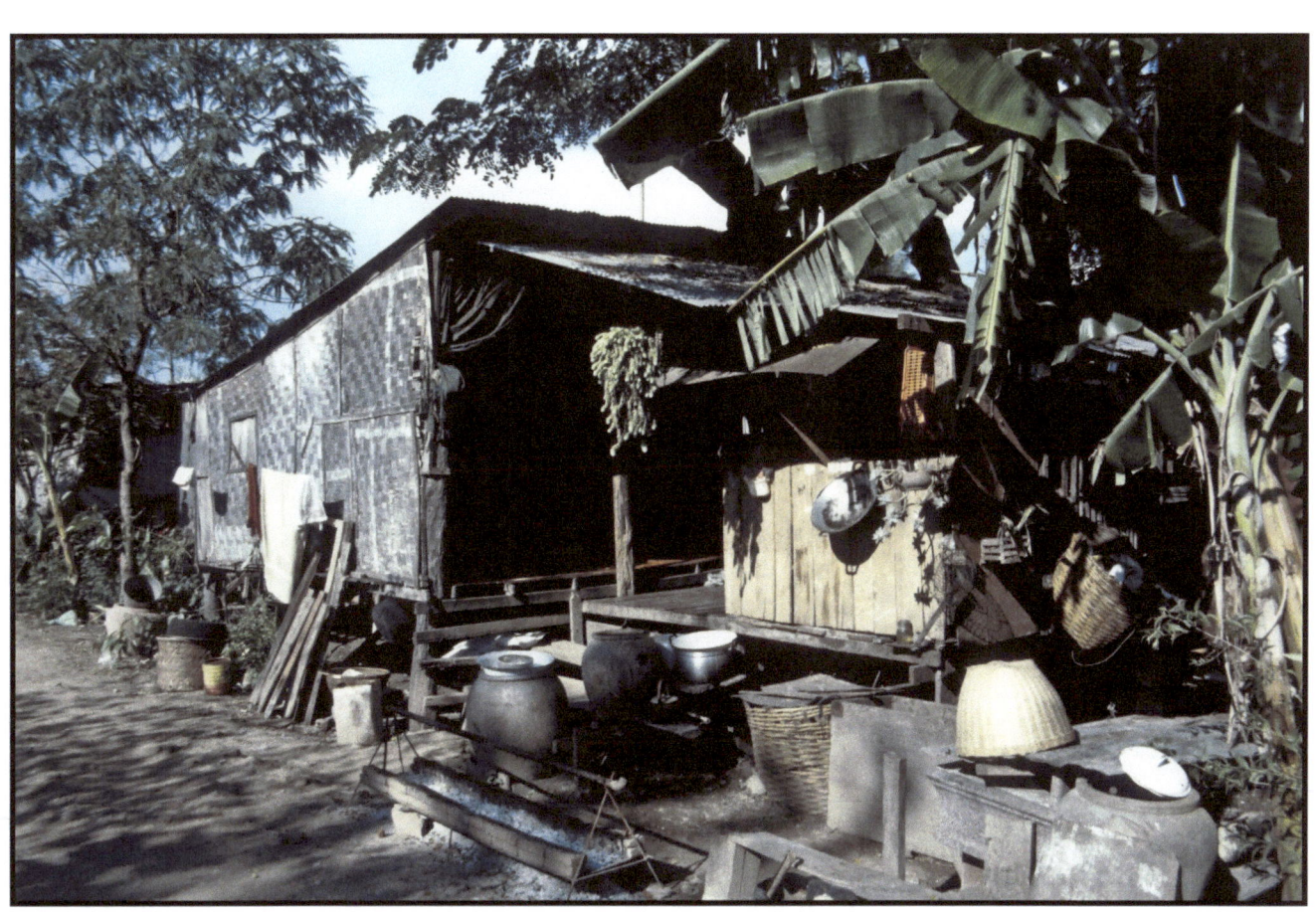

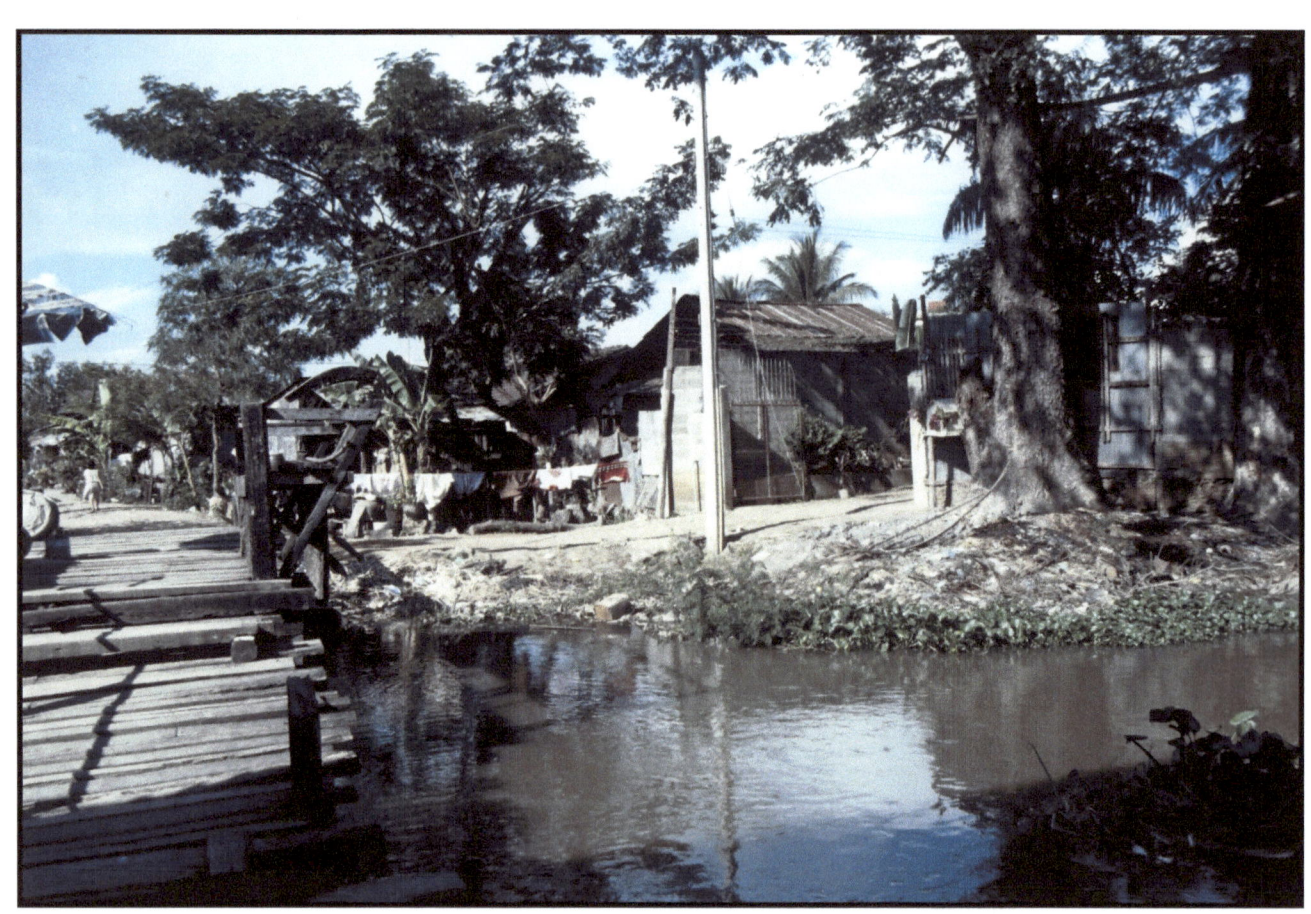

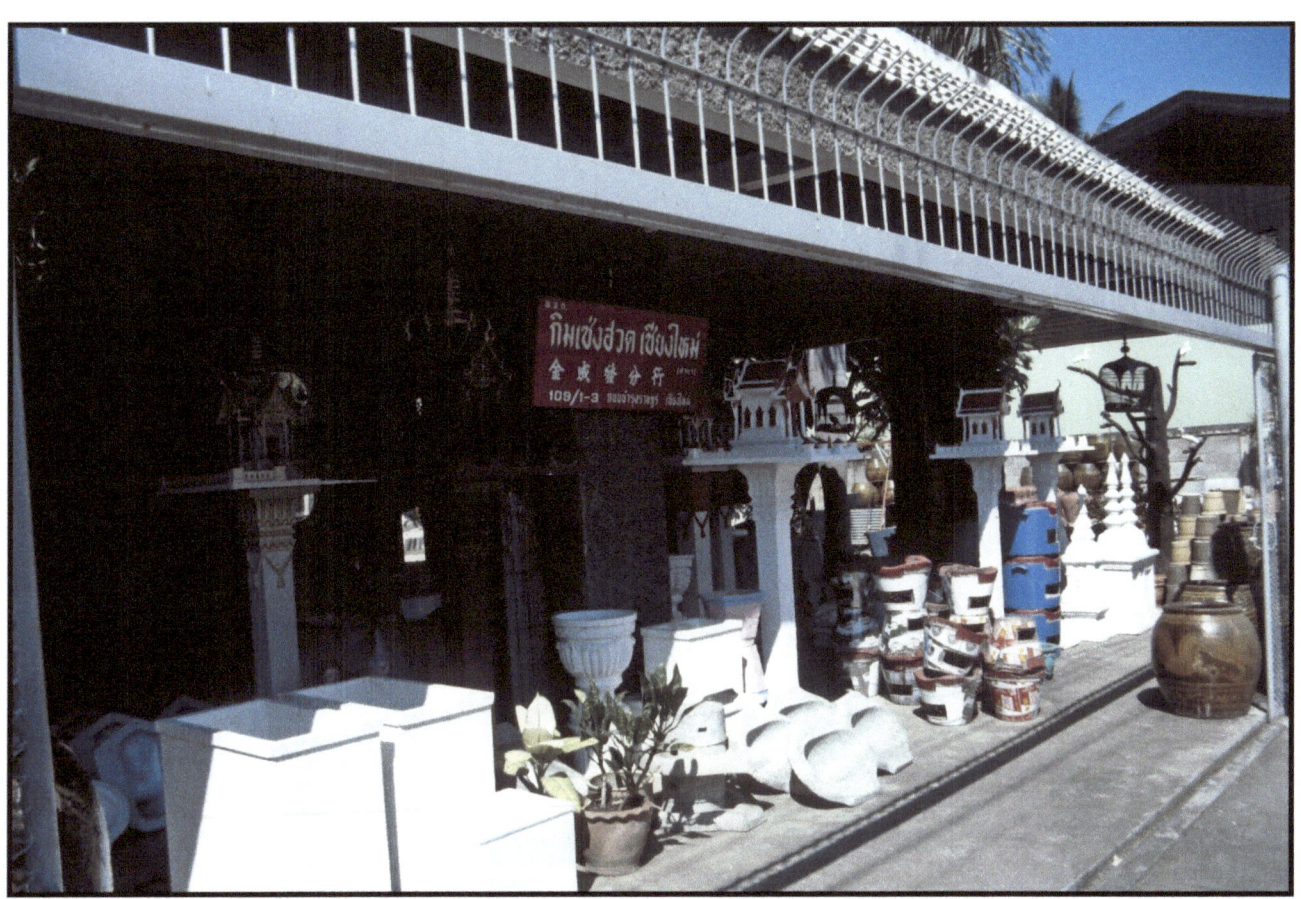

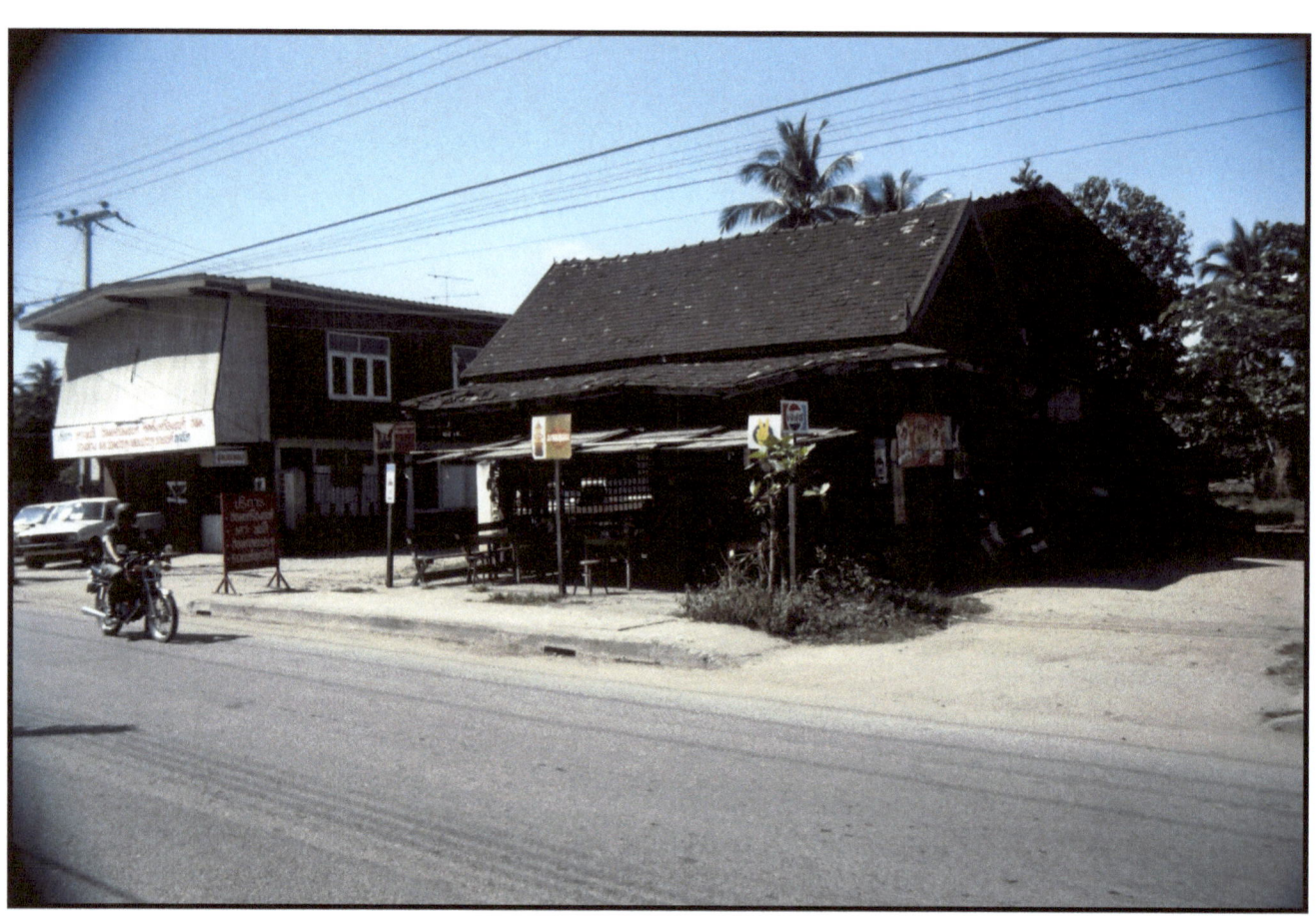

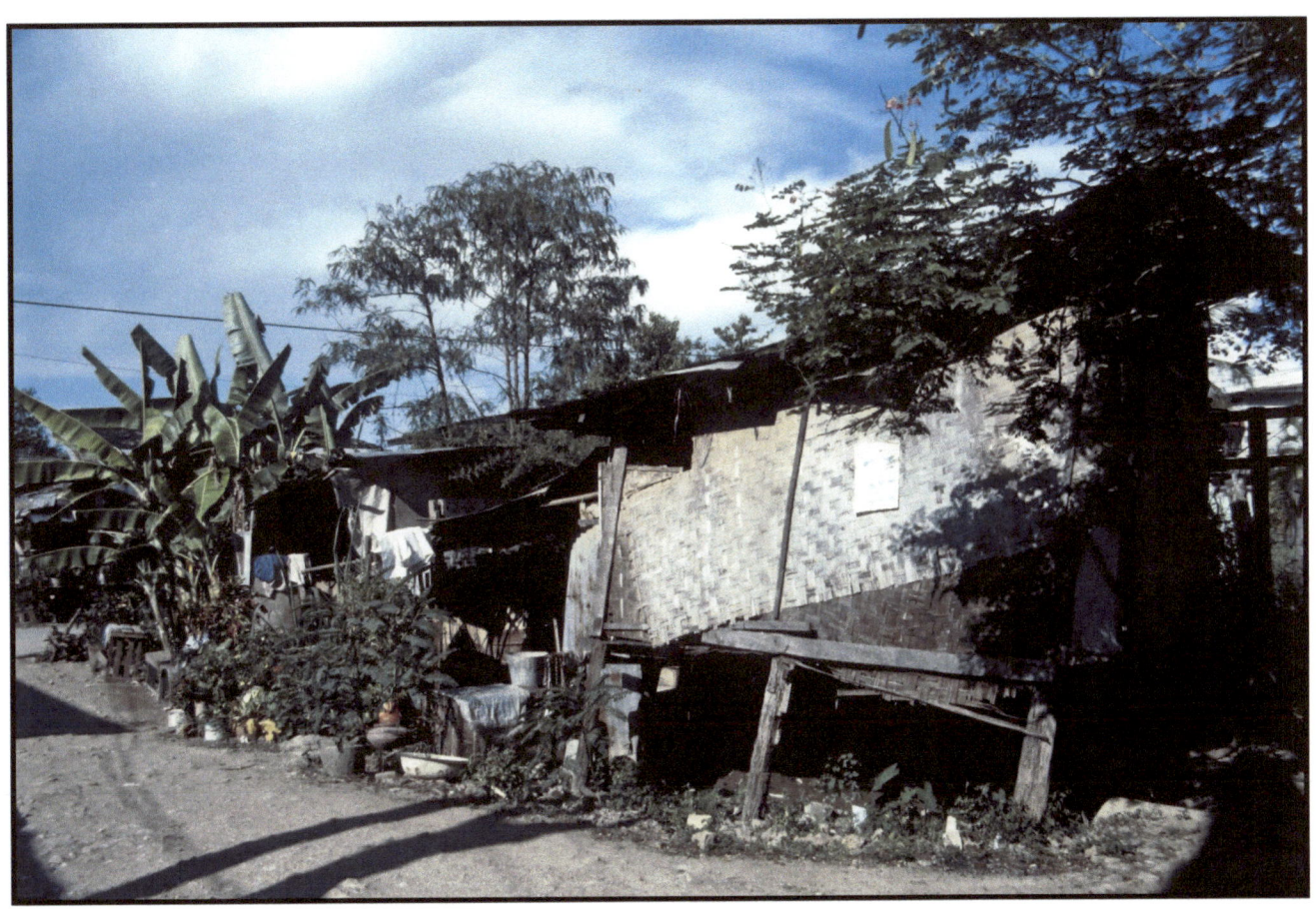

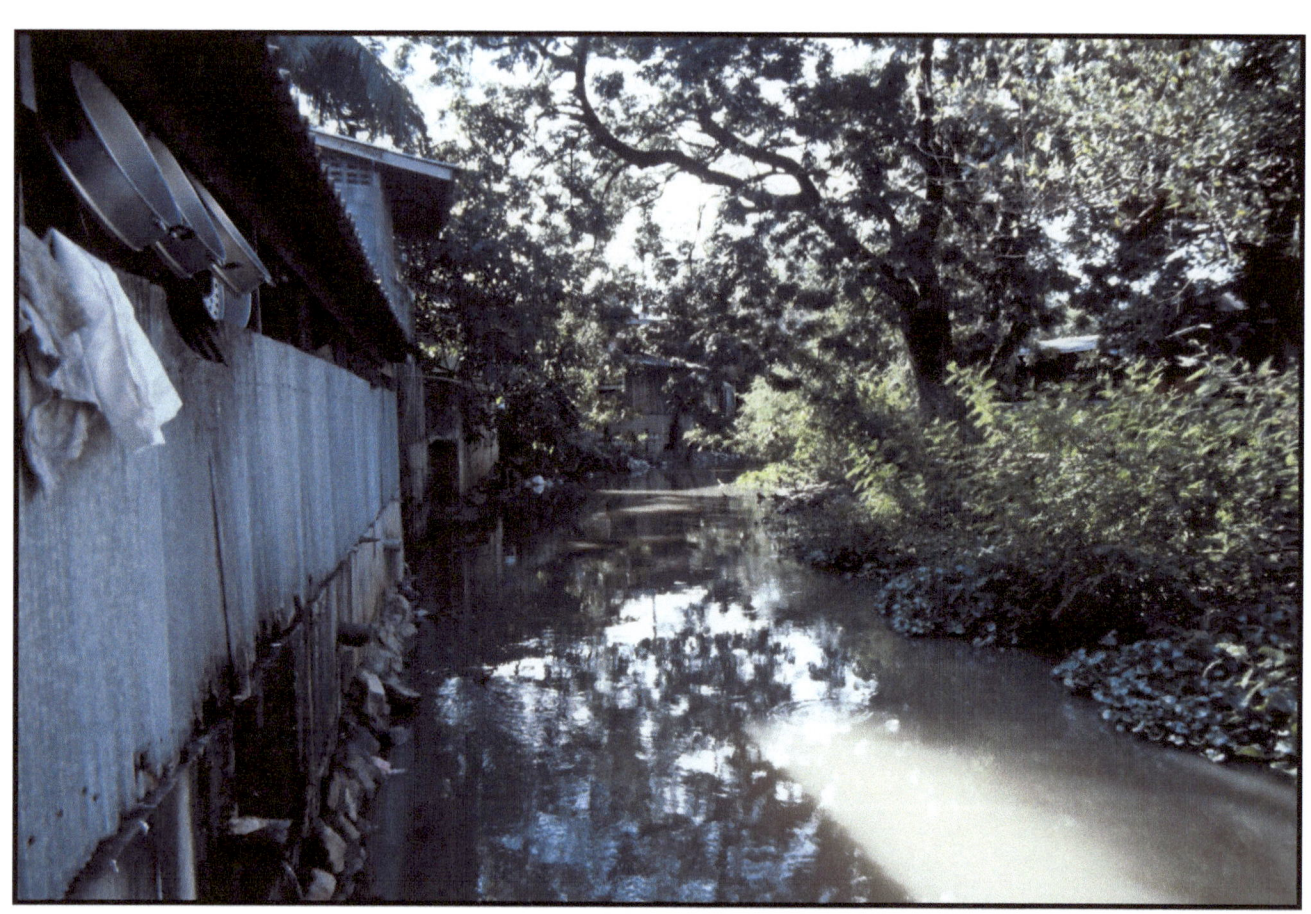

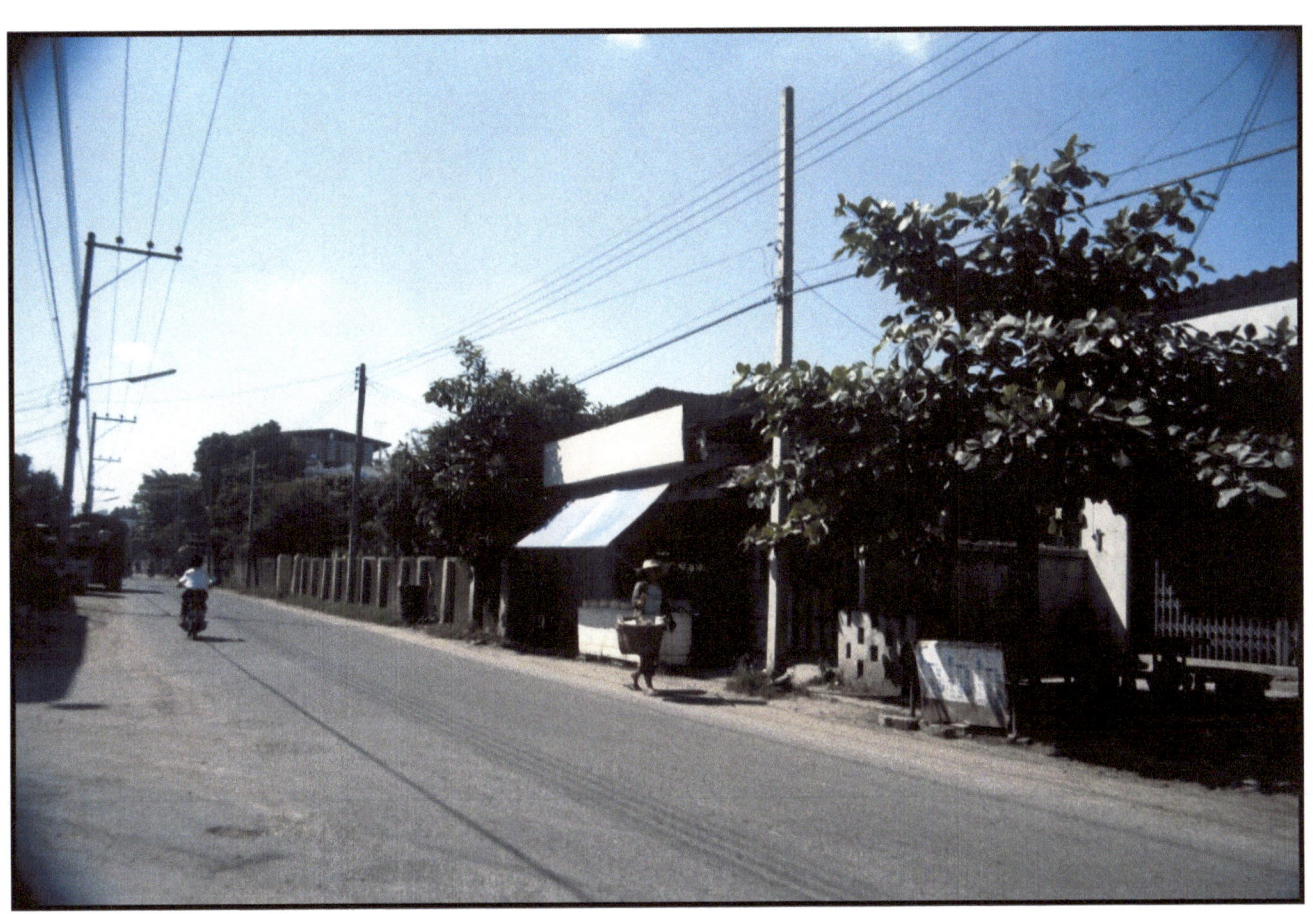

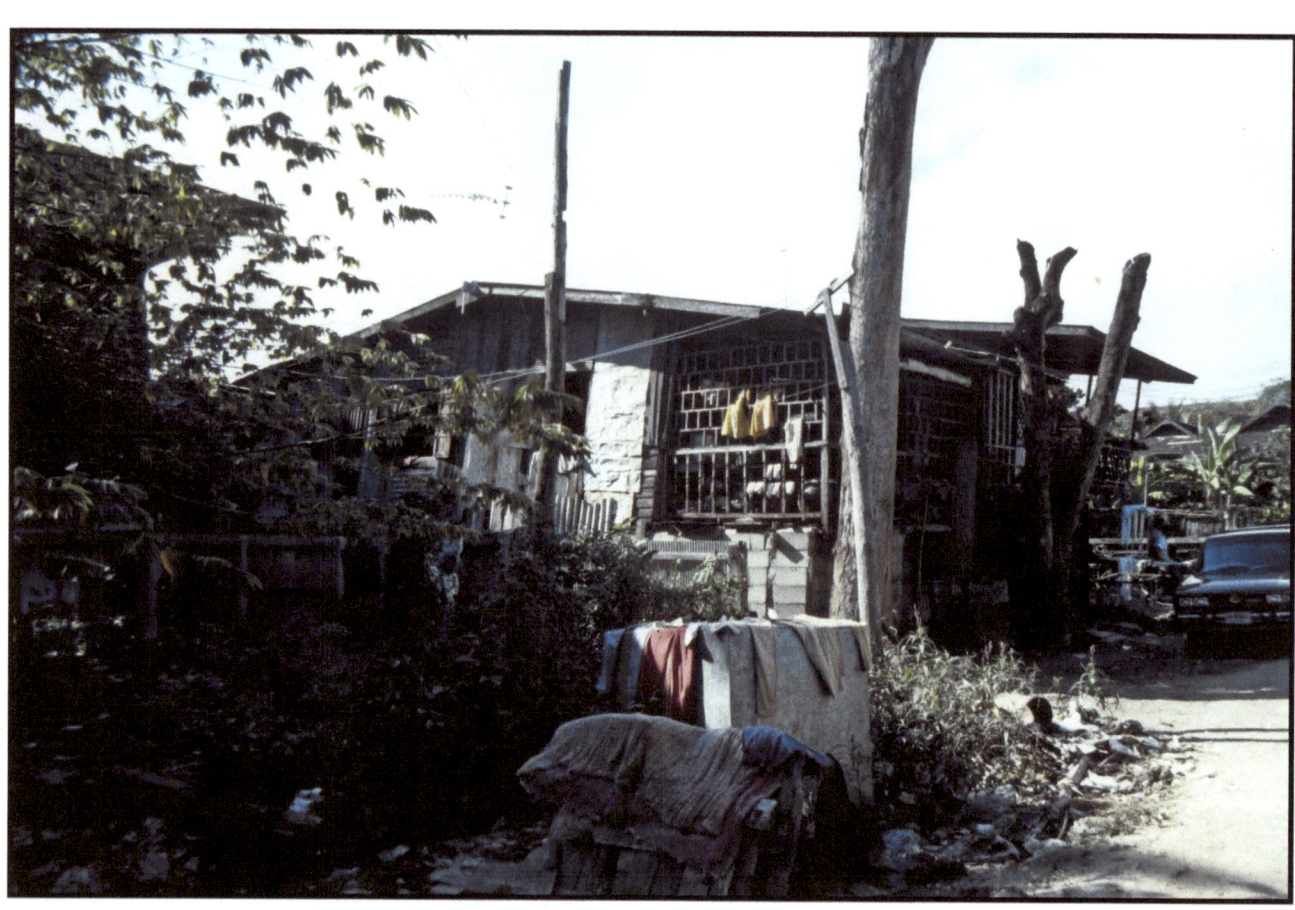

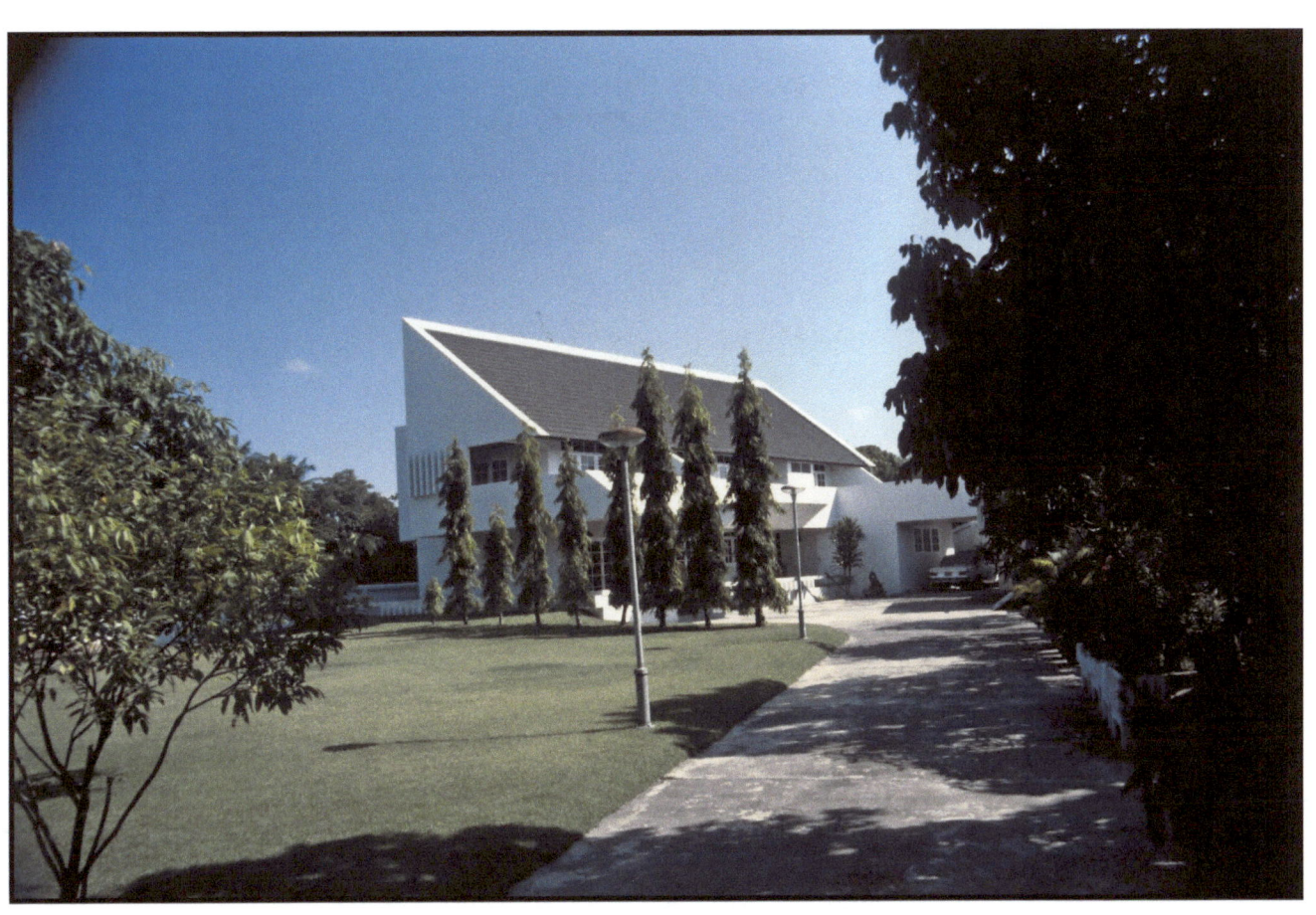

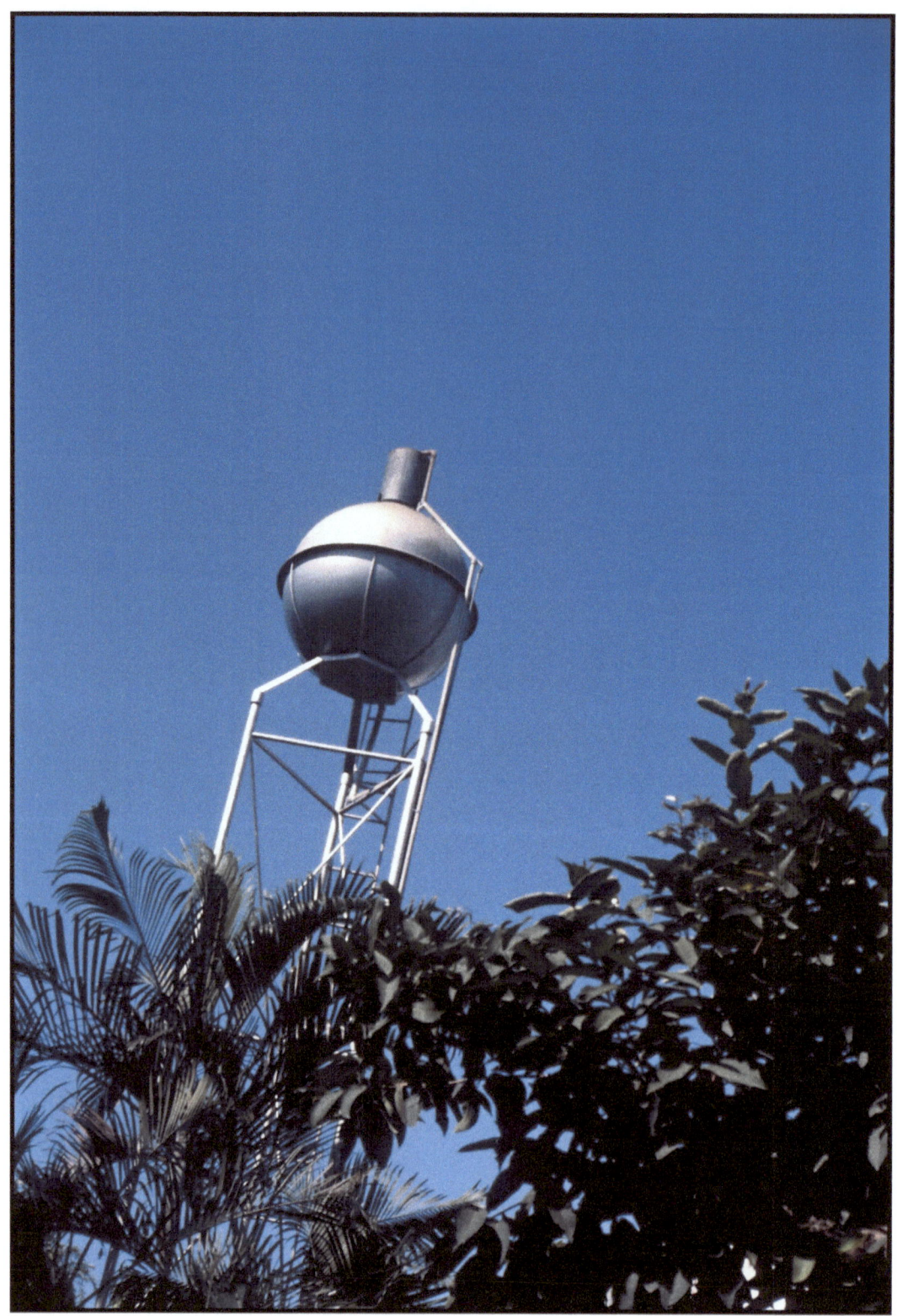

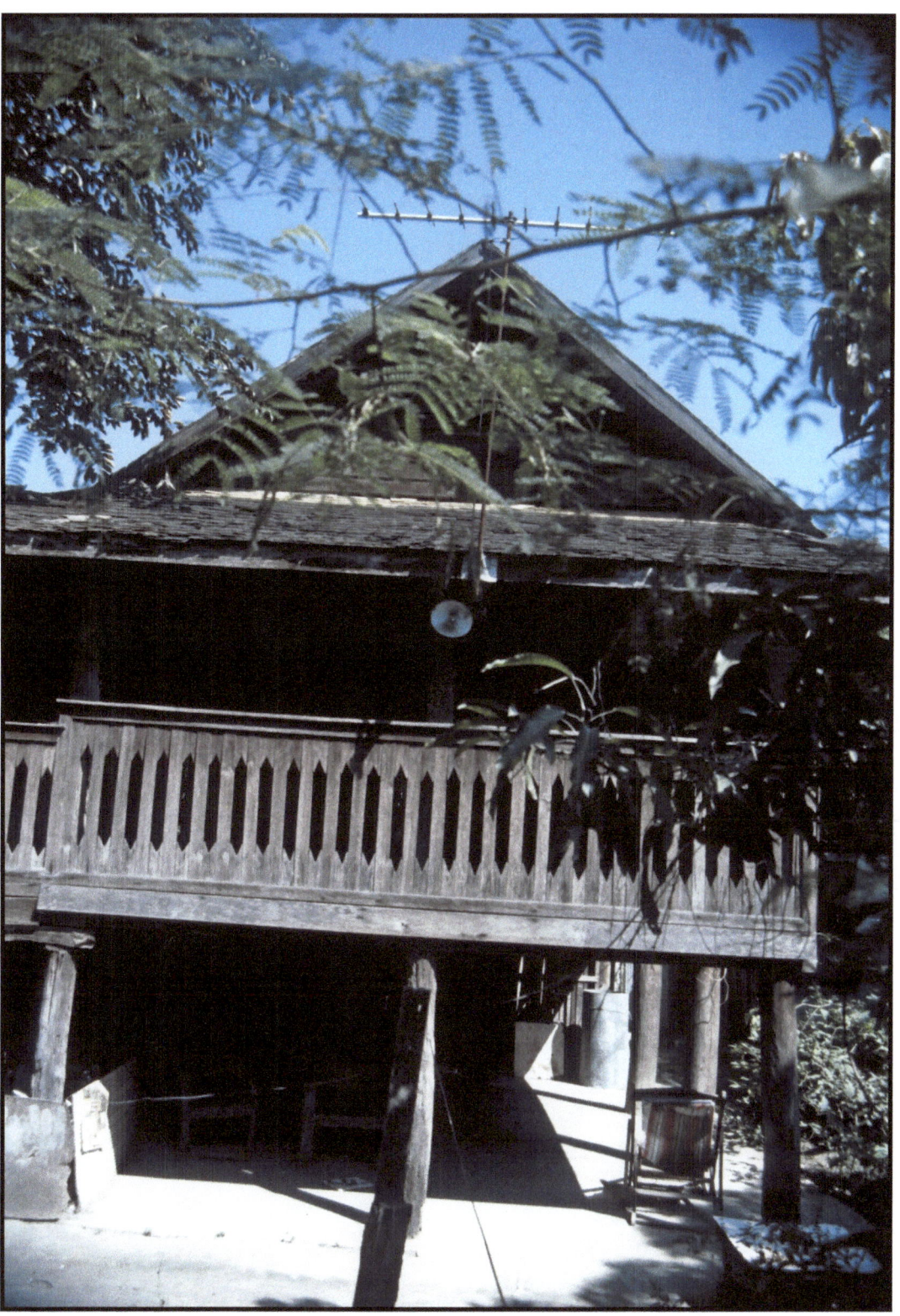

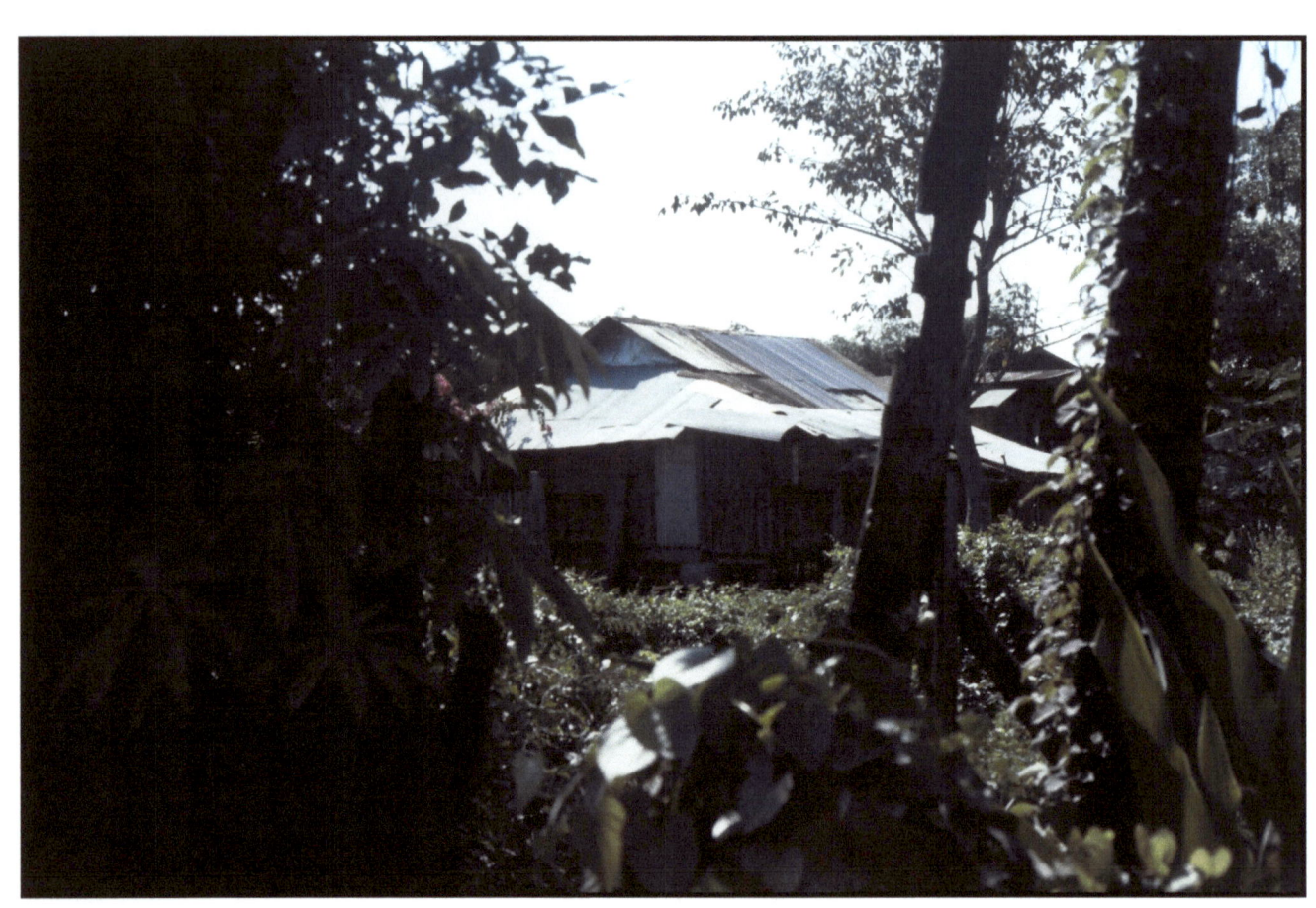

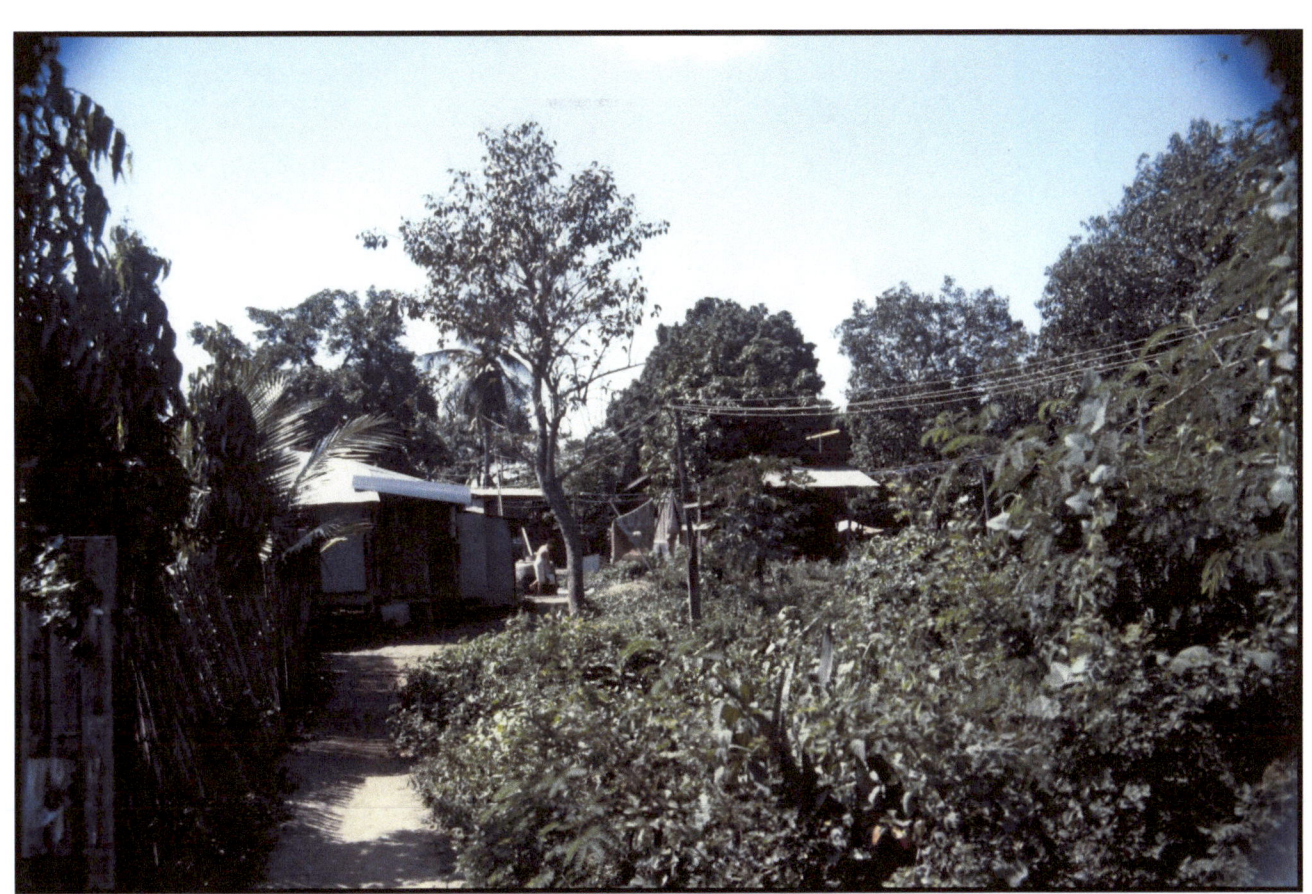

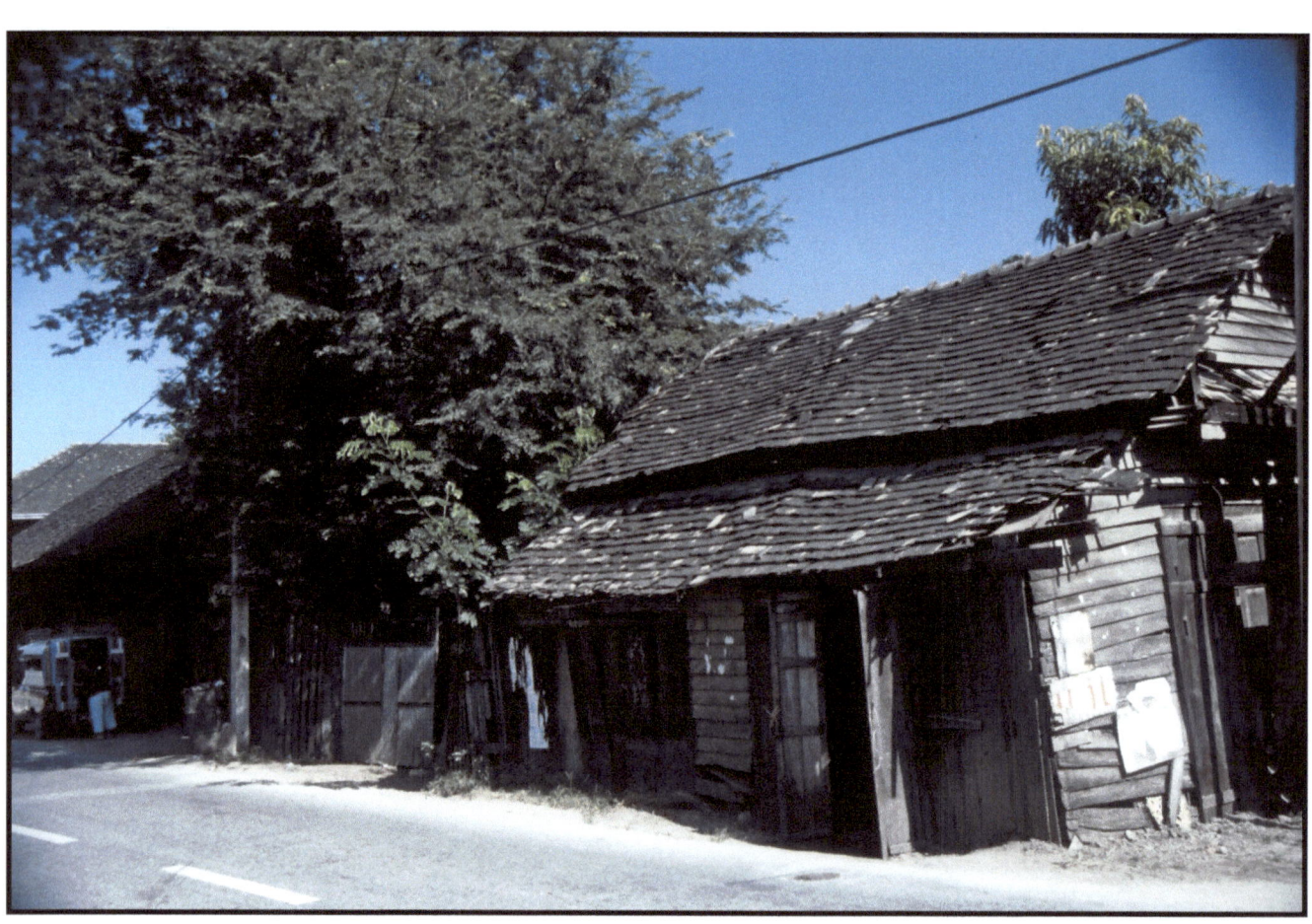

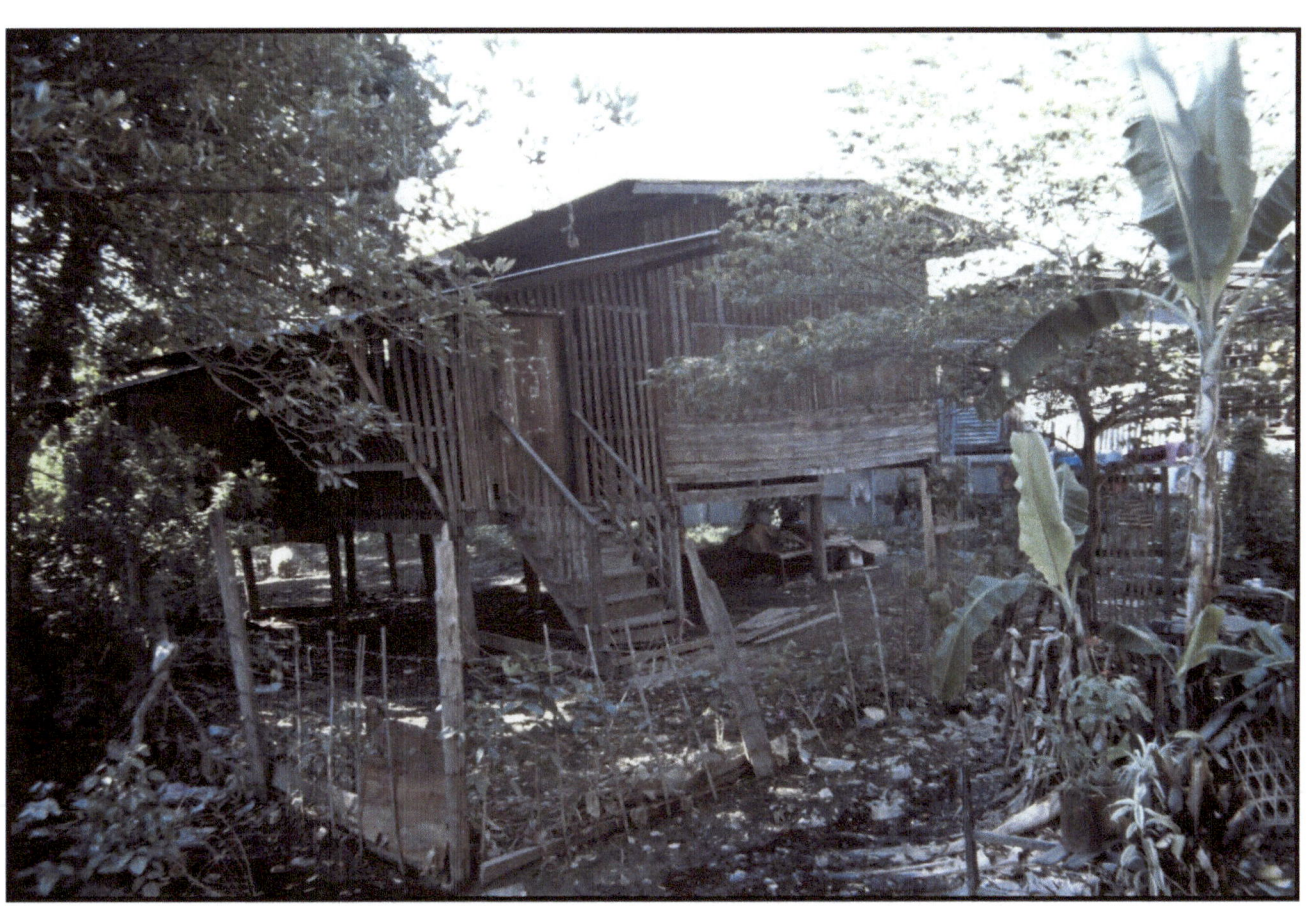

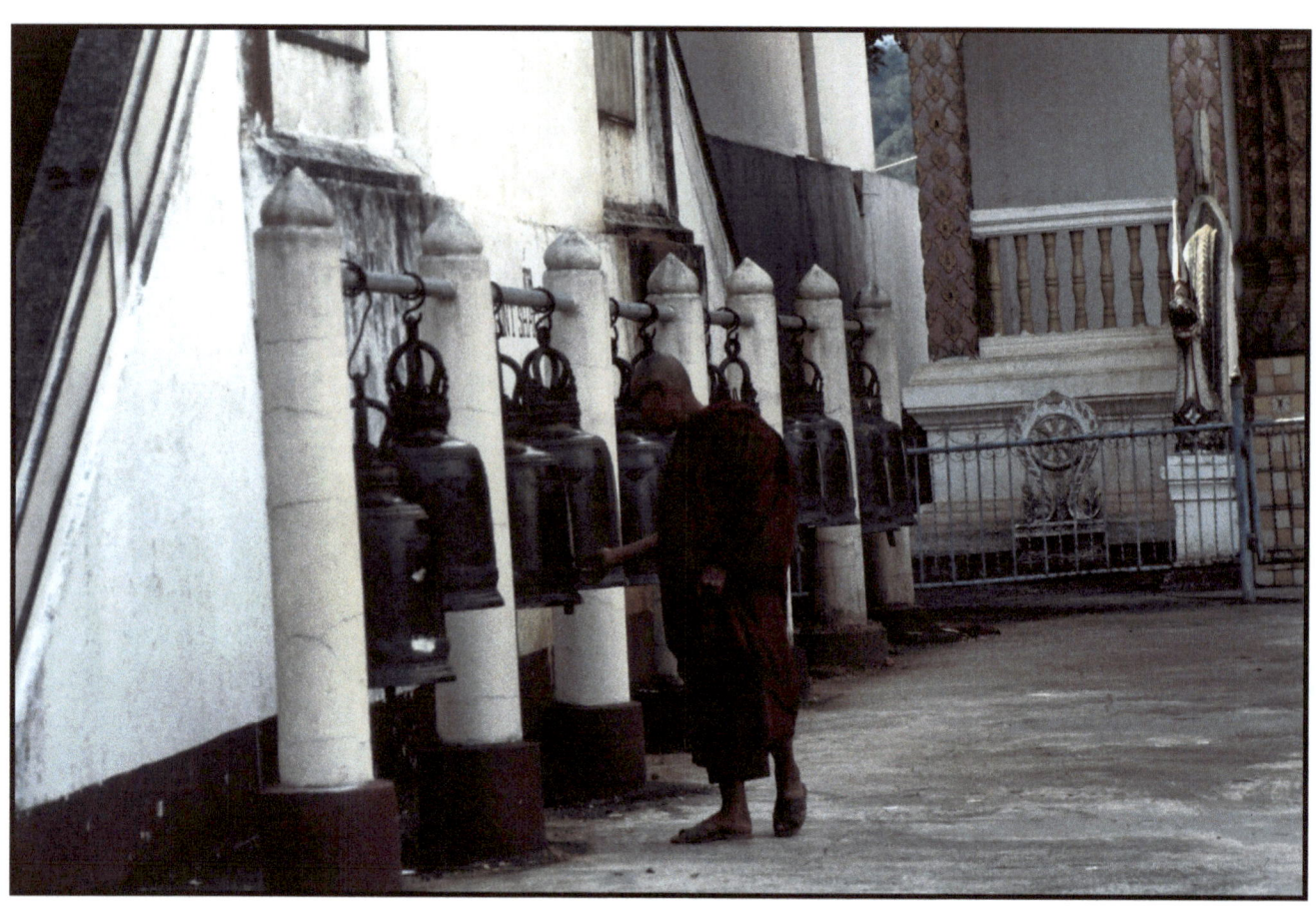

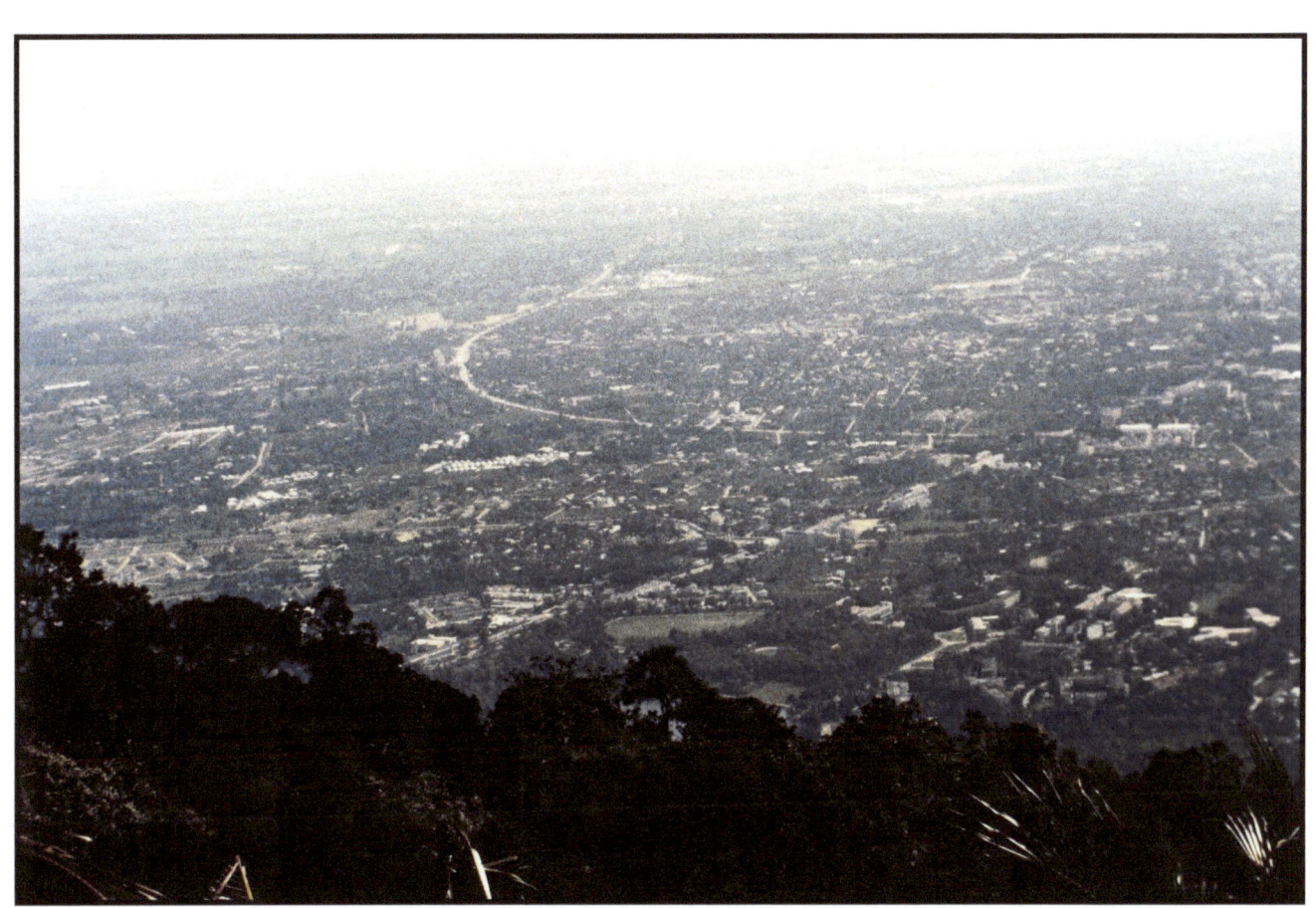

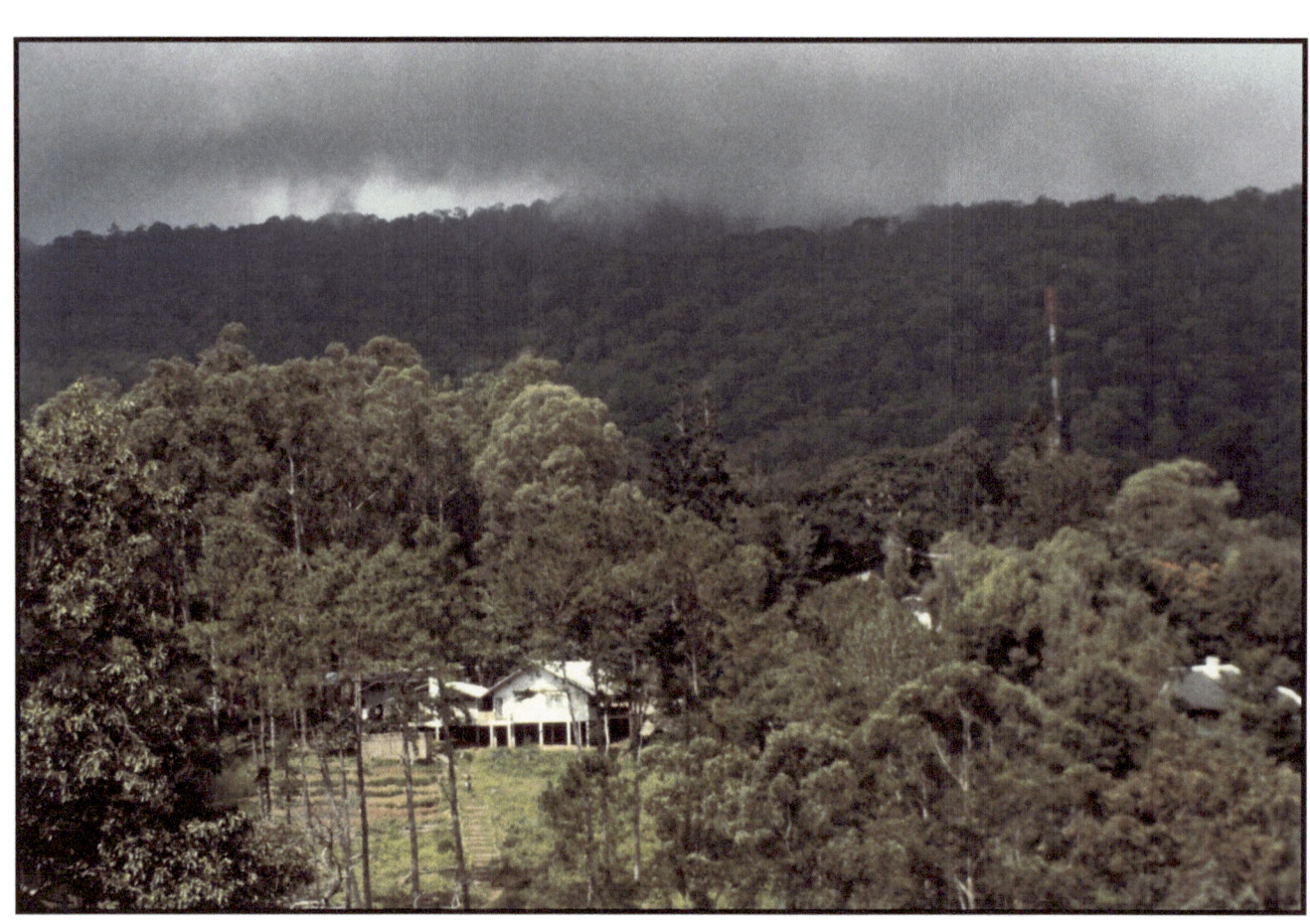

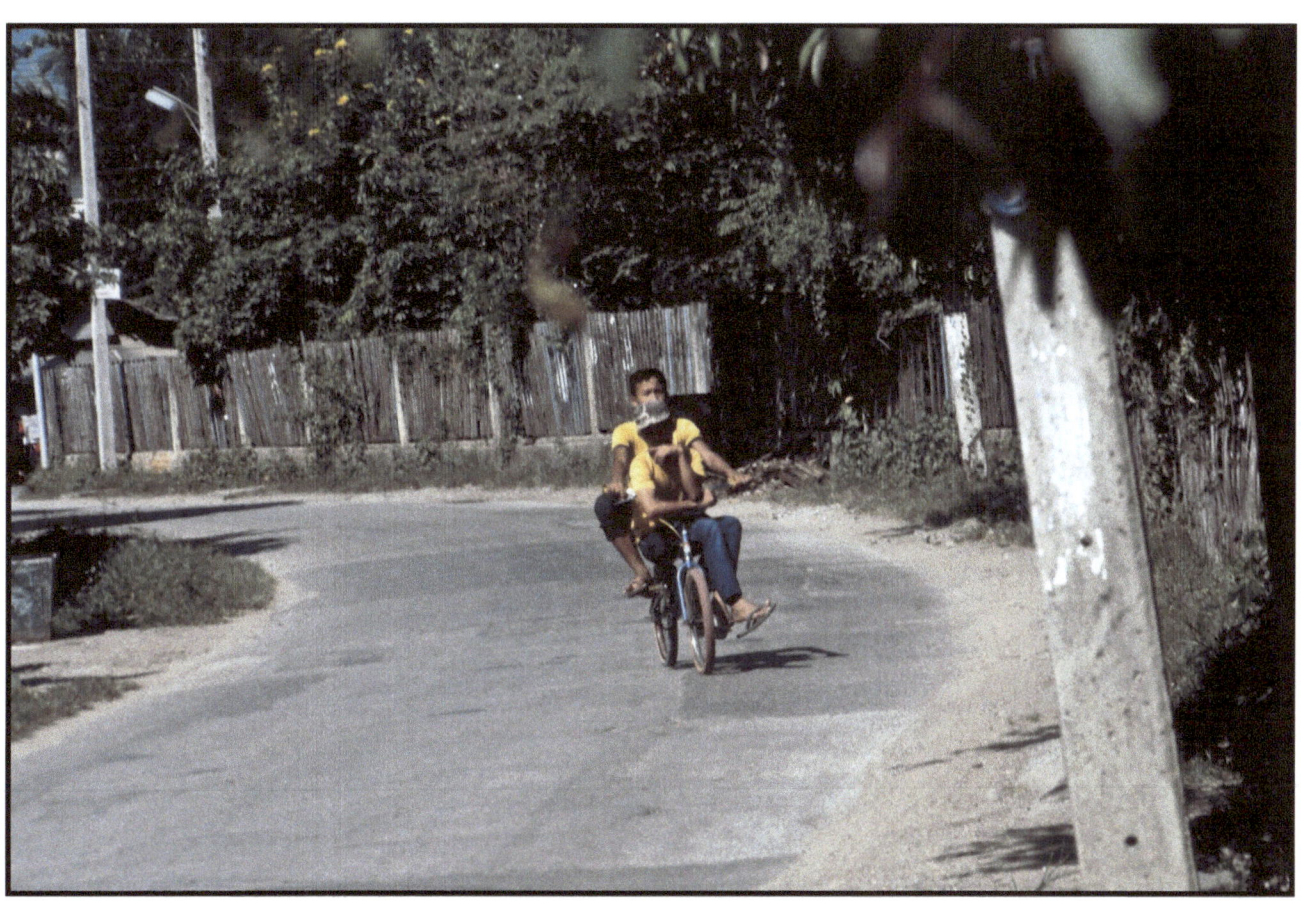

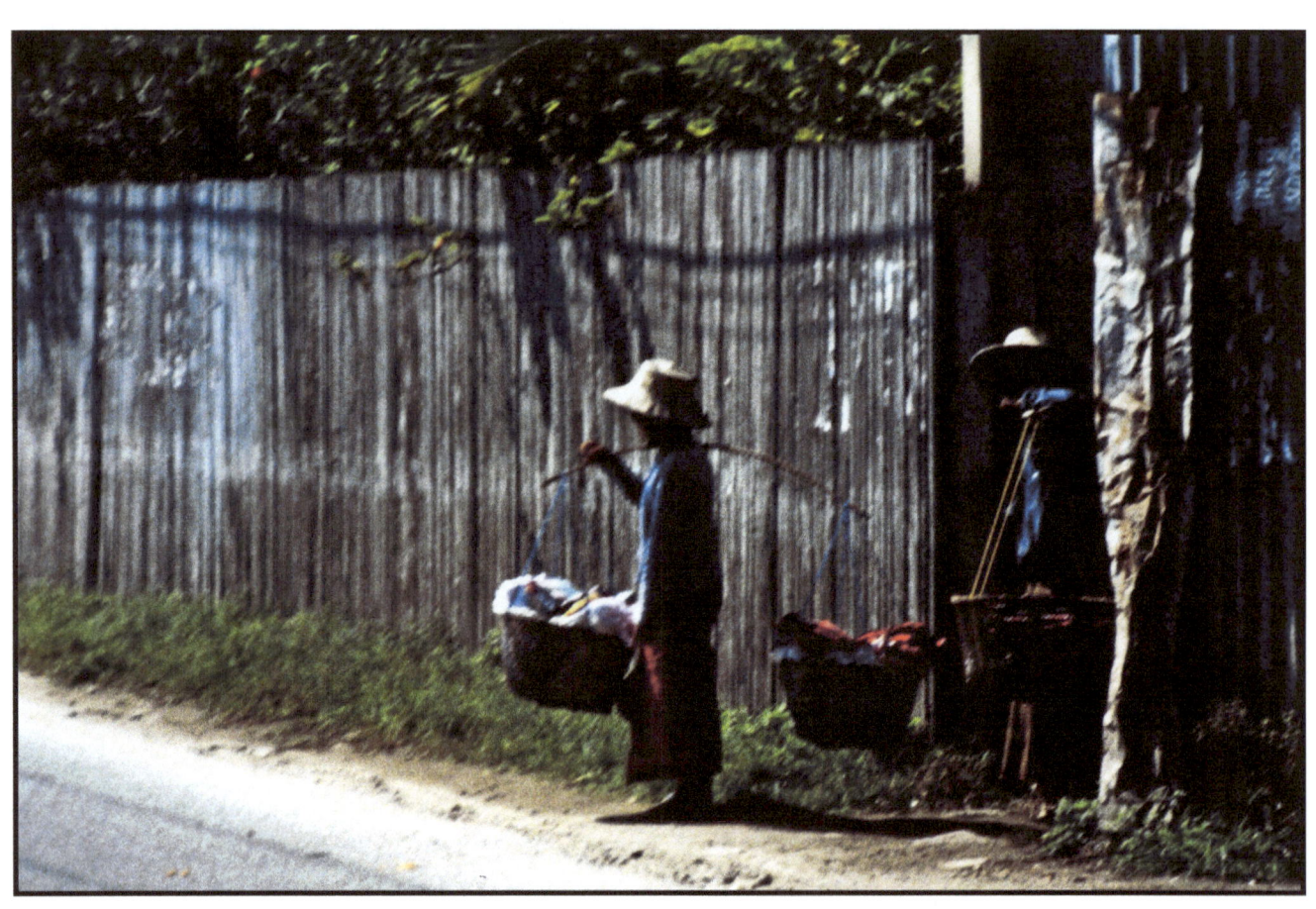

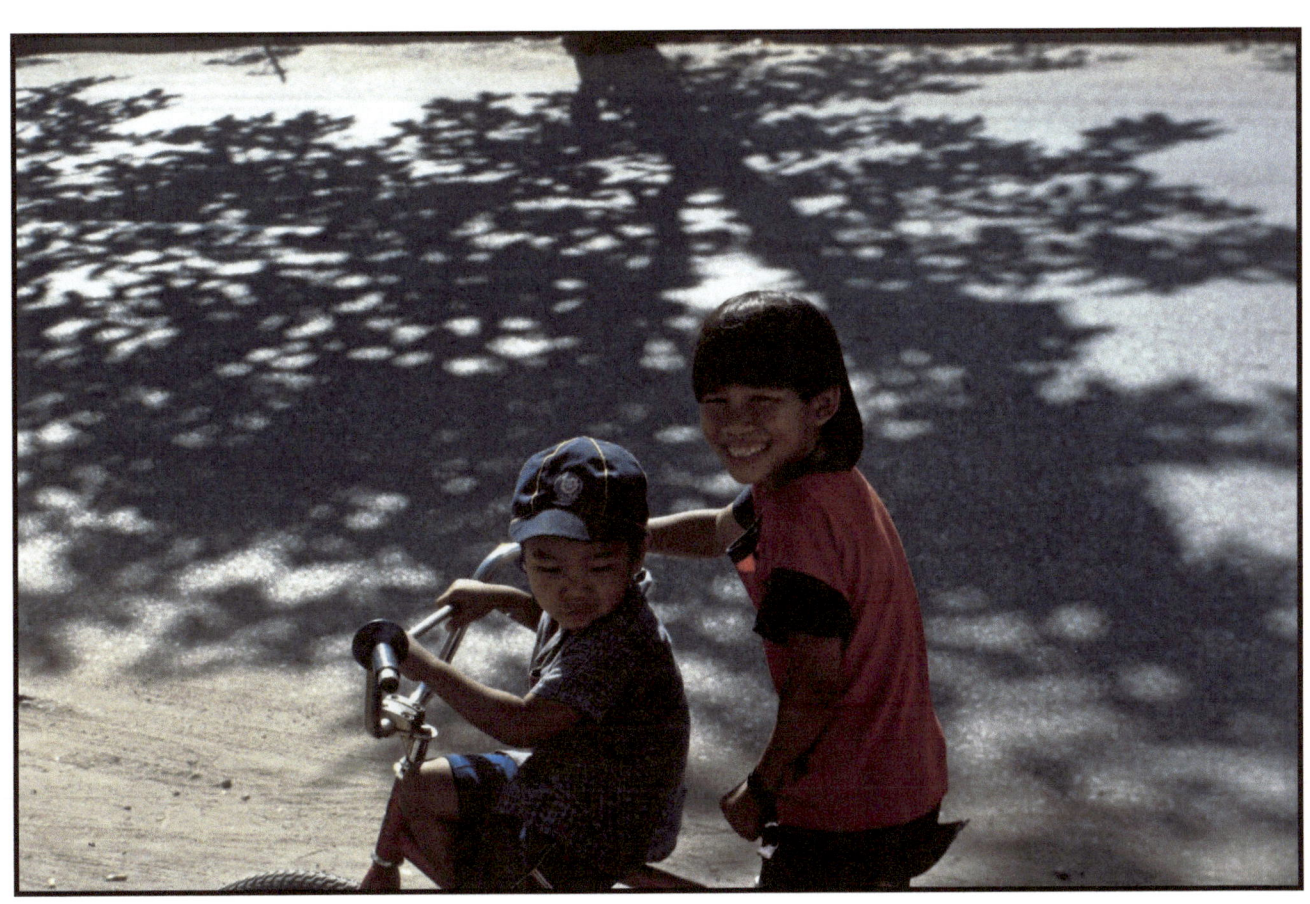

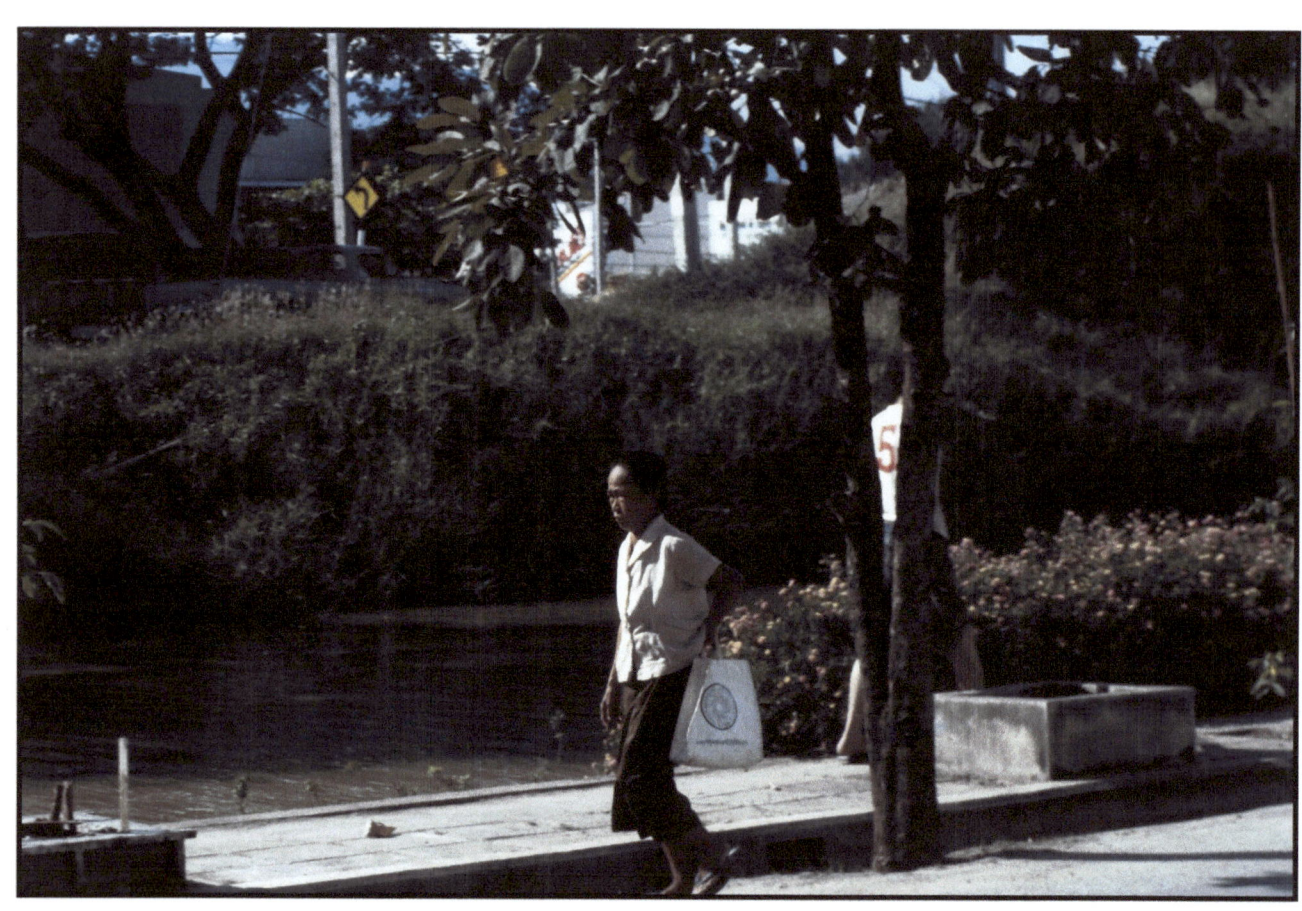

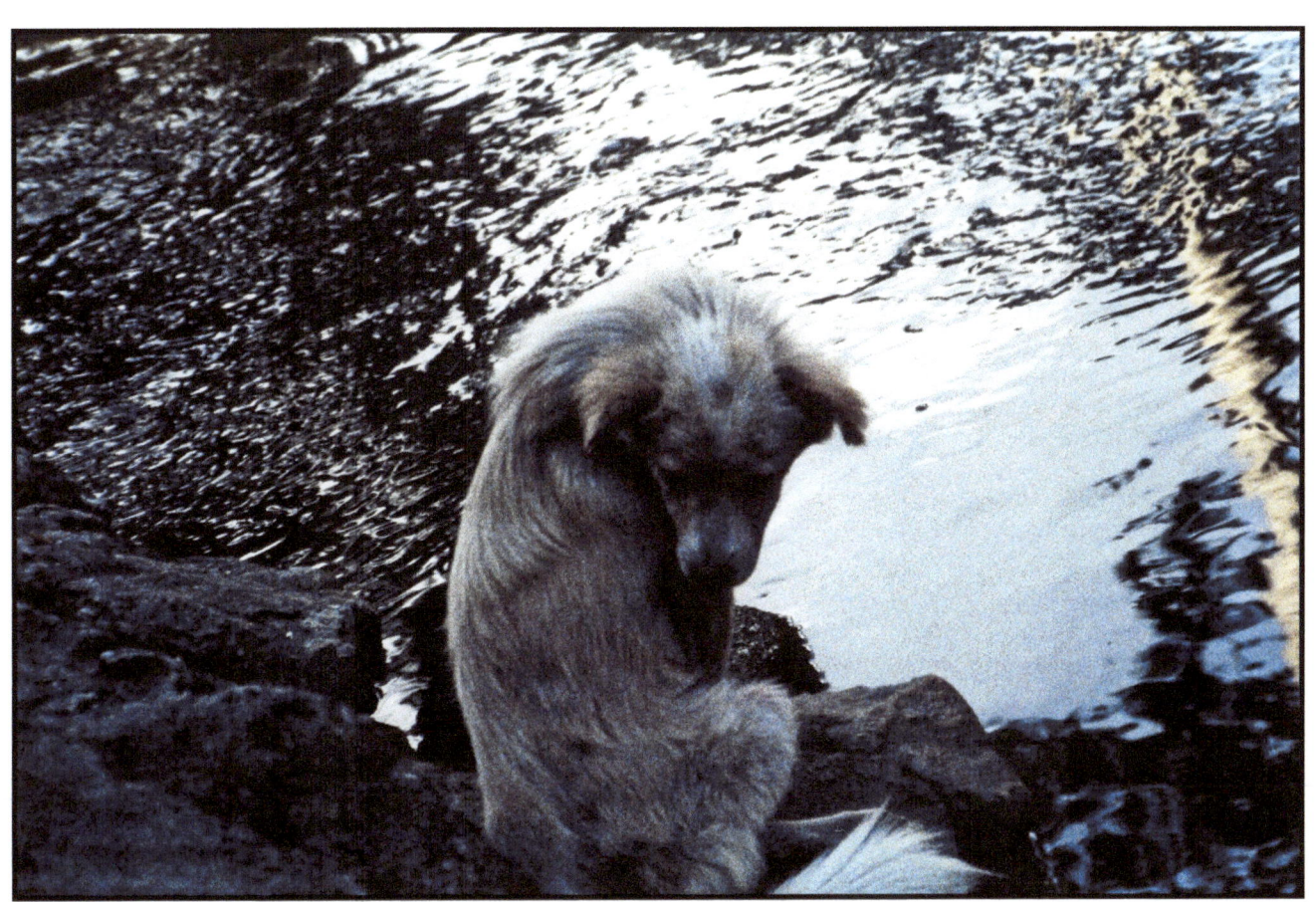

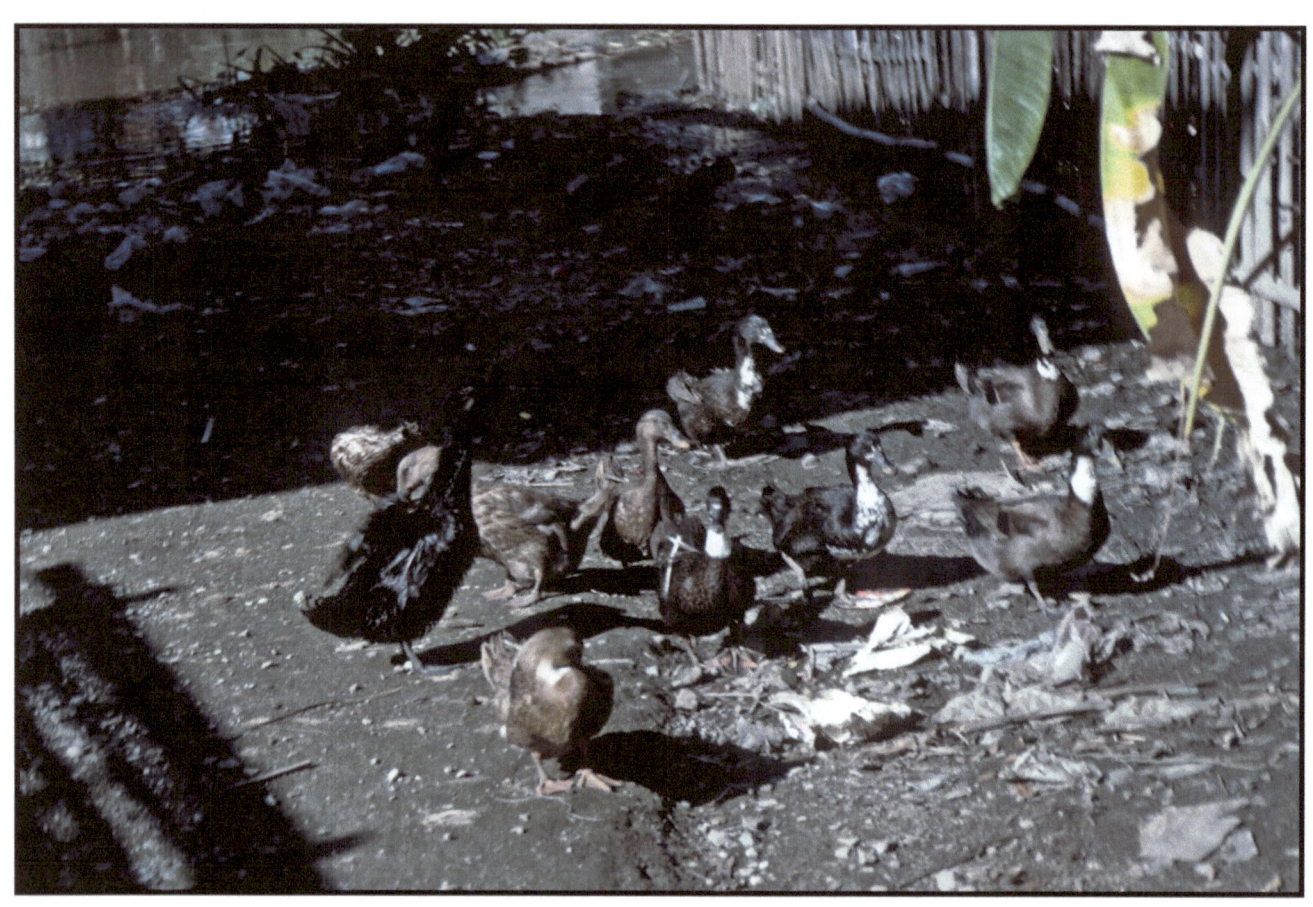

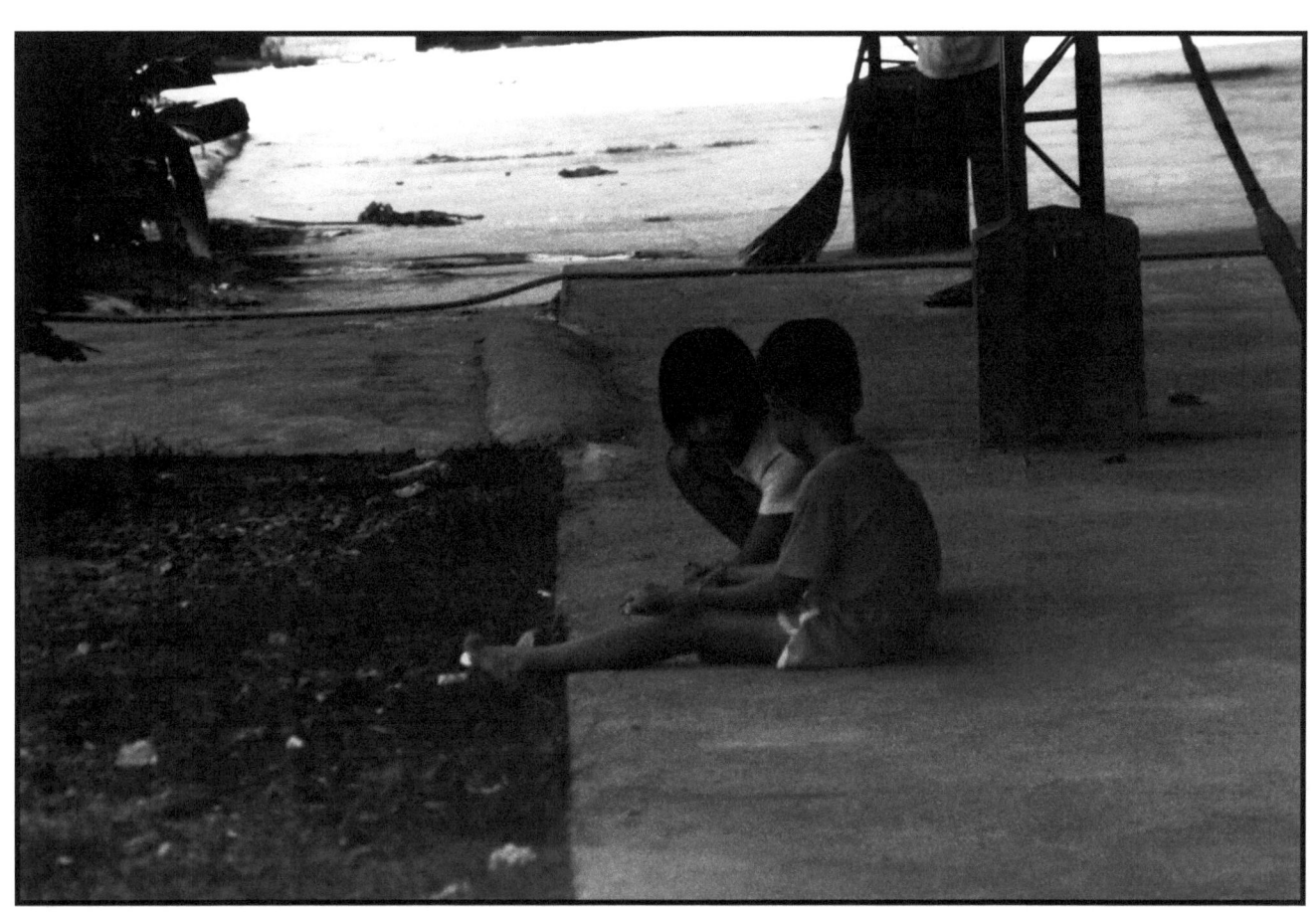

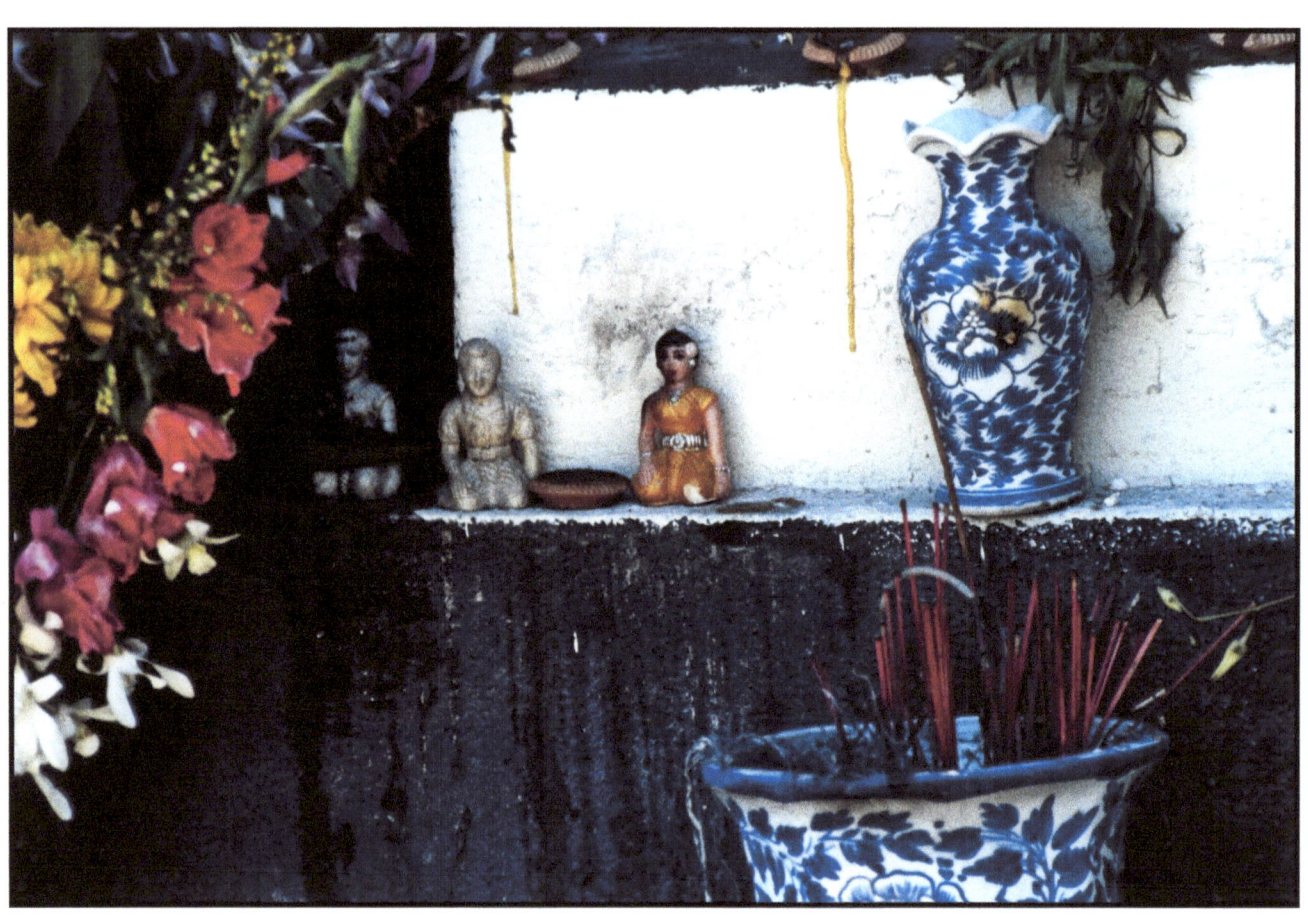

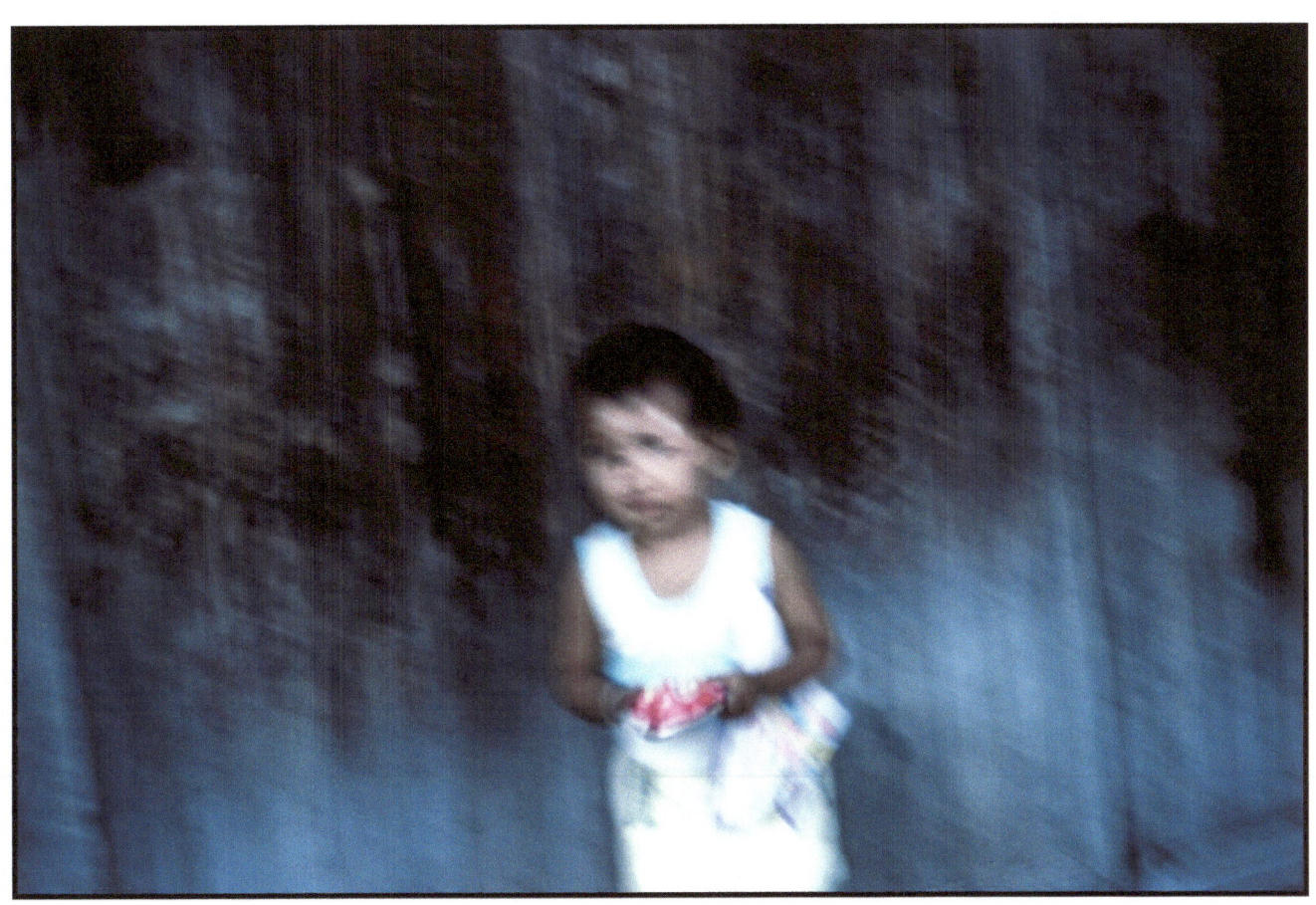

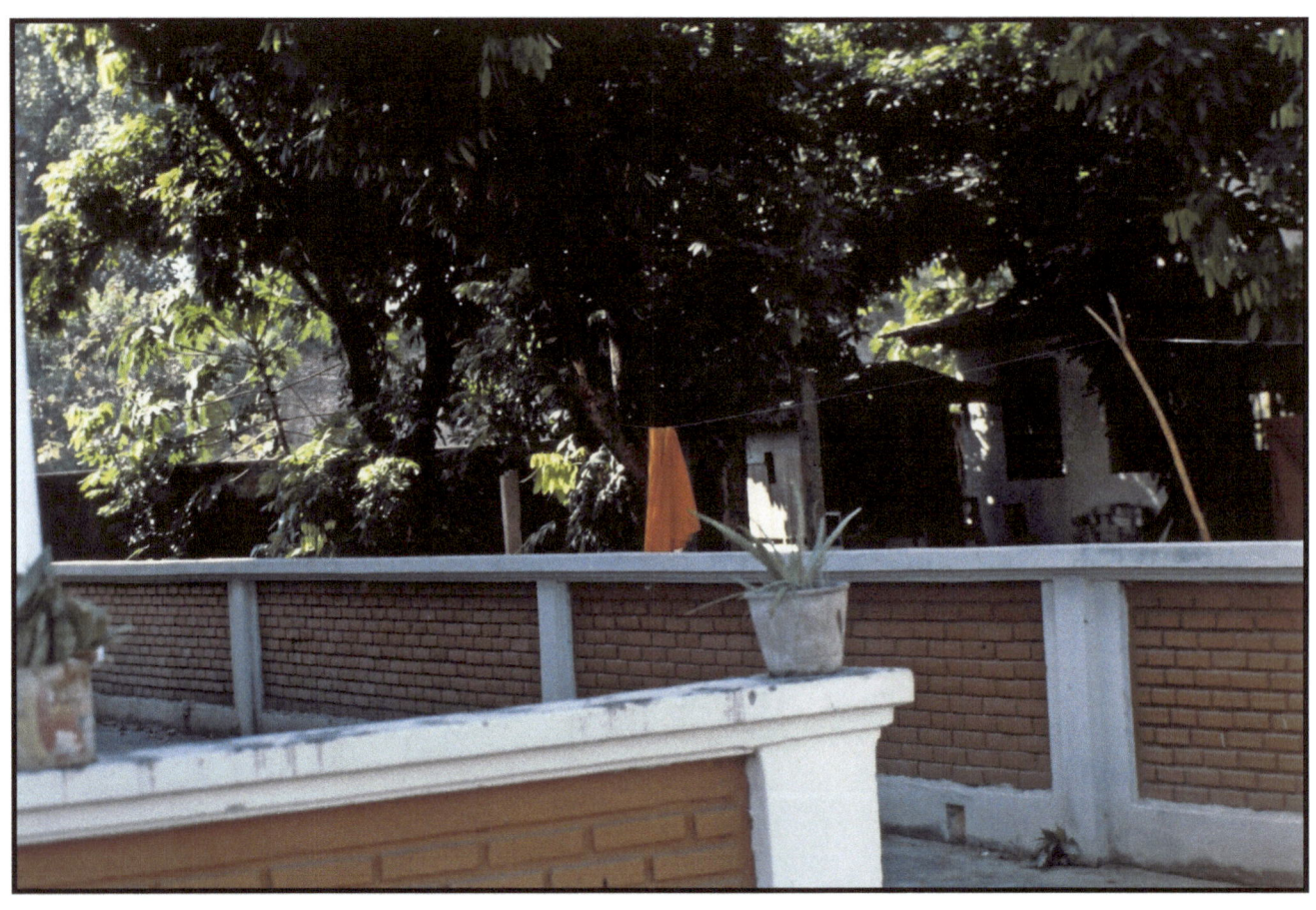

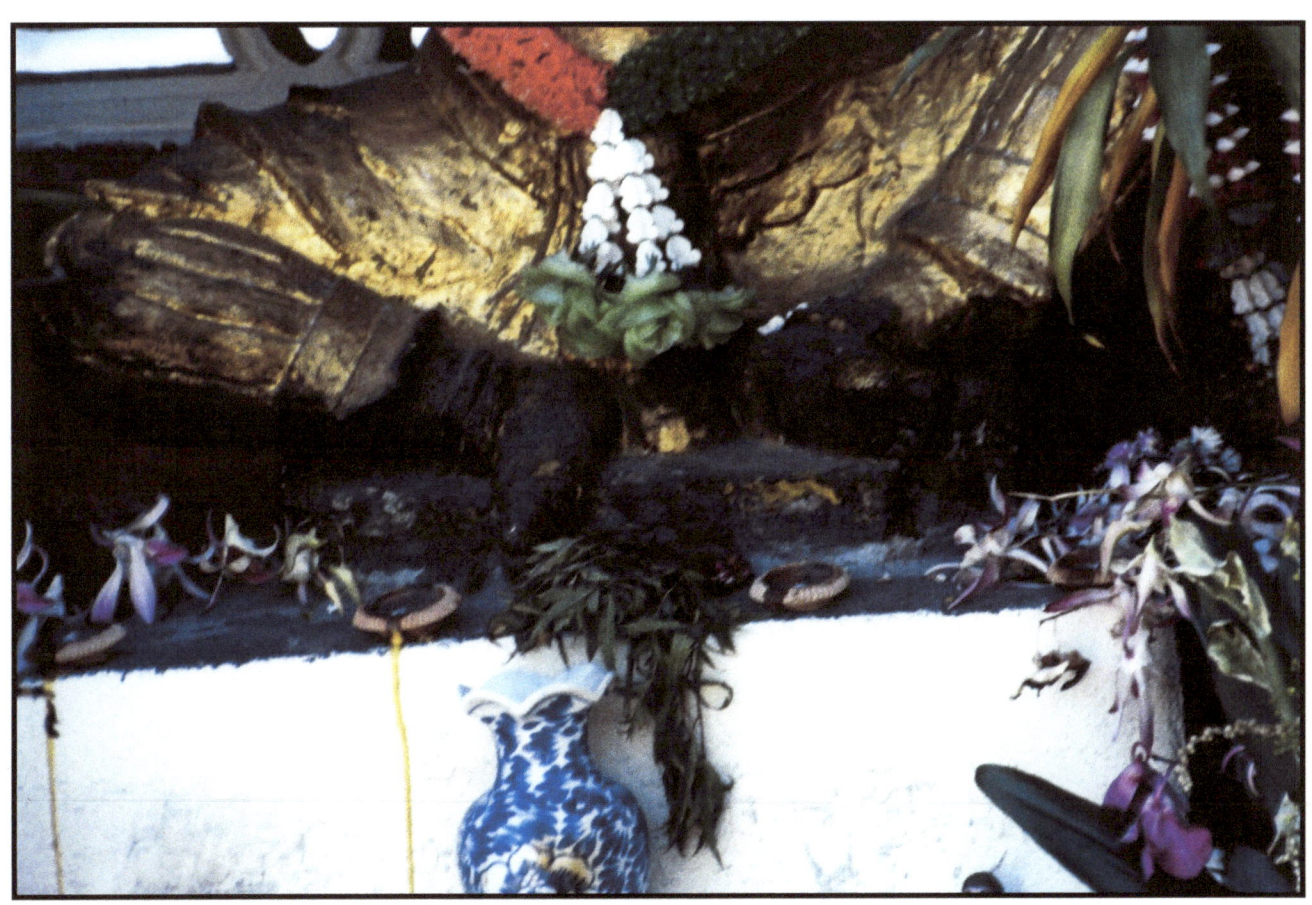

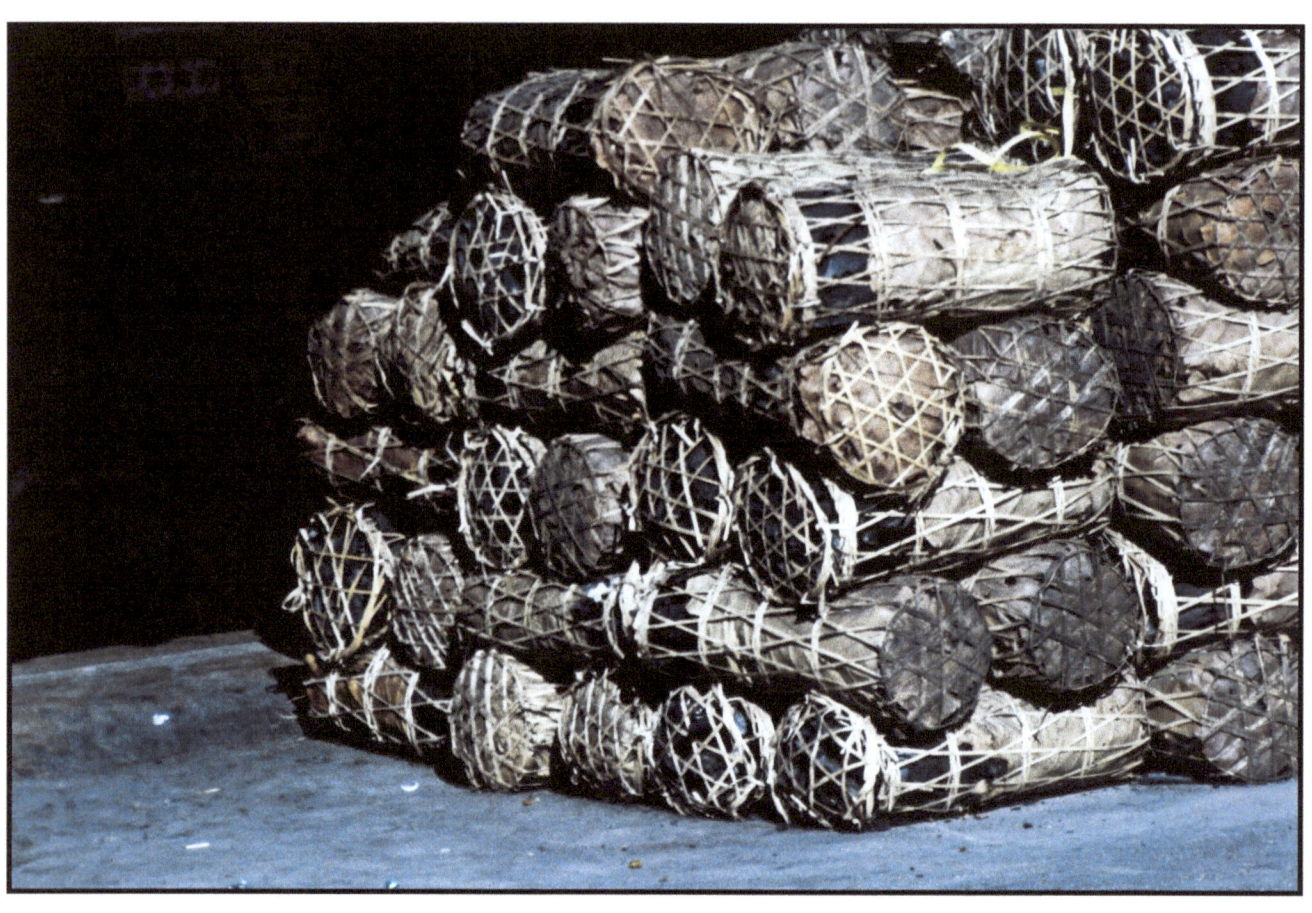

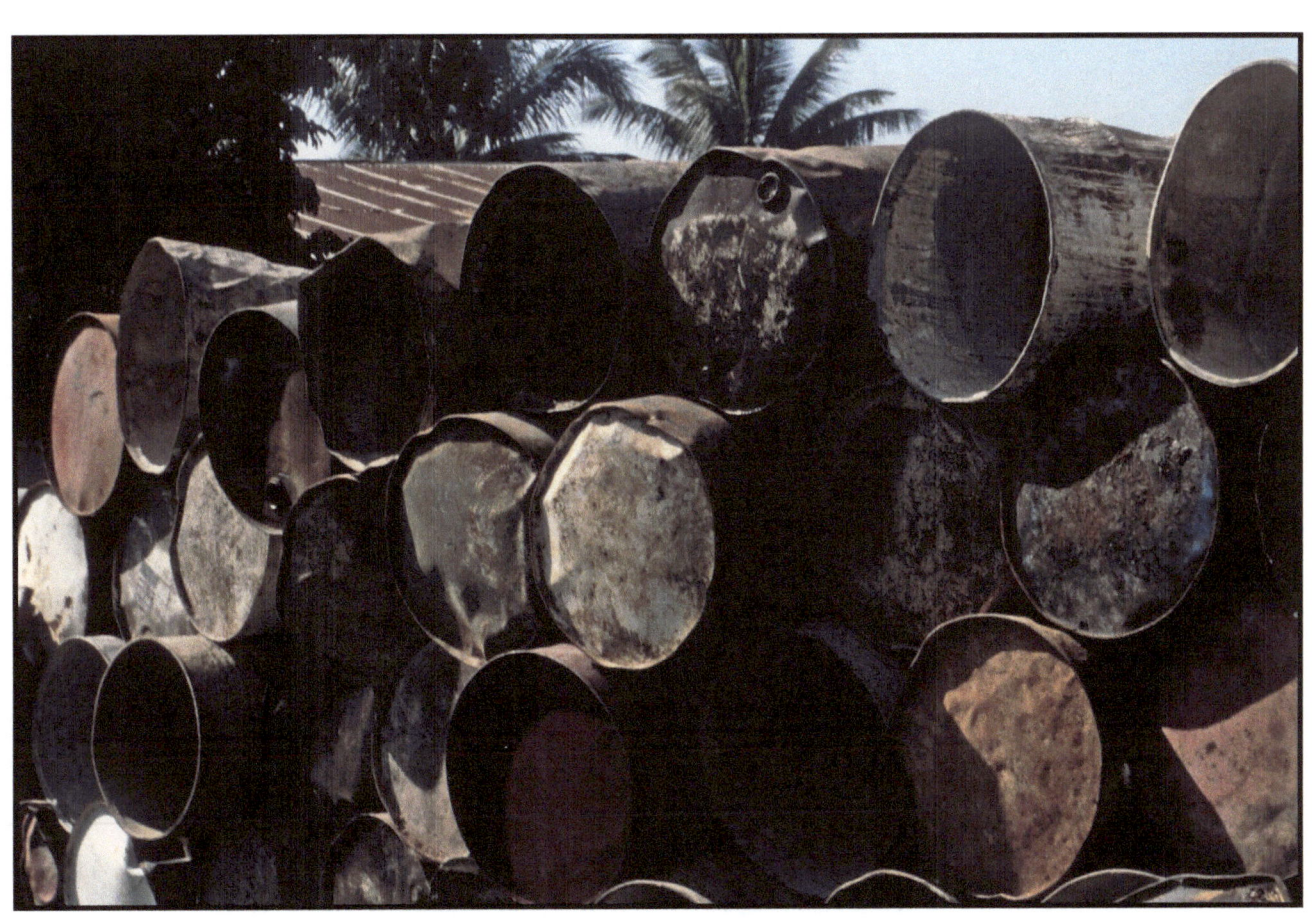

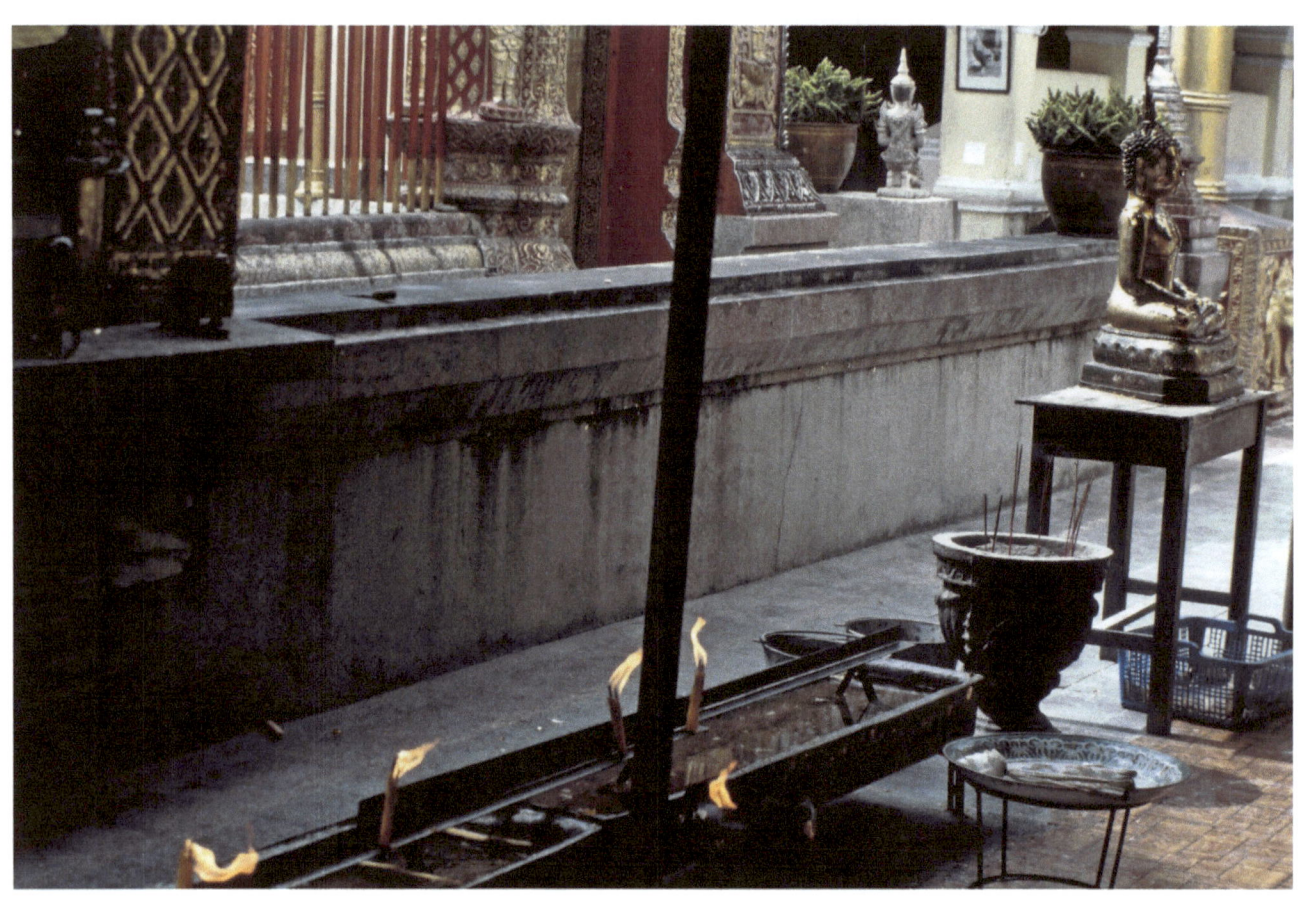

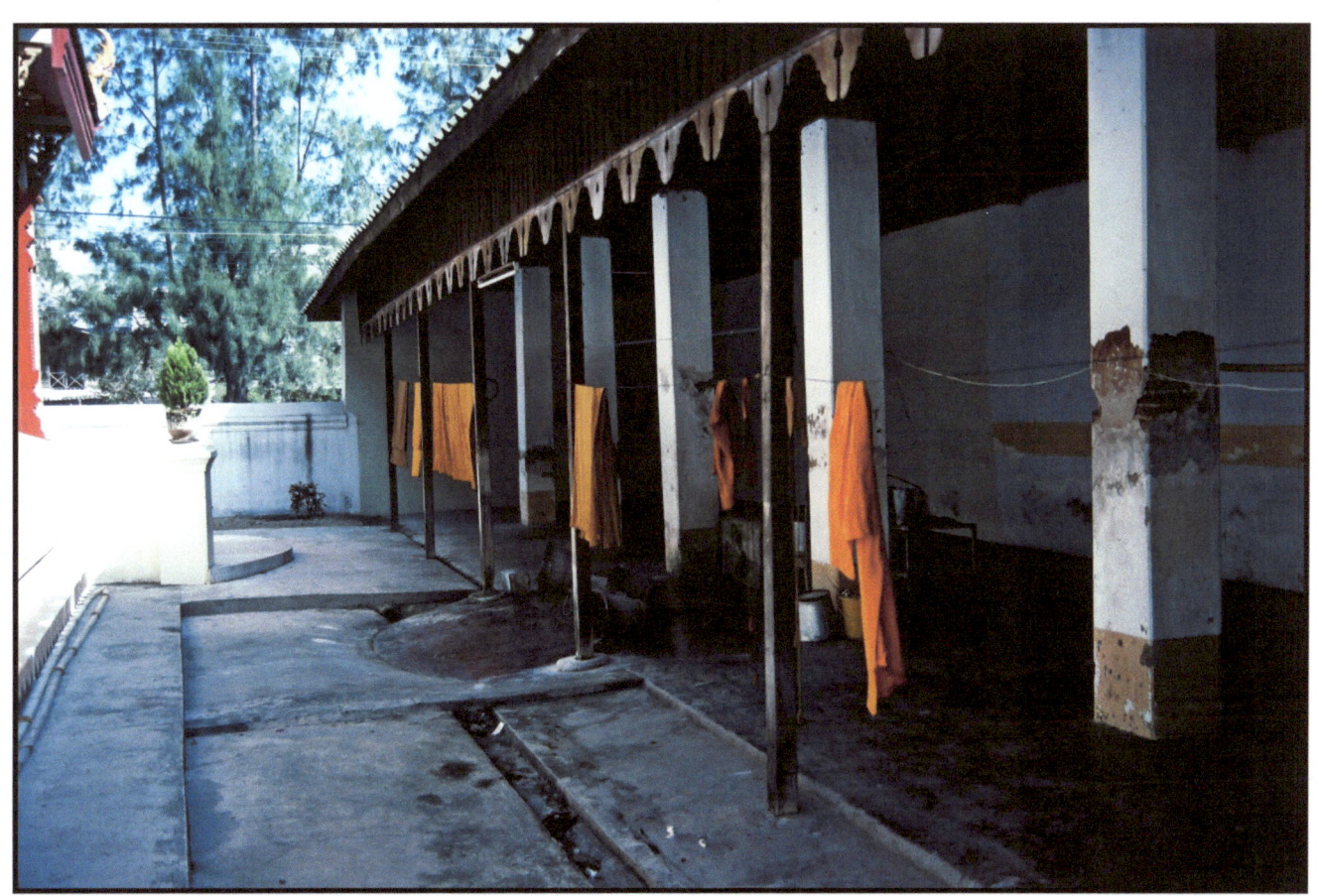

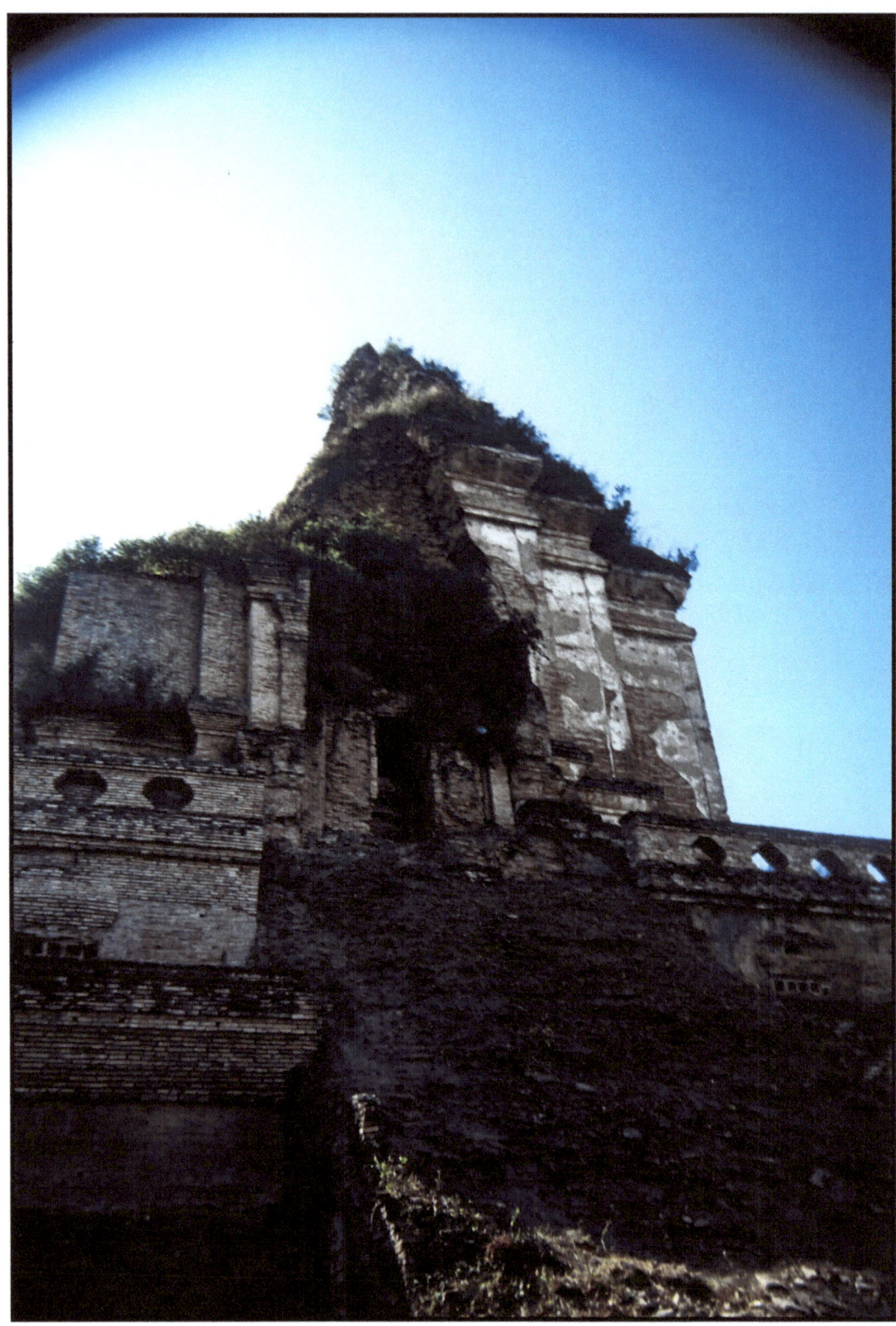

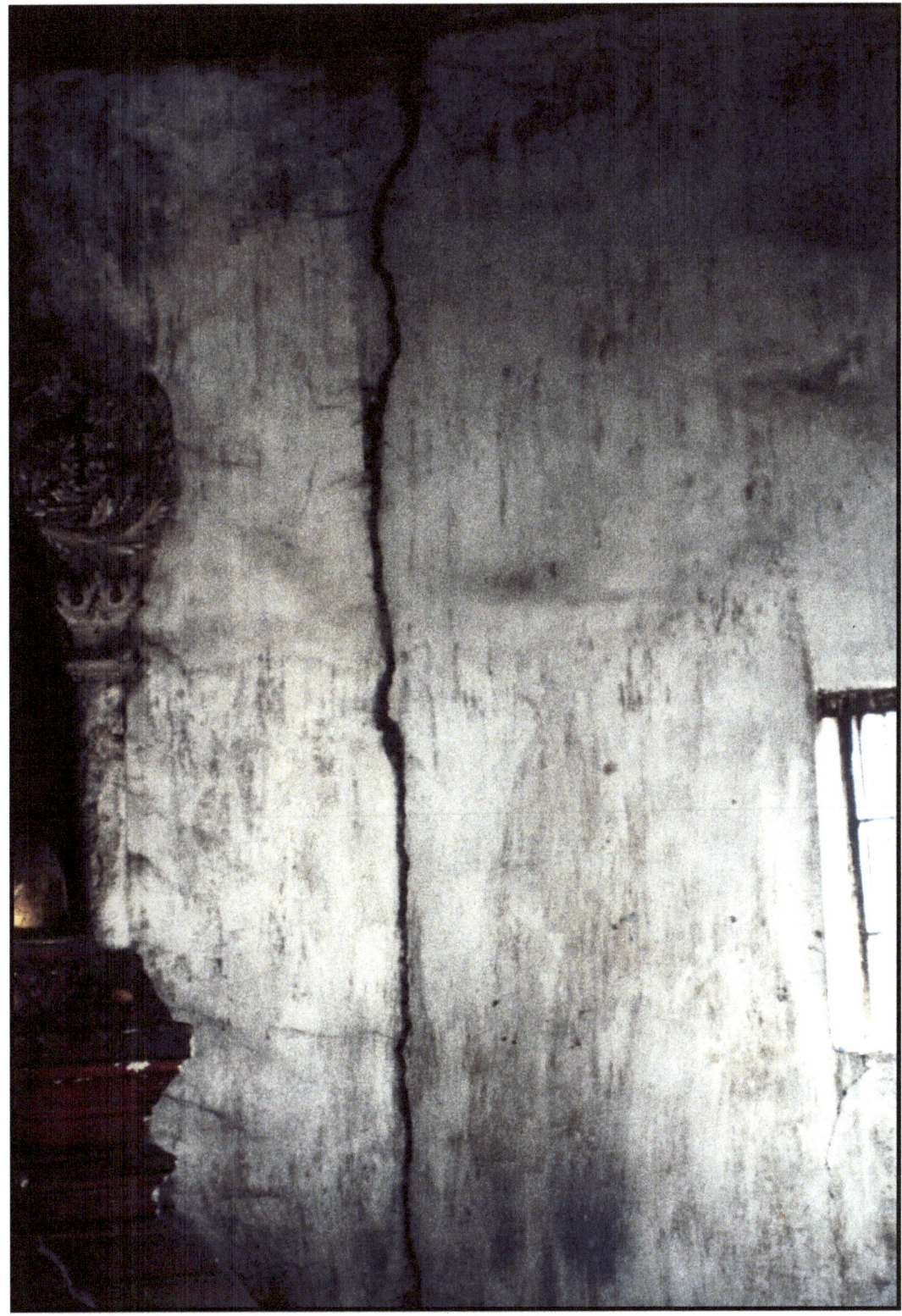

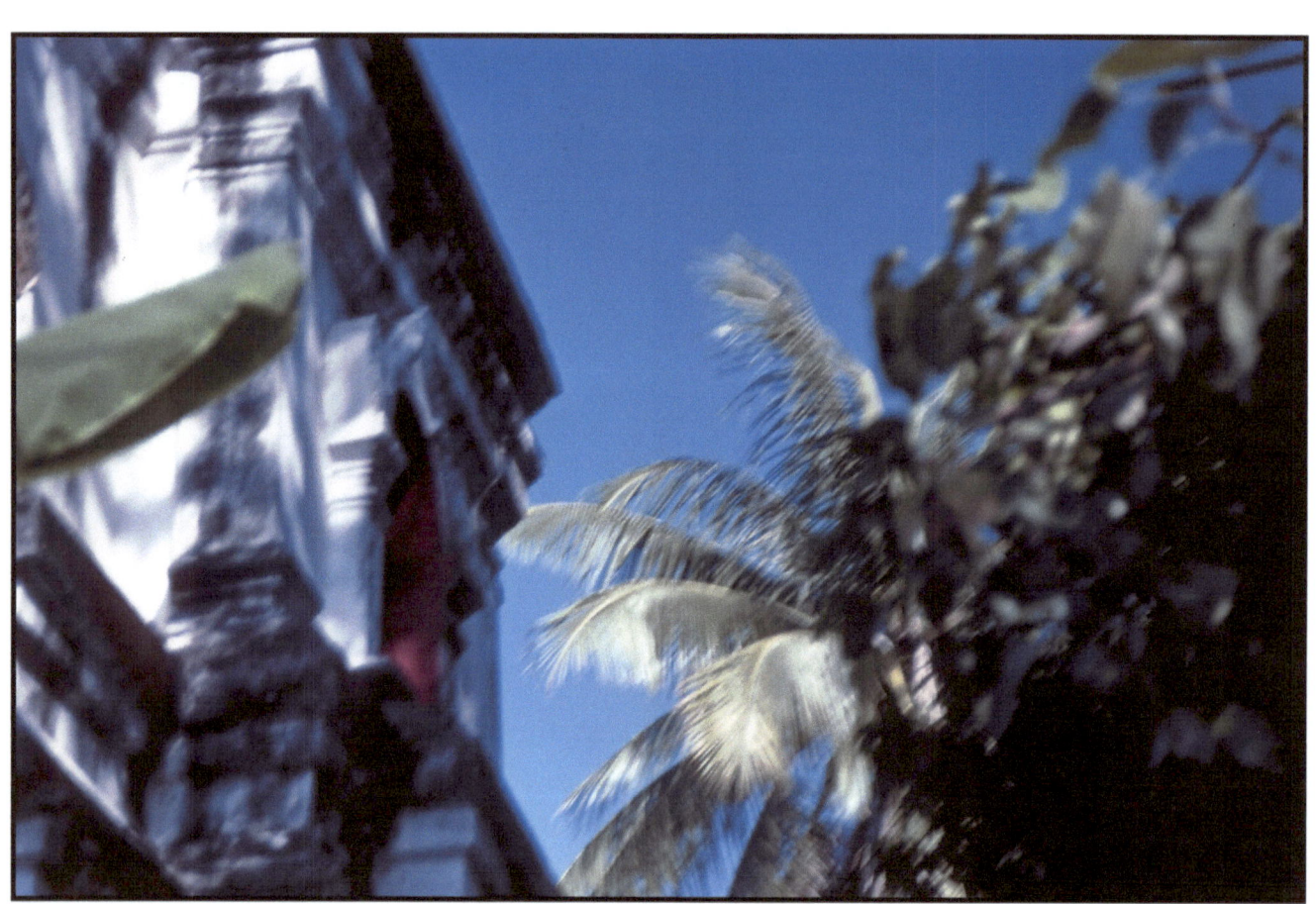

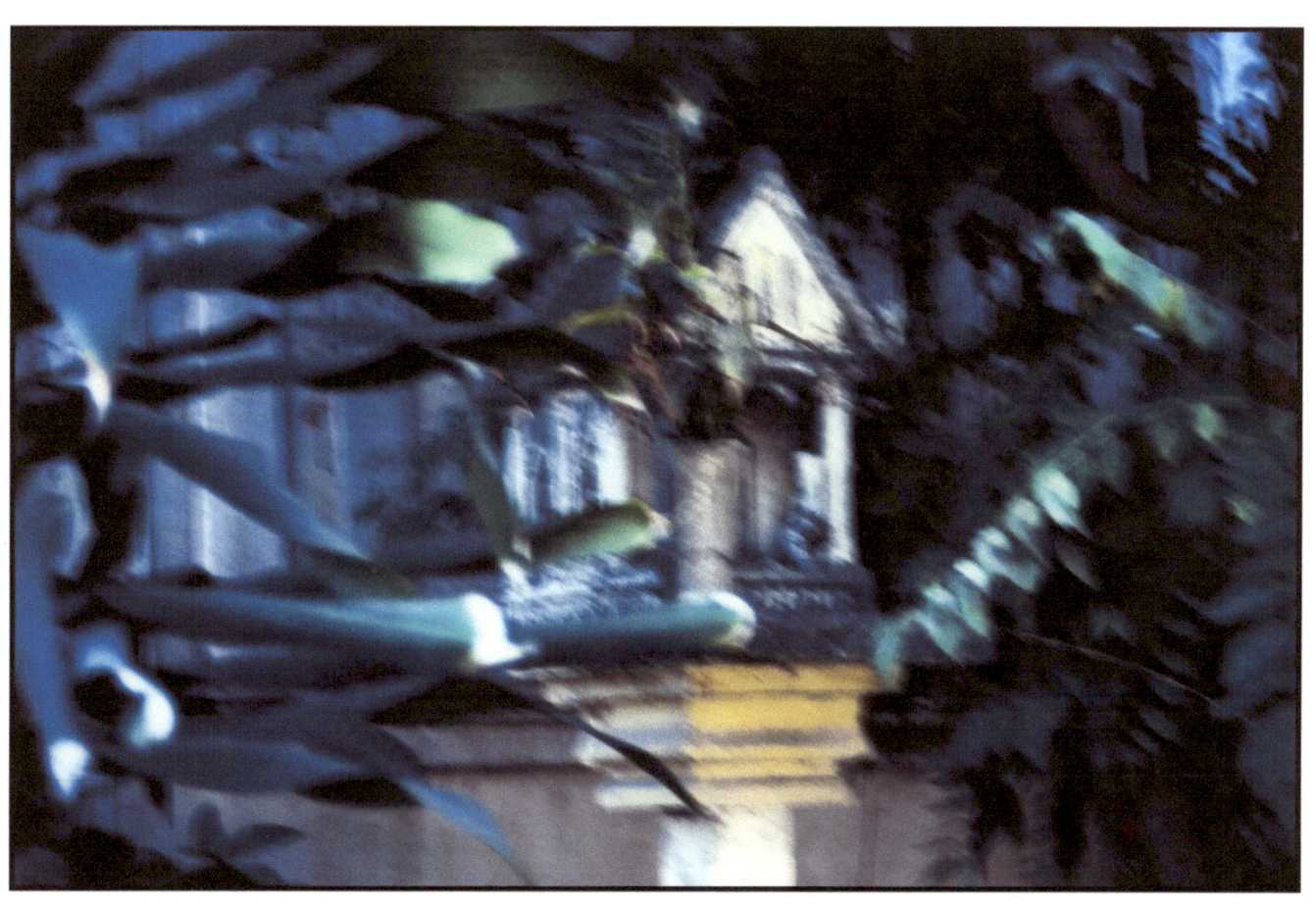

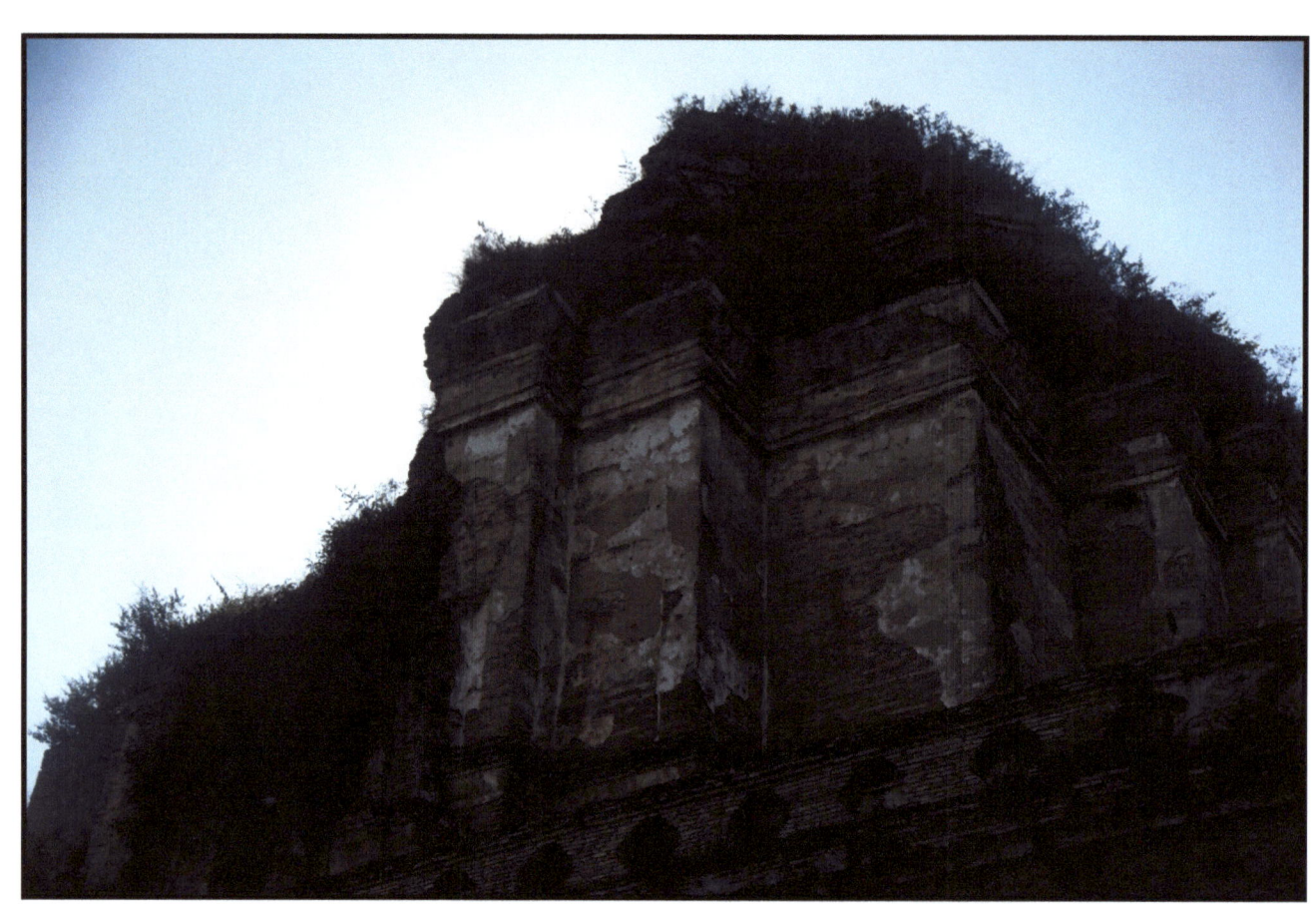

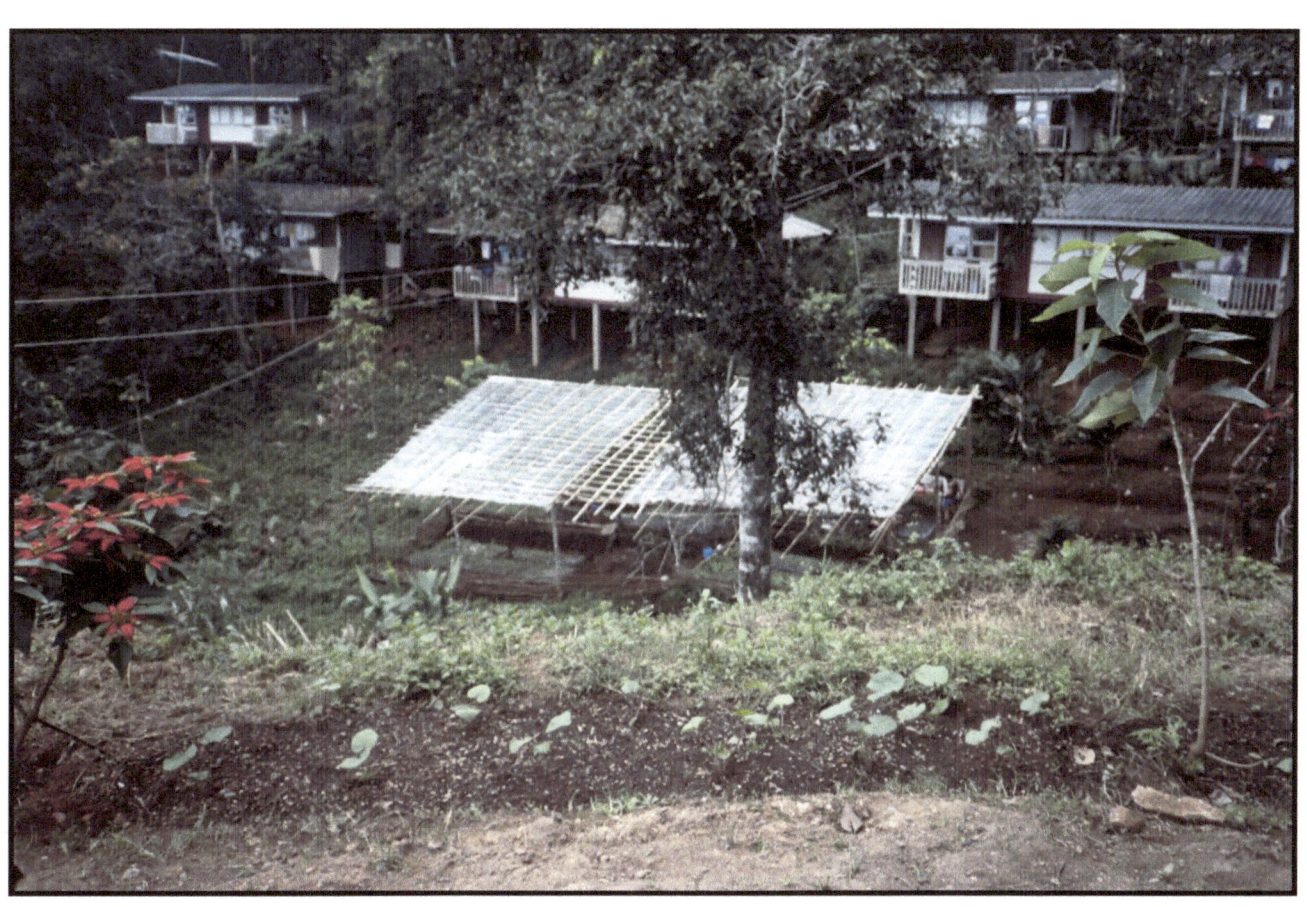

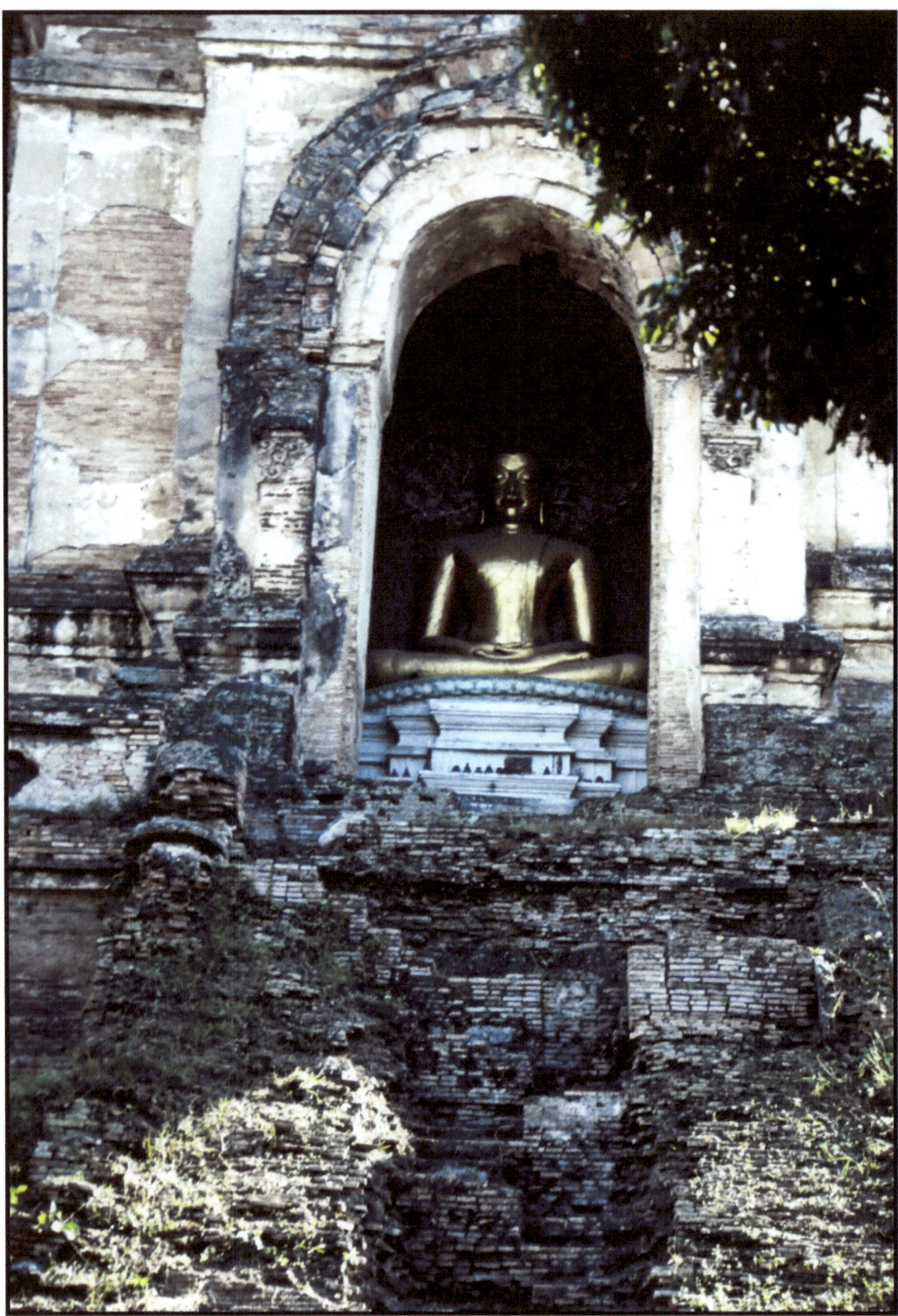

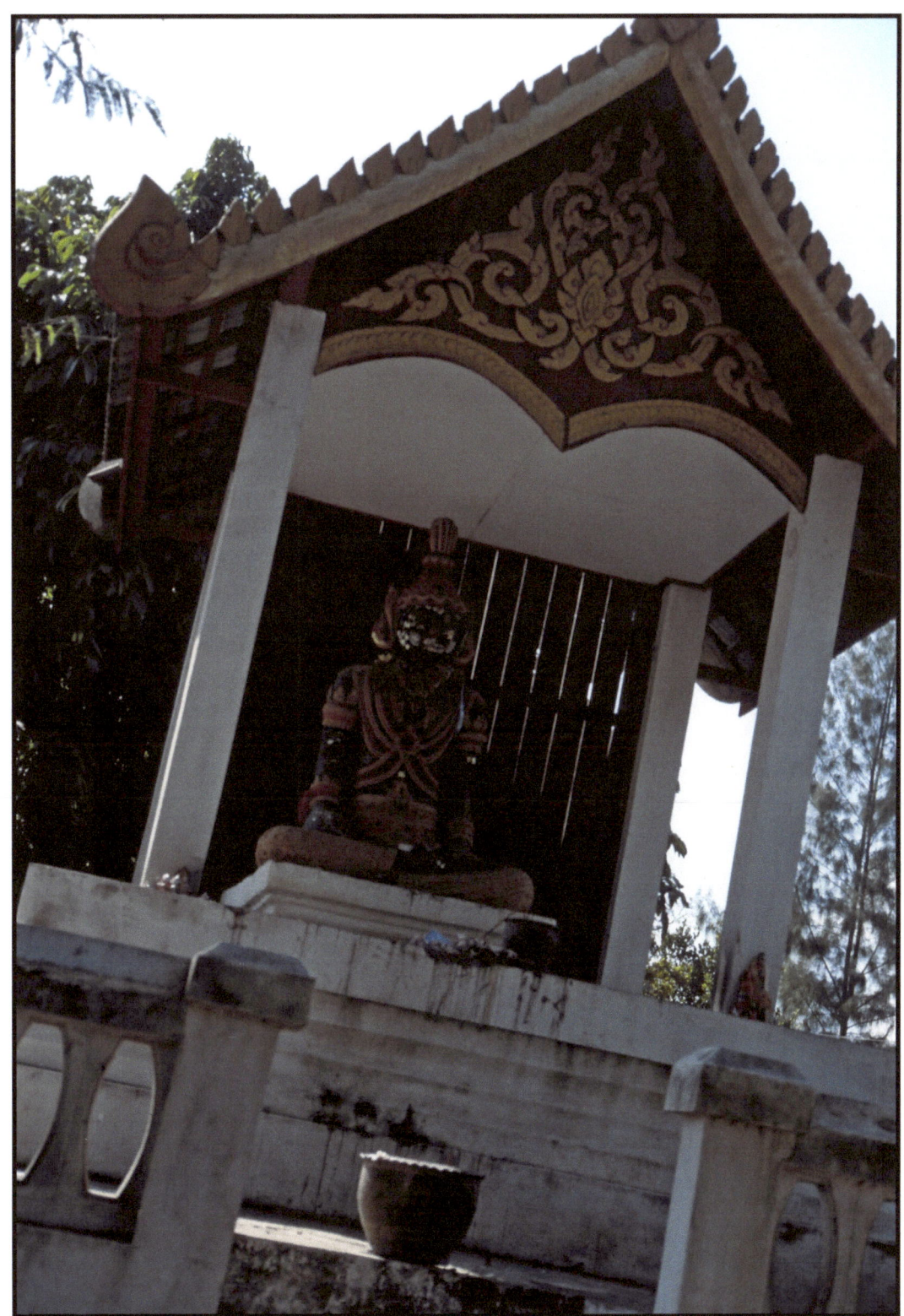

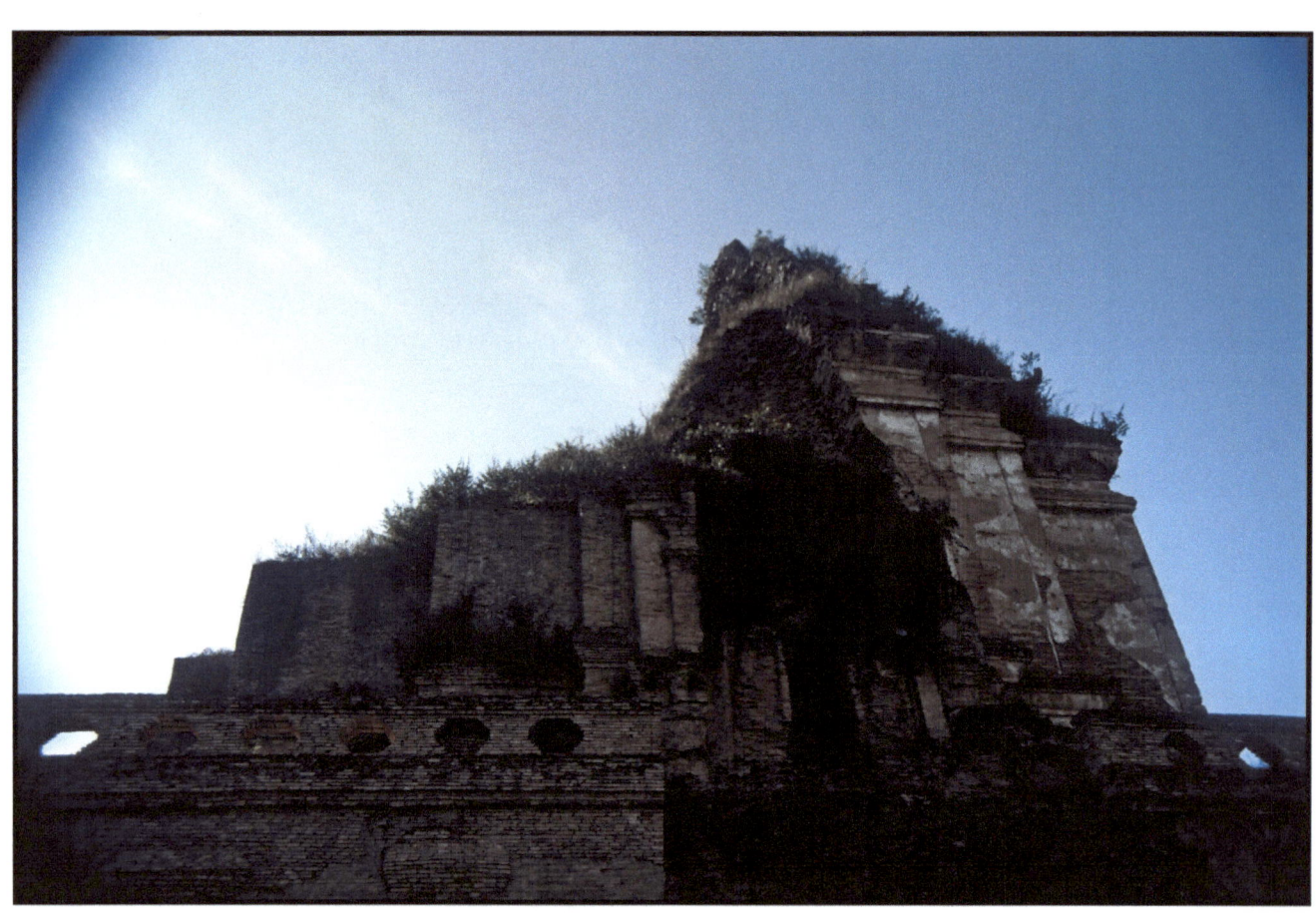

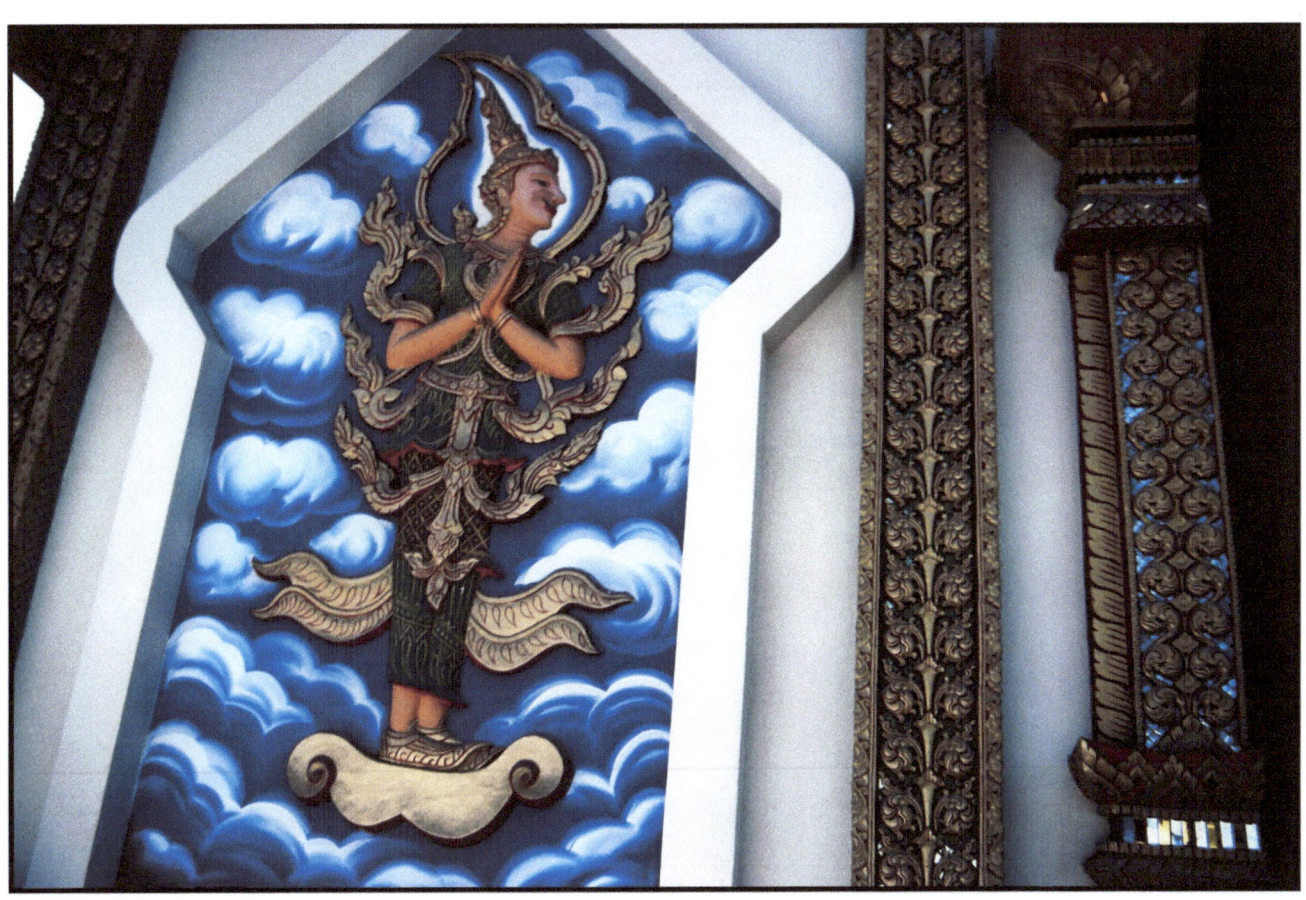

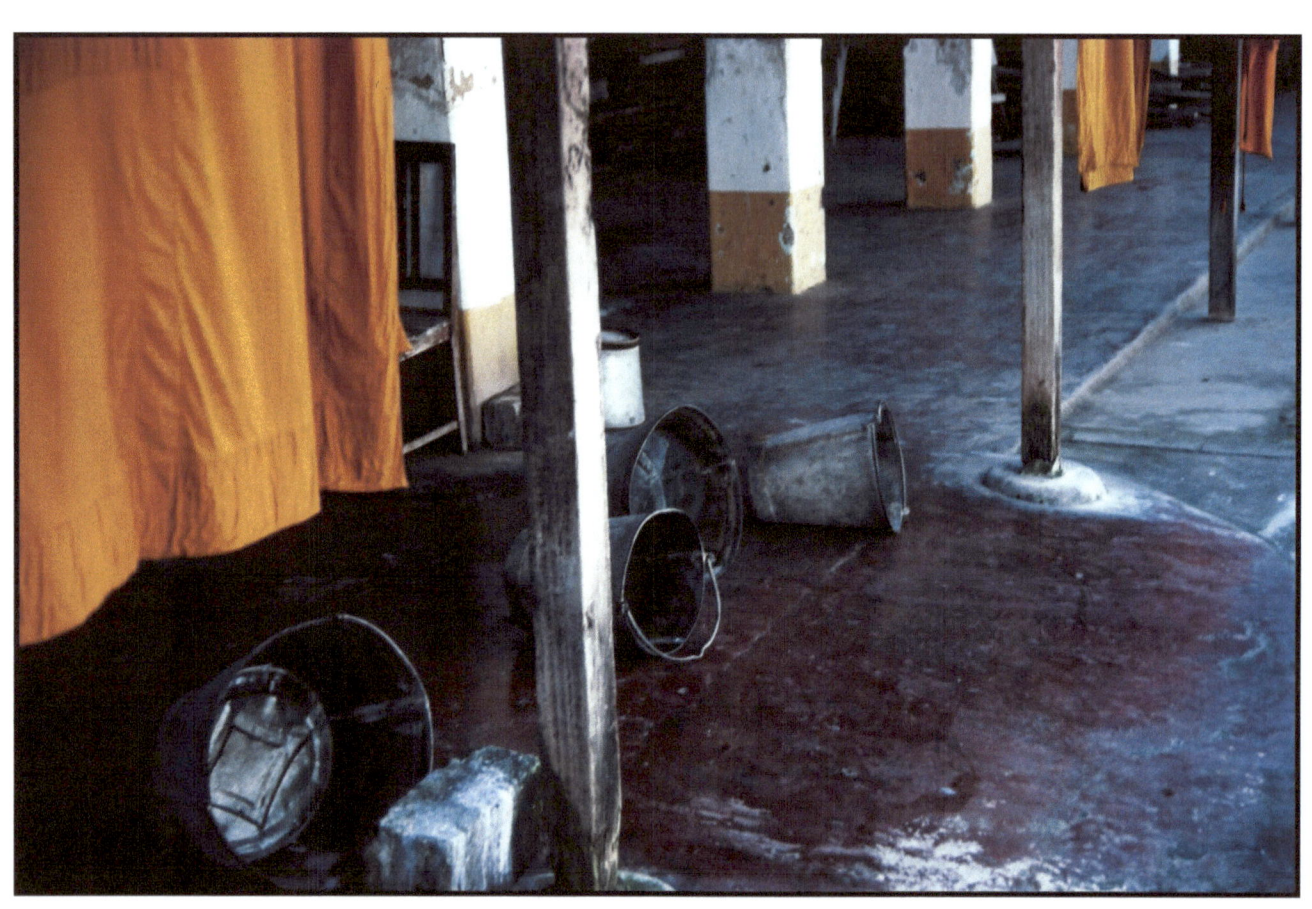

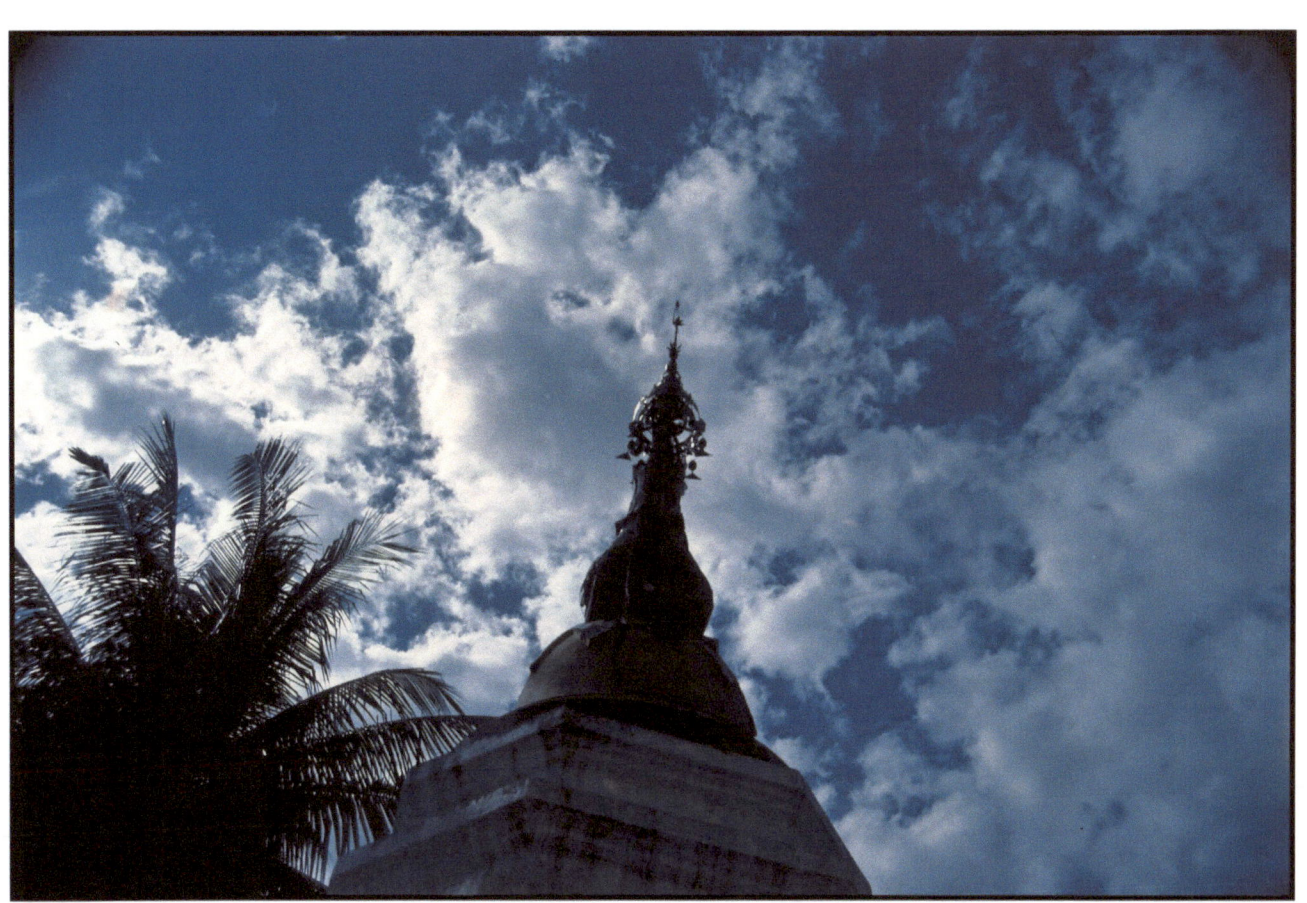

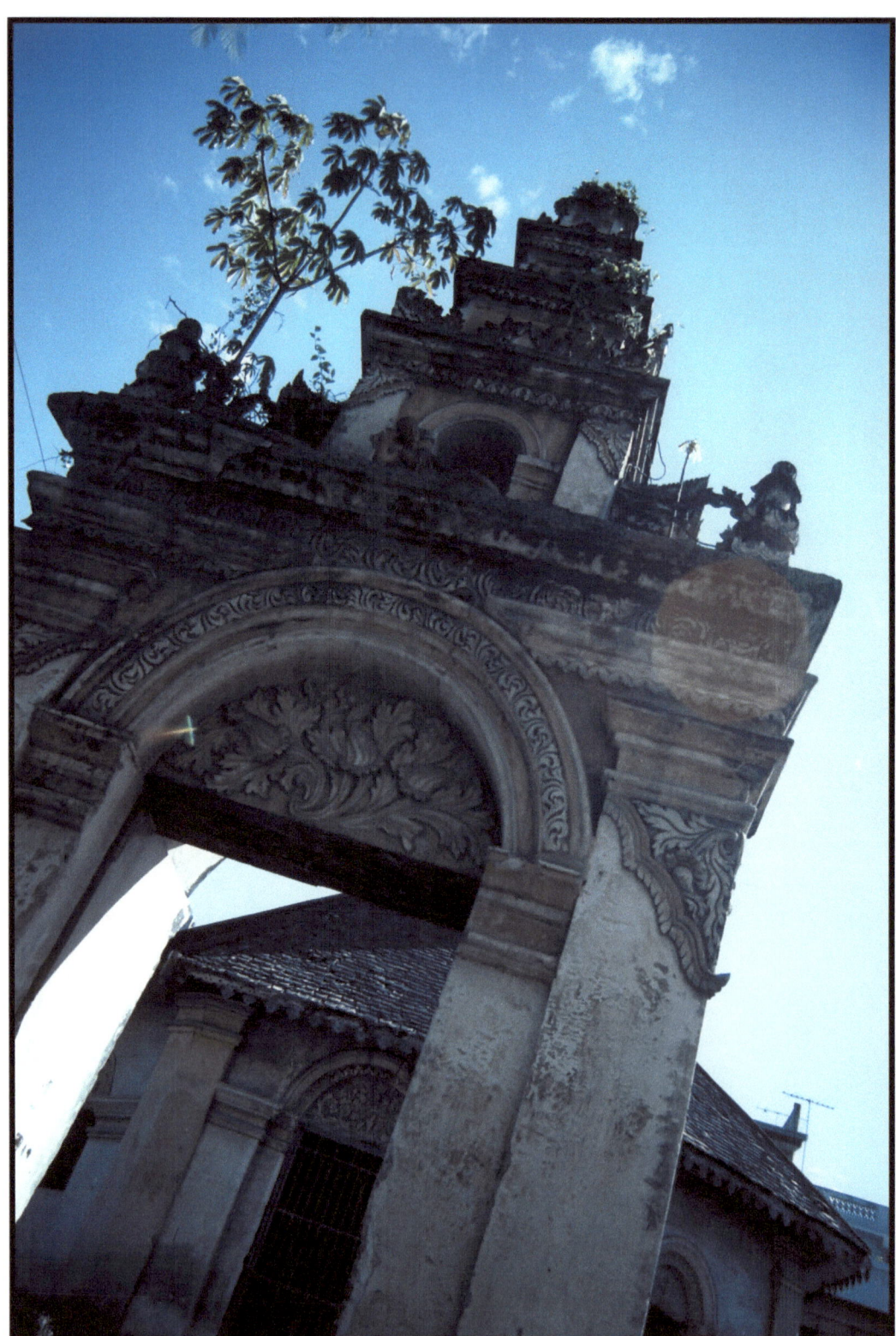

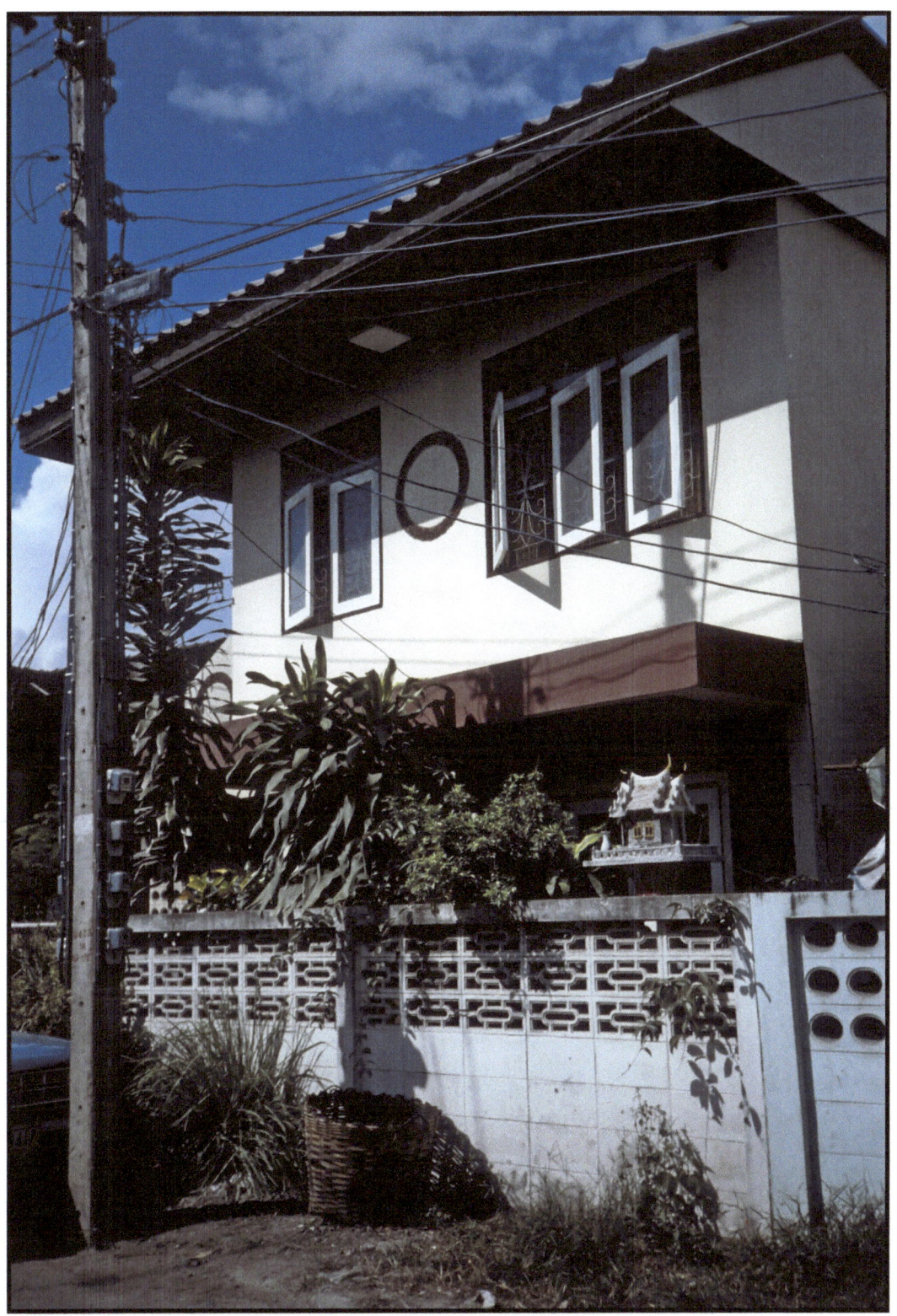

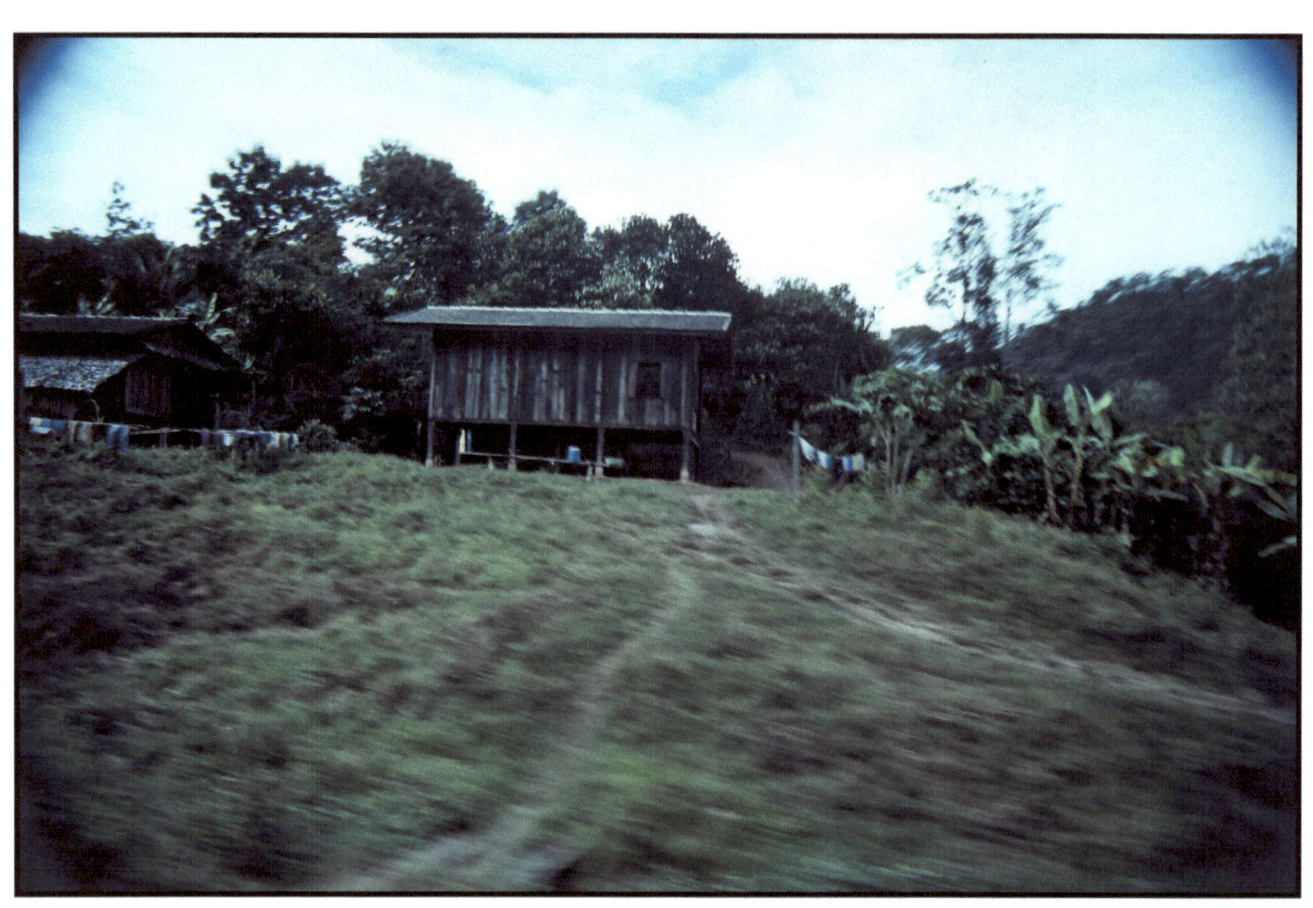

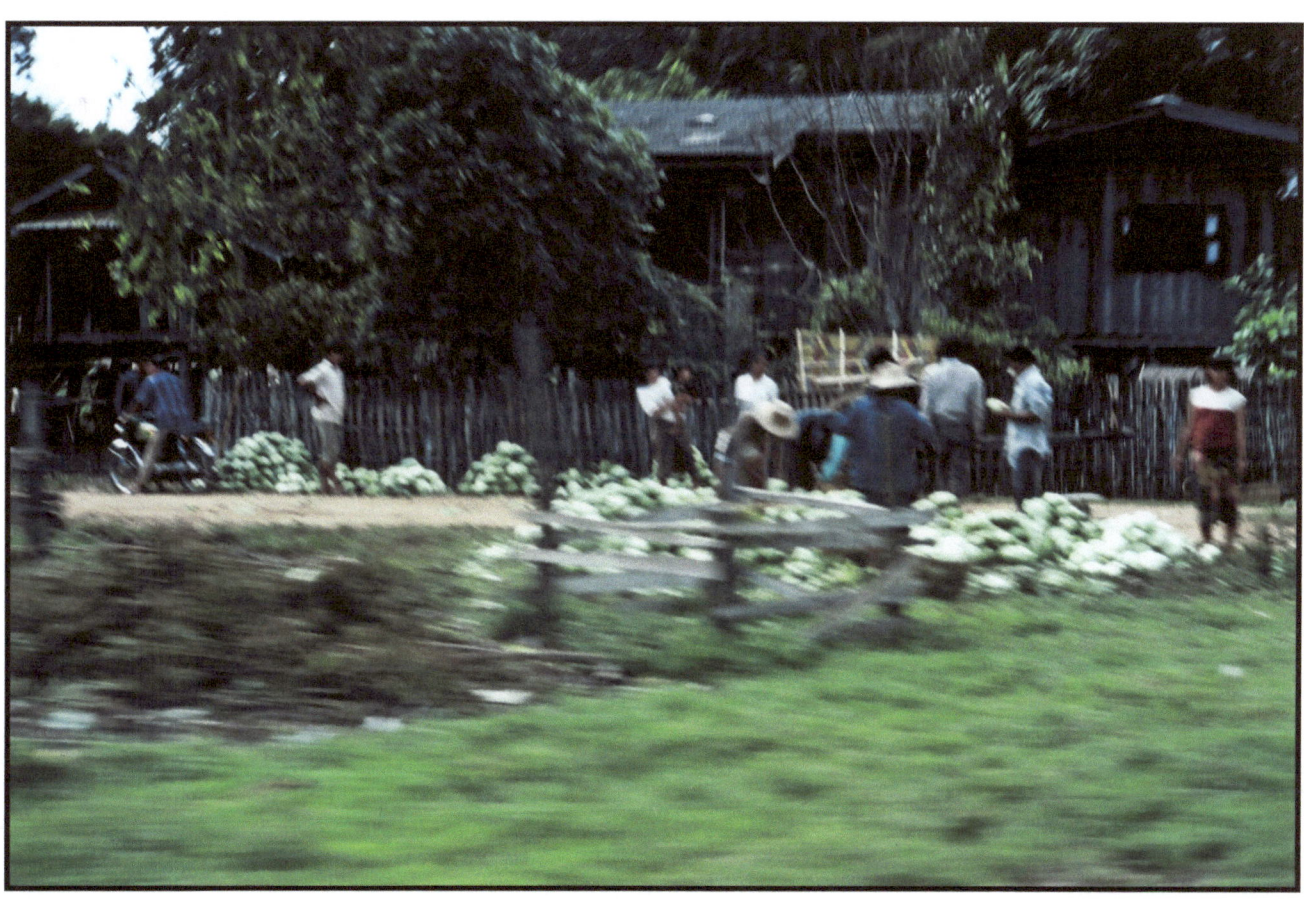

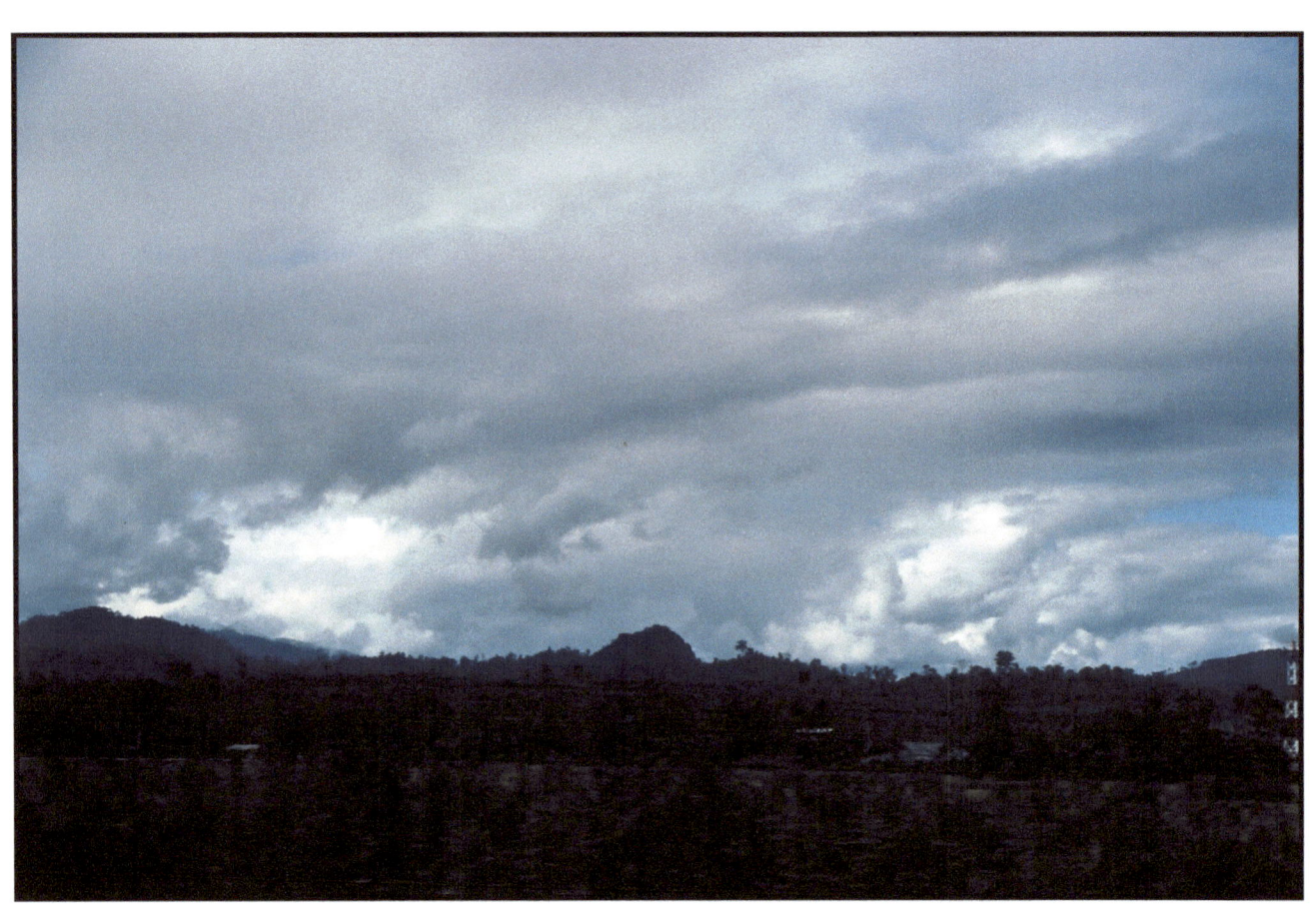

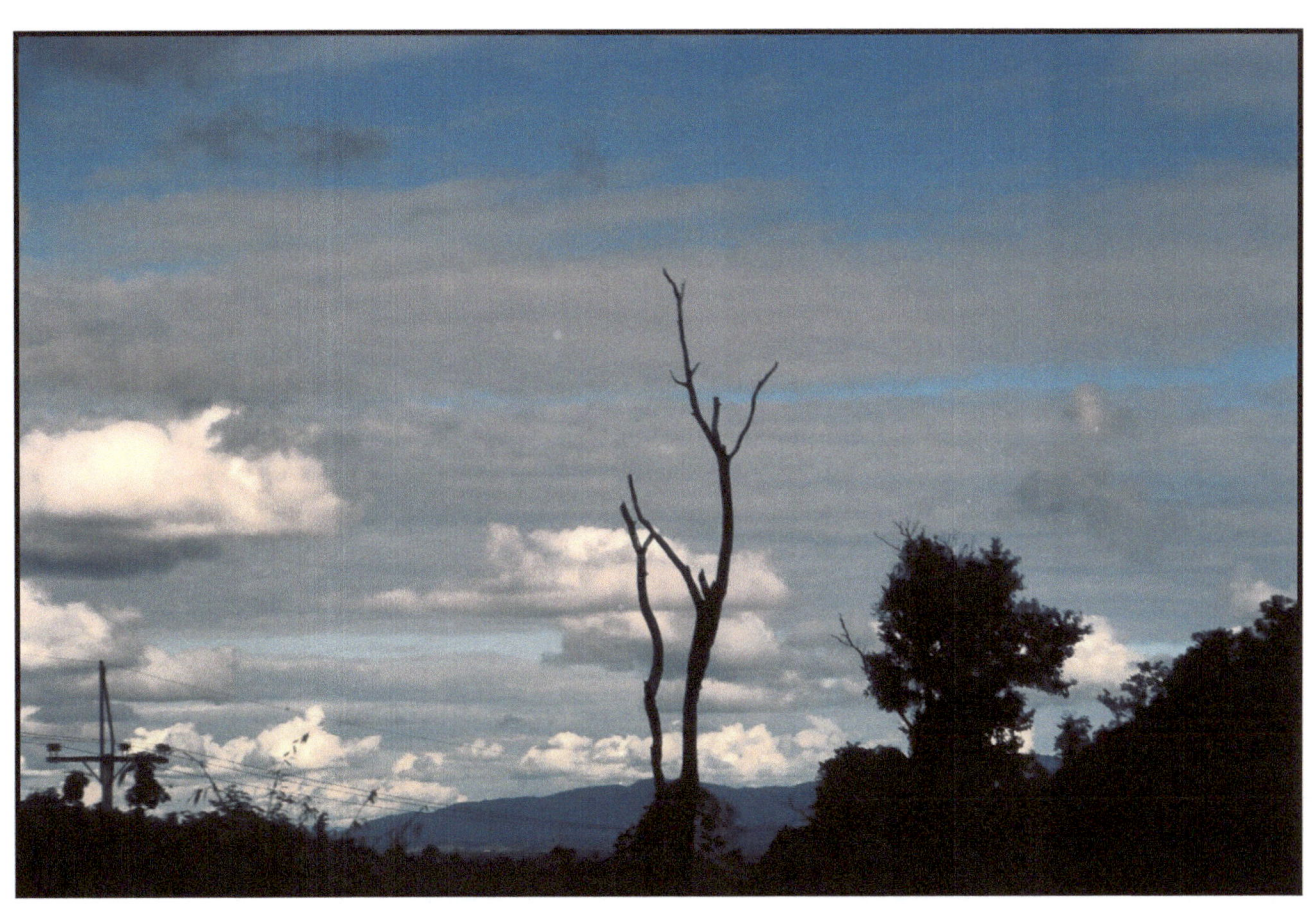

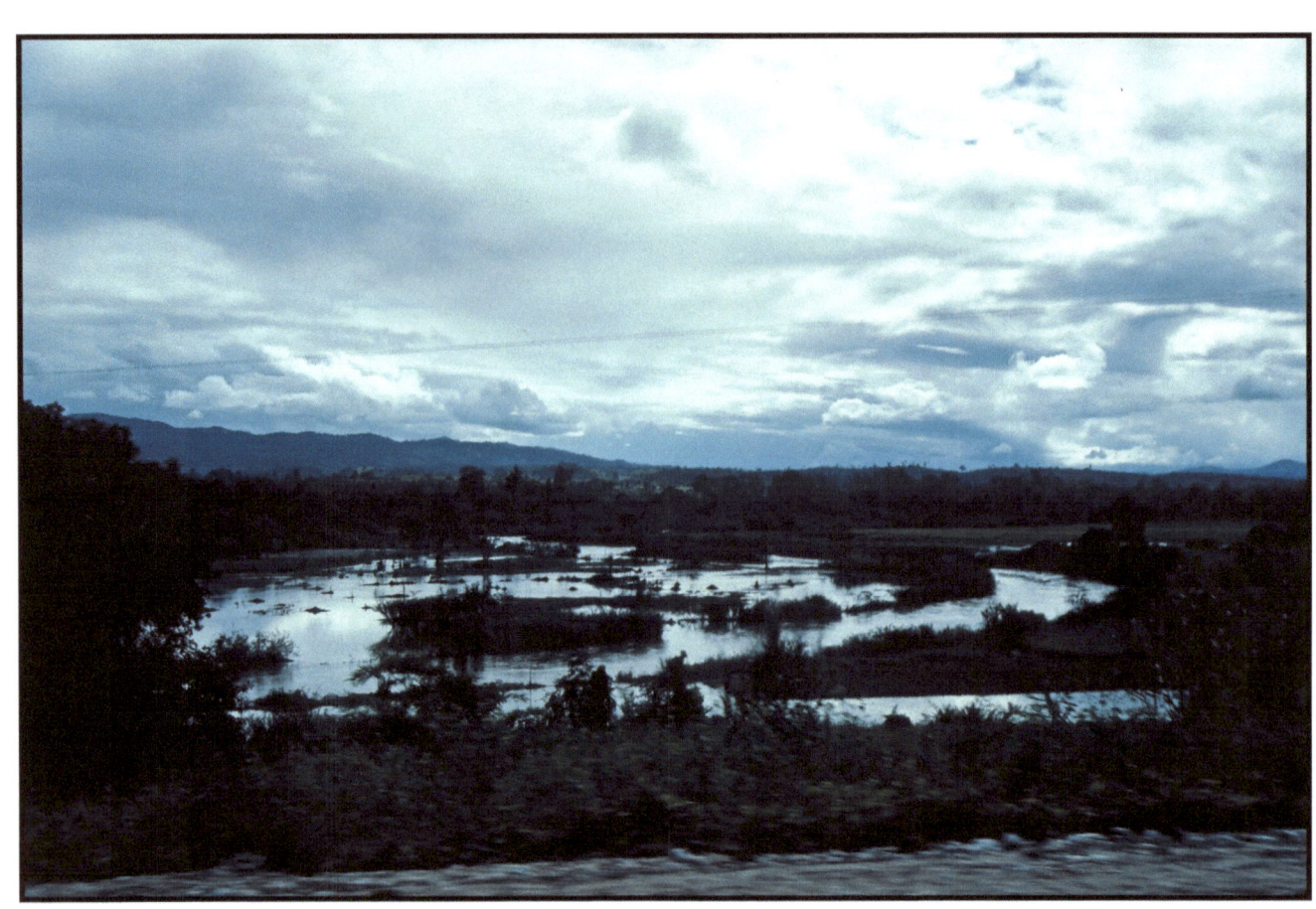

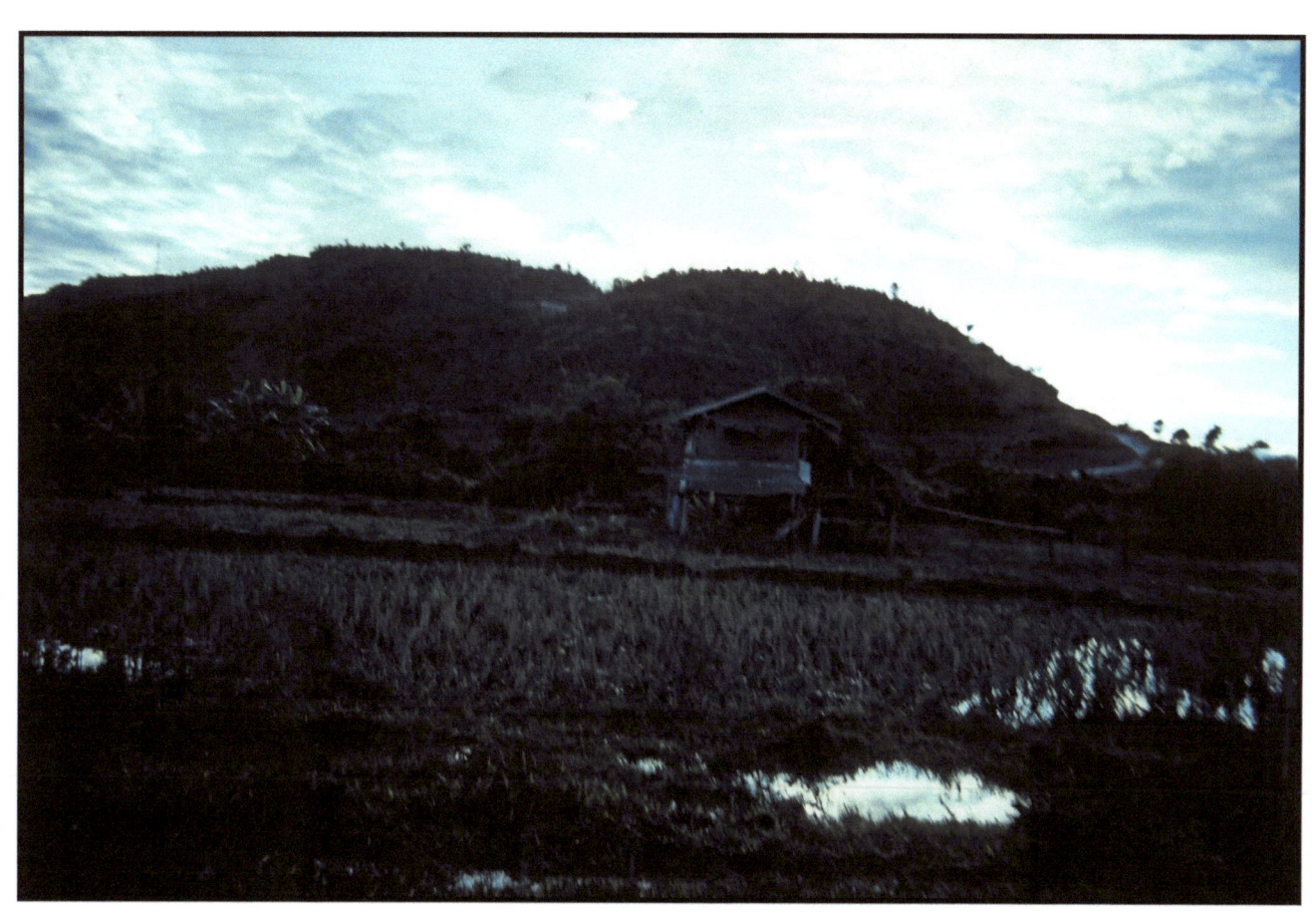

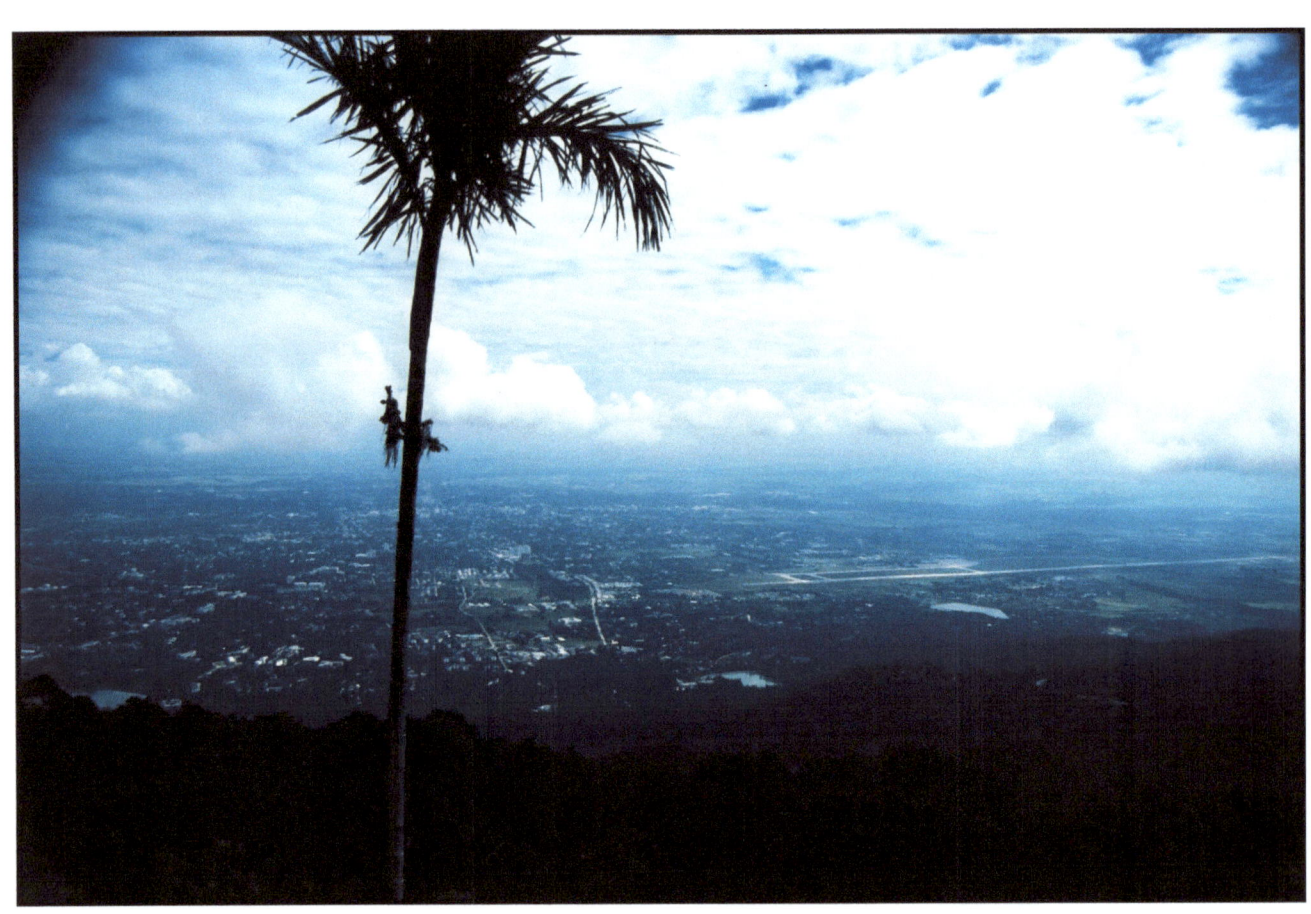

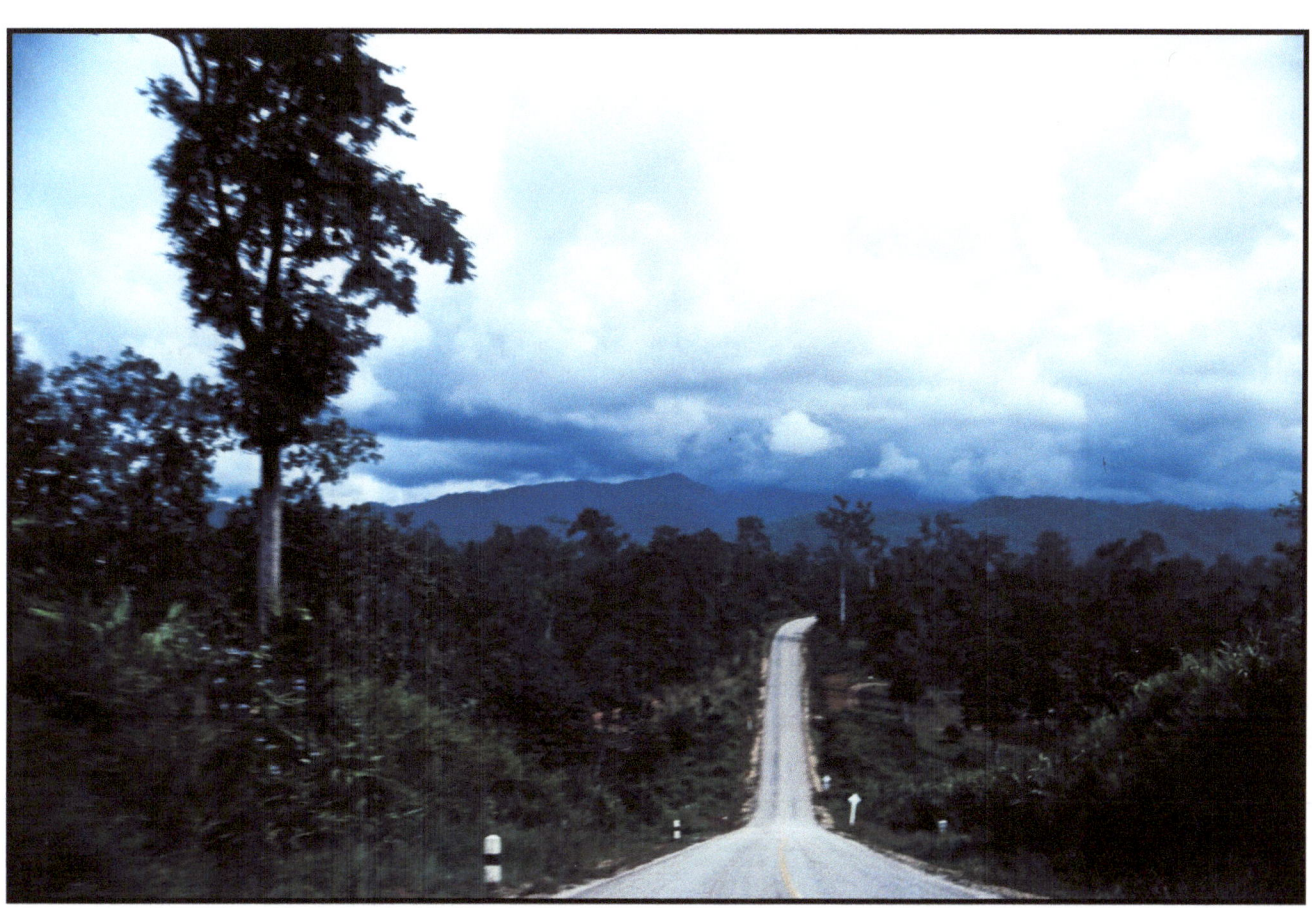

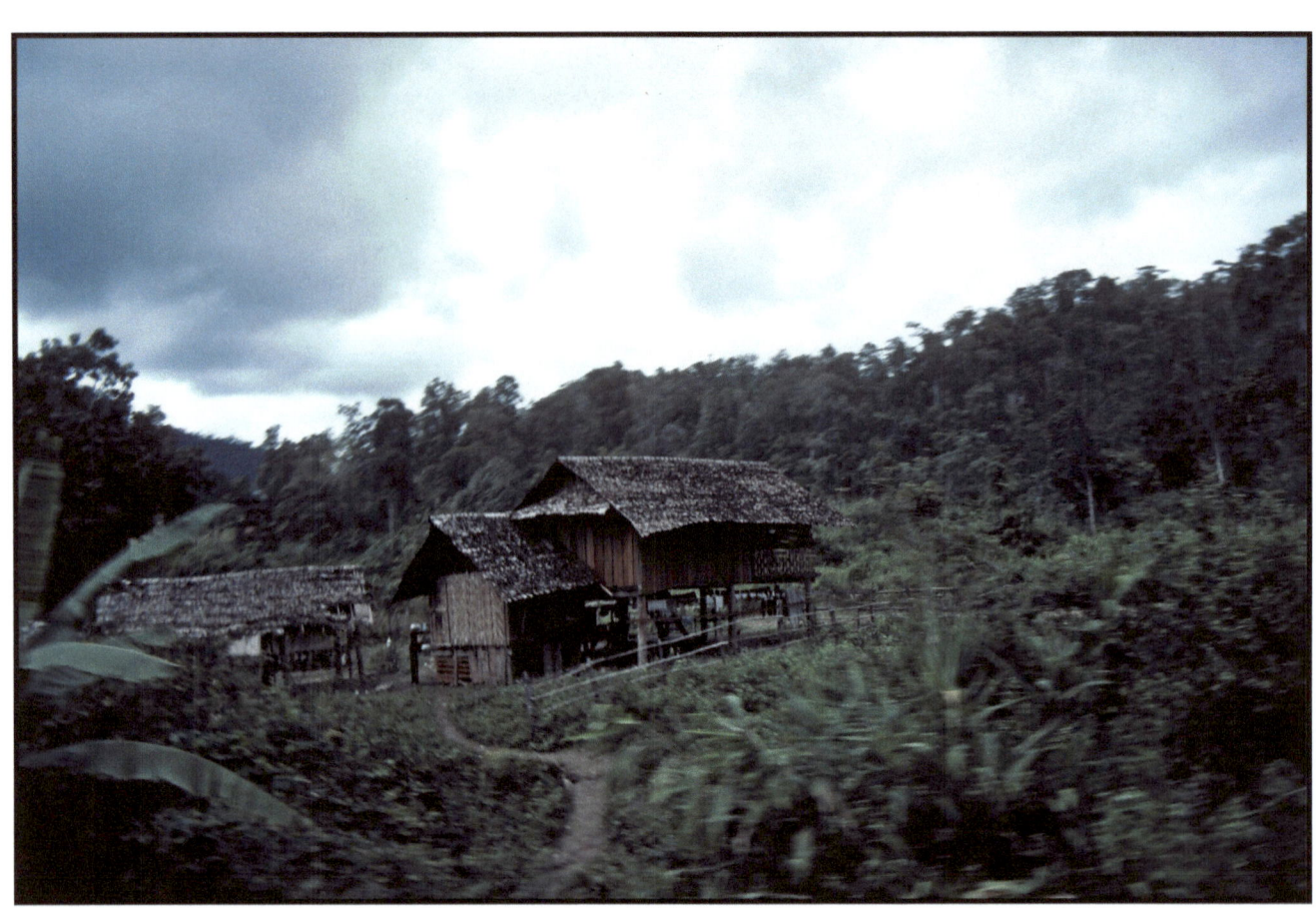

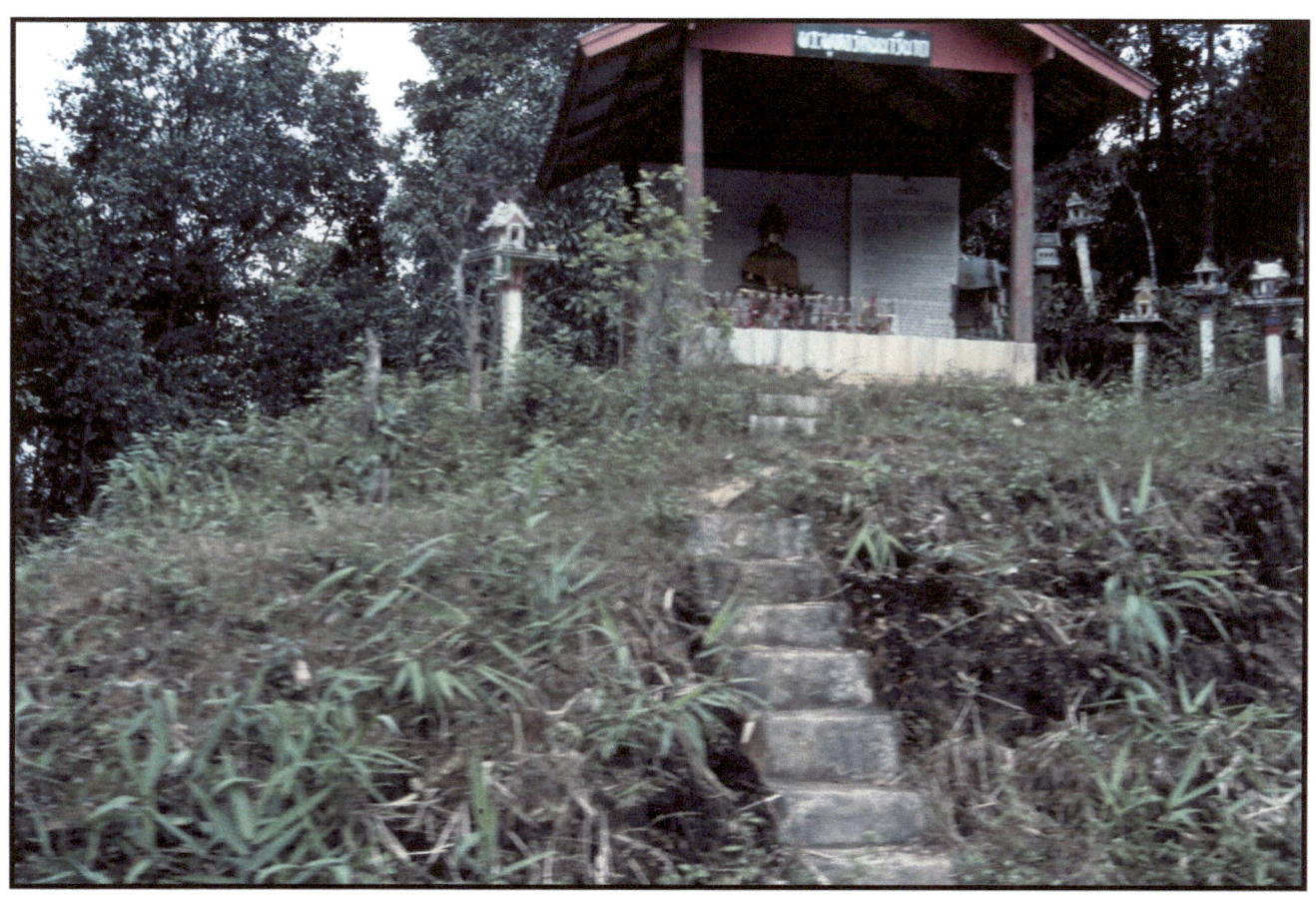

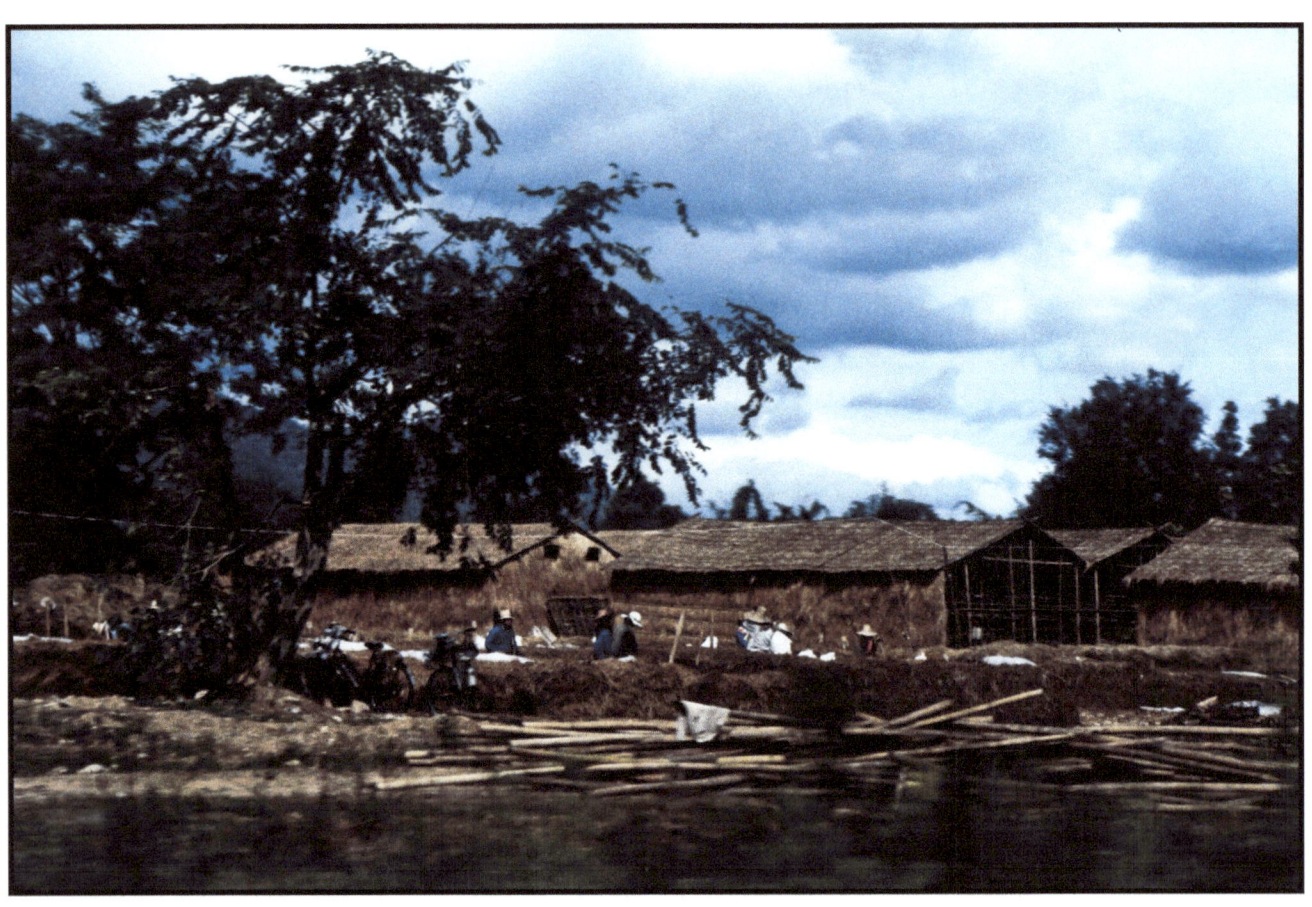

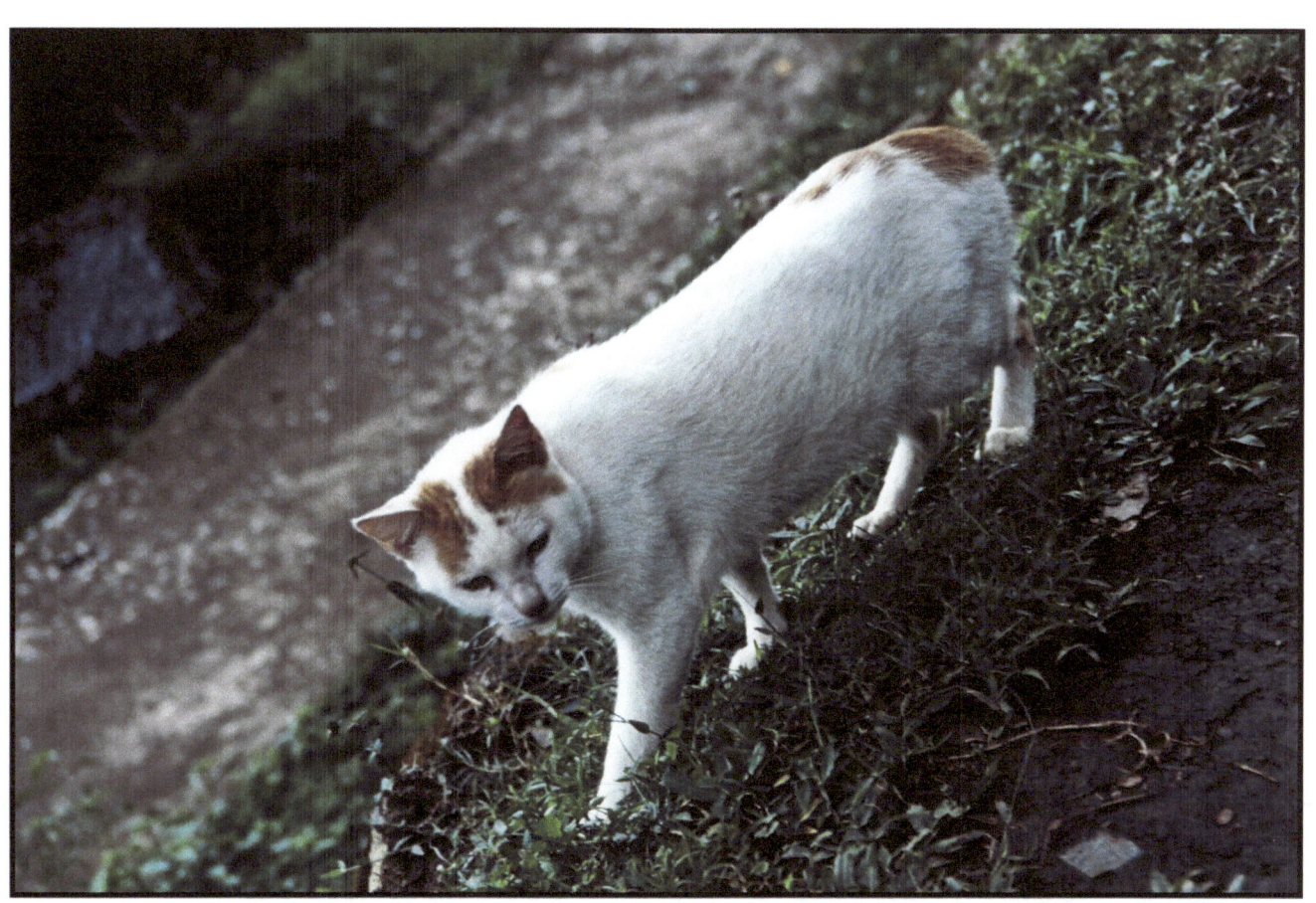

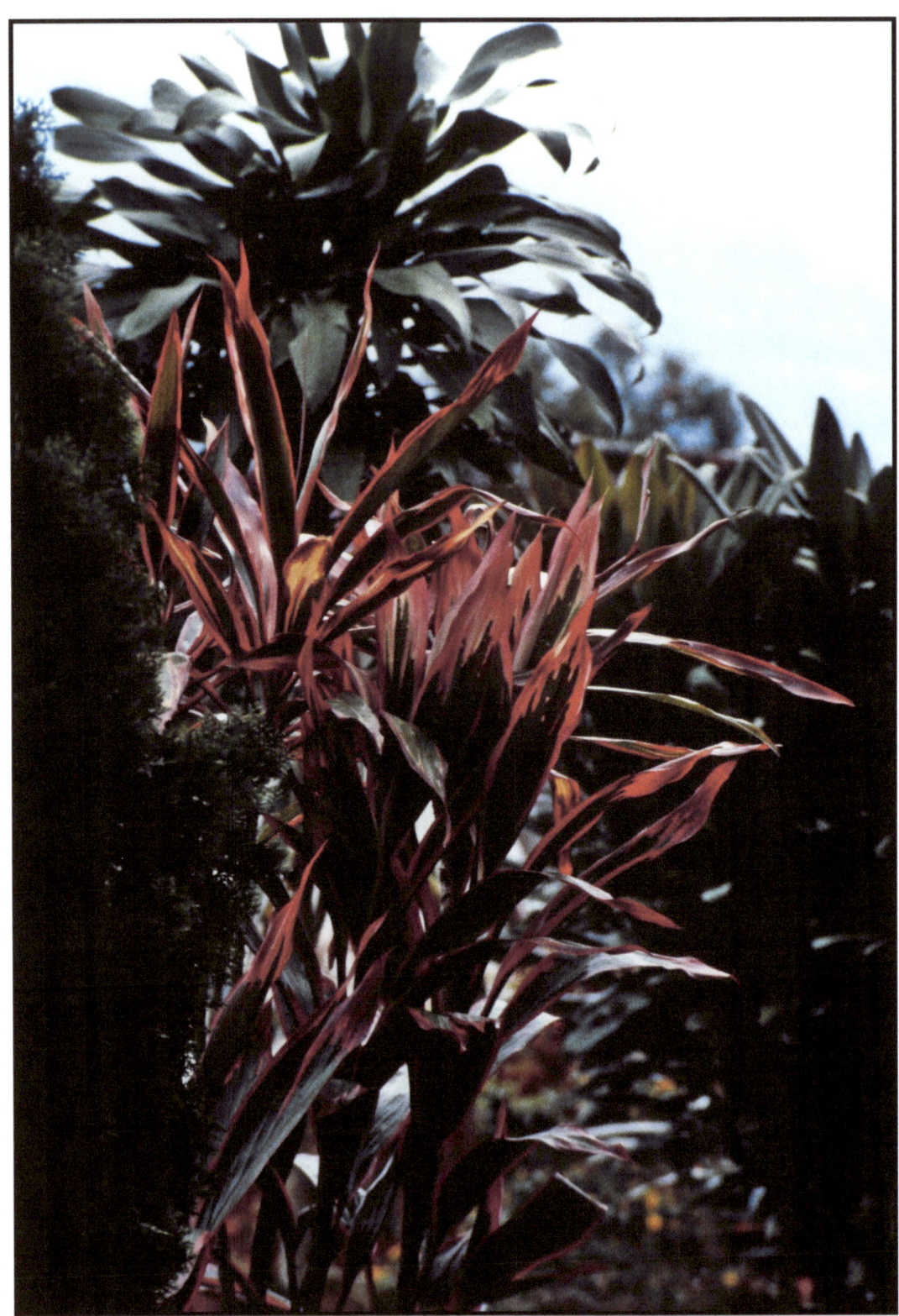

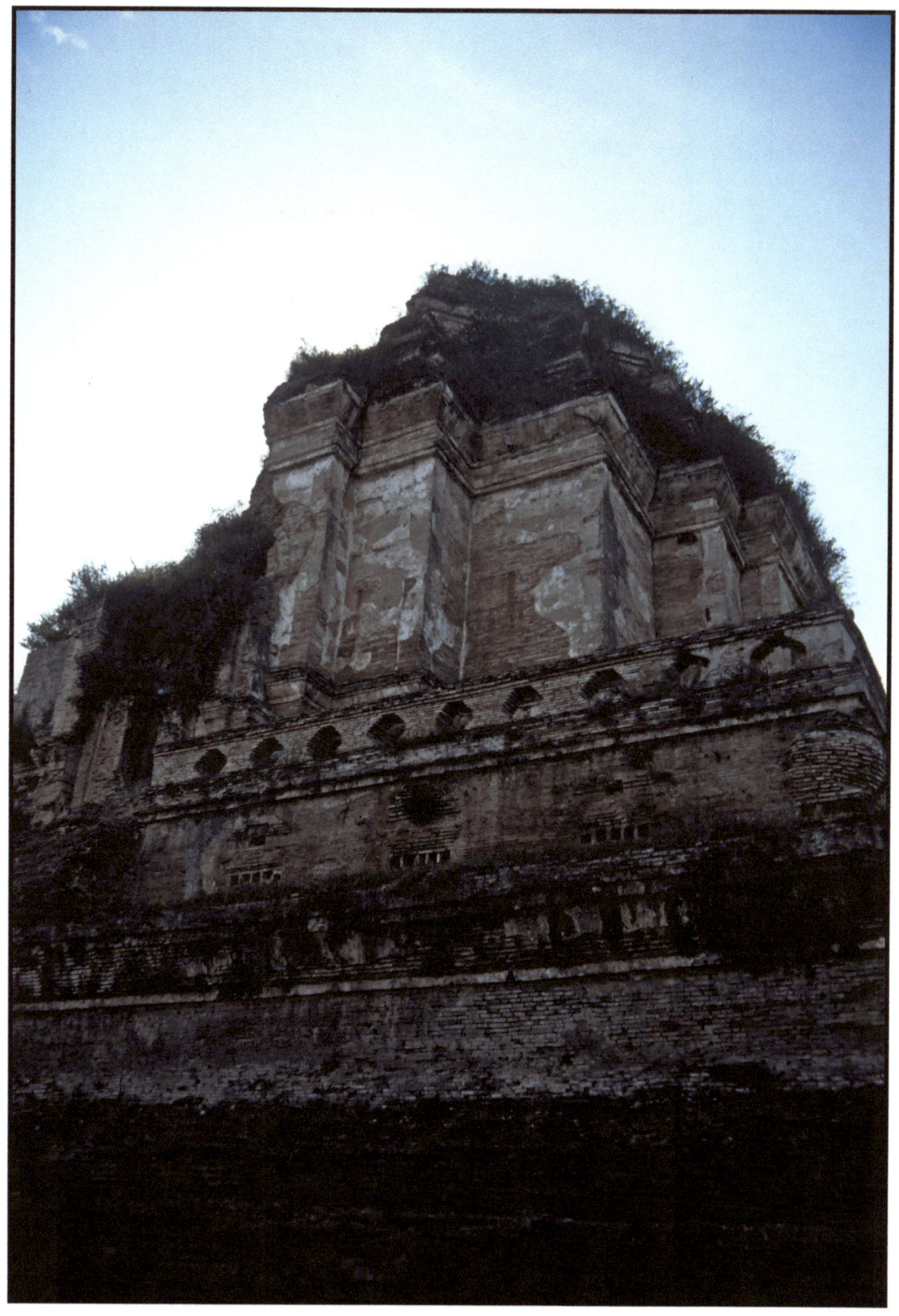

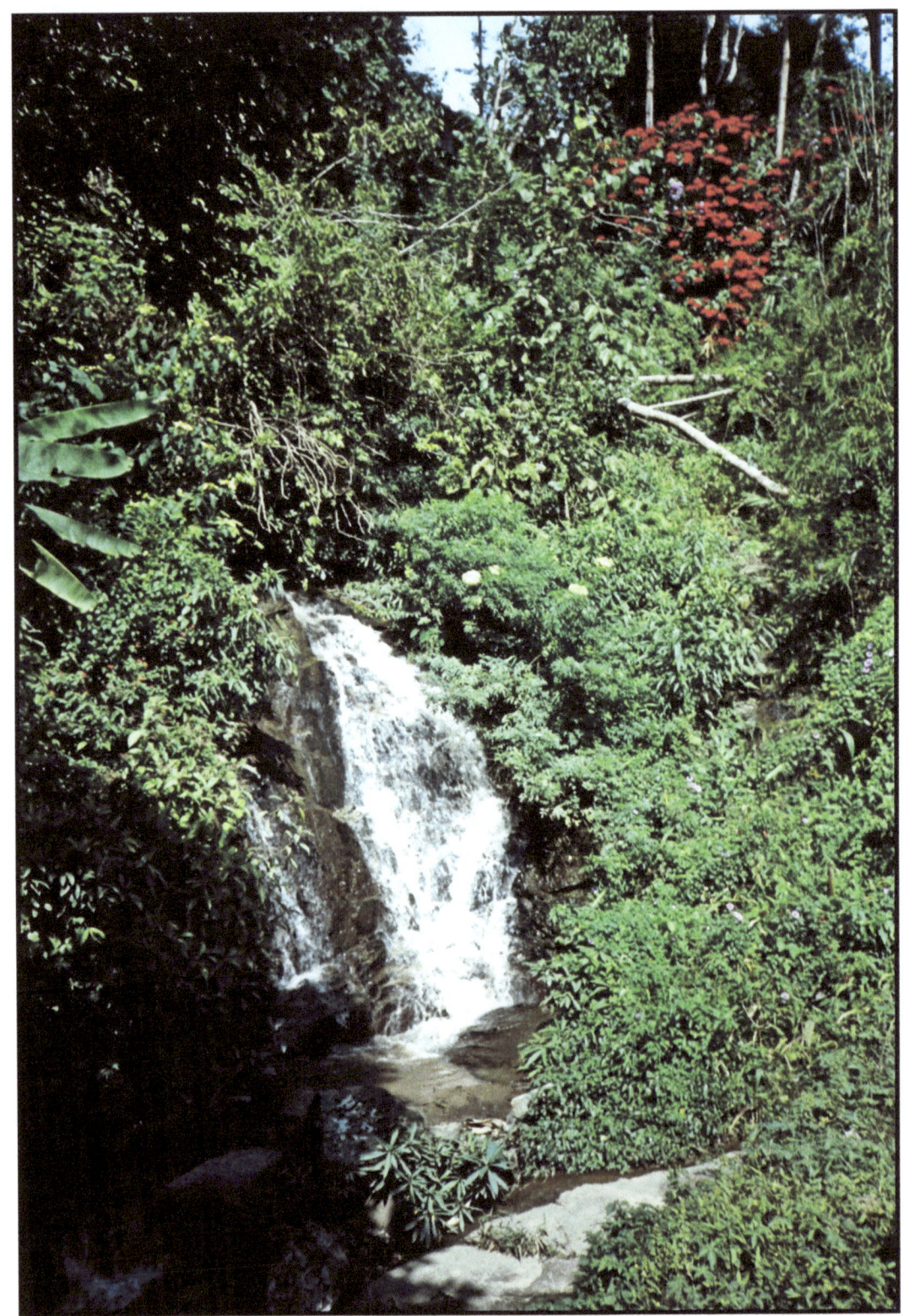

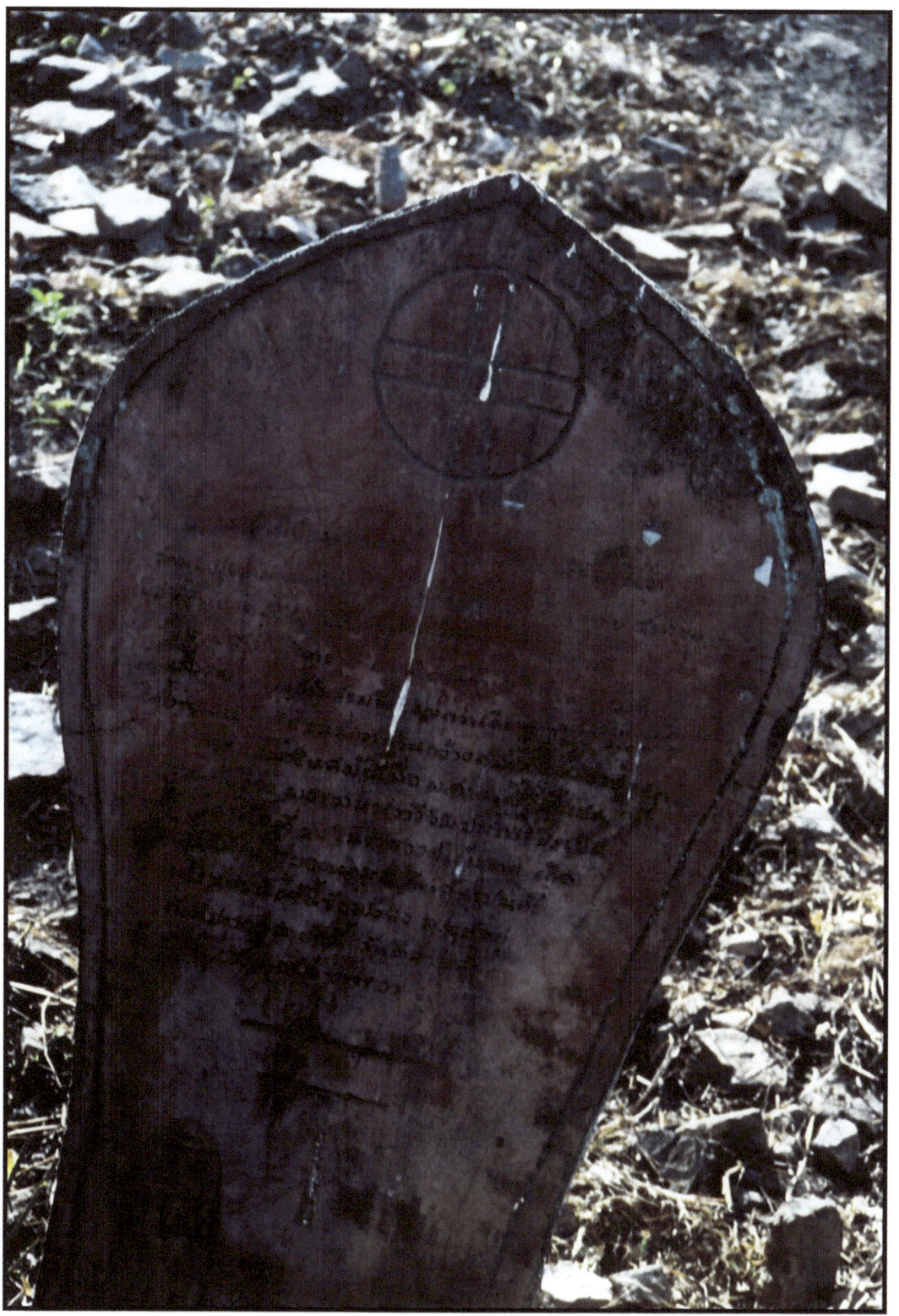

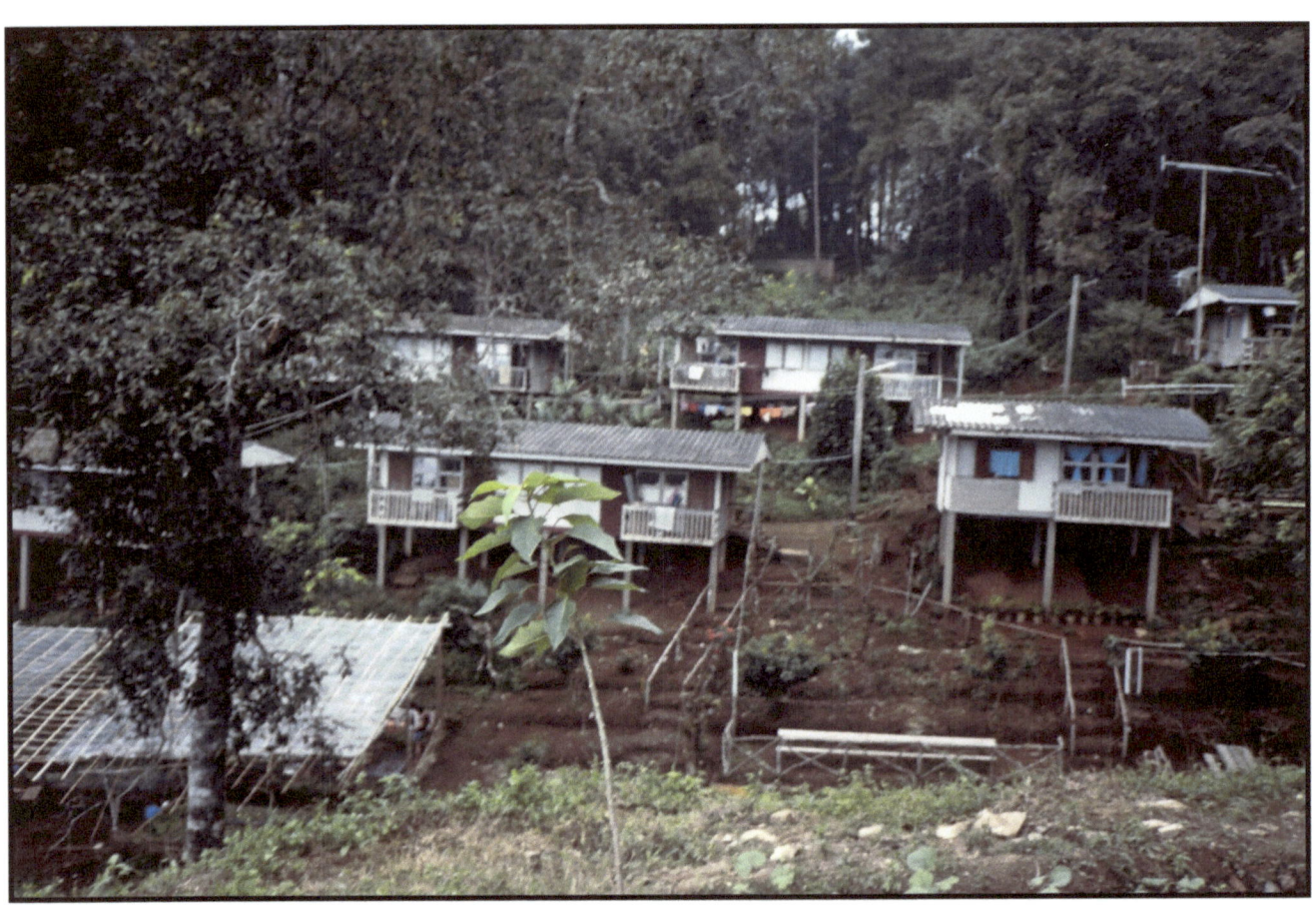

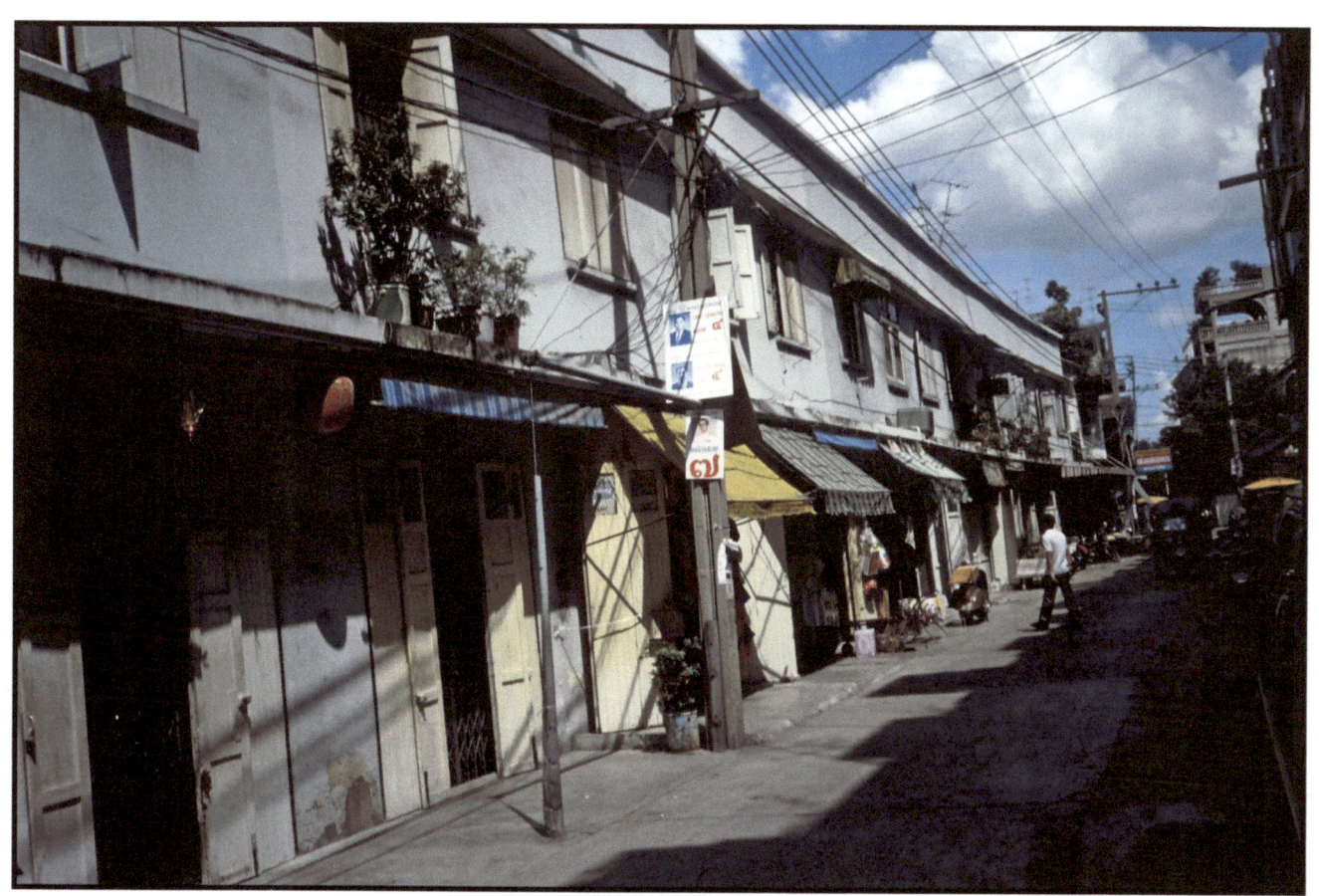

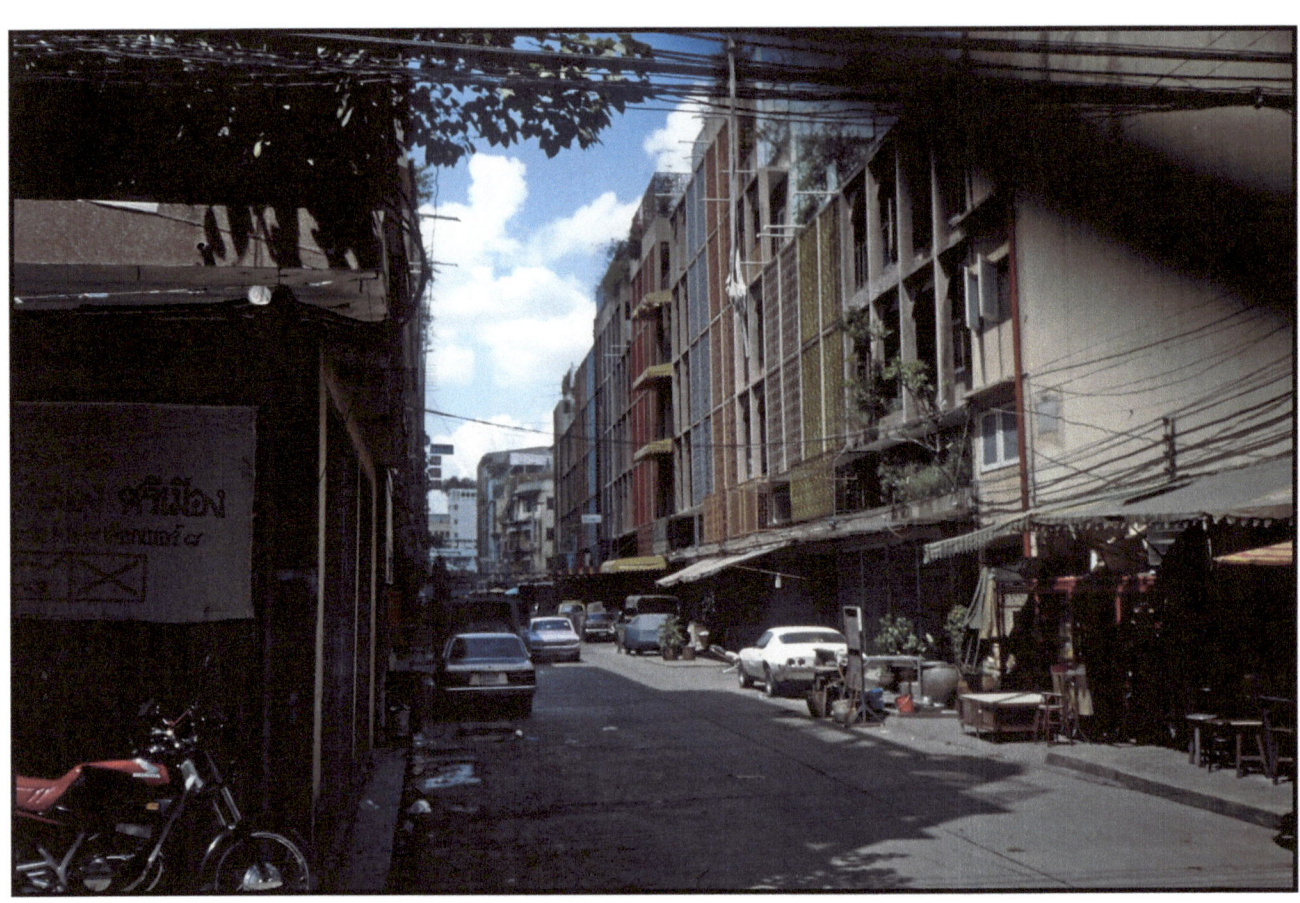

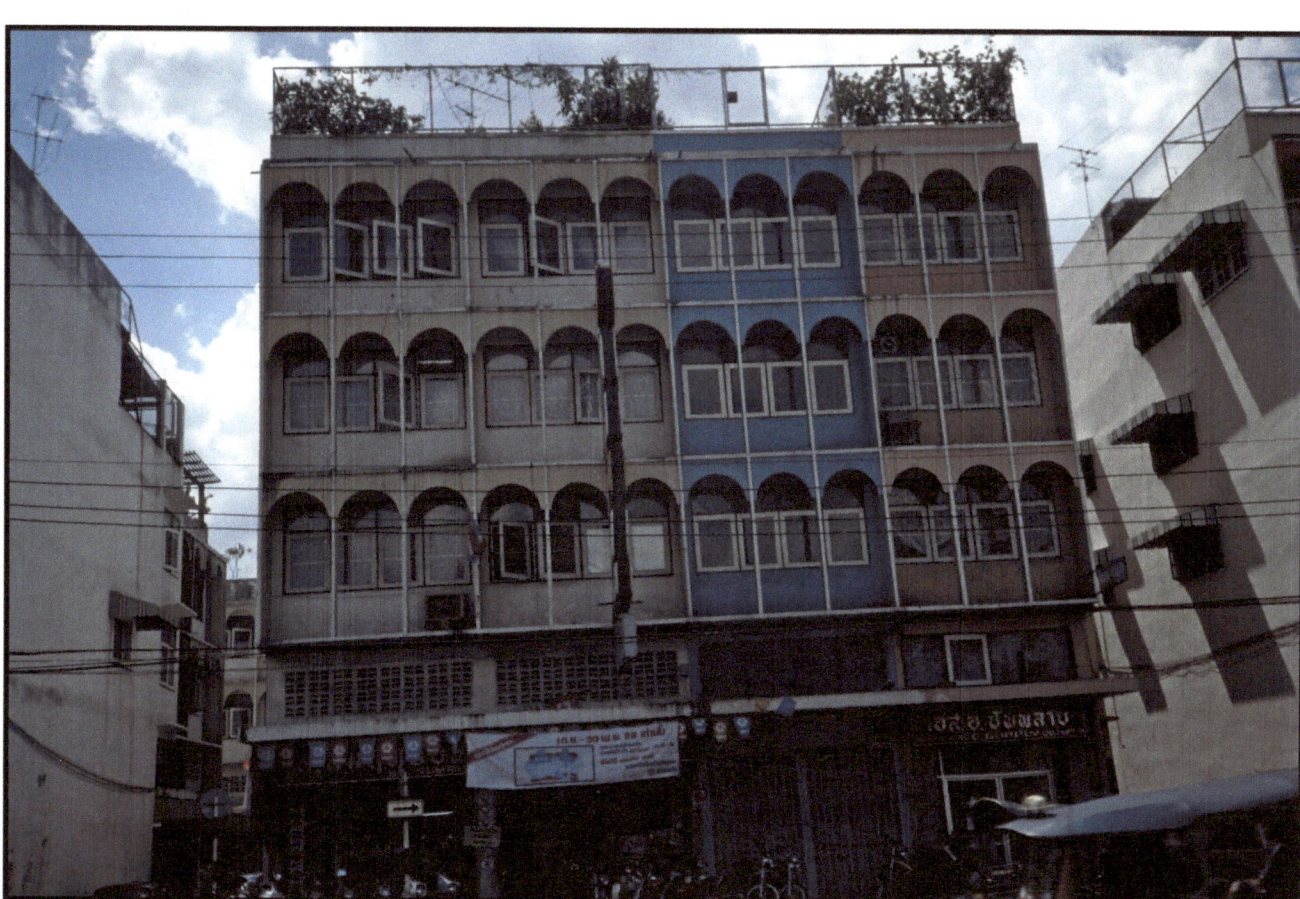

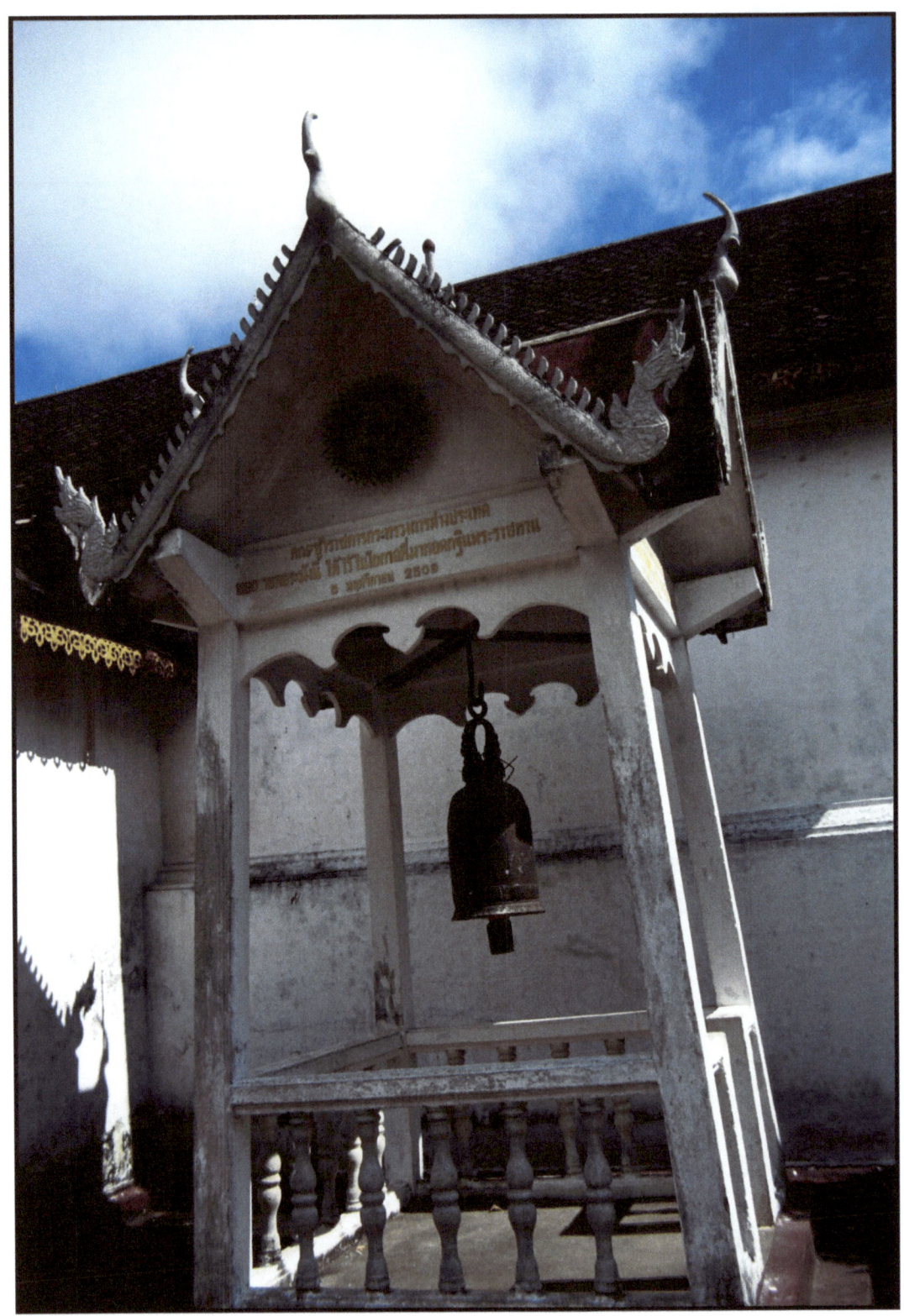

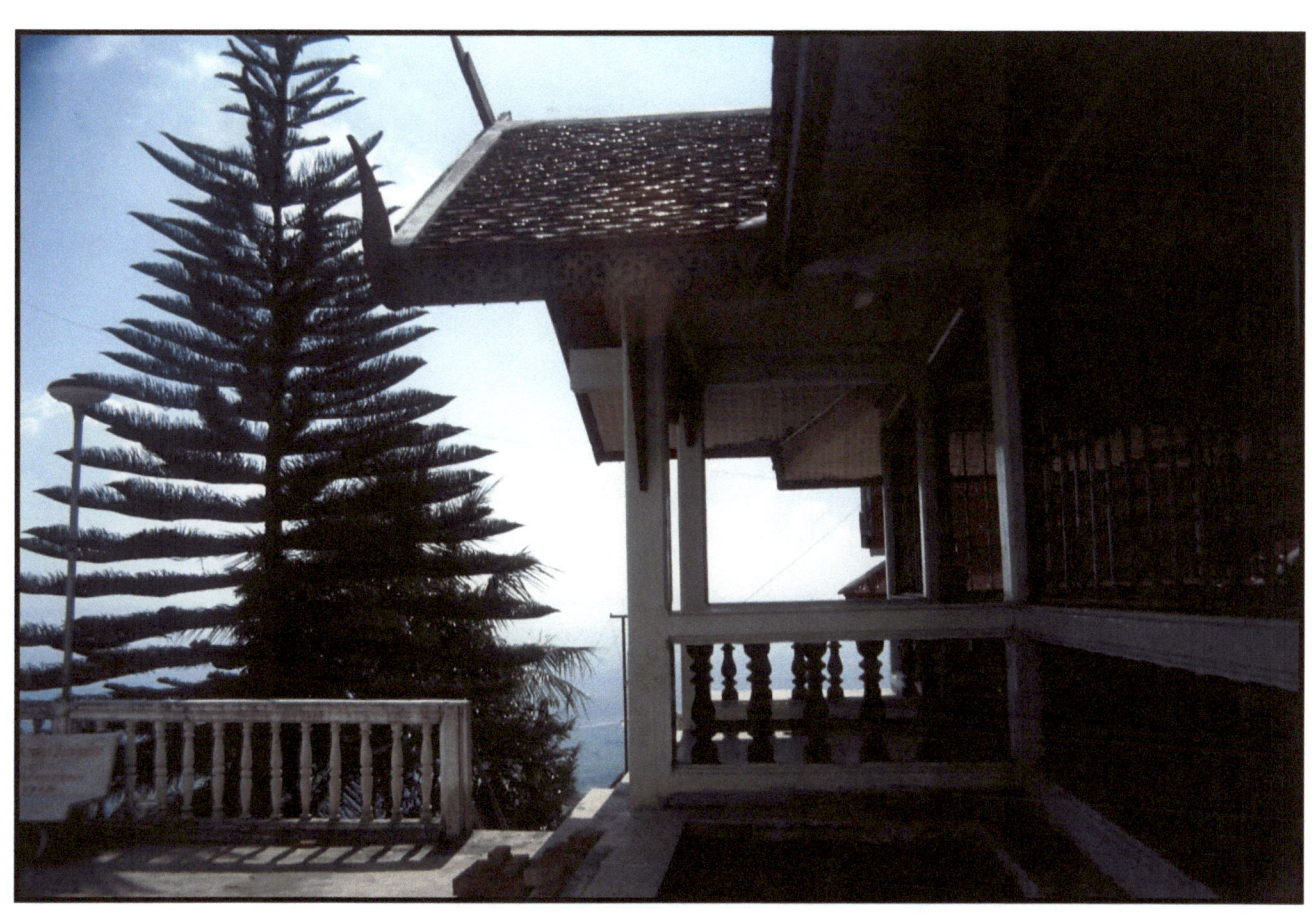

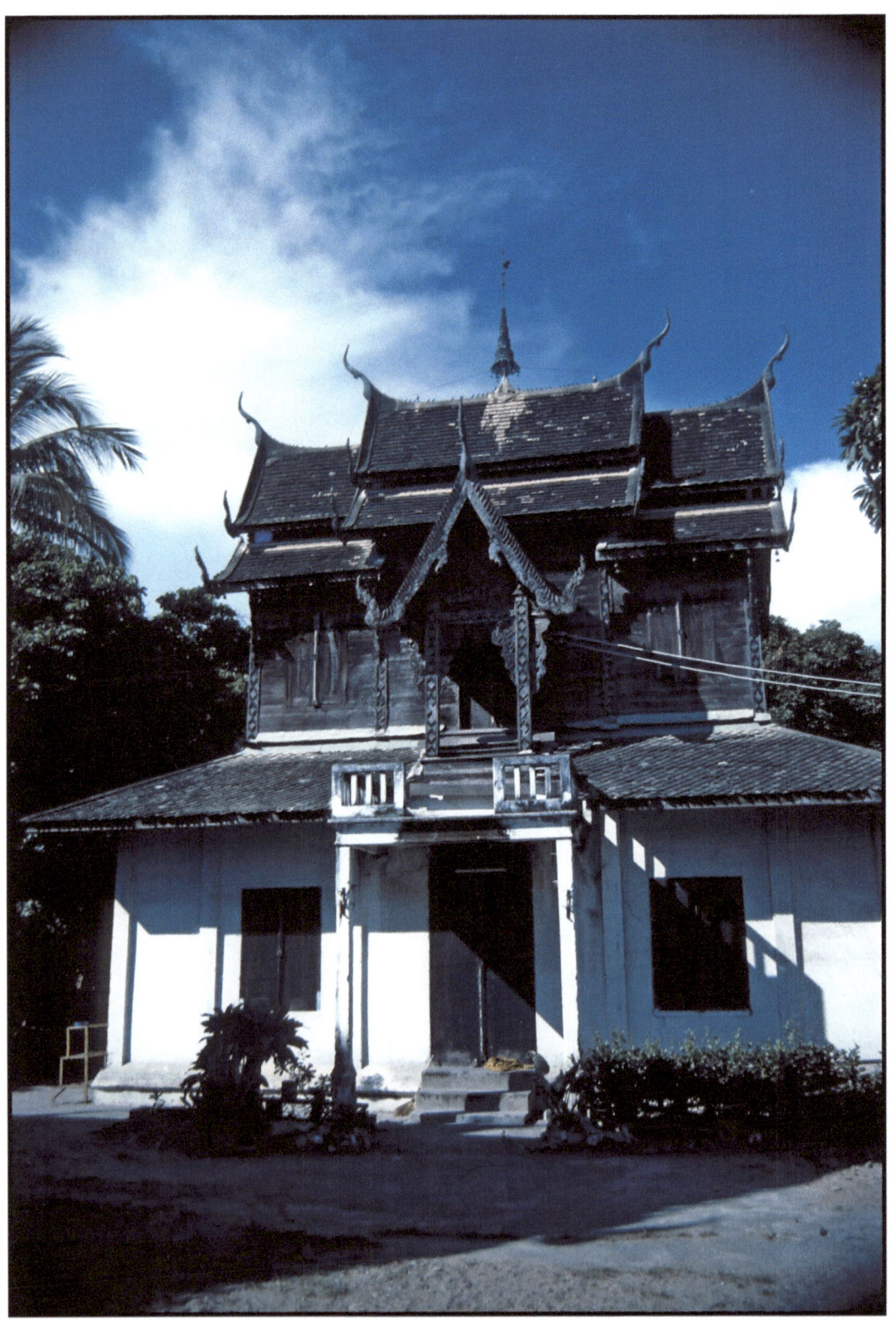

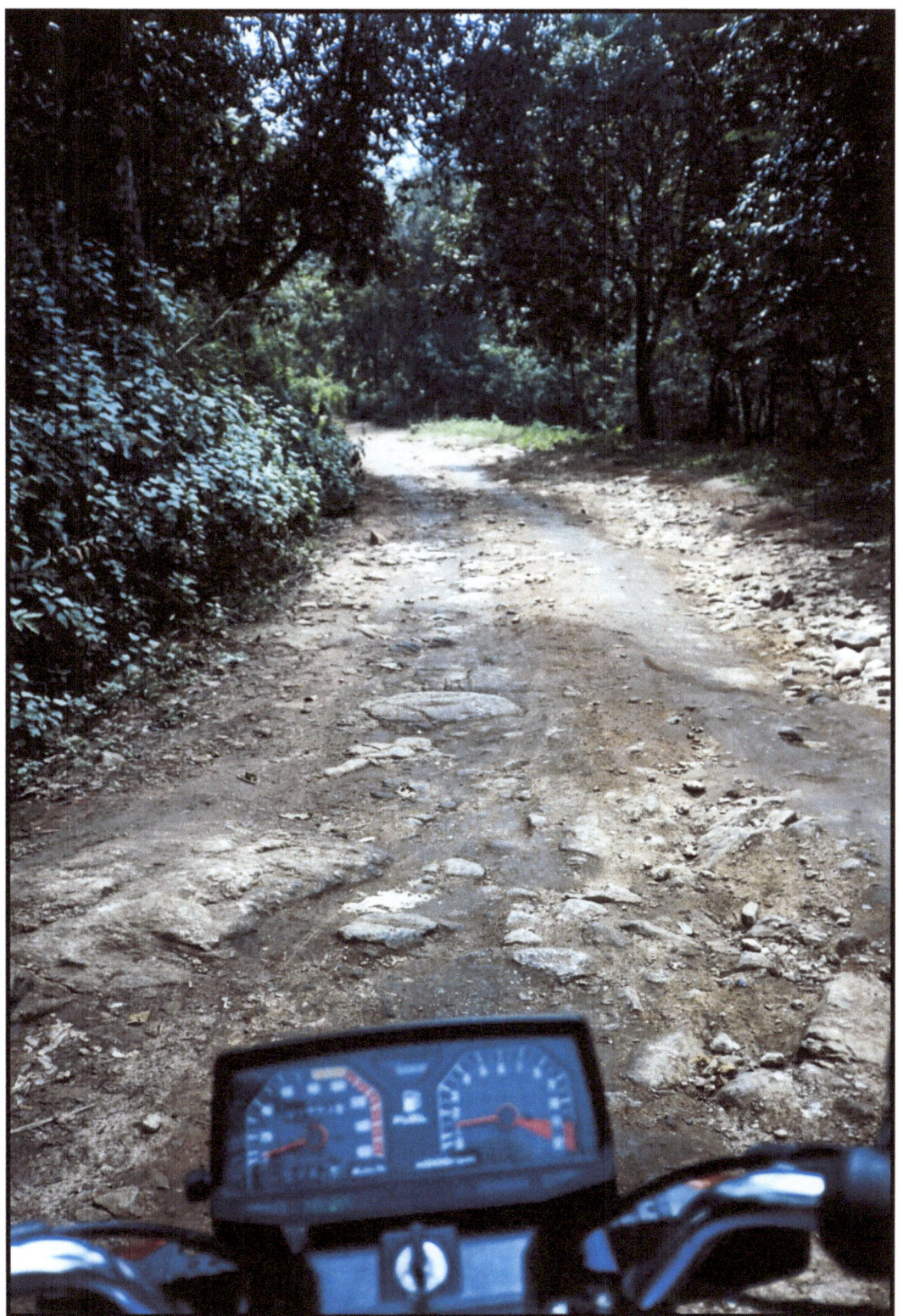

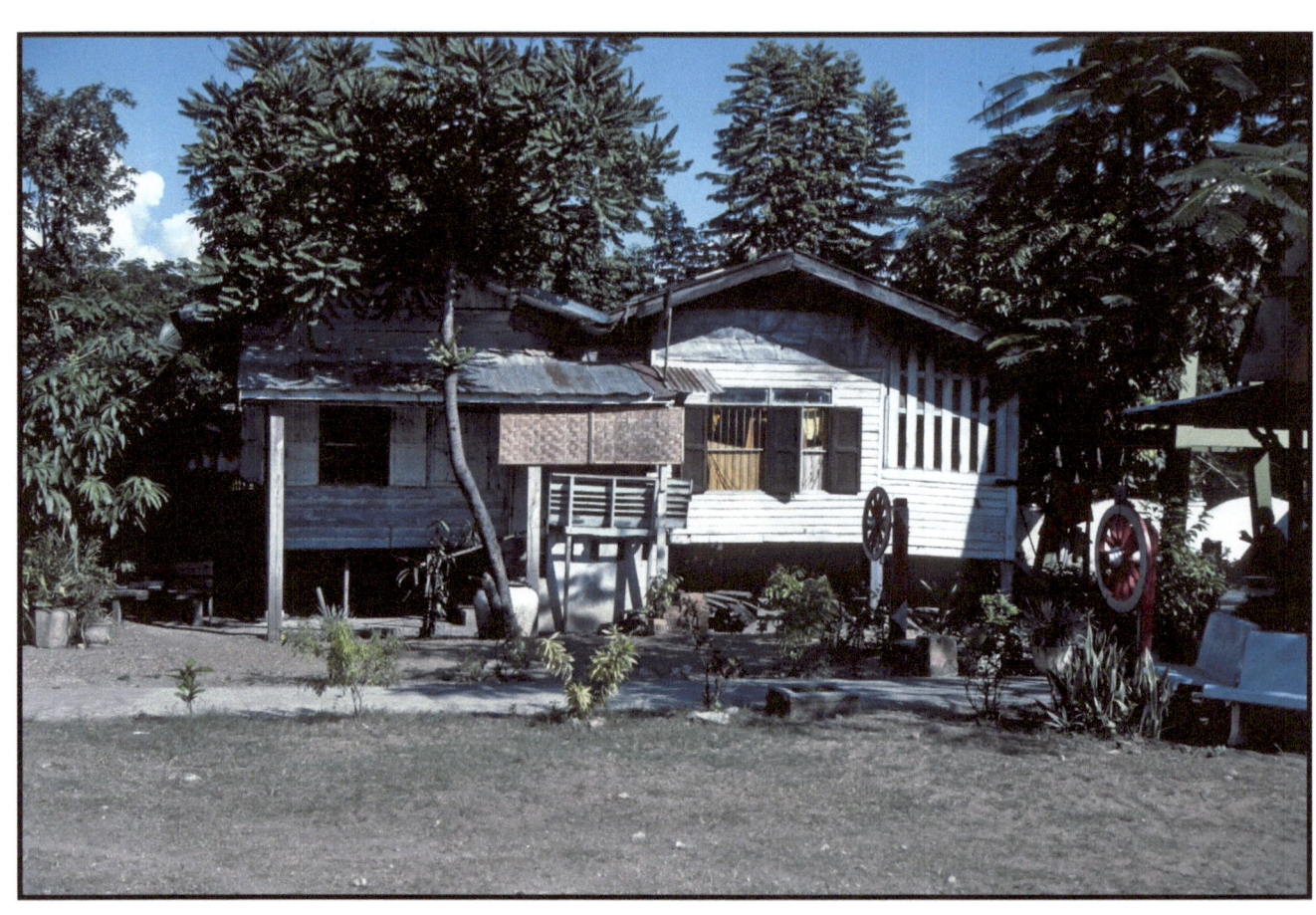

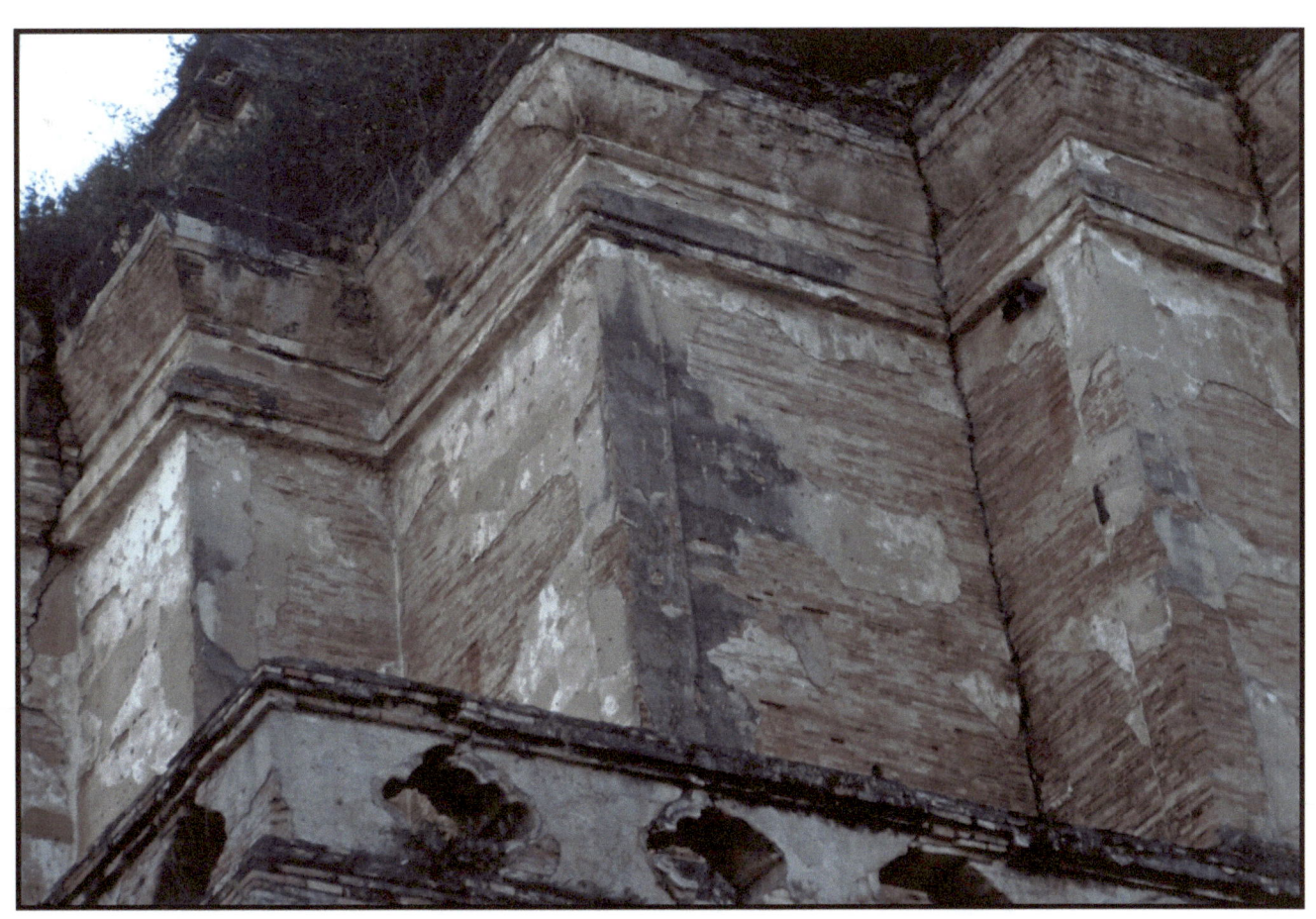

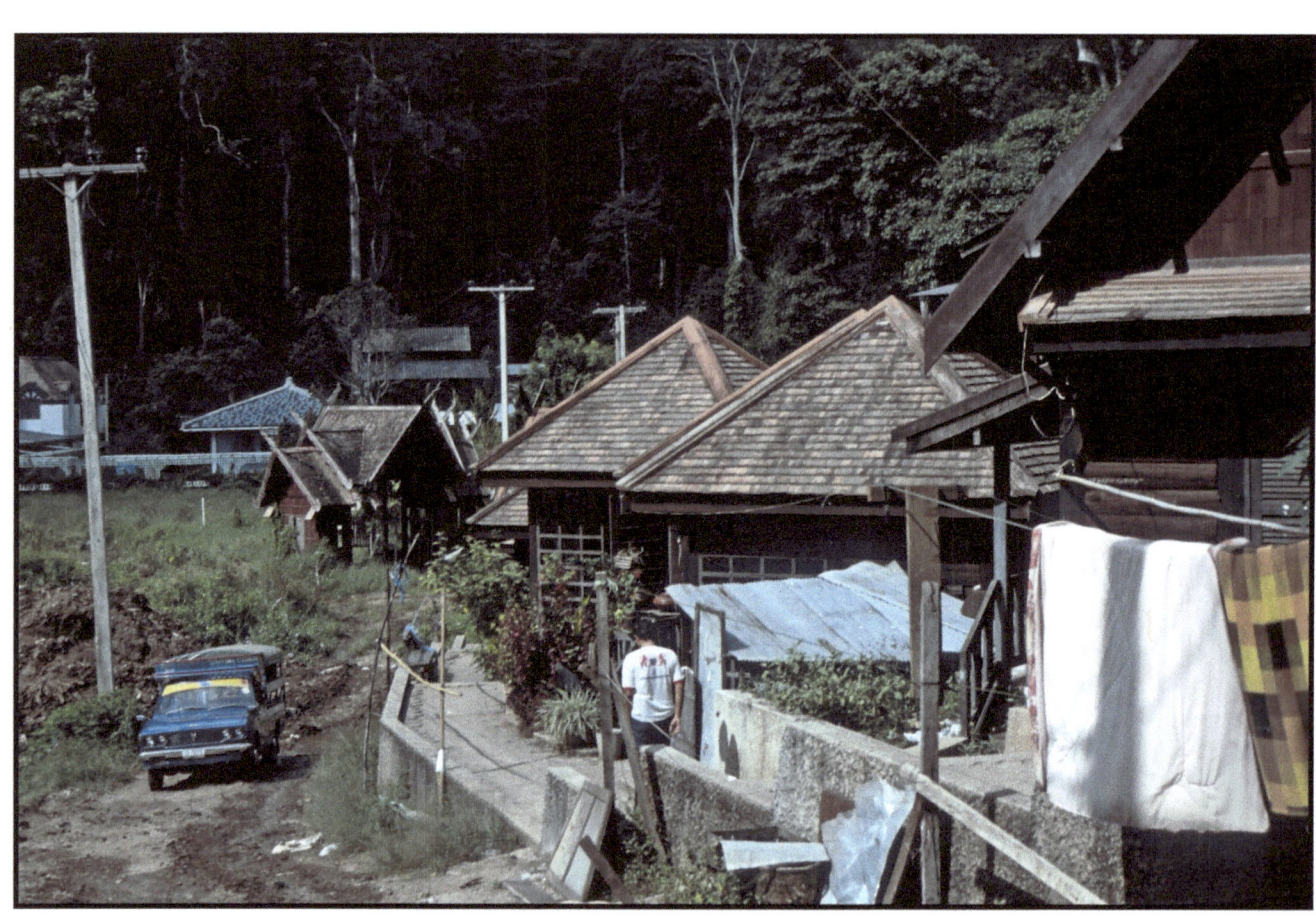

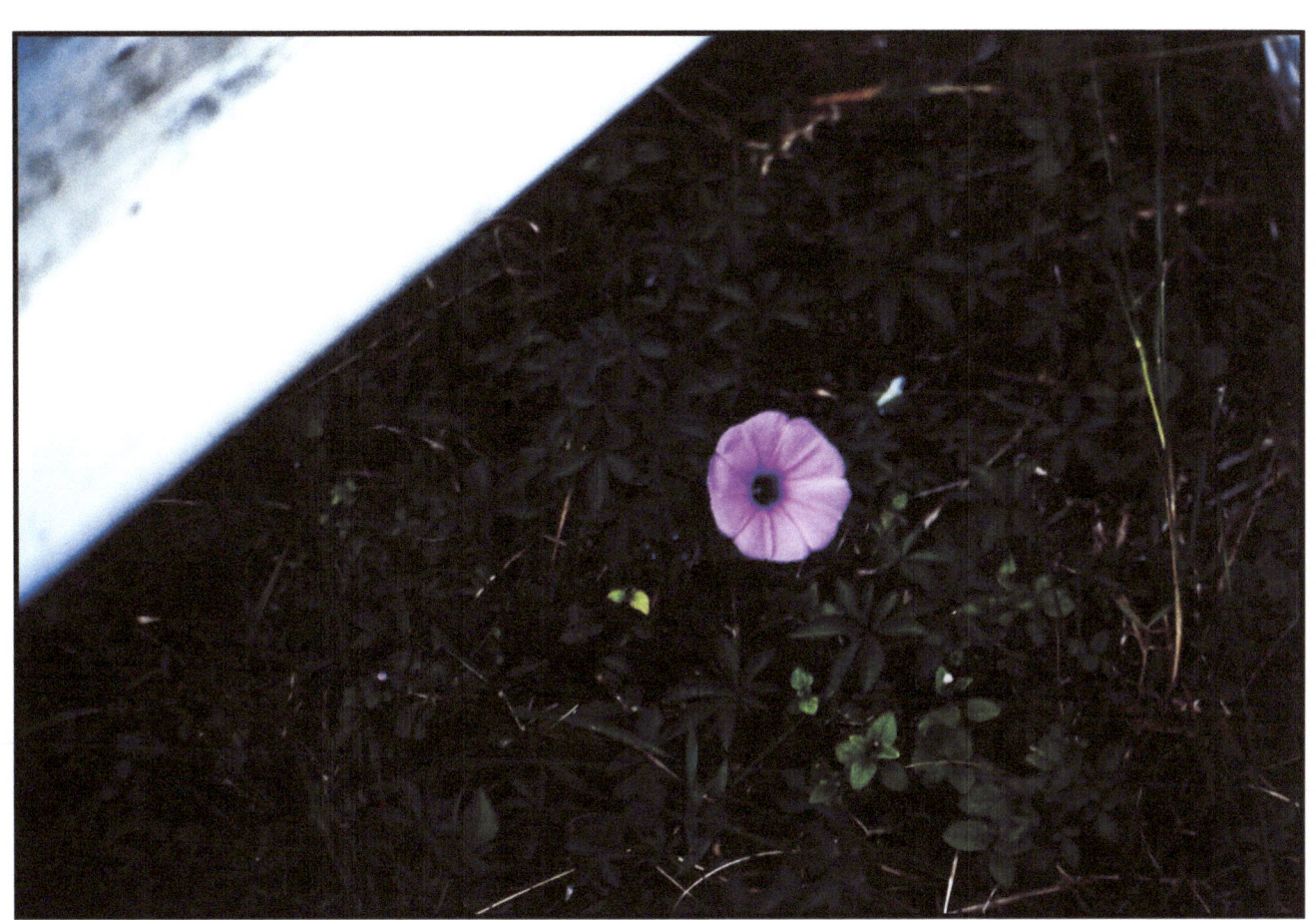

www.ingramcontent.com/pod-product-compliance
Lightning Source LLC
Chambersburg PA
CBHW051145220526
45473CB00003B/666

9781877792830